WHISKY RISING

•

To Rafa & Remy

13-Digit ISBN: 978-1-64643-361-2

10-Digit ISBN: 1-64643-361-0

This book may be ordered by mail from the publisher. Please include $5.99 for postage and handling. Please support your local bookseller first!

Books published by Cider Mill Press Book Publishers are available at special discounts for bulk purchases in the United States by corporations, institutions, and other organizations. For more information, please contact the publisher.

Cider Mill Press Book Publishers
"Where good books are ready for press"
501 Nelson Place
Nashville, Tennessee 37214

cidermillpress.com

Typography: Lydian BT, Proxima Nova

All photo credits are listed on page 637

Printed in Malaysia

23 24 25 26 27 TJM 5 4 3 2 1

First Edition

WHISKY RISING

THE DEFINITIVE GUIDE TO THE
FINEST JAPANESE WHISKIES AND DISTILLERS

FULLY REVISED & UPDATED

STEFAN VAN EYCKEN

CIDER MILL PRESS

BOOK PUBLISHERS

Contents

Acknowledgments

In Francois Truffaut's *Day for Night*, the character of the film director says, "Making a film is like a stagecoach ride in the old west. When you start, you are hoping for a pleasant trip. By the halfway point, you just hope to survive." There were times during the writing of this book when Truffaut's analogy seemed to apply. Invariably, however, the people involved—in ways big and small—helped make it into a pleasant trip.

I would like to express my gratitude to the many people working in the Japanese whisky industry who generously made time for me, welcomed me at their distilleries, shared their experiences and insights with me and put up with my endless queries. Special thanks to Osami Uchibori (former master distiller at Karuizawa Distillery) and to Hajime Asano for sharing his Nikka research materials with me.

A lot of my "research" took place at whisky and cocktail bars around Japan. Well-traveled lovers of the amber nectar often tell me that the best whisky bars in the world are to be found in Japan. I believe them and am grateful to the many bartenders I have had the pleasure of meeting along the way. A special word of thanks must go to Takayuki Suzuki (Park Hotel Tokyo) and Hiroyasu Kayama (Bar BenFiddich) for contributing original cocktail recipes to this book, and the late Osamu Futakata for putting his bar and collection at my disposal to take bottle shots.

At various points along the road, I was fortunate to be able to count on the support of people whose expertise and talent was much needed in preparing the artwork. I would like to thank Yukiko Koshima, the late Ryuichi Tanaka and Bonhams Hong Kong for their help with the photography; Hisashi Watanabe for his beautiful drawing of the mid-1980s "walk of shame" bottles; and Scott van Leenen for all-round technical support, often at extremely short notice.

Many thanks to Carlo DeVito for planting the seed for this project and seeing it through to completion; to my editor Pam Hoenig for weeding out my manuscript and spotlighting areas that needed clarification; and to the team at Cider Mill Press for their support and guidance. Thanks also to Tazlu Endo, my editor at *Whisky Magazine Japan*, for helping to

The author at Yamazaki Distillery

ease the strain of my travel expenses by commissioning pieces I could write in the margin of work on this book.

The original edition of this book has appeared in three different translations with minor updates. I am grateful to Michael Hsieh (Taiwan), Hideo Yamaoka and Yu Sumiyoshi (Japan) and Chesterfield Zhi (China) for the meticulous care and expert knowledge they have brought to bear on preparing *Whisky Rising* for their respective markets. Their feedback made it possible to remove various errors that had crept into the original manuscript.

I also wish to express my heartfelt thanks to the many readers who reached out to me in the years following the publication of the first edition of this book. There are times when writing feels a bit like throwing flowers into a dark cave. Words of appreciation go a long way in making the efforts involved seem worthwhile.

Last but not least, I owe an immeasurable debt of gratitude to my wife, Kyoko, and my sons, Rafa and Remy, for their understanding and patience. I wasn't always there while working on this book, even when I was home. It's good to be back.

Foreword

My first encounter with Japanese whisky wasn't in a bar; it was in the movie *Lost in Translation* (2003), set in Tokyo's Park Hyatt Hotel, where actor Bill Murray, playing an aging film star named Bob Harris, contemplates his life vis-à-vis his experiences in Tokyo, where he's been flown out to film a "Suntory Time" commercial for the company's whisky. While fictional, this was brilliant advertising for Suntory (called "Japandering," which is covered at length in the history section ahead).

Like Murray, I once had the pleasure of an extended stay in the Park Hyatt for work, and find that director Sofia Coppola's portrayal of the disorienting beauty and complexity of Japanese culture resonates with my experiences. Over numerous trips, I've fallen head over heels in love for the landscape and people of Japan, in spite of it being one of the most challenging cultures for an English-speaking visitor to penetrate. With this said, Stefan Van Eycken's insight into Japanese culture from a foreigner's point of view through the lens of whisky is invaluable.

As soon as I received his manuscript, I emailed my friend Ioanna, who runs a Japanese whisky bar with her husband, Hisashi, in Niseko, and she gushed about the author. "If there's anyone qualified to write a book about Japanese whisky, it's Stefan. I haven't read something new that I didn't read on Nonjatta (the website he edits) first, and the distillers respect him for reviewing their whiskies without bias. He's the only person I know who's visited every distillery in the country."

After diving in, I couldn't agree more. While I wish this book had come out a decade ago when you could still find old Japanese whisky—this would have been limited to Suntory in the U.S. market, as Nikka didn't arrive in the States until 2012—at a reasonable price, I believe the best years for the category are ahead. Indeed, many of the photos, interviews and tasting notes in the book feature brand-new distilleries and first releases in the making.

Whisky geeks will appreciate the level of detail shared in the distillery profiles, interviews and charts graphing subjects such as a distillery's pot stills, including year of installation, type, size and lyne-arm configuration. The organization of the data helps knowledgeable readers speculate how each might contribute to the character of the resulting whiskies, with the guidance of the author. The diagrams of the flow of grain whisky through the stills at Kirin's Fuji Gotemba distillery is one of the best explanations of the complex process of continuous distillation I've ever seen.

Stefan has given us a detailed history of the pioneers of Japanese whisky, distilleries not distributed in the U.S. I'd never read about and stories behind closed distilleries like Karuizawa and Hanyu, whose remaining stocks fetch thousands of dollars from collectors clamoring for the last drops.

Stefan has left these collectors a trail of crumbs to help locate these bottlings overseas, as well as whisky specialist bars in Japan where you can sample drams for a pretty price if you make the journey. For those putting together a wish list, there are detailed notes on many of the rarest bottlings from multiple producers including the vintage, alcoholic strength, cask number and wood type, finishing length, age and number of bottles. Complete catalogs with this level of detail are unheard of beyond rare whisky auctions.

Amongst his whisky bar suggestions are some amazing cocktail bars, including two of my favorites in Tokyo—Bar High Five in Ginza and Bar BenFiddich in Shinjuku. He's also included recipes, all original creations from two of Japan's most talented bartenders. Stefan's recommendations are a reflection of the trust and respect bar operators have for him, as their willingness to be present in this book—and share their collection with readers who make the pilgrimage—is a meaningful gesture within their culture.

For me, Stefan's overview is an instant classic that positions *Whisky Rising* alongside the whisky world's most heralded books. There isn't another guide on the market like it and, more importantly, it couldn't have been released at a more exciting moment in Japanese whisky history. As a bartender, I only hope that once distillers' stocks are replenished, the supply of excellent, reasonably priced Japanese malt whiskies will be plentiful once again.

—Jim Meehan, author of *The PDT Cocktail Book*

Introduction

As a child, my intake of liquids was severely limited in terms of variety by the fact that I had a profound dislike of fizzy drinks (not so much the flavor as the actual carbonation of said drinks) as well as milk products (because of a bad bottle of milk dropped off by the milkman one day). Until my late teens, that left only water on the menu at home. Then, I discovered whisky, which, not being carbonated and not being a dairy product, I had no reason to dislike. In fact, I quickly discovered I liked it a lot, the "water of life."

Whisky didn't exist in my parents' house—my mother rarely drank and my father preferred beer and high-proof rum—so that meant whisky came without any baggage or associations attached to it. It was an enchanting *terra incognito* just waiting to be explored. The first bottle I remember buying with my hard-earned pocket money was a single cask Scapa bottled by Cadenhead's—not your typical entry into the world of whisky. Following that purchase, I spent as much time visiting distilleries around Scotland as my limited budget allowed and started buying other obscure bottles of Scotch, looking for new taste sensations.

In 2000, I moved to Japan and I just assumed my days of "whisky immersion" were over, a bit like a passionate surfer who found himself in the Sahara. Nothing could have been further from the truth, of course, but at the turn of this century, "Japanese whisky" wasn't a category that many people got excited about. In fact, few people outside Japan knew there was such a category. In Japan, it was consumed (though not as much as in the past) but most people didn't think highly of their home-made whisky. It was booze and it did the trick, but it wasn't something people spent much time thinking, let alone raving, about.

Shortly after my arrival in Japan, discerning whisky connoisseurs abroad starting paying attention to Japanese whisky. This happened in the wake of a Yoichi single cask taking *Whisky Magazine*'s "Best of the Best" award in 2001, the first time a non-Scottish whisky had taken the top prize at a whisky contest. Eyebrows were raised and curiosity was piqued left and right, but interest in Japanese whisky was still a niche phenomenon and would remain so for another seven or eight years. At home, not much changed.

On one of my travels through Japan, I came across Karuizawa Distillery. I fell in love with it—the whiskies and the place—went back regularly and gradually realized that there was more to whisky than what was coming out of Scotland. I was exhilarated by the quality of the whisky being made in Japan but also more than a little baffled at the cold shoulder it was getting at home. Hard as it may be to imagine nowadays, limited releases of Japanese whisky lingered on the shelves of liquor stores for months, even years. I vividly remember buying some of the earlier Ichiro's Card releases with their labels literally falling off, because they'd been in stores for so long. Now, people would sell their mother-in-law without batting an eye just to get their hands on bottles like those.

The period between 2005 and 2009 was an exciting time for a whisky lover such as myself to be discovering Japanese whisky. The quality of all but the bottom-shelf blends was top-notch, prices were low or reasonable and there was very little competition from other interested parties. The fact that it was such an under-the-radar field—vastly underappreciated and completely uncharted—made it all the more appealing. I was keen to find out more about the marvelous Japanese whiskies I came across and the producers making them, but had a hard time finding any information, either in print or on the Internet, in Japanese or English.

Someone else was having similar trouble around the same time. In 2007, Chris Bunting, a U.K. journalist who had just arrived in Japan, set up the Nonjatta blog with the aim of making information on Japanese whisky available to whisky fans abroad. After a period of very frequent posts, Chris got increasingly busy with work and I noticed there was a lot that was starting to go unreported. I initially set up my own site, Tokyo Whisky Hub, to keep the international whisky community in the loop, but was persuaded it was more effective to post directly on Nonjatta. Shortly after the 2011 Tohoku Earthquake, Chris was forced to move back to the U.K. for personal reasons. Keen to keep the Nonjatta boat afloat, I took over the helm. It had always been our aim to make the site a group effort and a community forum, and for short periods of time we did have one or two people contribute on a regular basis, but it was a lot of work and most people just didn't seem to be able to find the time or justify the effort between work and other commitments.

Until 2016, Nonjatta was the most in-depth resource on Japanese whisky on the internet, but unavoidably, given the more informal and provisional nature of blogging, it was fragmentary and there was much that was out of date and of varying relevance and accuracy. I felt the time had come to finally put together a comprehensive resource on Japanese whisky in print, the sort of book I would have wanted when I started my explorations in the fascinating world of Japanese whisky. It still amazes me that there was no such book available when I sat down to write the first edition of *Whisky Rising*, not even in Japanese.

Whisky Rising was the first book to cover the history of Japanese whisky in detail. It was also the first historical account based on extensive archival research and original source materials (mostly in Japanese) rather than a rehashing of the same two or three stories that the history of Japanese whisky was reduced to in most published writing. The book also offered detailed technical information on all distilleries past, present and near future, and discussed approaches to whisky making as they varied from producer to producer. It was also the first book to help you find your way to and into the actual liquid.

The years since the publication of the first edition have seen unprecedented change on the Japanese whisky scene. The number of active distilleries has more than doubled since 2016, and those that were active when the first edition came out have seen a lot of change, too. As the years went by, the number of voices lobbying for a completely revised and updated second edition grew, but as so often, life took over and time was in short supply. The 100th anniversary of (proper) whisky making in Japan in 2023 provided the impetus to set time aside and focus on the task at hand. The updated manuscript was finished in September 2022. Errors notwithstanding, this second edition reflects the state of affairs on the Japanese whisky landscape in mid-2022.

The book is organized in three parts. Part 1 sketches the history of Japanese whisky. It borrows its subtitle ("On The Way") from a whisky released by one of the younger distilleries, Chichibu, in 2013 (with a follow-up in 2015 and 2019). Just like the name of that whisky was meant to capture something of the dynamism, forward momentum and open-endedness of the continuing adventure that is

Chichibu distillery, this part of the book aims to reflect the drive and energy, the creativity and determination of those who have helped shape the Japanese whisky scene. It's a scene that's young compared with the whisky-making traditions of Scotland, Ireland, the U.S. and Canada, but that doesn't mean whisky makers there are less "on the way" than those in Japan or other whisky-making regions with an even shorter history. We're all on the way. Not everyone knows it. Japanese whisky makers do and hopefully that's reflected in the concise history that is outlined in Part 1.

Being a macro-history of whisky in Japan, the emphasis is on key figures, defining moments, historically important releases and the general drinking culture. The big players get most of the spotlight here, so Suntory and Nikka loom large in these pages. The smaller producers or those who arrived on the scene when a lot of water had already flowed under the bridge are placed in a historical context in their respective chapters of Part 2.

The (in)famous Golden Gai neighborhood in Shinjuku, Tokyo at night

It's impossible to understand the many twists and turns of the story of Japanese whisky without looking at the political and socio-economic developments, both domestic and international, that have steered it. It's also impossible to understand the story of Japanese whisky without looking at aspects of taxation, so the taxman plays a big role in Part 1, too. It's a bizarre character—a bit like the weird uncle—so you'll be entertained.

Part 2 discusses how Japanese whisky is made. As will be clear from these pages, there is no one way of doing things, so each distiller has their own chapter with a historical introduction, technical details about the key equipment used, a description of the processes involved and a brief overview of the distillery's expressions. The key role played by the blender is placed in evidence in interviews with the three most prominent chief blenders in Japan at the time of writing. By necessity, Part 2 is of a more technical nature. I have tried to keep things as transparent and easy to follow as possible, but a basic familiarity with common distillation practice (Scottish and, to a lesser extent, American and Canadian) will be useful. I've tried to keep the geekery to a reasonable minimum. That means I have kept the technical focus limited to those aspects that would give you a deeper understanding of the whisky produced by a distillery. Knowing how many rolls are in a distillery's malt mill is not likely going to give you a deeper appreciation of the whisky you're sipping, so details like those have been omitted from the technical overview.

Japanese distilleries, on the whole, don't swap stock. Almost everything is done in-house. This partly explains why many whisky producers (especially the bigger ones) play their cards very close to their chest. I have done my best to be as comprehensive as possible in the distillery portraits, but in certain cases, the distillers were unable to share certain specifics with me, as per their internal regulations. Obviously, I had to respect that. In some cases, they did provide very specific information but requested that I adjust the level of detail in print to a point they were comfortable with. If you find yourself thinking, "Why is there no in-depth discussion of the yeast used at this distillery?" or some such, that is the reason why.

Much of the information in Part 2 was gathered during visits to the distilleries, by speaking with the men and women who are/were involved in the production process. From a writer's point of view, the post-2016 period is the worst time to be writing this part. In the early

21st century, most of the technical details in the distillery portraits would have remained accurate for years and years to come. Now, there is so much change, so much tweaking, so much research and development going on at distilleries in Japan that some of the information is bound to be "wrong" by the time the book rolls off the press. Pot stills may have been added, the fermentation time may have been adjusted or wood policy may have changed. I can't stop change, nor would I want to. The distillery portraits are therefore to be seen as snapshots in time.

I have visited most of the distilleries featured in Part 2 many times over the years. When I wrote the first edition of *Whisky Rising*, it was still possible to do a final tour right before publication. Currently, that is a very tall order. As mentioned before, there are now so many distilleries —and some of them in rather remote places—that "hitting" all of them in a short span of time requires a sabbatical, not to mention a serious expense account (neither of which I am in a position to negotiate). The COVID-19 pandemic also made it considerably more challenging to visit distilleries over the past couple of years as producers, understandably, prioritized the well-being of their staff. All in all, I am pleased that I did manage to visit most of the new distilleries, in spite of the challenges, as that is the most enjoyable part of writing about whisky for me, per-sonally: the experience of meeting those making the actual liquid in their natural habitat. In a few cases, I have had to revert to online tools of the sort that have become more prevalent at the workplace during the pandemic.

Many Japanese companies—and this includes many of the whisky producers in this book—value the concept of *kaizen*, which is usually translated as "continuous improvement," the opposite of "if it ain't broke, don't fix it." If you notice that some information in the distillery portraits no longer reflects reality when you are reading them, then chances are we'll be drinking even better whisky in five or ten years' time, or have more choice.

In another way, this was a great time to be writing Part 2. Back in 2016, when working on the first edition of this book, a handful of new distilleries had to be added to the Japanese whisky map. If, at the time, someone had told me I would need more than 20 new pins six years later, I would have told them stop dreaming. And yet, that's the reality now. It's a period of unbridled optimism and initiative, and I am thrilled that I am able to include history in the making in these pages. It's not often that one gets to witness the birth of a new dream, the beginnings of a brand-new whisky adventure, and here we have two dozen captured in words and images.

A word about the selection of the distilleries. "Making whisky" is a very vague concept in Japan. Legally speaking, "production" covers everything from sourcing whisky (mostly abroad) and blending it, with or without further aging, to making it from scratch, starting with the raw materials. To produce whisky in Japan, you need a license. So, to run a whisky distillery, you need a license, but having a license and shipping whisky out of your warehouse does not make you a distillery—not necessarily; not in my book. If it seems like I have missed a "whisky distillery," dig a little deeper into the production methods of the people behind the product and you'll understand why.

There are many new whisky distillery projects currently in progress, and by the time you're holding this book, several new pins will have to be added to the map, but I had to draw the line somewhere, so this book covers all Japanese whisky distilleries that were active by September 2022—in as far as this was public knowledge, of course.

Distilleries come, but they also go. In the course of writing the first edition of this book, the iconic Karuizawa Distillery—my first love—was razed to the ground. The last chapter of Part 2 is dedicated to this and other lost distilleries. It's sad to see dreams come to an end but as whisky lovers we are fortunate that there is still whisky from most of these lost distilleries around—not much and it's not cheap, but it's still around for the savoring. Until the last drop has been consumed, the spirit of these lost distilleries lives on.

Part 3 of this book spotlights the actual liquid. It covers ways of drinking, includes 10 original cocktail recipes using Japanese whiskies created at my request by two immensely talented Japanese bartenders, lists 50 bars where the odds are high you will be able to find some quality Japanese whisky, has a section on iconic Japanese whisky series and reviews of 33 absolutely stunning drams.

Before we dive in, I'd like to briefly mention a few conventions followed in this book. Japanese whisky makers spell whisky without an "e," like in Scotland, so that is the spelling used throughout this book. To avoid confusion, I have reserved the % symbol for references to abv (alcohol by volume). In all other contexts, I've used "percent." Japanese names are written in Western order, so in the case of Kihei Abe, "Kihei" is the given name and "Abe" the family name. Japanese words that foreign readers may not be familiar with have been italicized. The word "sake" is slightly ambiguous. In Japanese, *sake* is a general term for alcoholic beverages. Basically, it means "liquor." The beverage called "sake" in English is usually referred to as *nihonshu* in Japan. *Seishu*, the legal term, is less commonly used in conversation. In this book, sake (not italicized) is used to refer to the alcohol beverage made from fermented rice.

There are various ways to transliterate Japanese words into the Latin alphabet, each with its own advantages and drawbacks. To give an example, the Japanese word for "brewery/distillery" can be transcribed as *jyozo, jouzou, jōzō, jôzô* or *jozo*. I have opted for the last one, which is a simplified version of the Hepburn romanization system (the third option without the macrons). This is the system most used in English-language newspapers and media. In the case of my example here, it's the way you will most often see it romanized on bottle labels by producers themselves as well. It doesn't tell you which sounds are long, but that is the case with the spelling system used by most languages in the world anyway, including English. With the simplified Hepburn system, odds are you will get close enough to the correct Japanese pronunciation. You can check my theory for yourself—*jozo* is pronounced by putting the first syllable of "Joseph" together with the "zo" of "ozone."

And with all that under our belt, we are ready for a wild ride through the history of Japanese whisky.

●

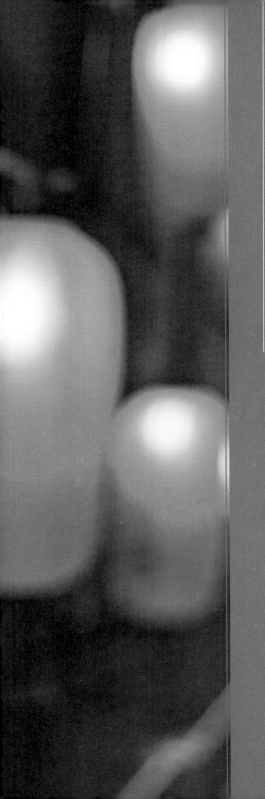

Part I

ON
THE
WAY

Autumn in Karuizawa

A History of Japanese Whisky

BEGINNINGS

As story beginnings go, that of Japan's love affair with whisky is so cinematic it feels almost staged. It takes place in the margin of an epochal event and starts with a transaction that seems of little significance. Later on, of course, as the story develops, this will be reinterpreted as the fateful moment. This sort of beginning has become such a worn-out dramatic device in historical fiction that (screen)writers would almost certainly steer away from it nowadays, for fear of being labeled "unimaginative." Fortunately for us, this isn't fiction.

On July 8, 1853, Commodore Matthew C. Perry illegally entered Edo Bay with his Black Ships, demanding treaty negotiations with the Japanese. This was risky business, at the time. Under the Tokugawa shogunate, a policy of national seclusion had been implemented. Since 1633, no one was allowed in or out of the country—some strictly regulated exceptions aside—on penalty of death. Seeking to end Japan's isolationist stance, Perry initiated negotiations with local officials. Records indicate that during the diplomatic maneuvering, together with a letter from President Millard Fillmore, a white flag and a few other "gifts," the U.S. delegation handed some whiskey to the Japanese representative. The Japanese told Perry never to come back. Perry replied he would be back to receive their answer a year later.

Clearly, patience was not one of Perry's virtues. Half a year later, he had returned with more ships . . . but also more whiskey. As they say, every cloud has a silver lining. After initial resistance, Perry got permission to land in Kanagawa, near the site of present-day Yokohama.

On March 13, 1854, some presents were brought ashore, including: a barrel of whiskey "for the Emperor"; 20 gallons of whiskey each for Commissioner Hayashi and Abe, Prince of Ise, 1st councilor; 10 gallons for each of the other five councilors; and 5 gallons for each of the other four commissioners. We don't know if the whiskey had anything to do with it, but this time around, things worked out well for Perry. On March 31, 1854, the Treaty of Peace and Amity between the United States and Japan was signed aboard Perry's ship, the Powhatan. Apparently, there was liquor involved there, too. The Kanagawa Treaty brought to an end 220 years of national seclusion and precipitated the signing of similar treaties with other western powers.

Unfortunately, there are no details available as to the sort of whiskey that was gifted by Perry. Most likely, it was rye whiskey, but there is no way of knowing. We also have no idea how the whiskey was received by the Japanese, i.e., whether they liked it or not. Apparently, the barrel never made it to the emperor, so *some* people must have liked it quite a bit.

By the end of the shogunate (1868), people in Japan knew there was such a thing as "western liquor" (*yoshu*), but as a category it was seen as an oddity and far removed from everyday life. The abolition of feudalism resulted in enormous social and political changes. During the 1870s and 1880s, Japan's social and economic institutions were radically reformed along the lines of models provided by Western nations. "Civilization and Enlightenment" became the political slogan of the Meiji Restoration and a voracious appetite for new ideas, and interest in new technologies and new industries, marked the new era.

It was in this climate that the first attempts at making "Western liquor" in Japan took place. Rather than copying the production methods (which nobody in Japan was familiar with, anyway) people tried to approximate the characteristics of the liquid (imagined, in most cases) by using ingredients and techniques that were familiar to them. There was already a practice of making Japanese liquors by steeping leaves, bark and roots of various plants in mirin, a type of rice wine used in cooking. The first attempts at making ersatz Western liquor involved little more than replacing mirin with alcohol and adding sugar where needed. Although there was a history of illicit manufacture of liquor in Europe and the U.S. in the eighteenth and nineteenth century, no recipes developed by bootleggers and moonshiners there were circulating in Japan. Everything was trial and error.

According to lore, a medicinal tradesman by the name of Kurayoshi Takiguchi, working out of a shop in Takekawa-cho, Kyobashi, was the first to make western liquor in Japan. His claim to fame was a simple concoction he made in 1871, consisting of shochu (a clear distilled spirit commonly made from rice, sweet potatoes, barley or sugarcane) to which *Rubia tinctorum* (madder) steeped in sugar syrup was added. Other people with a background in making medicinal potions soon followed suit.

It's easy for us to be dismissive of these crude attempts at making Western-style liquor. From a business point of view, however, the enterprise had its appeal. There was no need for special equipment and products could be made in small batches. Risk was low, profits high. Since the general consumer had no frame of reference—that is to say, no or very scant familiarity with the "real deal"—these domestically made versions were welcomed with curiosity and interest, for the most part. There was also another incentive. At the time, alcohol was considered a pharmaceutical component, so making liquor by mixing alcohol with flavorings and colorings fell outside the scope of the liquor tax regulations that were in place. It was seen as falling under medicinal practice rather than liquor production. It wasn't until October 1901, when the new "Law on Taxation of Liquor and Beverages Containing Alcohol" was enacted, that these Western-style liquors were taxed.

Up until the first years of the twentieth century, most alcohol (meaning pure alcohol) used in Japan was imported. Its primary use was as a solvent in the production of gunpowder and in the pharmaceutical industry. For this, a high level of purity was required, which Japanese distillers (using batch distillation, like in shochu production) were unable to achieve. In 1902, serious producers in Japan started to import continuous stills from Germany and France. Continuous stills can produce a much purer distillate than pot stills can (up to 95%abv) and are much more cost efficient (once the process is set in motion, it can run indefinitely). Three years after the first continuous stills were imported, the domestic industrial production of pure alcohol was a viable business. By the 1910s, supply exceeded demand.

On the back of this development, a new market for industrial alcohol opened up. Traditionally, shochu was produced by means of single distillation in a pot still (usually not made of copper, though). In 1911, a new type of shochu was created by adding a small amount of shochu (as it was known and made until then) to pure alcohol that had been made in a continuous still and then reduced in strength. This new-type sho-chu became a big hit, especially in the Tokyo area. It's not too hard to understand why factories with continuous distillation equipment were doing good business. On the one hand, they were producing industrial alcohol for various nonbibulatory purposes; on the other, they had the base to make new-type shochu as well as ersatz Western liquor.

In the same year, the last obstacle hampering the development of the domestic production of Western-style liquor was removed. In the wake of Perry's visit, Japan had been forced to accept and sign treaties with foreign countries that contained provisions relating to foreigners and trading that smacked of semi-colonialism. These came to be known as the "unequal treaties" and resulted in, among other things, the for-mation of enclaves in the treaty ports where foreigners lived and could trade outside the provisions of Japanese law. Also, Japan was limited to a maximum import duty of 5 percent *ad valorem* (the assessed value of the product). Because of this, Japanese producers of Western-style liquor felt they couldn't compete with the real deal being exported to Japan by foreign producers.

Towards the end of the nineteenth century, Japan had managed to renegotiate many of the unequal treaties. By 1899, the treaty ports were gone, and in 1911, Japan formally regained tariff sovereignty. Unsurprisingly, the playing field was then slanted in Japan's favor as taxes on imported goods were raised substantially. Foreign products had become very expensive by 1911 so it made good economic sense from then on for Japan to attempt to make "Western liquor" in-house.

By the end of the Meiji era (1912), two producers dominated the ersatz Western liquor market in Japan. In the Kanto area (east of Japan), Denbei Kamiya—who had gained experience working for an importer in Yokohama—was the go-to man. His sweet wines and Denki Bran (liter-ally, "Electric Brandy") were very popular there. In the Kansai area (west of Japan), the Settsu Shuzo company ran the show.

Kamiya never moved beyond the ersatz field. Denki Bran is still pro-duced—now by Godo Shusei—and the recipe is still as secret as it was back then. It can be sampled at the Kamiya Bar, the oldest Western-style bar in Japan (established in 1880), which is located near Kaminarimon, one of the major tourist spots in Tokyo. Settsu Shuzo, on the other hand, played a crucial role in the move from ersatz to authentic whisky, even though the company wouldn't be able to take credit for it. Before we can focus on that move, however, we need to zoom in on two characters who would go on to play a major part in the development of Japanese whisky.

SHINJIRO TORII

Shinjiro Torii was born in 1879 as the second son to Chuube Torii, who ran a money exchange business in Osaka. After two years at the Osaka School of Commerce, Torii started an apprenticeship at a local pharmaceutical wholesaler, Konishi Gisuke Store. Torii was 13 years old at the time.

In addition to medicines, owner Gisuke Konishi also handled wines, brandies and whiskies, so in the course of his apprenticeship Torii came into contact with various types of western liquor. As blending was an essential skill at the drugstore, Torii also acquired a general knowledge of chemistry. After a little over three years, Torii moved to Konishi Kannosuke Shoten, a paint-and-dye wholesaler in Bakuro-machi, Osaka, where he further honed his blending skills, this time blending coloring materials. He stayed for three years and then set out on his own.

In 1899, Torii opened a small store called Torii Shoten in Nishi-ku, Osaka. In the early years, he sold mostly wines and canned foods. Torii had developed a strong interest in western liquor, but the general consumer in Japan didn't share that enthusiasm in those days. Western liquor constituted a mere 0.3 percent of the market at the time and the few people who drank imported wine and the like regarded it as medicine more than anything else.

While working at Konishi Gisuke's, Torii had come into contact with a Spanish wine

Shinjiro Torii in his younger years

trader by the name of Sellés. After Torii set up his own business, he continued to visit Sellés at his home in Kobe to learn about European wines and cuisine. On one of his visits, he had the chance to try an authentic port wine. Torii was so impressed by it that he immediately resolved to focus his energy and resources on the sale of authentic wines on a mass scale. He changed the name of his shop to Kotobukiya Liquor Shop and started bottling and selling unadulterated, authentic wines. Unfortunately, consumers in Japan were far from enamored with the wines Torii was offering. At the time, people in Japan expected wine to be sweet. Torii's wines were considered to be too sour and bitter, so they didn't sell.

Torii found himself sitting on a huge stock of unpopular wines, but he put his blending cap on and got to work. He collected all kinds of sweeteners and flavorings and blended those with the Spanish wines, in search of a taste that would appeal to the Japanese palate. In 1906, he released his first creation, Mukai-Jishi Jirushi Sweet Wine (Double Lion Brand). It sold but Torii wasn't quite satisfied yet.

The big breakthrough came in 1907. Torii had continued to tweak his recipes and finally reached a result he was happy with. Inspired by a red disk he had seen printed on an imported perfume, he named his new product Akadama Port Wine. Torii felt the *akadama* (red ball) was a good, strong iconic image to market his "uniquely Japanese" wine under. It evoked the sun, source of all life, as well as the Japanese flag. Torii promoted his new product tirelessly—apparently, he visited potential clients by bike—and even took out newspaper ads (the first one in 1909). In 1922, Torii set up an itinerant opera troupe (the Akadama Musical Troupe) to help promote the brand around the country. It was disbanded after one year, but it indicates how important marketing was for Torii, even in the early days, and illustrates the lengths he was willing to go to to make his products a success. Akadama Port Wine became a big hit. It's fair to say that, without this sweet wine, the history of Japanese whisky would have been very different.

But Torii wasn't only flogging wines. By the end of the Meiji era, he was selling his own "whiskies." These were, of course, whiskies of the ersatz type. Hermes Old Scotch Whisky dates from 1911. Needless to say, it was neither "old" nor "Scotch" and most definitely not what we would call "whisky" nowadays. Truth in labeling was clearly not a concern in those days. The label does reflect the zeitgeist, however—

Kotobukiya products from the early days with Akadama Port Wine on the left

in particular the rise of militarism during the Meiji Restoration—in stating "S.T. Hermes & Co." were "purveyors to the Imperial Army and Navy Department and all Noble Families." Similarly, the view of western liquor as a kind of medicine is exemplified by the back label, which reads: "World Wide Reputation in Homes and Hospitals."

During World War I, the Japanese economy flourished and Western liquor became more popular. Being far removed from the conflict, Japan was in an ideal position to pick up the slack in commercial sectors neglected by European wartime economies. The wartime economic growth led to inflation, however, and there was much resentment, especially in rural areas, over the uneven rise of the economy and the impact on people's livelihoods. At Kotobukiya, business was good, even when the inflation hit, and sales were increasing.

An interesting anecdote that set the stage for the production of authentic whisky in Japan dates from these years. One day, Torii had filled an old wine cask with alcohol for blending and then forgot about it. When he returned to it several years later, he was pleasantly surprised by the way in which the liquid had been transformed—in color, aroma and flavor—by the time spent in wood. Not one to waste such a serendipitous discovery, Torii bottled it and put it in the market. Sold as

Torys Whisky in 1919, it was gone in no time. Obviously, since this was a product that was developed accidentally, he couldn't make more of it. In 1920, he launched a new product, Whistan, a bottled whisky and soda. Sales of this were less than spectacular, however. People clearly enjoyed the "accidental whisky" more than the bottled highball.

From the feedback he got, Torii felt that a "whisky era" loomed on the horizon. He was convinced that, in the not so distant future, people in Japan would enjoy drinking authentic whisky on a regular basis. His next goal, a very ambitious one, was to create an authentic whisky suited to the Japanese palate. There was a lot of opposition to this plan, both inside the company and among Torii's friends and supporters. The arguments were the usual ones: 1) nobody had managed to produce whisky in the Scottish tradition outside of Scotland, and 2) following Scottish practice meant maturing whisky, which in turn meant no income for years and years. Torii's counterargument was that the sales of his Akadama Port Wine could easily make up for the lack of cash flow from the whisky operation in the beginning.

The first step was to set up a proper malt whisky distillery in Japan. Torii had requested Mitsui Bussan, a powerful trading company, to be on the lookout for a Scotsman who could be lured to Japan to help set up the distillery. An acquaintance, Dr. Moore, suggested an alternative. He knew of a young Japanese fellow who had studied whisky making in Scotland a few years earlier. Surely, he would be the right man for the job. Torii knew exactly who Dr. Moore was talking about. In fact, Torii was one of the people who had seen the young man off in July 1918. Enter Masataka Taketsuru.

MASATAKA TAKETSURU

Masataka Taketsuru was born in 1894, the third son of Keijiro Taketsuru, who ran a sake brewery in the village of Takehara, near Hiroshima. Although the family's background was in salt farming, Taketsuru's branch had taken up sake making, with considerable success. Masataka's earliest memories were of a world of sake. He became familiar with the strenuous work involved in sake making and his path seemed clear: following in the footsteps of his father. Seeing as his two older brothers had ended up in faraway places with obligations of their own, Masataka was expected to continue the sake business. History had something else in mind for him, though.

Taketsuru studied chemistry at Osaka Technical High School (now Osaka University), but when a new course in zymurgy (the study of fermentation) was introduced, he promptly signed up. While studying with Dr. Sentaro Tsuboi, Taketsuru developed a strong interest in western liquor. In 1917, Taketsuru was introduced to Kihei Abe, the owner of Settsu Shuzo, by an alumnus of his school, Kiichiro Iwai. Settsu Shuzo was the leading producer of industrial alcohol and western-style liquor in Kansai at the time. Taketsuru told Abe he was hoping to acquire experience at a western distillery before taking over his father's business. Abe was

Masataka Taketsuru in June 1918

impressed, and invited Taketsuru to join Settsu Shuzo, which he did, in March 1917. It's safe to assume his father was none too happy. Not only did his son not graduate, he chose industrial alcohol and synthetic liquor production over the traditional craft of sake making.

Taketsuru started at Settsu Shuzo as a chemist, but it wasn't long before he was put in charge of western liquor production. Shinjori Torii bought some of his supplies from Settsu Shuzo, so it's highly likely Torii and Taketsuru met there. Scotch whisky imports had increased and more and more people in Japan were discovering what the real McCoy tasted like. Understandably, there was growing concern among domestic liquor producers that their cheap imitations would fall out of favor before long. Kihei Abe was keen to move beyond the ersatz phase and find ways to make genuine whisky in Japan. In order to facilitate that, he decided to dispatch one of his employees to Scotland to "steal the fire." Surprisingly, he entrusted this important mission to his recent recruit, Masataka Taketsuru.

Taketsuru was elated but his parents were less than thrilled and were opposed to the plan, still clinging to the hope that their son would take over the sake brewery. Abe managed to persuade them. In the end, Taketsuru's parents decided to turn the brewery over to relatives.

In July 1918, Taketsuru was ready for his trip to Scotland. Boarding the *S.S. Tenyo Maru* to San Francisco, he was seen off by his parents and family as well as Torii and Tamesaburo Yamamoto (of Dai-Nippon, later Asahi, Breweries). Unbeknownst to anyone at the time, these two men would hook up with Taketsuru at different critical points in his life later on.

After arriving in the U.S., Taketsuru spent some time at a winery near Sacramento that was operated by Japanese émigrés. In November, he managed to get on a military vessel sailing from New York to Liverpool, and finally arrived in the U.K. on December 2, 1918.

Taketsuru registered for classes in chemistry at the University of Glasgow as well as the Royal Technical College. One of his first contacts in Glasgow was Isabella Lilian (Ella) Cowan, a medical student at the University of Glasgow. Ella introduced Taketsuru to her family in Kirkintilloch, a small town northeast of Glasgow, and in early 1919, he took up residence there.

On April 17, 1919, Taketsuru traveled from Glasgow to Elgin, in the heart of the Speyside region. The plan was to visit J.A. Nettleton, the author of *The Manufacture of Spirit* (1893), which was the reference work on distillation at the time. Taketsuru had been studying his book and he was hoping Nettleton could help him further his studies and set up an apprenticeship at a distillery. Nettleton was keen to help and outlined a preparatory program of daily technical lectures at his house, but the fees involved were prohibitively expensive. Taketsuru had a map of distilleries with him and decided to cold call some of them. The first was closed. At the second one, he had more luck.

Longmorn is an iconic distillery now—every distiller's "second favorite"—but at the time Taketsuru knocked on the door, it was relatively new (built in 1894). J.R. Grant, the general manager, was happy to have the visitor and agreed to a five-day apprenticeship (April 21–25). Much to Taketsuru's delight, there

Taketsuru at Longmorn Distillery in April 1919

was no fee involved. In the course of those five days, distillery manager R.B. Nicol and his staff told Taketsuru everything there was to know about the whisky-making process. He also learned about the importance of casks—ex-sherry casks were preferred at that time—and the use of caramel to adjust the color of the whisky.

Taketsuru was keen to get some hands-on experience at a grain whisky distillery, too. In the early summer of 1919, he managed to arrange a two-week placement at Bo'ness Distillery, owned by James Calder & Co. at the time. Taketsuru familiarized himself with the continuous distillation process using a Coffey still and enjoyed himself so much that he asked for a week extension. The request was granted and Taketsuru used the extra time to gain experience in the fermentation room there.

Taketsuru had plenty to be happy about. Every season brought new thrills: Longmorn in the spring, Bo'ness in the summer, the vineyards of Bordeaux in the fall . . . and marriage in the winter. In the course of his year living with the Cowan family, Taketsuru had grown fond of one of the girls—not Ella, but her older sister Rita (Jessie Roberta Cowan). On Christmas Day 1919, Taketsuru proposed to Rita and she accepted. He indicated he was willing to stay in Scotland for her—how *that* would have changed the course of Japanese whisky history!—but she knew it was his dream to make genuine whisky in Japan, so she assured him she was happy to support him in Japan.

Rita and Masataka Taketsuru got married on January 8, 1920, despite familial unhappiness about the move on both sides. Mrs. Cowan wanted them to get an annulment and Ella wasn't tickled pink

Masataka and Rita Taketsuru

either. Taketsuru's parents back home were livid and got in touch with Kihei Abe, his employer, who quickly traveled to Glasgow to try and sort things out. Abe also had his own reasons for being disappointed in this development. He had a daughter, but no son, and was concerned about the future of his business. Taketsuru was an obvious candidate to bring into the family, but that clearly wasn't a possibility now that he had tied the knot with a Scots lass.

Shortly after they got married, Masataka and Rita Taketsuru moved to Campbeltown. With the help of Professor Forsyth James Wilson, Taketsuru's advisor at the Royal Technical College in Glasgow, Massan (as Rita called him) secured a longer apprenticeship at Hazelburn Distillery. In the course of his five months there, he kept a detailed notebook. This "Report of Apprenticeship: Pot Still Whisky" (called the "Taketsuru Note" for short in Japan) became the blueprint for whisky making in Japan.

In November 1920, Taketsuru was back in Japan, with Rita by his side. He was keen to start making genuine whisky, but quickly discovered things had changed quite a bit since he left. The wartime boom had ended and the economy was faltering. Facing financial difficulties, Settsu Shuzo had decided to scrap its plans to make whisky in the Scottish tradition and to stick to its old ways. Abe promoted Taketsuru to chief engineer and put him in charge of making ersatz whisky and fortified wine. Taketsuru found it soul-crushing to have to revert to the old tricks of faking whisky after his time in Scotland. In 1922, he resigned from Settsu Shuzo. Through an acquaintance of Rita's, Taketsuru found work teaching applied chemistry at a local junior high school. He was happier doing that than making imitation whisky.

1923–1934

By 1923, serious preparations were being made at Kotobukiya to set up a proper malt distillery—the first one—in Japan. In June 1923, Taketsuru entered the employment of Torii. According to Taketsuru (writing 50 years later) his contract stipulated that 1) Taketsuru would be solely responsible for whisky making, 2) that all necessary funds needed to accomplish this would be supplied by Torii, 3) that the contract would be for 10 years, and 4) that an annual salary of ¥4,000 would be set aside for him. The big surprise here is the extraordinarily high salary. At the time, on average, a college graduate entering the workforce could expect to make a little over ¥1,000 a year and to be able to live very comfortably on that. It's not impossible that Taketsuru's memory was playing tricks on him, half a century after the fact. On the other hand, it seems that this kind of salary had been set aside for a potential Scottish expert. It's not implausible that Taketsuru negotiated the terms of his contract based on the argument that his skills were equivalent to those of such an expert.

Next came the search for an appropriate site for the distillery. There are conflicting reports about this. The Suntory version is

Yamazaki Distillery in the late 1930s

that Torii traveled around the country looking for a suitable location. According to Nikka lore, Taketsuru set off around the country to select a distillery site. It's not impossible, of course, that both men were looking—together or independently. Whichever the case, it's clear that there was disagreement on this point. Taketsuru was of the opinion that Hokkaido was the perfect place to set up a distillery, this on account of its similarities in terrain and climate with Scotland. Torii, on the other hand, felt that the remoteness of the place would strain the company's finances. Transport by sea would most definitely guzzle up extra money. Torii also wanted the distillery to be closer to the company's seat. Unsurprisingly, the man bankrolling the enterprise had the final word.

By October 1, 1923, the purchase of the land on which the distillery would sit had been finalized. The location was the village of Yamazaki, on the border between Kyoto and Osaka. Based on his experiences in Scotland, Taketsuru led the construction of the distillery buildings and the installation of the equipment needed. Some of the latter was imported (from Scotland and the U.S.), but most of it (including the pot stills) was made in Japan based on Taketsuru's notes. A little over a year and a whopping 2 million yen later, the distillery was ready. The official start of malt whisky making in Japan was 11:11 a.m. on November 11, 1924.

As distillery manager, Taketsuru had about 15 people working under him. With the exception of one office worker, all of them were employed on a seasonal basis (from October to May). During the first whisky season, things didn't go as anticipated. In fact, the spirit running off the stills left a lot to be desired. The kilning and the difficulty in controlling the distillation temperature were suspected to be the main culprits. As soon as the season was over, Taketsuru was sent back to Scotland to engage in further study. He spent August and early September there and sought the advice of his friends at Hazelburn. Shortly after he left, the distillery closed.

The staff at Yamazaki distillery kept their fingers crossed for the next few years. The story goes that Shinjiro Torii stayed in the distillery day in and day out to follow up on the maturation of the whisky in the barrels. He was far from satisfied with how it was progressing and couldn't understand why it wasn't of the same quality as the Scotch whisky he knew, given the fact that the method of production was the same. Torii spent a lot of time blending, hoping his skills would be able to transform the somewhat flawed components into a quality product. Keen to get feedback from professionals, he took samples around to banquet halls and wholesalers for tastings. His strategy was to slip in a control sample of Johnnie Walker in the hopes that his guinea pigs would choose one of his creations over the control sample. Apparently, this never happened.

Taketsuru's notebook

For years, raw materials were going into the distillery but nothing was coming out, which strained the company finances. To replenish the coffers, Torii developed new products left and right: Palm Curry (curry powder), Le.Te.Rup (lemon tea syrup), Smoca (tooth powder), Torys Sauce, Yamazaki Shoyu (soy sauce), Torys Pepper, Torys Tea and so on. Even though many of these products became hits, Torii had little interest in pursuing them long-term. This wasn't about diversification. It was simply a strategy to keep his whisky business, and the company, afloat.

In April 1929, Torii launched the first whisky coming out of Yamazaki distillery, Suntory Whisky Shirofuda (*shirofuda* means "white label"; later it would be called Suntory White). This was also the first product to carry the brand name Suntory, a composite of sun (the red disc of Akadama) and Shinjiro's last name, Torii. The advertisements for Shirofuda were bold and brash: "Give it a try! The era of blind faith in imported liquors is over. Why not enjoy the finest whisky made in Japan. Suntory Whisky!" Unfortunately, Shirofuda turned out to be a big flop. It was sold for ¥3.5 a bottle, which was quite ambitious given the fact that Johnnie Walker Black Label retailed for about ¥5 in those days. The price wasn't the main obstacle, though. Consumers were put off by the burnt taste and the smoky smell. In 1930, the follow-up was released, Akafuda (red label; later it would become Suntory Red), and two years after that, Tokkaku. Sales were similarly disappointing. In 1931, production at Yamazaki distillery was suspended. Kotobukiya was running out of stock in the warehouse, but they were also running out of money to pour into the whisky operation. Around the same time, interpersonal relations seem to have suffered, too.

Kotobukiya Distillery staff in 1929; the mustachoed man in the middle is the distillery manager

In November 1928, Kotobukiya bought a brewery from Nichiei Jozo in Tsurumi-ku, Yokohama. In late 1929 or early 1930, Taketsuru was transferred there. On paper, he was still distillery manager at Yamazaki, but in reality, he had his hands full as manager of the brewery. Taketsuru had never worked in beer brewing, so it was an opportunity to learn. It was clear, however, that the transfer was a *de facto* demotion. We can only speculate as to why Torii removed Taketsuru from Yamazaki distillery. Disagreements and clashes of opinion had probably taken their toll on the relationship between the two men. At the same time, the transfer may have had something to do with the fact that, by the late 1920s, Shinjiro's eldest son, Kichitaro, had developed an interest in the whisky business. In 1931, Taketsuru was asked to escort Kichitaro to Scotland on a whisky study trip. Kichitaro Torii passed away in 1940 at the age of 33. Because of his premature passing, he didn't have the chance to make his mark in the company. Unwittingly, however, he may have played a part in shaping the history of Japanese whisky.

In the early 1930s, the Japanese government's industrial policies promoted monopolistic organization. The aim was to increase productivity and relieve the pressure of international competition. Initially, this aim was pursued by encouraging mergers. As far as the beer industry was concerned, the government's rationalization scenario included Kirin and Dai Nippon only. In 1933,

1932 advertisement for Suntory Whisky Shirofuda

Kotobukiya sold the brewery they had bought just a few years earlier to Tokyo Beer, which was part of Dai Nippon. This development left Taketsuru very embittered, all the more so because it happened without his knowledge. Approaching the end of his contract with Kotobukiya, it was clearly time for Taketsuru to start weighing his options.

Taketsuru left Kotobukiya in March 1934, but this time round, he didn't gravitate towards teaching. His plans were more ambitious.

1934–1937

On June 8, 1934, Taketsuru sat down with a group of potential business partners in Osaka to discuss the idea of setting up a drinks company. Taketsuru was 39 years old at the time. Two of his main backers (Matashiro Shibakawa and Shotaro Kaga) he had most likely met through Rita, who taught English to their wives. A third, Count Yasutoshi Yanagisawa, he may have met during his time in Scotland.

The initial purpose of the company was to produce apple juice, hence the name Dai Nippon Kaju (The Great Japan Juice Company). The starting capital was ¥100,000, which was modest compared with what Shinjiro Torii had set aside to build his distillery in Yamazaki, and the first general meeting took place on July 2, 1934, again in Osaka. Among other things, it was decided that the company's headquarters would be in Tokyo, with a branch office in Osaka. Taketsuru was appointed executive director; there was no president.

As said, the initial focus of the company was on producing apple juice. Some have interpreted this as a cool-down strategy so as to not appear to be competing straight away with his former employer. It's more likely that it was part of a well-thought-out and sound business plan. From his experience at Yamazaki, Taketsuru knew very well that the first years in a distillery's life were the hardest. There were kinks to iron out, but more crucially, whisky needed time to mature. There was just no way around that. Torii had his Akadama Port Wine to offset the lack of cash flow during the first years of whisky production at Yamazaki. Taketsuru needed a similar cash cow.

As far back as 1920, Taketsuru felt that Hokkaido was the ideal place in Japan to set up a distillery. The notebook he kept during his apprenticeship at Hazelburn Distillery makes mention of this. Hokkaido was also the largest apple-producing region in Japan. The Hokkaido Exploitation Office had introduced young plants from Rochester, New York, in 1874. The following year, the apple trees planted at the office

A 1937 advertisement for Nikka apple juice

site in Sapporo bloomed for the first time, and farmers started incorporating apple culture into their management system. Yoichi was the first area to do so.

In 1933, Taketsuru had visited Ebetsu and Yoichi. A year later, he decided to go for Yoichi. The winters were cold, but not horribly so, and the summers were cool because of the proximity to the Sea of Japan. The apple connection and the availability of cheap land were obviously important considerations, as well.

Taketsuru had no experience whatsoever making apple juice. The only thing to guide him in the process was a copy of C.W. Radcliffe Cooke's *A Book about Cider and Perry*, which he had ordered when he was in Scotland with Kichitaro Torii in 1931. It soon became apparent that that wasn't enough. In fact, the whole apple plan quickly went

Yoichi Distillery in the early days

pear-shaped. The apple juice became cloudy in the bottle, the glue used for the labels became musty, and the drink itself was found to be too sour. On top of all that, it was also very expensive—five times the price of lemonade.

Much of the apple juice was returned and a lot of money was lost. In October 1935, a shareholders meeting was convened and the purpose of the company was redefined to also include brandy and whisky making. During the last days of that year, an extra ¥200,000 was pumped into the company. Obviously, Dai Nippon Kaju was heavily in debt.

In February 1936, a copper pot still arrived at the Yoichi factory. It had been made by Watanabe, the company responsible for the stills at Yamazaki. At Dai Nippon Kaju money was tight, so the budget only allowed for one still. It took a little over a month to prepare the factory for distillation and another five months for the license to be granted (August 26, 1936). New products like jam and ketchup were marketed that year. Whisky wasn't a make-it-today, sell-it-tomorrow product, however. It was four more years before the first whisky produced at Yoichi would see the inside of a bottle.

Meanwhile at Kotobukiya, Torii and his staff had developed a new product. Kakubin (literally "square bottle") was launched in 1937 as a

Kakubin bottles of varying sizes

12-year-old expression and was well received. At the time, there were about 6,000 cafés and 1,300 bars in Tokyo. The highest concentration was in the Ginza district of Tokyo. The tortoise-shell Kakubin bottle became a familiar sight at many of these places and quickly became very popular. Thirteen long years of hard work and persistence were finally starting to pay off.

1937–1945

In the summer of 1937, Japan's invasion and occupation of China escalated into a large-scale war. After the attack on Pearl Harbor (December 7, 1941), the Sino-Japanese war became part of a greater conflict, the Pacific Theater of World War II. One would expect the calamitous events of this period to have had a negative impact on the development of whisky in Japan. In reality, the opposite was true.

The Japanese Navy was largely modeled after the British Navy. What rum was to the British naval personnel, whisky became to the Japanese. As Suntory puts it: "Liquor is inherent in war. In fact, many young men got their first taste of Suntory whisky when in uniform. The production volume of Akadama Port Wine and Suntory Whisky continued to rise to new heights each year." At Dai Nippon Kaju, the situation was similar. The following tables illustrate the impact of the war on whisky production at both companies.

TABLE 1: DAI NIPPON KAJU, SALES 1934–1945

	sales in thousands of yen
1934	0
1935	55
1936	66
1937	139
1938	193
1939	300
1940	1,136
1941	1,250
1942	2,489
1943	3,422
1944	5,830
1945	9,024

TABLE 2: KOTOBUKIYA, YAMAZAKI FACTORY, *KURADASHI* (LIT. LEAVING THE WAREHOUSE), 1930–1945

	sales in kiloliters
1930	17
1931	39
1932	88
1933	102
1934	109
1939	204
1940	291
1943	650
1944	771
1945	487

The big jump in 1940 at Dai Nippon Kaju is partly explained by the fact that, in October of that year, the company came under the command of the navy. The other half of the story is that in June, the company released its first products, Rare Old Nikka Whisky and Nikka Brandy. In both cases, the component spirits were quite young, making blending a challenge, but Taketsuru felt the quality was good. The packaging was appealing and the timing proved to be fortunate. By 1940, alcohol imports had virtually dried up, so there was little competition for Taketsuru's first creations at Dai Nippon Kaju.

The figures for Kotobukiya show a big leap in 1943. In that year, the navy instructed the company to use their liquor manufacturing technologies to produce aircraft fuel. In June 1943, Kotobukiya was ordered to build a factory in Okinawa for the production of butanol and ethanol. This project ate up one-fifth (2 million yen) of the company funds. In January 1944, they were told to build a factory in Surabaya, Indonesia. Later that year, the Osaka factory (which had been set up in 1940 to make "grain whisky") was designated as a naval munitions plant. Brown and white sugar (from Okinawa and Taiwan, respectively) was taken to the factory by truck and turned into butanol.

As the war in the Pacific entered its final phase, many of the factories pumping out butanol and the like were destroyed. Kotobukiya's head office in Sumiyoshi-cho burned down in the Osaka air raids of March 1945. The Okinawa factory was destroyed in April, rebuilt and then destroyed again in June. The same month, the Osaka factory was also bombed. Fortunately (for the development of Japanese whisky, that is) neither Yamazaki nor Yoichi suffered the same fate. Precautions had been taken at both distilleries to protect the stock. At Yamazaki, casks were moved to tunnels in the mountains. At Yoichi, warehouses were constructed around a swamp, with plenty of separation between them, to minimize the losses in the event of fire. Miraculously, both distilleries survived the war with all of their stock intact.

Rare Old Nikka Whisky

An interesting episode from the final days of the war that is usually not spotlighted relates to the construction of the Usuki factory. After the destruction of the butanol plant in Okinawa, the navy asked Shinjiro Torii to build a new factory in the coastal town of Usuki, in Oita prefecture (Kyushu). On the morning of August 15, the groundbreaking ceremony took place. This is a traditional Shinto ritual held before

An original Torys bottle

construction of any sort in Japan to pacify the spirits of the land. It's led by a priest who prays for safety, happiness and protection from disaster. At noon the same day, Emperor Showa addressed the nation via public radio, announcing the end of the war. It must have been a moment of mixed emotions for those present at the groundbreaking ceremony. The Usuki factory was completed in 1947, but set up to serve a very different purpose from that originally anticipated: to assist in the production of Torys Blended Whisky, a new product launched the year before.

There is no doubt that the war was a draining period but, in hindsight, it's clear that there were certain benefits for both companies. Because they were directed by the military, they had privileged access to raw materials. Barley was a scarce resource during the war years but both Kotobukiya and Dai Nippon Kaju had a steady supply coming in. Another plus was the huge thirst for whisky in the military. Special products were developed for them, like Kotobukiya's 1943 Ikari-jirushi Whisky (literally "anchor brand"). According to Dai Nippon Kaju, the navy bought so much whisky that they became the sole customer of the company during the war years; none of their products were available in shops. In November 1944, Dai Nippon Kaju came under the control of the Imperial Army. This led to a tug-of-war for whisky between their old customer, the navy, and the new folks pulling the strings, the army.

The patronage of the military turned out to be a triple blessing for both companies: access to raw materials (and land), booming sales and money saved because promoting products was unnecessary. Given the fact that changing situations always have a delayed effect in the world of whisky-making (because of the time-lag that is the maturation process), this triple blessing also set them up for a smooth postwar transition.

1945—1952

The immediate postwar years were a period of great confusion. Food shortages were severe. Triple-digit inflation wrecked people's lives and black market inflation, which was even higher, was unreal. A bottle of whisky sold for ¥120 by the producer would fetch ¥1,500 on the black market. This was the equivalent of 132 pounds/60 kg of rice at the time, which is significant, since most people were on the verge of starvation. Bona fide producers of whisky (of which there weren't many to start with) were struggling to get hold of barley and other raw materials. Importing was out of the question as international trade was extremely limited and highly regulated. Unsurprisingly, given the profit involved in black-marketeering, lots of whisky with highly suspect credentials started flooding the market. In the best cases, it was like a return to the ersatz whisky days of the Meiji era. In the worst cases, it could kill you.

Soon after the war, it became clear that there was one segment of the population with a thirst for whisky that rivaled that of the Imperial Japanese navy and army: the U.S. occupation forces. As early as October 1, 1945, General Headquarters (GHQ) requested Kotobukiya to deliver whisky to them. For the higher echelons of the U.S. military, Torii produced Rare Old Whisky, the label indicating it was "Specially Blended for American Forces." For the G.I.'s, he created Blue Ribbon Whisky. Since the Osaka factory had been leveled during the last months of the war, these whiskies were made at the new Domyoji factory. The irony is that what went into those bottles was, of course, originally produced with the Japanese military in mind. It was a hard pill to swallow for Shinjiro Torii. Sixty-six years old, the self-confessed patriot

Rare Old Whisky (1945)　　　　Blue Ribbon Whisky (1945)

found himself flogging whisky to the occupation forces. What pulled him through was his determination to keep going without having to let any of his 500 employees go. Rare Old and Blue Ribbon were sold until 1949.

Torii wasn't neglecting the Japanese consumer in the meantime, though. On April 1, 1946, Kotobukiya released a new product, Torys Blended Whisky. "Tastes good and inexpensive," was the catchphrase. "Purity and Palatability Guaranteed," said the label. Torys Blended was a 3rd grade whisky and its success sparked a veritable 3rd grade whisky boom. To understand what that means—"3rd grade"—we need to make a little detour via the tax office.

Tax(ing) Matters (Part 1)

In 1940, the Liquor Tax Law was enacted. This obviously had to do with the fact that the government needed to find extra income to fund the war effort. In the Liquor Tax Law, alcohol beverages were classified into nine categories (at present, there are ten) and the tax was simply based on quantity. For comparison, the table below shows the figures involved for three of the categories, in ascending order of alcoholic strength: *nihonshu* (sake), shochu and whisky. *Zoukokuzei* is the tax levied at the time of production; *kuradashizei* is the tax due when the liquid leaves the *kura* or warehouse.

TABLE 3: LIQUOR TAX LAW 1940, TAX RATES FOR 3 CATEGORIES

	sake	shochu	whisky
zoukokuzei	45	48	50
kuradashizei	55	55	70
		yen per *koku*; 1 *koku* = about 180 liters	

As the war intensified, more money had to be found. On April 1, 1943, the tax was raised significantly. The *zoukokuzei* remained the same, but the *kuradashizei* was substantially increased. In addition, a grading system was implemented. For whisky, this was based on a combination of abv (alcohol by volume) and the amount of "authentic whisky" mixed in (the mix ratio). The table below indicates the abv (%), the mix ratio and the two types of tax levied for the three categories of whisky. In what follows, the mix ratio is to be understood as the amount of "authentic whisky" mixed in, expressed as a percentage of the total volume of the product. To avoid confusion with the abv, the % symbol is dropped for the mix ratio. When a figure is in square brackets, it refers to a limit that is excluded, i.e., 0–[5] means that the mix ratio is lower than 5 percent.

TABLE 4: WHISKY TAXATION, GRADING SYSTEM 1943

	3rd grade	2nd grade	1st grade
abv	37–39%	40–42%	43%
mix ratio	0–[5]	5–[30]	30+
zoukokuzei	50	50	50
kuradashizei	350	470	570
	(yen per *koku*)		

An important stipulation regarding "authentic whisky" was that it had to be over three years old.

In 1944, the *zoukokuzei* was dropped, but on the *kuradashizei* front things kept getting worse. It was raised to 600 per *koku* for 3rd and 2nd grade whisky, and 1,000 per *koku* for 1st grade whisky.

Economic controls continued in place during the postwar recovery period, but in 1949, the first steps were taken to reduce the role of the government and deregulate the economy. Price controls and subsidies were abolished in April 1950 and the market mechanism was largely restored. A free—not completely free, but *freer*—economy meant free competition, of course.

Torys Blended Whisky had sparked a 3rd grade whisky boom. This was an easy field to enter into for any liquor producer. The mix ratio for 3rd grade whisky was under 5 percent. The remainder was blending alcohol, which was not defined in terms of raw materials and production methods used. It was, for all intents and purposes, a more-or-less neutral base alcohol. What this meant was that one could make "whisky" without using a single drop of "authentic whisky" (i.e. malt). Anyone who had access to neutral spirits and a knack for approximating the color, aroma and/or flavor of whisky could make 3rd grade whisky.

According to Suntory, Shinjiro Torii put "a large amount of genuinely produced whisky into Torys Whisky." Obviously, this had to be under the legal limit of 5 percent. At Dai Nippon Kaju, Masataka Taketsuru was reluctant to make 3rd grade whisky. He didn't consider such a product worthy of his time and skills and definitely not worthy of the name "whisky." His focus was on the 1st grade category, for which the mix ratio was 30 percent or more.

Around 1950, the average price of a 3rd grade whisky was around ¥300. A 1st grade whisky cost considerably more: around ¥1,350. To give an idea of how much this was at the time, the average annual salary was ¥100,000. The man in the street, obviously, couldn't afford 1st grade whisky. In fact, 1st grade whiskies weren't even sold in most liquor stores, rather in department stores, where well-heeled folks would pick them up as special gifts.

By 1950, Dai Nippon Kaju was in a tight spot. It was all fine and well to have lofty ideals, but they needed to generate profits. The people at Kotobukiya were promoting Torys left, right and center and sales were spectacular. At Dai Nippon Kaju, the figures were depressing. Because of the high inflation during the postwar years, various costs (ranging from raw materials to salaries) had gone up considerably. Because of the company's adherence to the 1st grade whisky category, it was hard to offset those costs. Towards the end of the 1940s, the situation was so severe that they had trouble making their liquor tax payments to the government.

A 1957 advertisement for Rare Old Nikka Whisky

Mamoru Takahashi, head of the National Tax Administration Agency, urged Taketsuru to start selling 3rd grade whisky. Reluctantly, he gave in. In August 1950, he addressed his employees. "Don't forget the pride we take in making whisky," he said, "but understand the situation." The following month, the company entered the 3rd grade whisky field with Rare Old Nikka Whisky (also referred to as Special Blend Whisky). Like Torii with Torys four years earlier, Taketsuru used the highest mix ratio allowed under the regulations. Rare Old Nikka Whisky was first released as a pocket bottle (180ml, 37%abv, ¥150). This was followed up, in May and October 1951 respectively, with a 720ml round bottle (*marubin*, ¥600) and a 500ml square bottle (*kakubin*, ¥380).

Rare Old Nikka Whisky seems to have done the trick for Dai Nippon Kaju. In 1950, net profits went up fourfold compared with the year before; the year after, sales doubled. They still weren't quite there, though. Taketsuru hadn't used any artificial colorings or flavorings in making Rare Old Nikka Whisky, and seeing as aged malt was only a small component of the product, as per the regulations, the liquid in the bottle was perceived to be "thin" and weak in flavor. Experiments with homemade caramel were carried out to try and stabilize the color. Another issue was the price point. Even though it was relatively cheap, it was still more expensive than Torys (640ml, ¥360).

In 1950, Kotobukiya launched a product that would go on to be their best performer in the decades to follow, Suntory Old. Torii had conceived the product (including the label design) a decade earlier, but 1940 was a turbulent year. The wartime climate was hardly conducive to promoting a high-quality product, so the plans were shelved. In 1950, Torii was ready. Suntory Old (760ml, 43%abv, 1st grade) was sold in a distinctively shaped brown bottle, not unlike the famous blended Scotch whisky Buchanan's De Luxe but more rounded. Because of its similarity in shape with the traditional *daruma* doll, Suntory Old came to be known affectionately as "Daruma."

"Old" was clearly the buzzword in those days. Judging from an advertisement in *Newsweek* in 1956, however, Suntory Old really *was* old—at least, by the standards of those days. The ad states that the whisky was "carefully distilled from choice Golden Melon barley . . . aged 8 to 15 years in oak sherry casks." At the time, no one else in Japan would have been able to come up with a product with such specs.

A Suntory Old bottle from the late '50s/early '60s

1952–1964

On April 28, 1952, a little over seven months after the signing of the San Francisco Peace Treaty, Japan formally regained its sovereignty. After the end of the Korean War (1953), the Japanese economy entered a period of high growth. The model of the "American way of life" (as perceived by people in Japan through films, TV dramas, magazines and advertising) became an ideal to aspire to. Having a TV, a refrigerator and a washing machine in an American-type suburban house was the ultimate dream for the Japanese middle class. The first supermarket in Japan, Kinokuniya in Aoyama, opened in 1953. A lively bar and café scene developed and the enjoyment of western liquor became a social phenomenon. Whisky was everywhere. Until 1958, it was the most consumed type of liquor in Japan. Afterwards, it was overtaken by beer—spectacularly so, it has to be said—but whisky remained firmly in second place for decades.

At Dai Nippon Kaju, they realized that the times they were a-changing. Up until 1952, their main market was Hokkaido. This accounted for 60 percent of their sales. What they wanted next was national name recognition. In view of that, some structural changes were implemented in 1952. In April, the headquarters was moved from Yoichi to Nihonbashi, Tokyo. In August, the name of the company was changed to Nikka Whisky Co. Ltd., which made sense, since they hadn't produced juice since 1945. By November 1952, a new bottling plant, located in Azabu, Tokyo, had been set up. They clearly meant business. Things were far from easy, though. Looking back on his life in later years, Taketsuru said the year 1953 was the hardest one. What he resented most of all was having to beg for loans at banks. In the summer of 1954, two of the founders (Shotaro Kaga and Matashiro Shibakawa) sold their shares to Tamesaburo Yamamoto, the president of Asahi Beer. As a result of this, Asahi (together with the Sumitomo bank) held a 51 percent share in Nikka. This would prove to be a significant help later on.

At Kotobukiya, as it was still known then, a new wind was gently blowing through the company as well. Around this time, Keizo Saji began to stand in for his father more frequently. Keizo Saji was the second son of Shinjiro Torii. (When Keizo entered junior high school, he was adopted by relatives on his mother's side, which explains the different family name.) Saji had joined Kotobukiya in October 1945, shortly after his return from the navy. He advocated a more scientific approach to prod-uct development and set up a research lab at the com-pany in February 1946, the Institute of Food Chemistry. Apparently, Torii taught his sons nothing about whisky making. Maybe he felt that it was better for them to find their own way into the pro-cess, just like he had. In that sense, Saji was self-taught.

Keizo Saji in the director's office at the laboratory in Osaka, circa 1946

Tax(ing) Matters (Part 2)

In 1953, the Liquor Tax Law was amended. This involved a few changes, some in name only, others more substantial.

First of all, a recategorization took place: 1st grade/2nd grade/3rd grade whiskies in the old system were now special grade/1st grade/2nd grade whiskies, respectively, in the new system. The new structure was as follows:

TABLE 5: WHISKY TAXATION, GRADING SYSTEM 1953

	2nd grade	1st grade	special grade
abv	37–39%	40–42%	43%
mix ratio	0–[5]	5–[30]	30+

As far as the mix ratio is concerned, a change of phrasing was adopted. The term "authentic whisky" (*honkaku* whisky) was changed to *genshu*. This is a difficult term to translate. It is a composite of *gen*, which means original/primitive, and *shu*, which is a blanket term for alcohol. It means different things for different types of liquor. In the context of whisky, "unblended alcohol" is to be understood as "undiluted malt whisky."

This change in terminology seems like a trivial detail but it isn't. "Authentic whisky" was defined as "made from grain which is malted, fermented, distilled and matured for three years." *Genshu*, however, doesn't include the last part of that definition, the three-year minimum maturation period. The day it runs off the stills, malt distillate is *genshu*. Clearly, the tax authorities were being pragmatic. At the time, 80 percent of all whisky consumed was 2nd grade whisky (the lowest grade). Demand was huge. To assist the producers in creating "whisky" expediently, the three-year maturation minimum was erased. As a "whisky" producer, you were in total control of the lead time: no more waiting, if you didn't feel like waiting. But pragmatic decisions can have far-reaching consequences. Quality must have suffered, except in cases where the producer chose to uphold higher standards. Baffling as it may seem, the three-year minimum maturation period still hasn't been reinstated, *anno* 2022.

The 2nd grade whisky field was very lucrative but it was also very competitive. The table below lists the main players with their respective price points in 1953.

TABLE 6: DOMESTIC WHISKY PRODUCERS, MAIN PRODUCTS IN 1953

	price (yen)	bottle size (ml)	price per 100ml
Ocean (*kaku*)	330	550	60
45	330	550	60
Ideal	330	550	60
Nikka (new *kaku*)	340	550	62
Nikka (*maru*)	500	720	69
King	500	720	69
Silver (*maru*)	500	750	67
Torys	340	640	53

In terms of price as well as market share, Torys was unbeatable. It wasn't until November 1956 that Nikka managed to put out a product at the same price, Marubin Nikky (640ml, 37%abv, ¥330). They put as much quality malt into it as the regulations allowed, but didn't succeed in pushing Torys off the throne. Marubin Nikky was discontinued in 1964. Torys is still around, although the recipe must be quite different nowadays.

With so many products vying for the attention of the consumer, brand building took on key importance. One way in which the big players went about promoting their flagship whiskies was by setting up official bars. This wasn't a new strategy. Kotobukiya opened the first Suntory Bar in 1938, in Umeda, Osaka. The first Torys Bar opened in Ikebukuro in 1950. From the mid-'50s on, however, there was a veritable explosion of "official bars." Kotobukiya alone was said to have had 35,000 bars nationwide featuring the Torys or Suntory brand at this time. The Torys bars were instrumental in wiping away the murky image that bars had up until then. Drinks and snacks were priced the same at every single one of these places. A whisky straight was ¥40; a highball (a *Torihai*) ¥50 and a gin fizz ¥100. The bars offered relief after a hard day of work and the ambience was such that women could enter without trepidation. Interestingly, their bars did not want men and women to come together.

Torys bottles from yesteryear

Separately was fine. Presumably, this was a way to discourage couples from frequenting the bars. Maybe this made them good pick-up places. One thing is for sure, the bars must have been popular, because other producers soon followed suit and set up their own.

Advertising and PR was another area in which Kotobukiya pulled out all the stops. In April 1956, Keizo Saji started publishing a magazine called *Yoshu Tengoku* (Western Liquor Heaven). It was conceived as an educational magazine, but educational with a twist. Featuring popular mature content—playful but intelligent—and a smattering of nudity, it was meant to be "a textbook for liquor and play" (*sake to asobi no tekisuto*). Initially, the circulation was around 20,000. The magazine was distributed to Torys bars around the country and quickly became very popular. People would flock to the bars to read the latest issue. At the height of its popularity, 240,000 copies were printed.

It was Keizo Saji's conviction that they weren't just selling a product, but "a lifestyle in which the product was present." Starting in 1958, a team of 10 highly talented people was entrusted with creating advertisements that exemplified that belief. Two particularly humorous Torys ads are worth singling out. Both date from 1961. For the first, Takeshi Kaiko came up with the tag line "More 'human' is what I want to be." The second one, the "Dream Campaign" (conceived by Hitomi Yamaguchi) took Japan by storm. Here, the catchphrase was "Drink Torys and go to Hawaii!" At a time when going to Hawaii seemed like an unattainable dream, this campaign captured the imagination of the people and whet their appetite for overseas travel. Both ads (and many, many more) feature the lovable character of Torys, designed by Ryohei Yanagihara. Uncle Torys is the proverbial man in the street, the sort of character everyone knew from real life: in his late thirties, single, a stand-up guy, a little spineless but stubborn, with a soft spot for the ladies but clueless when it comes to taking action. Even now, Uncle Torys is still alive and kicking.

The people at Kotobukiya were aware of the importance of advertising, but they also knew that effort and creativity in that field was meaningless without a quality product. As Shinjiro Torii put it: "No matter how much our products are advertised, they must be of superior quality. Ads cannot be created unless we have confidence in our products. If our valued customers complain of false advertising, that's the end of our success. First and foremost, we have to create the absolute best products."

Yoshu Tengoku covers

Torys "More 'human'..." advertisement (1961)   Torys "Dream Campaign" advertisement (1961)

In May 1960, Shinjiro Torii presented his final creation (Suntory Royal) at a grand 60th anniversary event held at the Shin Osaka Hotel. The flavor profile was based on a detailed study of the distinctive palate of the Japanese and the blend was developed in close collaboration with Keizo Saji and Kan Sato, the company's second chief blender. Upon tasting his son's final test blend, Shinjiro closed his eyes and said: "The aroma brings to mind a flurry of falling cherry blossom petals." The following year, he handed the reins of the company over to his son.

At Nikka, they weren't resting on their laurels either. Even though the mid-1950s and early '60s were dominated by 2nd grade whisky, Nikka kept producing special grade whiskies, too. In November 1955, they launched Gold Nikka (43%abv, ¥2,000). The year after, in June 1956, they introduced Black Nikka (43%abv, ¥1,500). In a way, it was ahead of its time. Ten years later—by then in *kakubin* (square bottle)—it became a big hit. It's still being sold today.

In October 1962, Nikka launched their most expensive product, Super Nikka (43%abv). It was priced at ¥3,000. A college graduate's first salary would have been around ¥18,000 at the

An Uncle Torys toothpick holder

time. Super Nikka held special significance for Masataka Taketsuru. His wife, Rita, had passed away the previous year and, as part of the grieving process, he poured all his energy into developing a new blend. The result was Super Nikka. Taketsuru insisted on a presentation befitting of the liquid and had bottles hand-blown for it. Each bottle had to be hand-matched with a glass stopper that fitted the neck. The production cost of the bottle alone was ¥500, more than what a bottle of 2nd grade whisky retailed for. Per year, only 1,000 bottles were produced.

Just a few weeks before Super Nikka was launched, Nikka decided to boost their 2nd grade whisky presence in the market by replacing Marubin Nikky with Extra Nikka (37%abv, 640ml, ¥330). With the help of Dentsu, a large and prestigious advertising agency, they managed to make Extra Nikka the second best-selling whisky in Japan, after Torys.

A 1957 advertisement for Gold Nikka and Black Nikka

The original Super Nikka (1962)

Tax(ing) Matters (Part 3)

In 1962, the Liquor Tax was amended again. This time there were two major changes. The first involved a slight bumping up of the mix ratio of the lower grade whiskies, but a lowering of the mix ratio threshold for special grade whiskies. For ease of comparison, the table below shows the old mix ratios (dating back to the 1953 amendment) along with the newly stipulated ratios.

TABLE 7: WHISKY TAXATION, GRADING SYSTEM 1953 VS 1962

	2nd grade	1st grade	special grade
abv	37–39%	40–42%	43%
mix ratio 1953~	0–[5]	5–[30]	30+
mix ratio 1962~	0–[10]	10–[20]	20+

The other change was the adoption of an ad valorem tax for expensive liquor. The tax was applied to items (not only whisky, but premium sake, wine, etc., too) of which the price exceeded a certain threshold. For whisky, it only applied to special grade products. In 1971, it was expanded to also apply to 1st and 2nd grade whiskies.

The early 1960s were a period of great optimism and enterprise in the Japanese whisky world. Keizo Saji was now running Kotobukiya. One of his first goals was to break into the beer business. This was seen as a fool's dream at the time, given the utter domination of the domestic beer market by three huge companies. Towards the end of April 1963, the first product—Suntory Beer—was launched. Two months earlier, the company name had officially been changed to Suntory. Selling the beer proved to be a harsh exercise in marketing from the ground up, but that's a story that belongs in a different book.

Saji was also looking beyond the domestic market. In May 1962, he had established Suntory de Mexico SA in Mexico City to begin manufacturing Torys whisky locally. The plan was to take the country by storm but it soon became clear that was wishful thinking. Production in Mexico started in late October 1963. It's unclear how exactly whisky was made there, i.e., whether malt from Yamazaki distillery was exported in bulk to Mexico and blended with locally produced blending alcohol, or whether malt whisky was produced in Mexico, too. Maybe a bottle or two survives in an attic or on a dusty shelf somewhere in Mexico. It would be interesting to compare the Torys made in Mexico with that produced back home around the same time.

Back home, whisky production got a serious boost at both Suntory and Nikka in 1963. At Suntory, malt whisky production at Yamazaki distillery was ramped up considerably. Since 1958, the distillery had been working with four pot stills. In January 1963, there were eight. This meant production capacity increased threefold. At Nikka, on the other hand, a Coffey grain whisky production facility was set up in Nishinomiya. The cost involved was a staggering 150 million yen. Both companies were clearly getting ready to shift gears.

1964–1972

In February 1964, Nikka launched a new product called Hi Nikka (720ml). It was a 2nd grade whisky, but the abv was 39%. This was unusual. Most 2nd grade whiskies were bottled at 37%abv, the lower limit for the category, because less alcohol meant more profit. Hi Nikka was priced at ¥500. They started selling it in the Tokyo area, and then did a nationwide rollout. The following month, Suntory launched Suntory Red. Size? 720ml. Abv? 39%. Price? ¥500. From a distance, it's easy to ascribe a cause-effect relationship to these events. It's doubtful, however, that Suntory could have produced a product with the same specs as Nikka at such short notice—unless inside information was circulating, of course. Again, we'll never know. The thinking in the Suntory camp was that the time had come to offer those who liked Torys an alternative that was a step up.

A selection of old Suntory Red bottles

The events of early 1964 sparked what became known as the "500-yen whisky war." Sanraku Ocean, the third-biggest player (the result of the merger of Sanraku and Ocean in 1962), came out with M&S, which—surprise, surprise—was 2nd grade whisky, bottled at 39%abv and priced at ¥500 for 720ml. Other producers soon followed suit. The year after, the "whisky war" entered its second phase.

In September 1965, Nikka released a new version of Black Nikka. In the early 1960s, Masataka Taketsuru had initi-

A 1965 advertisement for Black Nikka showing the Coffey still (on the left)

ated a project to produce proper grain whisky. Up until then, blended whiskies were made with so-called "blending alcohol" in Japan, which could be anything and usually wasn't aged in wood. Keen to follow Scottish practice and make blends with grain whisky, Taketsuru set up a grain whisky distillery in Nishinomiya. This was done with considerable help from Tamesaburo Yamamoto of Asahi Bakushu. The first grain whisky was produced there in October 1964, and a year later the first product incorporating the grain whisky made at Nishinomiya was launched. That was the new version of Black Nikka. It was a 1st grade whisky (42%abv, 720ml) that retailed for ¥1,000.

Nikka promoted their new Black Nikka—which replaced the original *toku kaku* (special grade, square bottle)—with the following tagline: "Tastier than *kaku*–1,350 yen products have become a thing of the past at Nikka." The reference here was to their own *kaku* (the old Black Nikka). One of the reasons why Nikka felt the taste eclipsed their old version of Black Nikka was because the new product was made with grain whisky rather than blending alcohol.

The phrasing was a bit unfortunate, though, and this soon led to major trouble with Suntory. At the time, Suntory had a product in the market—their famous Kakubin (affectionately called *Kaku* by consumers)—which also retailed for ¥1,350. Suntory felt that the *kaku*

Vintage Torys
promotion goods

reference in Nikka's tag line was to *their* Kakubin, i.e., that the new 1st grade Nikka product was tastier than Suntory's special grade product. Suntory accused Nikka of misleading advertising and slander, and sent a letter of protest to all liquor shops in the country. In it, they also addressed another point they were bothered about in Nikka's promotion of the new Black Nikka.

Obviously, Nikka was proud that they had created a product incorporating grain whisky distilled in a traditional Coffey still and advertised this in their promotion for the new product. Suntory objected to Nikka's claim that grain whisky was more flavorful than blending alcohol and that it boosted the flavor of a blended whisky. Suntory's argument was that, in Scotland, grain whisky was considered to be a "silent" component, and that its only function was to thin the flavor of malt whisky, to make it more easy to drink—in other words, that it didn't add flavor.

On November 5, 1965, Suntory launched Gold Crest. Size? 720ml. Abv? 42% (1st grade). Price? ¥1,000. The "1,000-yen whisky war" was about to start. For the next six months, both companies battled it out in the media, including full-page newspapers ads.

The following years were a period of fierce competition. In 1966, Suntory released a double-sized Red (1,440ml). They priced it at ¥900 and marketed it with the hook "twice the whisky, 100 yen cheaper" (the 720ml bottle was ¥500). By then, Red had overtaken Torys and accounted for 60 percent of the company's whisky sales. Suntory also made double-sized versions of Torys and White, following the success of the big Red. Nikka's answer came in 1967: a big Hi-Nikka, priced at ¥1,000 (twice the price) but the consumer was getting some extra liquid, since this came in 1,600ml bottles. Whisky fans would have endless debates about which was the better choice—the big Red or the big Hi-Nikka—and that was the point of the whole exercise, of course. The rivalry would live on into the 1970s. In 1976, Nikka started selling a jug-style bottle of Hi Nikka (1,920ml; ¥1,380). Suntory responded with Red Jumbo, which came in exactly the same bottle and at the exact same price.

In the larger scheme of things, these whiskies offered great value for the money. For the sake of comparison, Johnnie Walker Red retailed for around ¥5,000 at the time, which was 10 times more than these whiskies. There would have been a difference in quality, of course, but the way whisky was drunk in Japan at the time (mostly highball style) this wouldn't have been much in evidence.

During the "whisky war," companies came up with various strategies to sway and/or tie the consumer to their product. It became almost *de rigueur* to include a small gift for the customer—a shot glass or some such—anything that could influence a purchase at the liquor shop. Another strategy was the "bottle-keep" system, which was introduced at bars around this time. The beauty of the system was its simplicity: the customer would buy a bottle at the bar, and keep it there with his/her name on it. It was a stroke of genius: it tied the customer not only to the product but also to the bar. An added bonus was that it prevented tampering, i.e., bars refilling bottles with cheaper (read: low-quality) whisky and/or diluting the whisky little by little. The consumer bought a closed bottle so the authenticity was not in doubt. This meant peace of mind for the drinker as well as for the company whose name was on the label.

Tax(ing) Matters (Part 4)

In 1968, the mix ratios for the three grades of whisky were revised again. The table below illustrates the shift:

TABLE 8: WHISKY TAXATION, GRADING SYSTEM 1962 VS. 1968

	2nd grade	1st grade	special grade
abv	37–39%	40–42%	43%
mix ratio 1962~	0–[10]	10–[20]	20+
mix ratio 1968~	7–[13]	13–[23]	23+

Aside from the obvious bumping up of the relative quality of whiskies across the board, what's significant here is that, from 1968, it was no longer possible to make whisky—that is to say, blended whisky (which all Japanese whisky in the market was, at the time)—without using any malt whisky component(s). Completely fake, ersatz whisky was finally a thing of the past.

Between 1964 and 1972, whisky production in Japan went from 58,000 to 166,000 kiloliters. Whisky was ubiquitous as a recreational drink and enjoyed by people from all strata of society.

Looking at statistics, it's clear that the populace wasn't just drinking more, it was drinking better—or at least, wanted to drink better. In 1964, whiskies bottled at 37%abv, i.e. the lowest quality allowed, constituted 64.5 percent of all whisky sales. By 1972, this figure had dropped to a mere 16 percent. The chart below shows the market share of 2nd grade, 1st grade and special grade whiskies in 1964 and in 1972, side by side. This reveals a migration from 2nd grade whiskies to 1st and special grade whiskies.

Fig. 1 Japanese Whisky Market Share Per Grade, 1964 vs. 1972

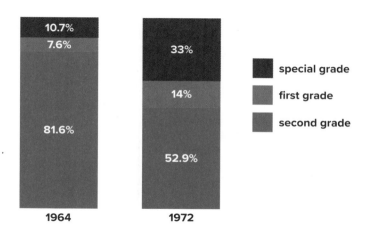

Second grade whiskies were still selling like hotcakes in the late 1960s and early 1970s, but 1st and special grade whiskies were slowly becoming less marginal. Suntory dominated 90 percent of the special grade market. Nikka, on the other hand, had barely managed to make a dent in that market, in spite of a decade of concerted efforts. In October 1968, Nikka launched G&G (Gold & Gold, 760ml, 43%abv, ¥1,900). Up until then, special grade Nikka products were sold mostly as gifts at department stores. They didn't really have a presence at bars and other watering holes. When G&G was launched, the Nikka sales team decided to try to do something about that. They visited as many bars in Ginza as they could and of the 1,400 bars in the district, 800 agreed to put G&G on the shelves.

In November 1970, Nikka's other special grade product got a makeover. The tedious process of working with handblown bottles was dropped and henceforth Super Nikka was sold in machine-made bottles of the same shape (760ml, 43%abv, ¥3,000). The eye seeks pleasure, too, but at the end the day, it's the liquid in the bottle that counts.

In June 1971, Japan announced the adoption of comprehensive external economic measures. This involved the liberalization of imports, the lowering of tariffs, efforts to remove nontariff barriers and the promotion of the liberalization of capital. From an early stage, whisky producers in Japan were aware of the impact a new free trade system would have on their business. An advertisement for Suntory Reserve (760ml, 43%abv, ¥2,700), launched in 1969 to commemorate the company's 70th anniversary, carried the catchphrase: "Don't call it a Japanese product. Call it an international product."

Suntory's advertisement for Reserve can be seen as symbolic of whisky makers' determination to compete against the increase in foreign brands in the domestic market. The days of divvying up the cake at home in peace and quiet were over. Holding on to one's piece of the cake, or getting a bigger one, meant making alliances and sharpening one's tools and that's exactly what whisky makers in Japan did during the transition to a free trade system.

1972–1984

Anticipating increased competition from abroad, both Nikka and Suntory expanded their toolbox. It wasn't just about making more whisky, however; it was about making better whisky. This meant having a wider variety of blending components at one's disposal. Unlike in Scotland, where swapping stock was (and still is) common practice, whisky producers in Japan had (and still have) to create that variety in-house. Nikka had set up a second malt distillery in Sendai in 1969. Suntory established a grain whisky facility called SunGrain in Chita, Aichi prefecture, in 1972 and a second malt distillery in Hakushu, Yamanashi prefecture, the year after.

It was clear that quality had to be the focus for Japanese whisky producers. At the end of 1972, import tariffs were lowered. As a result, Scotch whisky became considerably cheaper. To give an idea of the figures involved, Johnnie Walker Red dropped in price from ¥5,000 to ¥3,500, a drop of 30 percent. Unsurprisingly, Scotch whisky imports jumped up almost immediately. In 1973, the figures tripled, that is,

Suntory Reserve

品質と風格を贈りましょう

'69 NIKKA SUMMER PRESENT

An advertisment promoting Nikka gift sets for the summer of '69

compared with what the pre-free trade situation was like (in 1970). Even though domestically produced whisky was still by far the most consumed whisky in Japan (it still is at the time of writing), the trend was significant enough to keep domestic whisky makers on their toes.

Towards the end of 1972, a new player emerged on the Japanese whisky scene, Kirin-Seagram. In August 1972, Kirin-Seagram was established and a distillery was set up at the foot of Mt. Fuji. The idea was to have a comprehensive whisky manufacturing plant where everything (from malt and grain whisky distilling to blending and bottling) could be done on one site. Fuji Gotemba distillery was completed in November 1973, a month after the beginning of the oil crisis.

The 1973 oil crisis accelerated the inflation caused by the "Nixon Shock" (which included a 10 percent import surcharge on all goods coming into the U.S. and led to a plunge in the value of the dollar) two years earlier. This heightened the propensity to save and negatively impacted consumer demand. It also led to a decrease in industrial investments, especially investments in plants and equipment. Strangely enough, neither of these trends manifested themselves on the whisky scene in Japan. Whisky still sold well. In fact, in pretty much the same way that people were hoarding toilet paper, they were stockpiling whisky. Retailers around the country were begging for more stock, and producers were scrambling to satisfy the increased demand.

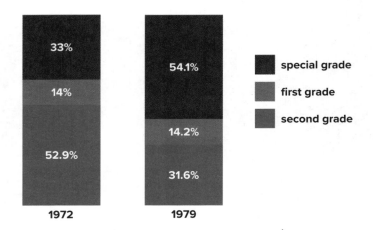

Fig. 2 Japanese Whisky Market Share Per Grade, 1972 vs. 1979

Between 1972 and 1979, the consumption of liquor in general increased by 25 percent, but the consumption of whisky shot up by 118 percent. This seems bizarre given the fact that whisky was seen more and more as a luxury product, but it indicates the extent to which people were willing to pay more for a better drinking experience. By the end of the 1970s, special grade whisky outperformed the lower grades by a wide margin (Figure 2).

From the mid-1970s, super-premium or "prestige" whiskies started appearing on the market. In July 1976, Sanraku Ocean released Karuizawa Single Malt, priced at ¥15,000 a bottle (43%abv, 720ml). In October 1976, Nikka released Tsuru (43%, 760ml). The product had been in development since the 40th anniversary of the company (1974). It contained lots of malt whisky from both the Yoichi and Sendai distilleries and came in a beautiful *noritake* decanter. Tsuru turned out to be the last product that Masataka Taketsuru had a hand in creating; he passed away on August 29, 1979, at the age of 85.

In June 1977, Suntory trumped the competition's premium whiskies with The Whisky (43%abv, 760ml). It came in a specially designed *arita jiki* porcelain decanter and retailed for a whopping ¥50,000. This was almost a third of an average worker's monthly salary at the time. It's difficult to gauge whether the liquid was worth the steep price tag. Specimens that have managed to survive the decades often come to us with significantly lower fill-levels, because of evaporation, so there's no telling what the liquid was like when it was just released.

Even though special grade whiskies were in the spotlight in the 1970s, producers weren't neglecting the lower grades. In March 1975, Nikka released Black-50 (1st grade, 40%abv, ¥1,000), which was aimed at young people wanting to drink authentic whisky at a reasonable price. It was a vatting of Yoichi and Sendai malt and Coffey grain whisky and was mild and soft. The packaging, on the other hand, was meant to project "strong and masculine."

In the 1970s, most people were drinking whisky *mizuwari* style (literally, "divided by water"; see page 508 for more on this). This made it very similar in alcoholic strength to sake, which tends to be around 15%abv. Suntory saw potential here for 2nd and 1st grade whiskies. Sake was usually drunk as an accompaniment to food. Surely, whisky drunk long could be promoted as a novel alternative. In February 1972, Suntory launched Operation Chopsticks (*Nihonbashi Sakusen*). The idea was to persuade eating establishments where chopsticks were used (sushi places, izakayas and so on) to put whisky on the drinks menu. Initially, people in the industry were resistant to this suggestion. Their objections were mostly practical, whisky taking up extra shelf space in their cramped quarters and so on. Suntory quickly came up with some elegant solutions. They started offering whisky in 50ml min-iature bottles, which customers could use to make two mizuwaris without having to bother the wait staff. They also pushed "baby size" (180ml) bottles, which could be consumed in one sitting with a few people. Again, customers could take care of their own needs as long as they had their little whisky bottle, a pitcher of water, some ice on the side and a glass for each person who wanted to partake. When the customer(s) left, the miniature or baby bottle would be empty and could be discarded. For full-sized bottles, the alternative was the "bottle keep" system, which took up space, for sure, but it encouraged customers to come back. Suntory Old became particularly popular in the wake of this campaign.

Nikka Black-50

Tax(ing) Matters (Part 5)

In 1978, the mix ratios for the three grades of whisky were bumped up again. The table below illustrates the shift:

TABLE 9: WHISKY TAXATION, GRADING SYSTEM 1968 VS. 1978

	2nd grade	1st grade	special grade
abv	37–39%	40–42%	43%
mix ratio 1968~	7–[13]	13–[23]	23+
mix ratio 1978~	10–[17]	17–[27]	27+

Having access to good malt whisky was clearly becoming more important. This was not an obstacle for whisky makers who didn't have malt distilleries of their own, however. With the liberalization of trade, it quickly became apparent that there was a relatively cheap way to get hold of good quality malt whisky: bulk imports from Scotland.

An interesting development in the margin of the "whisky theater" run by the big producers was the emergence of a so-called "ji-whisky" scene, which gained momentum in the first half of the 1980s. Many small liquor producers started pushing their whiskies, spotlighting them as alternatives to the established brands of the big producers. Most of these producers had been making whisky on and off since the post-war years, but usually as a side business. Towards the end of the 1970s, skyrocketing whisky sales in Japan encouraged them to prioritize and push their whiskies. This led to a veritable *ji-whisky* boom around 1983.

The prefix "*ji*" is often translated as "craft," as in the "*ji-beer*" phenomenon, which emerged in Japan in the mid-1990s and is generally translated as "craft beer." However, at the time of the *ji-whisky* boom, there was no such thing as a "craft [fill in the blank]" movement, so referring to this as "craft whisky" is not only anachronistic, but it also conjures up associations that are inconsistent with what *ji-whisky* producers were doing. Most *ji-whisky* producers didn't really have the infrastructure, equipment and/or know-how to properly make whisky from scratch. Some used makeshift equipment to distill malted barley. Most of them relied on malt and/or grain whisky imported in bulk from abroad (mostly Scotland, but also the U.S. and Canada). Some of them didn't actually produce a single drop of what they bottled. Nowadays, we would call some of them rectifiers, processors, blenders, NDPs ("non-distilling producers," a term coined by Chuck Cowdery in the context of American whiskey for brands with no stills) or charlatans.

In the early 1980s, provenance and authenticity were irrelevant to most whisky drinkers in Japan, so these smaller brands were welcomed with curiosity and seen as "locally made" alternatives to the ubiquitous "big brands." In Japanese, *ji* means "(this) land" or "place," so a better translation of "*ji whisky*," both linguistically and in terms of how it was perceived by the consumer, would be "local whisky." The irony is that lots of whisky sold by *ji-whisky* makers contained components that were made on the other side of the world, very far from "that place."

In the early 1980s, the increase in whisky consumption in Japan was starting to slow down. Between 1980 and 1983, it rose by just 4.7 percent. Liquor taxes were raised in 1978, 1981 and 1984 and this resulted in price instability. Between 1978 and 1984, with producers adjusting their prices in between the increases in taxation, it seemed like whisky prices kept going up year after year. By 1984, prices were about 50 percent higher on average than prior to 1978.

The other part of the story here is the "shochu boom." During the 1960s and early '70s, shochu had come to be seen as a poor, working-class, unsophisticated drink. Many newly affluent Japanese dismissed it as cheap rotgut—something for farmers and fishermen. By the mid-'70s, there was very little love or demand for the colorless spirit. In the U.S. and Europe, however, a "white liquor revolution" was underway. In 1974, vodka consumption surpassed that of bourbon in the U.S. Inspired by this example, and convinced that the trend could catch on in Japan, Takara Shuzo started developing a high-quality shochu meant to revive the product's image. They launched Jun (meaning "purity" in Japanese) in 1977. A unique filtering process was used to create a shochu with a more naturally smooth taste and a light aroma—something that conjured up the image of "purity."

The rest is history, as they say. Jun caught on and sparked a veritable shochu boom. Takara started marketing canned shochu highballs as Can Chu-Hi (a combination of the last syllable of shochu and the first syllable of highball). None other than John Travolta was roped into advertising the product in a series of memorable commercials (check "Tokyo Drink" on YouTube!) and it took off. Younger people, unaware of the low esteem in which shochu was held by their parents (or maybe partly because of it), took a real liking to this new-image shochu and the premixed cans of shochu with fruit flavors. Other producers quickly jumped on the bandwagon and a boom was in the making.

Sales were helped tremendously by the government's policy of taxing shochu at a much lower rate than other alcoholic beverages. A producer of whisky paid a little over 50 percent of the retail price to the taxman for a bottle of special grade whisky, whereas a shochu maker only had to cough up 14.4 or 8.7 percent, depending on the type of shochu.

In 1982, sales of shochu were up by 16 percent over the previous year; in 1983, they rose by 29.7 percent, and in 1984, by a spectacular 45.2 percent. That year would turn out to be pivotal. For the first time in decades, whisky consumption in Japan dropped and not by a little bit but by a painful 15.6 percent. There was a new kid on the block, and whisky was headed for the doghouse.

1984—2001

To have an idea of the extent to which the decline in whisky consumption in Japan over the next two and a half decades would impact domestic whisky makers' businesses, it's useful to view the picture from the top. In 1983, almost 380,000 kiloliters of whisky were consumed in Japan; by 2007, that figure had dropped to a miserly 75,000 kiloliters. In other words, over those 24 years, the whisky market in Japan shrank to 20 percent of what it was at its peak. Figure 3 on page 73 illustrates which companies were hurt the most.

It shouldn't come as a surprise that the company that stood to lose the most was at the forefront of developing strategies to elevate the whisky market.

The strategy highlighted in most official versions of Japanese whisky history is the introduction of the single malt category and the premiumization of the blended whisky market. To commemorate the 60th anniversary of whisky making at Yamazaki, Keizo Saji felt the time had come to put together a single malt rather than yet another blended whisky. It took Saji and chief blender Kan Sato two years to develop a profile they were happy with. In March 1984, Suntory launched Suntory Pure Malt Whisky Yamazaki (43%abv, 700ml, ¥10,000). Initially, it didn't carry an age statement. Starting in 1986, it was sold as a 12-year-old.

The original Yamazaki (1984)

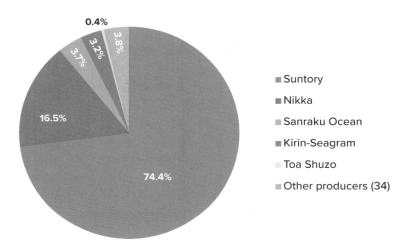

Fig. 3 Whisky Market Share by Producer, 1983

0.4%
3.8%
3.2%
3.7%
16.5%
74.4%

- Suntory
- Nikka
- Sanraku Ocean
- Kirin-Seagram
- Toa Shuzo
- Other producers (34)

Suntory	74.4%
Nikka	16.5%
Sanraku Ocean	3.7%
Kirin-Seagram	3.2%
Toa Shuzo	0.4%
Other producers (34)	3.8%

Nikka also had an anniversary to celebrate in 1984 and they were thinking along similar lines. To mark the 50th anniversary of the company, they created Nikka Single Malt Hokkaido 12 Year Old (43%abv, 700ml), which went on sale in November. Nikka's new item was limited to 10,000 bottles per year and retailed for ¥12,000 a bottle.

In the early 1980s, special grade whiskies outperformed 1st and 2nd grade whiskies combined, but after 1983, sales of special grade whiskies started slipping and their share of the market fell under 50 percent again. Undeterred, Nikka started releasing a plethora of new special grade products. In December 1984, they started selling two pure malts (what we would call "vatted malts" nowadays): Black and Red. Pure Malt Black was of the Highland type, and heavy on the Yoichi malt, whereas Pure Malt Red was of the Lowland type and contained proportionally more Sendai (i.e., Miyagikyo) malt. They were no-frills products (in simple 500ml bottles with very basic labels, sold without any promotion whatsoever) aimed to appeal to young people who couldn't care less about branding but wanted a good-quality, easy-drinking whisky at a reasonable price (¥2,500). In June 1987, a third pure malt was added to the lineup, Pure Malt White, which contained a generous amount of peated Islay malt. Red and Black are still part of the Nikka portfolio at the time of writing. White was discontinued in September 2015.

In October 1985, Nikka launched a new blended whisky. This wasn't a new product just for the sake of it, however. The concept behind it was novel, too. Takeshi Taketsuru wanted to create a blended whisky that would give the drinker the sort of experience the blender had in the lab, uncut, as it were. He called it From The Barrel (500ml) and bottled it at 51.4%abv, which was almost unheard of in those days. It offered a great drinking experience at a very reasonable price (¥2,800 when it was first launched) but it had to swim upstream in the market, a whisky full of character and flavor launched when people preferred their whisky light and smooth.

From The Barrel was followed in October 1986 by another new blend, which, again, went against the grain, this time, in a literal sense. The Blend of Nikka (45%abv, 600ml, ¥5,000) reversed the habitual malt-grain ratios in blended whiskies by

Nikka's first single malt, Hokkaido 12yo (1984)

Takeshi Taketsuru

favoring the malt rather than the grain components. It was said to contain more than 50 percent malt. A month after it went on sale, Nikka added a 17-year-old expression of The Blend of Nikka (¥10,000).

In 1985, the marketing department at Suntory was keen to launch a Hakushu single malt. The blenders, however, felt it was way too early and insisted the plan be shelved indefinitely, until the time was ripe.

Following the peak of 1983, another strategy to try and boost whisky sales was implemented by domestic producers. This was a complement to the premiumization strategy, namely, economization. This strategy has been de-highlighted in Japanese whisky history because, unlike the products that came out of the premiumization drive, those that were developed for economization purposes are now seen as somewhat of an embarrassment. They are long gone, except on the secondary market where specimens still float around, and have been written out of the official histories.

In 1983, Suntory released a 1st grade whisky called Q. It came in three versions: Q1000, Q500 and Q250 (40%abv). The number was a reference to the volume (in ml). The presentation was designed to be everything that whisky wasn't perceived to be: slick, hip and modern. It didn't look like anything their dads would have picked up, and that was the point, of course: reeling in young people. It was dirt cheap (¥2,200 for the liter version) and "light & smooth" as it said on the bottle. Commercials on TV featured the band Duran Duran.

Kirin-Seagram's answer, released in August of 1983, was News 1000, News 500 and, sure enough, News 250 (40%abv). Again, the design was meant to distance the product from anything that looked like whisky. Again, the label said it was "light & smooth." The 1-liter version spelled it out clearly: "This whisky is light & smooth. You can enjoy it on the rocks, with water or with anything you like. This whisky can create your new lifestyle." Almost prescription-like, it also said "one liter per month" on the label. News was sold at the exact same price as Q and was also heavily advertised. Kirin-Seagram's commercials must have cost them a pretty yen. They featured *Airwolf* star Jan Michael Vincent, who, at the time, was one of the highest paid actors on television.

In 1984, Nikka and Sanraku Ocean put their equivalents of Q and News on the market. In July, Nikka released Yz (1st grade, 40%abv) in 900, 450 and 225ml versions with the 900ml version priced at ¥2,000. In September, they launched a 2nd grade product called no Side, developed for drinkers on a very tight budget. It came in the three sizes listed above, as well as a jumbo bottle (1,920ml) and was half the price of Yz. Bottled at 35%abv and made with malt, grain and spirits, it was sort of halfway between a whisky and a vodka. The same goes for Sanraku Ocean's MOO (2nd grade, 35%abv), which went on sale in November of that year. It came in 900ml and 450ml bottles and was priced the same as no Side (¥1,000 for 900ml). The name was a reference to "sMOOth." It's unclear whether the pun on the Japanese word *mu* (pronounced like "moo" but shorter, and meaning "nothingness") was intentional or not. It cost next to nothing and tasted like it, too.

There were also special grade products styled in the same hip, contemporary way and aimed at the same younger demographic. In order not to alienate young people, prices were kept as low as possible. There was only one size (500ml) and the strategy was to set the price at the same level as a 1,000ml 1st grade product. Basically, it boiled down to choosing between more booze or better booze for the same price. Suntory 21 (1983, 40%abv, 500ml) was a rank up from Q and advertised by the internationally renowned French piano duo, the Labèque sisters, with the tagline "after 20 comes 21," a reference to the drinking age in Japan and moving on to better things the year after. Kirin-Seagram's Saturday 1 and Saturday 2 (1984, 40%abv, 500ml) was a sort of yin-yang pair branded as a "High Performance Whisky," whatever that meant. Saturday 1 was "Light & Smooth," whereas Saturday 2 was "Mellow & Body." Kirin-Seagram explained on the label: "Saturday is the high-quality whisky for the new age suitable for sophisticated men wishing to relax and express their desired way of life." We don't know what sort of beverage they had in mind for sophisticated *women* wishing to relax and express *their* desired way of life.

A selection of "modern whiskies" from the mid- to late '80s

Other dubiously memorable products from the immediate post-peak period include Suntory's Cobra (2nd grade, 39%abv, ¥1,000 and 500ml) and Sanraku-Ocean's 30-0 (1989, 1st grade, 30%abv, 500ml), pronounced "thirty-love," as in tennis, a reference to the unusually low bottling strength. If you come across any of these whiskies, don't pass up the chance to try them. It's an educational experience, that's for sure. Blind you would never guess you were drinking whisky. In some cases, you'd actually think someone had added a bit of mouthwash to a shot of vodka. Exactly how producers managed to create whiskies that didn't taste like whisky is a mystery, but then again, regulations were (and still are) very lax in Japan when it comes to making whisky.

As is clear from these examples and from other whiskies released in the run-up to and during the bubble economy in Japan in the late 1980s/early '90s, lightness was everything. In advertising and even on the products themselves, "light" was the key word. "Light" and "smooth" sold—not just whisky, but other types of liquor as well. A famous catchphrase coined by a Fuji TV writer during the bubble years was "*karucha-poi*," which literally means "culture-like" but is also to be understood as a pun on the Japanese word for light, *karu(i)*. What people wanted then (what they needed) was "lightness" or *leggerezza*, the Italian, which, carrying connotations of "a lack of control in behavior because of scant seriousness and frivolous negligence" (Devoto-Oli), is more appropriate. It's quite interesting to contrast this with the recession climate of 2013, when the new buzzword in drinks advertising in Japan was "rich."

Tax(ing) Matters (Part 6)

In the early 1980s, the extremely complicated Japanese liquor tax system and its implications for foreign trade became a regular issue at official meetings between the European Commission (EC) and Japan.

Since the 1943 amendment of the Liquor Tax Law, alcoholic beverages were taxed at different rates in Japan depending on the liquor type, the alcoholic strength and the grade. The latter, in particular, was unusual among industrialized countries. In Japan, however, it was considered part of a strategy to ensure vertical fairness. The thinking behind this was that liquor, not being a daily necessity, ought to be taxed by taking into account the tax-bearing ability of prospective customers. Higher tax rates were applied to high-quality products, likely to be consumed by people in higher income brackets, and vice versa. This pursuit of vertical fairness resulted in excessive categorization and grading of liquor, often based on fairly arbitrary stipulations to do with abv, contents of raw materials and manufacturing method. In spite of it being idiosyncratic, the grading system applied to all liquor, regardless of whether it was domestic or imported.

According to the European Commission, the differentiation built into the Japanese liquor tax system had the effect of discriminating against European imports. In other words, it was a nontariff barrier. The first major issue had to do with the fact that the grading system for whisky and brandy was Japan-specific. It didn't make any sense in the context of Scotch whisky or any of the other traditional whisky-making regions, for that matter. As explained in the Tax(ing) Matters excursions above, the whisky grading system was based on abv and mix ratio. In Europe—meaning Scotland—there was simply no equivalent of 2nd grade whisky. Whisky couldn't be bottled and sold as "whisky" if it was under 40%abv. Diluting malt whisky with neutral spirits or "blending alcohol" was also out of the question. Adding flavorings so the product would acquire the perceived characteristics of whisky was unheard of since the dark ages of whisky making in Scotland, pre-twentieth century.

Unlike sake (where grading was voluntary and by taste) the grading of whisky (and most of this applied to brandy, as well) was mandatory and automatic. This meant that, unless a Scotch whisky company could prove otherwise, its whiskies were automatically considered special grade, the category with the highest tax rate. Needless to say, very few Scotch whisky makers were tempted to go out of their way to prove that their blends contained under 27 percent malt whisky, just so they could take advantage of the 1st grade whisky tax rate. The following figures for fiscal 1985 speak volumes. Of all whiskies and brandies taxed in Japan that year, 83 percent of special grade products were domestically produced. For 1st and 2nd grade whisky/brandy, the figures are 99.9 and 100 percent respectively. With the negligible exception of the 0.1 percent in the 1st grade category, all imported whisky/brandy was in the special grade category and taxed accordingly, at a tax rate that was seven times higher than that of 2nd grade whiskies (¥2,098,100/kl vs. ¥296,200/kl).

The second major issue was that in Japan, tax rates for shochu were considerably lower than those for other spirits. The tax on comparable Western-style spirits such as vodka and gin was 4 to 7 times higher than that on shochu. Special grade whisky was taxed a staggering 41 and 26 times higher than the two types of shochu (B and A, respectively). The money that the taxman took from a bottle of special grade whisky was enough to buy an *isshobin* (1.8l bottle) of shochu and a little snack at your local liquor shop.

The EC felt that the grossly unequal taxation of "like"—that is to say, directly competitive or substitutable—products had a protective effect.

In October 1986, the Scotch Whisky Association (SWA) and other liquor interest groups from Europe and North America visited Japan to voice their objections and bring pressure to bear. In February 1987, the EC brought their case before the GATT (General Agreement on Tariffs and Trade) panel. Japan's counterarguments to the two main issues outlined above were: 1) that the grading system was created during wartime with the object of raising financial resources and that discriminating against imported products (of which there were none at the time) was not a motivating factor, and 2) that the lower taxation of shochu (which was seen as a lower-class beverage) simply had to do with vertical fairness.

During the GATT discussions, the EC was the main foreign actor. The U.S. was much less active. This was clearly not of the same order of importance as, for example, issues in the automobile industry. Canada was a fairly quiet observer, too. For obvious reasons, Britain was the leader of the EC pack. Scotch sales had been falling for three straight years after 1982 so there was cause for worry and a sense of urgency to take action where action could be taken. In the years leading up to the GATT panel discussions, Britain had repeatedly spotlighted the discriminatory effects of the Japanese liquor tax system on foreign imports. Margaret Thatcher was one of the more vocal critics and never failed to bring up the issue whenever Japanese politicians visited Downing Street.

It must be said that there were also voices in Japan calling for reform of the liquor tax system. In 1982, a study group set up within the Ministry of Finance had recommended a simplification of the categories and a concomitant reduction of the tax differentials. The influential newspaper *Nippon Keizai Shimbun (Nikkei)* advocated reform along the same lines. The main reason why nothing came of these and similar recommendations from within was that the powers-that-be spent much of the 1980s trying to push through something much bigger: the introduction of a mass indirect tax. (This was eventually introduced on April 1, 1989.)

Following the decision of the GATT General Assembly, a reformed liquor tax system was submitted to the Diet and enacted on December 24, 1988. The changes were substantial: whisky and other spirits were redefined; the grading system for whisky and brandy was abolished; the *ad valorem* tax was abolished, too, and replaced with a quantity tax only; and tax rates were reduced for beer, sake and whisky, but increased for shochu and liqueurs. Much to the dismay of shochu producers, the new liquor tax was implemented at the start of the next fiscal year, April 1989. Imports of Scotch whisky shot up immediately (65.3 percent in value and 29.7 percent in quantity). Against the background of falling shochu sales post-1985, the tax increase—which was dubbed "Thatcher *zozei*" (Thatcher tax increase) by shochu producers—seemed like a double whammy. Zooming out, the picture was slightly different, however. Even though whisky imports were on the up, overall the consumption of spirits was on a downward slope in the latter half of the 1980s in Japan.

This wasn't the end of the story. There was still a fairly large tax gap between shochu and whisky. Seen in terms of retail price, the tax on whisky was 36.3 percent, whereas that on shochu was 21.3 or 13.5 percent (depending on the type of shochu). After a few years, the EC reactivated their negotiations. This time round, they had allies on the ground: the biggest losers after the tax reform, Japanese whisky producers. By the early 1990s, 2nd grade whisky as a category had all but disappeared. With its tax more than tripled, its raison d'être was gone. In the Japanese whisky camp, the feeling was that the new tax situation had effectuated a migration from 2nd grade whisky to shochu among drinkers. The figures seemed to confirm their suspicion (see Figure 4 on page 85).

TABLE 10: SPIRITS MARKET SHARE IN JAPAN (%) 1987–MAY 1994

	1987	1988	1989	1990	1991	1992	1993	1994
Domestic whisky	26.7	27.0	23.4	19.6	18.1	17.1	15.8	13.4
Imported whisky	3.3	3.7	5.8	6.5	6.0	5.5	5.0	3.8
Shochu	63.8	63.1	61.2	63.1	65.0	66.9	69.3	74.5

Source: Abe, Atsuko

Seeking to level the playing field, Japanese whisky importers lobbied the government to further revise the tax difference between shochu and whisky.

In 1996, the World Trade Organization (WTO), the successor of the GATT, ruled that the difference in tax rate between shochu and whisky violated WTO rules. Shochu, whisky, brandy, rum, genever and liqueurs were considered to be "directly competitive or substitutable products" and therefore, the tax differential was seen as discriminatory. In response, the Japanese government raised the tax on shochu by 160 and 240 percent (for the two different types), whereas the tax on whisky was reduced by 58 percent. Calculated per degree of alcohol, this meant a de facto leveling. That doesn't mean the situation improved for whisky makers in Japan, but henceforth the downward trend in consumption could only be attributed to customer preference and the vagaries of trends.

The first whisky released after the implementation of the new liquor tax system was Hibiki. It was launched on April 3, 1989, alongside Suntory Whisky Crest, to mark the 90th anniversary of the company.

In creating Hibiki, the third chief blender Koichi Inatomi, a keen amateur viola player, was said to have been inspired by the 4th movement of Brahms' First Symphony. To symbolize the importance of time, a special 24-faceted bottle was designed for Hibiki. It was meant to represent the 24 hours in a day, as well as the 24 "small seasons" of the Japanese calendar (a traditional way of expressing seasons in Japan, defined by the ecliptic longitude of the sun): circular but multi-faceted. In contrast with the cool, slick design of the whiskies of the latter half of the 1980s targeting young drinkers, the presentation of Hibiki incorporated traditional Japanese elements. The name (meaning "resonance") was written by calligraphy artist Tansetsu Ogino. The label itself was made by paper designer Eriko Horiki using the traditional Echizen Washi method.

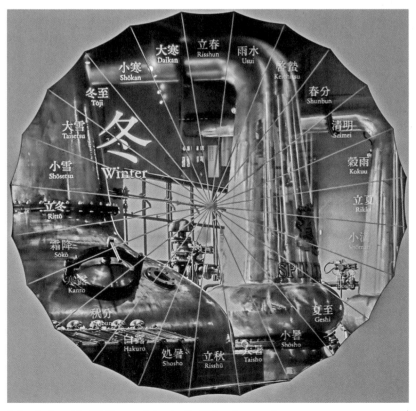

A visualization of the Hibiki concept showing the 24 "small seasons"

Initially released as a no-age-statement premium blended whisky, it was later designated as a 17-year-old. In 1994 and 1997, the fourth chief blender Seiichi Koshimizu created a 21- and 30-year-old expression, respectively.

On the single malt front, there was quite a bit of activity after 1989, starting with the release of Nikka's Single Malt Sendai Miyagikyo 12 Years Old (43%abv, 750ml, ¥10,000) to commemorate the 20th anniversary of the distillery. Rather than list all expressions released from this point onwards, I've included a handy reference "map" showing the development of the single malt category in Japan. It traces the core expressions released by the three main players (Suntory, Nikka and Kirin) from the mid-1980s up to the present day.

It's easy to paint a warped view of Japanese whisky during the last decade of the twentieth century by focusing on the premium segment of producers' portfolios. The reality was that, in terms of sales, this was very much a niche market. Single malts and premium blends didn't really contribute all that much to a company's bottom line. In the bread-and-butter department, sales of standard and bottom-shelf whiskies were still falling. Most of the cheap whiskies aimed at young drinkers (Q, News, Yz, no Side, etc.) were phased out around 1992–93. It was clear that these trendy whiskies had outstayed their welcome, which was rather lukewarm to begin with.

Suntory decided to give some of the old mainstays of the portfolio a bit of a makeover and/or create new variations. In March 1992, the company started selling a white-label variation of Kakubin, called Shiro-Kaku (white Kaku). Whereas the regular yellow-label Kakubin contained a balanced mix of ex-bourbon Yamazaki and Hakushu malt, together with grain whisky from Chita Distillery, the new Shiro-Kaku favored Hakushu malt in the mix. It was clearer and smoother in taste and was specifically designed to be drunk *mizuwari* style, with water. The new product was promoted as part of Suntory's "*oishii* [tasty] *mizuwari* campaign" that was launched at the same time.

Next in line for an update was the old powerhouse Suntory Old. In October 1994, the "new Old"—"Mild & Smooth"—hit the shelves. On TV, it was promoted in a series of memorable commercials in the shomin-geki style (a genre of realist films dealing with lower-middle-class family life). Under the motto "Old is New," the commercials depicted romantic situations that exemplified the catchphrase "*koi wa toi hi no hanabi de wa nai*" (love is not a bygone day's fireworks). The understated sentimentalism of the commercials made them a big hit.

Unlike most drinks commercials from the past, they are still a joy to watch. There was also a special Winter Blend that was meant to be drunk oyuwari style, with hot water, and advertised as "Old is Hot."

Other updates of old classics followed in 1995 (Royal Premium 12 Year Old), 1996 (Reserve 10 Year Old) and 1997 (New Royal 12 Year Old and New Royal Premium 15 Year Old).

Meanwhile, the people at Nikka had also put their thinking caps on. When the grading system came to an end in 1989, a regulation was put in place that stipulated that blended whiskies needed to contain at least 8 percent malt whisky. Looking to develop substitutes for ex-2nd grade whiskies, a new category was born, so-called "new spirits." It was harder to keep the quality of these products up, because whereas the old 2nd grade whiskies could contain up to 16.9 percent malt whisky (the mix ratio range was 10–[17] percent), the "new spirits" had to work with 7.9 percent or less. Nikka released Gold Nikky (39%abv, 720ml, ¥900) and White Nikky (37%abv, 640ml, ¥720) in August 1989. Fortunately for us, the company also developed products where quality came first.

In February 1990, Nikka released All Malt (43%abv, 750ml, ¥2,350). The concept behind this was totally novel. It was made from 100 percent malted barley, but it was a blended whisky. How could that be? From 1985, Nikka started distilling 100 percent malted barley in their Coffey stills on an occasional basis. Traditionally, grain whisky is made from corn with a bit of malted barley and sometimes rye added. Distilling malted barley in a continuous still had not been done before, at least not commercially. In Scotland, it didn't make economic sense to do so. A mash of malted barley distilled in a continuous still could only be called "grain whisky." So, why would one use a more expensive mash (malted barley) when the resulting whisky, after maturation, had to be called the same as that made from the standard—cheaper—corn-based mash? Nikka felt it was worth a try. In any case, the regulations in Japan were different. All Malt, a vatting of Coffey malt and pot still-distilled malt, was an immediate hit. In May 1997, in anticipation of the lowering of tax rates for whisky in October of that year, the presentation of All Malt was reconceived somewhat. From then on, it came in 700ml bottles and at 40%abv. This allowed the company to lower the price to ¥1,920, which was under the ¥2,000 threshold, where the biggest market for whisky was at the time.

Just after the tax rates were lowered, Nikka released a variation on Black Nikka. With Black Nikka Clear Blend (37%abv, 700ml, ¥1,000), they hoped to appeal to people who were used to drinking shochu. In order

Nikka's current Taketsuru lineup

to make the whisky more approachable and easier to match with food, a cleaner (nonpeat) profile was developed. Seeing as whisky didn't really sell all that much in high-class clubs and restaurants anymore, the target was shifted to the family circle: people enjoying a glass or two at home in the evening. This necessitated the development of different sales channels: convenience stores and supermarkets rather than specialist liquor retailers. All in all, sales of Black Nikka Clear Blend were pretty good. For a while, it was the best-selling whisky in convenience stores and supermarkets. In March 1998, two premixed low-alcohol offshoots went on sale: Black Clear Blend with Water (9%abv, 250ml, ¥158) and Black Clear Blend with Lemon Soda (8%abv, 250ml, ¥150).

The super-premium blended category also got some love and care from Nikka towards the end of the 1990s. In June 1998, Nikka Whisky Aged 34 Years (43%abv, 750ml, ¥60,000, 1,000 bottles) came out. At the time, this was the oldest Japanese whisky commercially released. Another 34-year-old blend was released the year after. The specs were the same but the label was different. It's unclear whether this was a new vatting or the same as the 1998 release but with a different label. A month later, in July 1999, The Nikka Whisky Sendai 30 Years Old (43%abv, 750ml, ¥50,000, 500 bottles) was released to mark the 30th anniversary of Miyagikyo distillery. These were all one-off prestige projects—very interesting for the connoisseur but with very little long-term impact. A bigger project was just round the corner, however.

In November 2000, Nikka launched what would become their flagship pure malt range, Taketsuru. The biggest shock about Taketsuru 12yo was the price point. At a time when a regular 12-year-old blended whisky would retail for around ¥5,000, this 12-year old vatted malt (Yoichi and Miyagikyo) was yours for less than half that price (40%abv, 660ml, ¥2,450). The idea was to get people hooked on good whisky again after a decade and a half of dumbing down the amber nectar and dressing it up as something else. The strategy paid off. In the first two months after the release, they sold 540,000 bottles. The 12-year-old arrived in the company of a Taketsuru 35yo (43%abv, 750ml, ¥50,000, 700 bottles). This was obviously pricier, but it sold out in a little over a month. In March 2001, the Taketsuru family got a 17- and a 21-year-old sibling (43%abv, 700ml, ¥5,000 and ¥10,000 respectively). These would go on to win Best Blended Malt in the World several times over.

In spite of all the positives highlighted above, the whisky ship was still sinking in Japan. Whatever producers did—raising the bar, going for the lowest common denominator and everything in between—it seemed like nothing could reverse the downward trend in whisky consumption. By 2001, the whisky market in Japan had shrunk to less than a third of what it had been at its peak in 1983. The situation was starting to get very uncomfortable for producers. How much longer could this go on?

**Fig. 4 Whisky Consumption in Japan
(National Tax Agency data, 'Sake no shiori')**

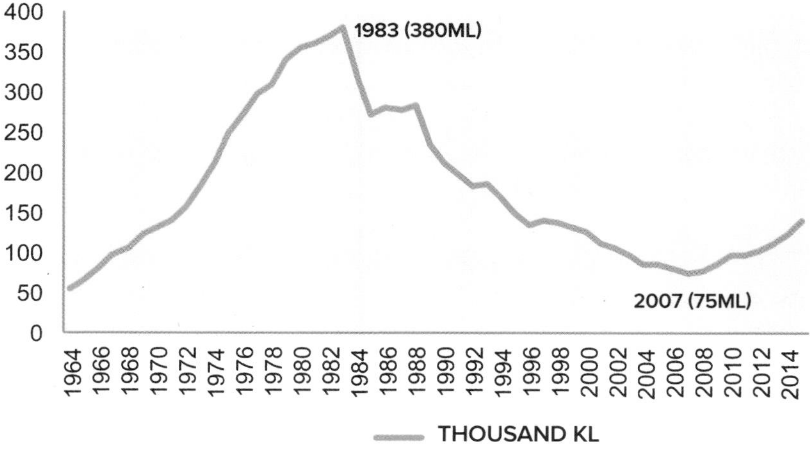

2001–2008

The year 2001 marks the beginning of a new chapter in the ongoing story of Japanese whisky, not because things on the ground changed—whisky was still unpopular and sales kept falling—but because of a change in perception abroad.

In February 2001, *Whisky Magazine* (published by Paragraph Publishing, U.K.) organized a blind tasting competition for the first time. Whisky producers from around the world submitted a total of 293 products, which were judged by 62 experts in Edinburgh, Kentucky and Japan. A Yoichi 10-year-old single cask got the highest score (7.79/10) in the Japanese whisky category, but it turned out this was also the highest overall score. The Best of the Best was not a Scotch, not a bourbon, but a Japanese whisky. Obviously, this result turned more than a few heads. The same year, Mercian's Karuizawa Pure Malt 12 Year Old picked up Gold at the International Wine and Spirits Competition (IWSC) in London.

In retrospect, it was fortunate that the first Japanese whiskies to get international recognition were single-cask/single-malt whiskies. During the 1980s and '90s, most people in the drinks business abroad assumed Japanese whisky was inferior to whisky made in Scotland. Most of this was based on hearsay or just plain bias. Admittedly, there was some pretty vile stuff out there. We're not going to rewrite history and say that the whisky scene in Japan was one big pot of gold at the end of the rainbow. It wasn't. However, there were many fine Japanese whiskies around. You just had to look beyond the bottom shelf of the liquor store. When people abroad did find Japanese whisky to be a pleasant drinking experience, the quip was that it was good because Japanese producers put a generous amount of Scotch malt into their better blends. If, in 2001, Japanese blended whiskies had snatched the top prize at *Whisky Magazine*'s Best of the Best or at the IWSC, that would have been the comeback. That the winners were single-cask/malt whiskies meant that they were entirely made in-house and that they won on their own merit—simple as that.

In 2002, Mercian's Karuizawa Master's Blend 10yo won Gold at the IWSC. In 2003, Yamazaki 12yo picked up Gold at the International Spirits Challenge (ISC). The year after, Hibiki 21 got Gold and Hibiki 30 was awarded the "Trophy" (the best among the Gold winners) at the same competition. Japanese whisky hasn't looked back since. In every single category—blended whisky, blended malt whisky, single malt whisky and single grain whisky—Japanese whiskies have received the highest accolades at the toughest whisky and spirit competitions worldwide. It would make for pretty boring reading to mention all of these awards.

Takeshi Taketsuru with the Best of the Best Award 2001

TABLE 11: JAPANESE WHISKY MAJOR AWARDS WINNERS 2001–2022

ISC	International Spirits Challenge
IWSC	International Wine & Spirit Competition
SWSC	San Francisco World Spirits Competition
WM	Whisky Magazine (e.g. Best of the Best)
WWA	World Whiskies Awards

2001

| WM Best of the Best | Yoichi 10yo Single Cask |
| IWSC Gold | Karuizawa Pure Malt 12yo |

2002

| IWSC Gold | Karuizawa Master's Blend 10yo |

2003

(no major awards)

2004

| ISC (Trophy) | Hibiki 30yo |

2005

| SWSC (Double Gold) | Yamazaki 18yo |

2006

| ISC (Trophy) | Hibiki 30yo |
| IWSC (Trophy) | Yamazaki 18yo |

2007

WWA (Best Blended)	Hibiki 30yo
WWA (Best Blended Malt)	Taketsuru 21yo
ISC (Trophy)	Hibiki 30yo

2008

WWA (Best Single Malt, 20yo)	Yoichi 1987
WWA (Best Blended)	Hibiki 30yo
ISC (Trophy)	Hibiki 30yo
SWSC (Double Gold)	Yamazaki 18yo

2009

WWA (Best Blended Malt)	Taketsuru 21yo
ISC (Trophy)	Taketsuru 21yo
SWSC (Double Gold)	Yamazaki 18yo
SWSC (Double Gold)	Yamazaki 12yo

2010

WWA (Best Blended)	Hibiki 21yo
WWA (Best Blended Malt)	Taketsuru 21yo
ISC (Supreme Champion)	Yamazaki 1984 Ltd Ed.
SWSC (Double Gold)	Yamazaki 1984 Ltd Ed.
SWSC (Double Gold)	Yamazaki 18yo
ISC Distiller of the Year	Suntory
WM Whisky Distiller of the Year	Suntory

2011

WWA (Best Single Malt)	Yamazaki 1984 Ltd Ed.
WWA (Best Blended Malt)	Taketsuru 21yo
WWA (Best Blended)	Hibiki 21yo
IWSC (Trophy)	Yamazaki 18yo
SWSC (Double Gold)	Hibiki 12yo
SWSC (Double Gold)	Yamazaki 18yo
SWSC (Double Gold)	Hakushu 12yo

2012

| WWA (Best Single Malt) | Yamazaki 25yo |

WWA (Best Blended Malt)	Taketsuru 17yo
ISC (Trophy)	Hakushu 25yo
ISC (Trophy)	Yamazaki 18yo
SWSC (Double Gold)	Yamazaki 18yo
ISC Distiller of the Year	Suntory

2013

WWA (Best Blended Malt)	Mars Maltage 3+25
WWA (Best Blended)	Hibiki 21yo
ISC (Trophy)	Hibiki 21yo
SWSC (Double Gold)	Hibiki 12yo
SWSC (Double Gold)	Yamazaki 18yo
SWSC (Double Gold)	Yamazaki 12yo
SWSC (Double Gold)	Hakushu 12yo
ISC Distiller of the Year	Suntory
SWSC Distillery of the Year	Suntory

2014

WWA (Best Blended Malt)	Taketsuru 17yo
ISC (Trophy)	Hibiki 21yo
ISC Distiller of the Year	Suntory

2015

WWA (Best Blended Malt)	Taketsuru 17yo
ISC (Trophy)	Hibiki 21yo
SWSC (Double Gold)	Yamazaki 25yo
SWSC (Double Gold)	Yamazaki 18yo
SWSC (Double Gold)	Hakushu 18yo

2016

WWA (Best Grain)	Fuji Gotemba Single Grain 25yo
WWA (Best Blended)	Hibiki 21yo
SWSC (Double Gold)	Hakushu 18yo
SWSC (Double Gold)	Hakushu 12yo
SWSC (Double Gold)	Hibiki Japanese Harmony

WM Distillery Manager of the Year	Koichi Nishikawa (Yoichi)
ISC (Trophy)	Hibiki 21yo

2017

WWA (Best Blended)	Hibiki 21yo
WWA (Best Grain)	Fuji Gotemba Single Grain 25yo
WWA (Best Single Cask Malt)	Chichibu Whisky Matsuri 2017
WM Distiller of the Year	Suntory
WM Craft Producer of the Year	Hombo Shuzo
WM Master Distiller/ Blender of the Year	Jota Tanaka (Kirin)
ISC (Supreme Champion Spirit)	Hibiki 21yo
ISC (Trophy)	Nikka Coffey Malt
ISC World Whisky Producer of the Year	Suntory Spirits
SWSC (Double Gold)	Yamazaki 12yo
SWSC (Double Gold)	Fuji Gotemba Blender's Choice Single Malt

2018

WWA (Best Single Malt)	Hakushu 25yo
WWA (Best Blended Malt)	Taketsuru 17yo
WWA (Best Blended Ltd)	Ichiro's Malt & Grain Japanese Blended Whisky Ed. 2018
ISC (Trophy)	Hakushu 25yo
ISC (Trophy)	Hibiki 21yo
ISC World Whisky Producer of the Year	Suntory Spirits

2019

WWA (Best Blended Malt)	Taketsuru 25yo
WWA (Best Blended Whisky)	Hibiki 21yo
WWA (Best Grain Whisky)	Fuji Gotemba Single Grain 25yo
WWA (Best Blended Ltd)	Ichiro's Malt & Grain Japanese Blended Whisky Ed. 2019
WM World Whisky Brand Ambassador of the Year	Yumi Yoshikawa (Venture Whisky)
ISC Master Blender of the Year	Ichiro Akuto (Venture Whisky)
ISC (Trophy)	Taketsuru 25yo
SWSC (Double Gold)	Tottori Mizunara Cask Single Malt

2020

WWA (Best Single Malt)	Hakushu 25yo
WWA (Best Grain Whisky)	Fuji Single Grain 30yo
WWA (Best Blended Ltd)	Ichiro's Malt & Grain Japanese Blended Whisky Ed. 2020
ISC (Trophy)	Fuji Single Grain 30yo

2021

WWA (Best Blended Ltd)	Ichiro's Malt & Grain Japanese Blended Whisky Ed. 2021
ISC (Trophy)	Hibiki 21yo
SWSC (Double Gold)	Akkeshi Sararunkamuy
SWSC (Double Gold)	Akkeshi Kanro
SWSC (Double Gold)	Saburomaru 0 The Fool Cask Strength

2022

WWA (Best Blended)	Akkeshi Shosho
WWA (Best Blended Malt)	Yamazakura Asaka Sherrywood Reserve
WWA (Best Label Design)	Yamazakura Asaka The First Peated
ISC (Trophy)	Hakushu 25yo

Japanese whisky was finally getting a bit of the spotlight on the international stage, not only at competitions but also in popular culture. Japanese whisky (in the form of Hibiki 17yo) got major product placement in Sofia Coppola's 2003 movie *Lost in Translation*. The plot revolves around a sad-sack, washed-up actor, played by Bill Murray, who is in Japan to film a whisky commercial for Suntory. Murray's line in the commercial has since become a cult catchphrase among fans: "For relaxing times, make it Suntory time."

Japandering: Sean Connery & Co.

The Urban Dictionary defines a "japander" (n.) as "a western star who uses his or her fame to make large sums of money in a short time by advertising products in Japan that they would probably never use," and "to japander" (v.) as "to make an ass of oneself in Japanese media." In our YouTube era, there is much less of this going on in Japan, but from the mid-1970s to the mid-'90s, "japandering" was a familiar trope in popular culture.

For Japanese whisky makers, the use of foreign celebrities—actors, actresses, film directors and musicians—in commercials was meant to add a touch of authenticity to their products. It was also part and parcel of the "approval of the West" strategy. I say "strategy" because the "approval" was not an expression of a widespread consensus among actual consumers in the West, but implied by having a famous star sip and endorse a whisky that wasn't even available in their home market—let alone appreciated and acclaimed.

One of the more memorable Japanese whisky commercials was Orson Welles' 1976 performance for Nikka's G&G. Looking slightly bored, Welles looks straight into the camera and says: "Hello, I'm Orson Welles. I direct films and act in them. What I aim for, of course, is 'perfection.' In a film, that's

Orson Welles in a 1977 ad for G&G

only a hope. But with G&G, you can rely on it. Perfection! G&G, Nikka Whisky." Welles' mischievous smile at the end of the commercial seemed to suggest his words were to be taken with more than a grain of salt.

Suntory was much more prolific in the field of advertising than Nikka, so it shouldn't come as a surprise that the best examples of "japandering" in Japanese whisky come from their stable. The following is a selection of the more entertaining commercials: Sammy Davis Jr. for Suntory White (1974), Francis Ford Coppola and Akira Kurosawa (shot while filming *Kagemusha*) for Suntory Reserve (1980), Duran Duran for Suntory Q (1983), Matt Dillon for Suntory Reserve Silky (1984), Lee Van Cleef for Suntory Old (1985), Keanu Reeves for Suntory Reserve (1992) and Mickey Rourke for the new Reserve (1996). As always, YouTube is your friend. They're all available for viewing there.

Sammy Davis Jr. for Suntory White

Interestingly, Suntory had a habit of using black musicians to promote their Suntory White. In addition to Sammy Davis Jr., they engaged the services of Herbie Hancock (1985), Ron Carter (1986), 14 Karat Soul (1988) and Ray Charles (1989).

The most amazing feat of Japanese whisky advertising was Suntory's 1992 commercial for Suntory Crest 12yo, featuring Scottish (!) actor Sean Connery. It wasn't Connery's first association on the screen with Japanese whisky. In the 1967 film *You Only Live Twice,* Sean Connery—as James Bond—can be seen briefly sipping some Suntory Old. Product placement in a movie was one thing, but a commercial was something else entirely. In Scotland, Sir Sean's Japanese whisky commercial didn't go down too well. The Conservative PM Bill Walker, among others, had a thing or two to say about Sean. "You know, the Suntory Scot, the one who exports jobs in the Scotch whisky industry. He's the one who's been telling us what we should be doing. Look at what he's doing to our whisky industry! He's promoting their biggest competitor." (March 23, 1992)

Finally, the plot of the 2003 movie *Lost in Translation* revolves around "japandering" for a whisky commercial. The movie was directed by Sofia Coppola, whose father, Francis Ford Coppola, had been in a Suntory commercial in 1980. It also contains an oblique reference to Sean Connery's Suntory commercial. When Bob Harris, played by Bill Murray, is asked to pose as 007 "Loger" Moore, he says: "I always think of Sean Connery. Seriously."

In reality, the times were far from relaxing for Suntory and other whisky producers in Japan. Getting attention and being lauded was all fine and good, but at the end of the day, it was the bottom line that mattered. Things were still not improving in that department, in spite of the exposure and recognition abroad. Exports were almost negligible at that point.

Whisky production in Japan was scaled back significantly in the early years of the new century. Whisky makers couldn't continue to keep making more than they were selling. Mercian's Karuizawa distillery and Toa Shuzo's Hanyu distillery stopped making malt whisky in 2000. Over at the big boys, the pot stills were cold more often than they were hot. Word has it that, in 2002 and 2003,

A Suntory Owner's Cask bottled in 2010

very little if any whisky was produced at Nikka's two distilleries, and that at Suntory's two distilleries, distillation only took place on Mondays. Visiting distilleries in those days was the equivalent of visiting ghost towns for the most part.

In 2004, Suntory tried something radical. Instead of selling whisky by the bottle or by the case, they decided to launch a program where individuals or small businesses could buy a whole cask of whisky, ready to be bottled. The so-called "Owner's Cask" program was announced on November 10, 2004. One hundred and three casks were made available for purchase. The oldest was a 1979 Yamazaki *mizunara* butt, priced at a staggering 30 million yen. At the time, that was a lot of money, the price of a house in Japan. Nowadays, a cask like that wouldn't be on the market for longer than a split second. Suntory stopped the program in June 2010, because they needed their casks more than they needed the money. What happened between then and now? The answer is as simple as it is unlikely: the highball.

Japanese Oak: Mizunara

During the last phase of the Pacific War, Japan had no access to imports. Obviously, the lack of oil, foodstuffs, medicines and other essential materials was of a different order of importance than the lack of barrels to mature whisky in. As explained elsewhere, however, there was significant demand for whisky during the war, so casks were needed. Reduced to finding domestic alternatives, whisky makers started working with Japanese oak—*mizunara*—which was mostly used for expensive furniture.

Mizunara means "water oak." This is because of the high moisture content of the wood. Japanese coopers quickly discovered that their homegrown oak was much more difficult to handle than European or American oak. There are less tyloses blocking the radial pores of the wood, so it is also more porous than other woods. Because of this, *mizunara* casks are prone to leaking. This is the main reason why *mizunara* staves are cut slightly thicker. Japanese oak also has more knots than European or American oak and doesn't grow as straight, making it additionally hard to work with. In order to be properly made into staves for casks, a *mizunara* tree needs to be at least 200 years old.

Mizunara wasn't just challenging to the cooper's skills, it was also challenging to the palate. In the early stage of maturation, *mizunara* tends to impart a very astringent woodiness to the whisky. Blenders regarded *mizunara* as a poor alternative to American and European oak. They felt it was too in your face in terms of aroma and taste. What they didn't know at the time of the Pacific War and shortly after was that *mizunara* wood needed time to work its magic. According to former Suntory chief blender Seiichi Koshimizu, the maturation peak of *mizunara* lies in the 20-year range. *Mizunara* casks lend themselves well to refilling. The aromas typically associated with *mizunara*-matured whisky are sandalwood, incense (the smell of Japanese temples) and coconut.

Nowadays, whisky matured in *mizunara* is held in high regard. Much of this has to do with Suntory's pioneering work in the area. *Mizunara* is an important component of several of their high-end blended whiskies and some of their single malt expressions. They cooper about 150 *mizunara* casks a year, which is very little, indeed. Other Japanese whisky producers also use *mizunara* but on an even more limited scale. The cost involved is substantial. A *mizunara* puncheon sourced from an independent cooperage in Japan can easily cost $5,000 and—even if money is no object—it's far from easy to get hold of.

Intrigued by the unique aromas and flavors that *mizunara* brings to the maturation process, not to mention the added hype it can bring to a product, whisky makers abroad started looking into incorporating Japanese oak into their production process. In October 2013, Pernod Ricard launched a Chivas Regal Mizunara for the Japanese market. Part of the blend was finished in *mizunara*, though for how long is anybody's guess. It sure is hard to detect any sort of *mizunara* influence in this product. In the summer of 2015, Beam Suntory released Bowmore Mizunara, the first Scotch single malt partially matured in *mizunara*. In the case of the Bowmore Mizunara, the secondary maturation period was three years. Here, too, you need the tastebuds of a catfish to be able to pick up the *mizunara* influence.

2008−2016

In April 2008, Suntory launched a new campaign. At the time, it seemed like just another run-of-the-mill attempt to get people to lavish some attention on the ugly duckling that whisky had become. Looking back, however, we know that it was instrumental in reviving whisky as a popular drink. If you were hoping for a spectacularly creative marketing trick, you're going to be disappointed. The focus of the campaign was the humble highball, more specifically, the Kakubin ("Kaku" for short) highball.

The people at Suntory didn't go for that other staple of "salaryman culture" from the 1970s and early '80s, the *mizuwari* (whisky and water), because they couldn't control the quality of the final beverage. No matter how good the whisky, if it was mixed with poor-quality water (e.g. tap water), the resulting drink wouldn't taste good. For a highball, you needed soda, so the chances of a bad mixer ruining the drinking experience were much smaller.

A 2016 advertisement for Kakubin Highball featuring actress Haruka Igawa

The Kaku-highball became a huge hit and sparked a veritable highball boom that had an impact far beyond the confines of whisky and soda. The marketing was handled well. Initially, the face of the campaign was actress Koyuki (who readers may remember from the 2003 movie *The Last Samurai*, in which she starred alongside Tom Cruise). Koyuki helped in attracting the attention of the male drinking populace.

In September 2011, she was replaced with Miho Kanno—an actress popular with young Japanese women—who reeled in the other half of the drinking populace. In January 2014, Kanno passed the baton to yet another actress, Haruka Igawa, who had popularity with both men and women.

Four years into the campaign, Suntory carried out a nationwide survey to gauge consumer response to the highball phenomenon. Sales figures showed signs of a steady recovery of the whisky market and it was clear the highball boom was responsible for that. The survey revealed some interesting trends driving it. Initially, Suntory's campaign was aimed at *izakaya* (after-work watering holes that also offer snacks and small plates) and restaurants. By 2012, however, the highball phenomenon had taken hold of people's home-drinking habits, too. Forty percent of respondents said they drank at least one highball a week at home. Most of the time (58.3 percent), home-drinkers made their own highball. The rest of the time (41.7 percent), they chose a canned highball for convenience's sake. Sales of ready-to-drink canned Kaku-highballs jumped from 38,000 cases (a case being 24 cans of 250ml) in 2009 to 6.2 million cases the year after.

When asked what they were drinking less of—in other words, what kinds of beverages the highball was replacing—people responded with *chu-hai* (shochu and soda), "sours" (a mix of shochu, soda and fruit syrup/juice/liqueur) and beer. What they liked most about the highball was that it was sparkling and clean tasting. In terms of demographics, highballs were most popular among people in their twenties. Half of the respondents who drank at least one highball a week at home said they drank with their partner. It was clear from the survey that the highball had a wide appeal and that things could only get better. And they did.

By the mid-2010s, the highball was literally everywhere. Suntory didn't have a monopoly on it, and other producers were also riding the highball wave. From the point of view of the consumer, it was a refreshing alternative to beer. It was also cheaper to make than it was to buy beer. This applied to the home-drinker but it also explains why the highball quickly became the darling of *izakayas* and restaurants; priced about the same as a beer, its margins were much better.

In 2014, whisky's rising popularity got another serious boost. This time it came from an unexpected corner: television.

Morning Drama (or *Asadora* in Japanese) is a serialized TV drama series produced by Japan's national broadcaster NHK that airs when

A selection of canned highballs available in 2016

most people are having breakfast. The series is immensely popular and watching it is a daily ritual for many people in Japan. From September 2014 to March 2015, Masataka Taketsuru—lightly fictionalized—was the focus of the morning drama. Pre-*Asadora*, only hard-core whisky fans in Japan knew who Taketsuru, or Massan, as his wife called him, was. If you live in Japan and don't know who Massan is now, people look at you as if you'd just crawled from under a rock.

One out of five Japanese followed the drama, so it's only natural that the number of whisky (and Nikka) fans increased in the wake of the series. At Nikka, sales jumped 124 percent in 2014.

Since 2008, sales of whisky in Japan have been rising steadily. However, whisky is not the sort of business where supply can be instantly calibrated to demand. As said before, in the early days of the new century, there was very little activity at the big producers' malt distilleries. The effect of this was felt around 2015 when stocks of mature whiskies in the range of 12 years old and upwards were very low. For entry-level products, like blended whiskies used for highballs, this wasn't a big issue. Those products tend to come without age statements so the recipes can be tweaked. They also lean towards younger malt and grain components, so catching up can be done relatively fast. In the premium category, however, the situation is very different. There, almost everything carries an age statement, and the youngest expressions are 10 or 12 years old. In that department, dealing with stock shortages is a major headache.

One solution was what I would call the "crossfade to NAS," NAS standing for "no age statement." This consisted of introducing a new no-age-statement expression for a given brand and then removing the youngest age-statement expression from the lineup. In May 2012, Suntory introduced a NAS expression of Yamazaki and Hakushu; in March of the following year, the respective 10-year-old expressions were discontinued. In October 2013, Nikka introduced a NAS Taketsuru; in March of the following year, the 12-year-old was history. In March 2015, Suntory launched Hibiki Japanese Harmony (NAS); six months later, Hibiki 12 was gone. You get the picture.

Another solution was tightly controlled allocation. This strategy was generally applied to older age-statement expressions. From around 2013, it was next to impossible to find a bottle of Yamazaki or Hakushu 18-year-old in liquor stores in Japan. The respective 25-year-old expressions were like liquid unicorns. They were supposed to exist but finding a specimen in the wild was a different story. These products weren't officially discontinued, but they were nowhere to be found.

A third solution was the "margin to center" strategy. In this case, it involved the creation of (a) core product(s) in the hitherto neglected category of single-grain whisky. In September 2012, Nikka launched Coffey Grain Whisky in Europe. In June 2013, it was also made available in the home market. They repeated this strategy in January and June 2014 with Coffey Malt Whisky. These products quickly became popular, especially on the mixology scene. In September 2015, Suntory created The Chita. In terms of branding, this was presented as a sibling of The Yamazaki and The Hakushu NAS expressions and priced only slightly cheaper. In commercials and campaigns, Suntory promoted The Chita as best enjoyed in a highball. Interestingly, the difference in category (grain as opposed to malt) was de-emphasized in the presentation of the product as well as in the advertising surrounding it.

The most radical solution of all was adopted by Nikka. Instead of bending over backwards to keep their portfolio intact and/or playing hide-and-seek with the consumer, they decided to axe a huge part of their core whisky range. On September 1, 2015, the entire single malt range—Yoichi 20, 15, 12, 10, NAS and Miyagikyo 15, 12, 10 and NAS— was discontinued en bloc and replaced with two new NAS expressions. Nikka also discontinued Pure Malt White and the blended whiskies Tsuru 17, G&G, Hakata, The Blend of Nikka, Malt Club, Hi-Nikka (only available in 720ml bottles from then on, as opposed to the larger plastic bottles prevalent in supermarkets around the country—up to 4 liters in volume), All Malt (only available in 700ml bottles, no longer in the larger bottles), Black Nikka 8yo and Black Nikka Special (only available in 700ml bottles, no longer in the larger bottles).

What remained (other than the aforementioned new Yoichi and Miyagikyo single malts) was: the Taketsuru lineup, the Black and Red Pure Malts, Coffey Grain and Coffey Malt, the brand-new premium blend The Nikka 12yo (which was released on September 30, 2014), From the Barrel, Super Nikka and the Rich Blend, Clear Blend and Deep Blend Black Nikka expressions. The prices of all these were raised, in the higher price brackets by as much as 50 percent. Suntory had already raised their whisky prices a few months earlier.

Regrettably, both Nikka and Suntory also froze their single-cask programs. This meant that the hard-core whisky fans who had followed and supported the companies through the lean years were suddenly left out in the cold. For smaller whisky producers, this presented an opportunity. Being small and flexible, they were perfectly suited to fill the niche that the larger companies couldn't (or wouldn't) take care of anymore: small-batch releases, limited editions and single casks. In this field, Ichiro Akuto of Venture Whisky was a trailblazer.

Ichiro Akuto had set up a new distillery in 2008, when whisky sales were at their most abysmal. At the time, people thought he was insane. In hindsight, his timing couldn't have been better. Six years later, when the big companies were struggling with low stocks, Akuto's warehouses were full. Needless to say, the order of magnitude was completely different—a few thousand casks vs. a little under a million over at Suntory, for example—but Akuto's playing field was much smaller and there was virtually no competition from the big companies by the mid-2010s. Something else happened that gave smaller producers a boost: a price explosion on the secondary market.

Towards the end of 2012, prices of Japanese whiskies on the secondary market started edging up. Before that, there was very little demand for Japanese whiskies on the online auction circuit. I still remember the days when people would sell Japanese whiskies at a loss, just to get rid of them. From the summer of 2014 onwards, Japanese whisky as a category outperformed whiskies from other regions in Scotland at auctions by a huge margin.

Figure 5, compiled by Johannes Moosbrugger of whiskystats.net, shows the price evolution of Japanese whisky on the secondary market in relation to the traditional whisky regions of Scotland from 2006 up until early 2016. The figures on the y axis indicate the price increase on the secondary market in comparison with the original retail price, i.e., 200 indicates that a whisky fetched twice its original price on the auction circuit. What the graph doesn't show is that retail prices of Japanese whiskies—especially those considered collectable whiskies—were raised considerably from around 2014 in response to people making a killing on the auction circuit. It's only natural the producers wanted part of the action, too.

Fig. 5

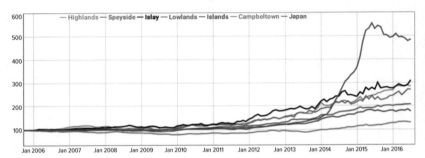

The price evolution of Japanese whisky on the secondary market compared with the traditional whisky regions of Scotland

Figure 6 shows a breakdown of the performance of Japanese whiskies on the secondary market by distillery. It is slightly misleading in that it seems to indicate Hanyu was the frontrunner and Karuizawa followed in second place. In reality, it was the other way around. One has to remember that this graph shows the increase in value with respect to the original retail price, not the absolute value of bottles. Average retail prices of Hanyu bottlings have always been much lower than those of Karuizawa releases. By actual value, Karuizawa is the most collectable of the lot. In fact, in March 2016, it managed to kick Macallan off the throne of The Whisky Magazine Index (a trading index for whiskies sold at live auctions), which is no mean feat.

On August 28, 2015, a single bottle of Karuizawa (1960, 52yo) was sold at Bonhams Hong Kong for a staggering HK$918,750 (US$118,000). The same buyer also picked up a complete set of Ichiro's Card Series (54 bottle) for HK$3,797,500 (US$490,000) the price of an average house in Japan. How did whiskies from two small Japanese distilleries

that had to stop producing because of poor sales suddenly get cata-
pulted to the top of the whisky pantheon?

In 2006, two gentlemen from England set up a company called
Number One Drinks. Marcin Miller, formerly of *Whisky Magazine*, took
care of business in Europe, whereas David Croll, who ran a company
importing Scotch whisky into Japan, was the man on the ground. They
started by distributing and bottling Hanyu, and in 2007, began working with Karuizawa, which had just become part of Kirin. They were so
keen on the whiskies slumbering in the Karuizawa warehouses that

Fig. 6

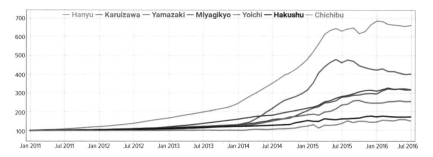

The price evolution of Japanese single malts on the secondary market

they offered to buy the distillery. Kirin wasn't having that, so plan B was
to acquire the entire remaining inventory. As it turned out, this took four
years to organize. In the meantime, occasional bottlings of Karuizawa
and Hanyu for Number One Drinks were shipped to Europe, where they
started to attract the attention of serious whisky reviewers and fans.
In 2010, four out of twelve gold medals awarded by the Malt Maniacs
were for whiskies sourced by Number One Drinks, including three
Karuizawas. In the summer of 2011, the transfer of the entire Karuizawa
inventory to Number One Drinks was finally wrapped up. The endgame
could begin.

There are various explanations for Karuizawa and Hanyu's rise from
zero to hero in the span of less than five years. One is the endgame
factor: closed distilleries with just a few hundred casks remaining.
Another is the fact that almost all of the remaining stock from these
distilleries was bottled as single casks (meaning there were lots of different releases to buy for collectors and hard-core fans). Big companies
generally don't want to get bogged down in the tedious labor involved

in bottling and selling products that are very limited and come and go in a flash, like single casks. For smaller companies, this is the field that suits them best. Logistically, it's ideal, too.

Another factor was the snowball effect of high praise—good reviews and super-high scores—from independent online reviewers (Serge Valentin of whiskyfun.com most prominently) and word of mouth on social media. This would explain why Japan was, in fact, last to latch on to the hype surrounding Hanyu and Karuizawa. Recognition through validation abroad plays a key role in many cultural areas in Japan, mostly on a subconscious level. It is certainly not limited to whisky, but also very much present in art, music and other fields in which evaluation is inherently subjective. I still remember the time when you could drive to Karuizawa distillery and buy any vintage from the 1960s up until 2000 for peanuts; the time when you would see Ichiro's Card Series in liquor shops around town with the labels falling off because they had been on the shelves for so long; the time you could walk to a large electronics chain with branches all over Japan (BicCamera) and pick a single-cask Yamazaki or Hakushu from a dozen different options any day of the week. I'm talking about 2010 here, not the Dark Ages. People in Japan simply weren't interested at the time. Now, "if only I had . . . " is the beginning of an oft-heard lament in whisky circles in Japan. Hindsight is 20/20, as they say. It was only when the noise abroad became louder that whisky fans in Japan turned their attention to Hanyu and Karuizawa. By then, it was too late. Buying a Karuizawa single cask in Japan was well nigh impossible because most of the stock bought by Number One Drinks had been reserved by foreign partners well before the resurgence of interest in domestic whisky in Japan. Whisky fans in Japan then started shifting their attention to anything and everything domestic they could get their hands on. In the span of five years (roughly 2010 to 2015) the pendulum had swung to the opposite end of the spectrum on the whisky scene in Japan: from almost zero interest in domestic whisky to an indiscriminate mad scramble for crumbs. A positive side effect of this was that it made the emergence of a craft whisky movement in Japan possible.

Encouraged by the highball boom and the hype surrounding Japanese whisky among whisky aficionados (including at home, by that stage), producers who had made whisky in the past became keen to give things another go. Following a 19-year hiatus, Mars Shinshu started distilling again in 2011. Sasanokawa Shuzo, another producer

Fig. 7 Development of Japanese Single Malt Category
(Major Brands, Standard Expressions)

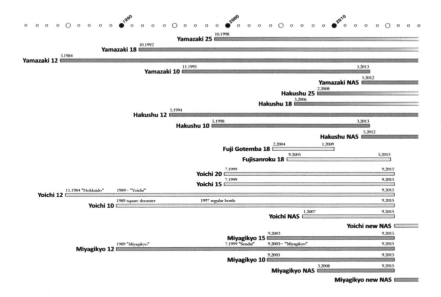

with a long history in small-scale whisky making, ordered their first copper pot stills in 2015 and started distilling in the summer of 2016. Wakatsuru Shuzo, another local whisky-maker, started contemplating a long-overdue refurbishment of its whisky production facility. Two completely new distillery projects (Gaia Flow's Shizuoka distillery and Kenten's Akkeshi distillery) were also initiated. Companies making beer and shochu started expanding into the whisky field as well. Towards the end of 2015, Hombo Shuzo surprised the whisky community at home by announcing their plans to build a second distillery in Kagoshima and have it ready for production by November 2016. In the span of a little over a year, Japan had almost doubled its distillery count. This was quite extraordinary in a country as resistant to change as Japan. Prior to this explosion, the last distillery to be added to the map was Chichibu. At the time, it was the first new distillery in more than two decades.

Clearly, the current craft distillery boom isn't just a case of synchronicity. Chichibu has a lot to do with it. It has provided a model for the new generation of craft distilleries—or a model for transformation for distilleries that had previously been active in small-scale whisky production. Unlike the *ji-whisky* boom of the early 1980s, the current craft whisky

boom is focused on the premium end of the market and on top-notch quality. Helped by the current whisky climate surrounding Japanese whisky, at home as well as abroad, Chichibu has demonstrated that it is possible for a small-scale producer to thrive on niche demand and to premiumize its image as a distillery. They have also shown that, given the right approach, it is possible to release excellent quality whiskies at a fairly young age (from 3 years old on). Gone are the days when distillers felt they had to wait a decade or more to enter the market. Three-year-old Japanese whiskies can now easily command the sort of prices that Suntory, Nikka or Ichiro would have charged for a 15-year-old single cask bottling five years ago. The appeal of this situation to new distilleries is obvious.

Meanwhile, one shouldn't lose sight of the fact that the big companies had ramped up production at their facilities in the wake of the highball boom. Suntory added two pairs of pot stills at Yamazaki distillery in 2013, and another two pairs at Hakushu distillery in 2014. By the end of 2016, all the distilleries owned by the three big companies were working hard to try and replenish their stocks in anticipation of a new "Golden Age" of Japanese whisky.

2017–

To say that the Japanese whisky scene *anno* 2022 is marked by an unbridled optimism is to point out the obvious. Whisky distilleries keep popping up all over the map. Point in case: I have had to add more distilleries to the middle section of this—the second—edition of this book, than there were featured in the original edition (written in 2016).

Figure 8 plots the number of licensed whisky distilleries since the liquor tax change of 1989, with a number of years—half a decade apart—prior to that added for historical context. Between 2001 and 2015, there were fewer than 10 active distilleries. The National Tax Agency had not yet released the figure for fiscal 2021 (which runs from April 2021 to the end of March 2022) at the time of writing, but other official information (e.g. new licenses issued during that fiscal year) indicate that there are now over fifty licensed whisky distilleries in Japan. And not a month goes by without a new distillery project coming to light.

The future (inside Warehouse No. 4 at Mt. Fuji Distillery)

Fig. 8

Licensed Whisky Distilleries
in Japan

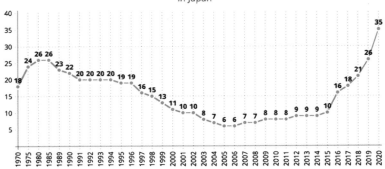

Figure 9 shows the production and consumption volumes of whisky in Japan since 2001. Other than the slight downward turn in 2020—due to the effects of the COVID-19-pandemic—the figures show sustained growth since the trough of 2007. That the growth is not of the same order as the increase in the number of licensed distilleries indicates that it is driven by quality: more producers making relatively small volumes of better whisky—at least, that is the hope.

Never before in the history of Japanese whisky have there been more bona fide whisky producers than now. But along with the increase in the number of whisky distilleries in Japan since 2016, drinks enthusiasts have become increasingly aware of a murkier side to the success story of Japanese whisky. While consumers were waiting for all the spirit laid down by the young craft distillers to turn into liquid gold, some whisky "producers" were doing their best to fill the shelves with "Japanese whiskies" in ways that—while not breaking any laws in Japan—would not be acceptable (not to mention: downright illegal) in other prominent whisky-making nations.

It's a well-known fact that whisky-making regulations in Japan are extremely loose. There is nothing that defines whisky as Japanese in terms of geographical indication. If you have a license to make whisky and you are putting something that can be called "whisky"—and there's considerable latitude here, too—in a bottle in Japan, you're making "Japanese whisky," to all intents and purposes, regardless of where

Fig. 9

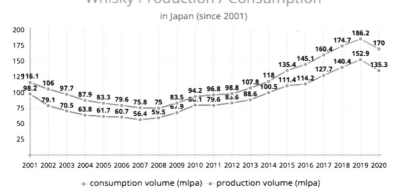

Whisky Production / Consumption
in Japan (since 2001)

- ● - consumption volume (mlpa) - ● - production volume (mlpa)

in the world the actual liquid was produced. There is nothing regulating the maturation of whisky—no vessels specified in terms of materials and/or size and no minimum period of maturation, either. Neutral spirit and flavorings can be mixed in without any problem, as long as it's mentioned on the back label. Worried about quality? Well, as long as 10 percent of the volume in the bottle is malt or grain whisky, you're good. Stills can be made out of any material. You can bottle under 40%abv. Interpreted positively, these loose constraints open up the field to creative R&D. But when demand is high and the money is easy, an open playing field can easily become a festering ground for opportunism and charlatanism.

The use of whisky imported in bulk from abroad by whisky makers in Japan has come under increasing scrutiny in whisky publications and on social media over the past few years, and with good reason. At its worst, its use comes down to "whisky laundering": whisky from Scotland, the U.S. or Canada enters the company and "Japanese whisky" in the bottle leaves the company, with the serious hike in "prestige" and price tag that comes with the latter category. It's worth keeping in mind, however, that the use of bulk-imported whisky is not a recent development. The practice is rooted in the fact that whisky producers in Japan operate as hermetically sealed businesses. There are no whisky brokers and—some recent and very limited exceptions aside (more about these below)—there's no swapping of stock. That leaves two options: create as much variety as possible in-house and/or bring in variety (or volume) from outside the country, in the case of whisky mostly from Scotland, and to a lesser extent, from the U.S. and Canada.

In 2018, H.M. Revenue & Customs—the U.K. government department responsible for the collection of taxes—listed 30 Japanese bulk importers of whisky. Only a third of those were companies that operated proper whisky distilleries of their own in Japan at the time. The list included the big boys as well as the smaller, so-called craft distillers. Interestingly, between 2013 and 2017, there was a fivefold increase in the volume of bulk blended malt (1.4mlpa in 2017), an eightfold increase in the volume of bulk blended whisky (0.7mlpa), and a threefold increase in the volume of grain whisky exported to Japan (1.7mlpa). Overall, the volume of bulk whisky coming into Japan from Scotland quadrupled in the course of those five years—and that's just looking at Scotland.

Then, of course, there is the remaining two-thirds on HMRC's list: "whisky producers" who didn't actually have the equipment to distill proper whisky. It didn't take savvy whisky enthusiasts long to put two and two together and to realize that there was something bizarre going on in Japan. Stock was brought in from abroad, moved around a bit— re-casked, re-vatted, blended—and then magically transformed into "Japanese whisky" once the liquid was bottled.

As said, historically, the use of bulk-imported whisky in Japan was nothing new. What was different, though, was the context. In the old days, there was no category of "Japanese whisky" to speak of and certainly no prestige associated with the concept of it. For the most part, it was a lowly-priced commodity. Hardly any of it was exported and if it appealed at home, it wasn't on account of it being Japanese. To draw an analogy, the use of bulk import whisky (to the extent that this was public knowledge at the time) would have been seen as the equivalent of a local baker in Japan using good butter imported from France to make pastries. What's the problem, right? They're using "the good stuff" and, as long as the price is reasonable, you're smiling as a consumer.

Fast-forward to the 21st century and things were completely different, of course. Japanese whisky had become a prestigious category. Exponents of the category picked up top awards worldwide, regularly besting competitors from more established whisky-producing nations, and prices were high across the board. No wonder the level of scrutiny was higher.

Clearly, the problem is not the fact that whisky imported in bulk was (and still is) used in Japan. The issue is transparency. As Ichiro Akuto, of Venture Whisky, points out: "We don't make grain whisky, so we simply have to import grain whisky from abroad if we want to create a blended whisky as a small craft producer. Also, blending whisky from all over the world is very informative." Ichiro's flagship blended whisky, Malt & Grain (White Label), contains whisky from all five major whisky-producing regions but he is upfront about it (no pun intended). The front label clearly states that the product is a "World Blended Whisky" and the back label clearly identifies the origin of the components. This is not a legal requirement, however. It's a simple matter of honesty—of ethics.

From the mid-2010s, a development in the U.S. further complicated matters for the Japanese whisky category: the appearance of so-called "rice whiskies." (The Fukano and Ohishi brands were trailblazers in this respect.) Here, the magic wand had shifted its powers from the adjective to the noun. That the liquid was made in Japan was beyond question. In fact, the raw materials themselves were grown in Japan, which is not the case with most whisky that is made from scratch in Japan. What was open to interpretation here, however, was whether it was "whisky."

Shochu is a traditional Japanese distilled spirit made from a wide range of base ingredients. The most common varieties are rice shochu, sweet potato shochu, and (unmalted) barley shochu. Just like in sake production, a mold called *koji-kin* is used to break down starch molecules into sugar molecules, which can then be processed by yeast cells. In terms of distillation method, there are two types: one is distilled in a continuous still to a very high ABV and then diluted for sale; the other, authentic, type is single distilled usually in a stainless steel still—wood stills are also used, copper being the exception—to a maximum abv of 45 percent. Most quality shochu is then aged in large earthenware pots or stainless / enamel-lined tanks. However, some shochu—rice and barley shochu, for the most part—is matured in oak barrels. To avoid confusion with whisky, the Japanese government put in place certain regulations in the shochu category. Most significant, in this context, is the fact that bottled shochu cannot exceed a certain, very low, absorbance value—meaning it must be markedly paler in color than whisky, by law. Whisky, on the other hand, must be made using malted grains in Japan. These regulations made it impossible for products to exist in a gray zone between categories.

In the U.S., however, all that's necessary for a distilled spirit to be legally sold as whisky is that it is made from a fermented mash of grain, stored in oak containers, and bottled at over 40%abv. The word "malt" does not appear in the regulations and the use of *koji-kin* is not a problem either. Therefore, despite their highly irregular production methods relative to standard whiskies sold in Japan and most other parts of the world, barrel-aged rice (and barley) shochu products manage to fit the whisky category in the U.S.

Shochu maturing in a barrel in Japan doesn't care about the color threshold, of course, and it *will* happen, depending on the cask types used and policies in place (or not) in the warehouse, that the liquid comes out darker than allowed. Up until recently, the shochu producer had three options when faced with a darker maturation hue: heavily filter it (but that can take the soul out of an otherwise excellent beverage); blend it with much lighter shochu before bottling to get it under the threshold; or sell it as a liqueur (but that requires a separate license and the price point will almost certainly be lower). None of those options are really attractive to producers, but losing money is even less attractive so one did what was necessary. Then, a fourth, more lucrative option presented itself like a *deus ex machina* coming from the U.S.: selling it as Japanese (rice/grain) whisky.

The proliferation of Japanese rice/grain whiskies, post-2016 in the U.S., led to bewilderment on a number of fronts, however. First off, here were products—some with rather impressive age statements—that were relatively easy to pick up at a time when Japanese whisky (even without age statements) was hardly anywhere to be found, and yet, a quick online search revealed that said products were not available in the home market. To some savvy consumers, this seemed to be a case of too-good-to-be-true.

Then, there was the flavor profile of these rice/grain whiskies, which was markedly different from what consumers were used to associating with the Japanese whisky category. For some, that was part of the attraction. According to shochu expert Stephen Lyman, "most if not all barrel-aged shochu currently sold as whisky in the U.S. is single distilled. This results in a much more flavorful new pot than would be expected from a double or triple distillation process, which is, I think, what makes these products so different, and sometimes wild or rough, compared to Japanese whiskies made in a Scottish tradition. There are no low wines in shochu production because the ferment itself is 15–18%abv prior to distillation, resulting in a 42–45%abv first run."

While the repurposing of shochu as Japanese whisky in the U.S. can seem like a win-win situation for everyone involved—the producers, the distributors, and the consumer looking for new taste sensations—there is potential for frustration. As Lyman points out, "shochu makers may be very good at making shochu, but they are not necessarily adept at making whisky, nor in the arts of barrel maintenance or blending. This certainly does not hold for all producers and some even have highly sophisticated barrel management programs and blending teams. However, one particular rice-shochu-as-whisky release that I tried smelled distinctly of acetone—not a favorable whisky profile. This risks diluting the reputation of Japanese whisky more broadly. I think, also, it risks damaging the reputation of the shochu producers if they're seen as opportunistic."

Aware that the reputation of the Japanese whisky category at large was at risk of being tarnished by these dubious practices, a working group was set up in 2016 within the Japan Spirits & Liqueurs Makers Association (JSLMA), consisting of the three largest producers (Suntory, Nikka, and Kirin) as well as the two leading craft distillers (Venture Whisky and Hombo Shuzo). The goal was to come up with a standard for Japanese whisky. It's a small miracle that the parties involved managed to reach an agreement. Debates were held until early 2021, and then in February—to the delight of many—the announcement was made that a standard had been established that would go into effect on April 1, 2021.

The standard specifies that, in terms of raw ingredients, malted grains must always be used (other cereal grains can be used as well but malted grains must be part of the mashbill) in conjunction with water extracted in Japan. Mashing, fermentation and distillation must be carried out at a distillery in Japan with the alcohol content after distillation not exceeding 95%abv. Maturation must take place in Japan, in wooden casks (note: not necessarily oak) not exceeding a capacity of 700 liters for at least 3 years. Bottling must take place in Japan at an abv of no less than 40%.

With further restrictions in place regarding labeling and the use of iconography and certain words that are considered evocative of Japan, the new standard was greeted by whisky enthusiasts at home and abroad as the dawn of a new era of absolute transparency. As usual, however, the reality is slightly more complex. First of all, this standard is not law but a standard self-imposed by companies who are part of the JSLMA. The definition of whisky by Japan's National Tax Agency remains unchanged and is unlikely to change in the near future. Further caveats are that there is currently no approval process and no penalties and that there is a transitional period until March 31, 2024, so we are not quite out of the woods yet. Another big loophole is that, for members of the JSLMA, disclosure that a whisky *doesn't* meet the standards of "Japanese whisky" must be made in at least one of the following ways: on the bottle label, on the company's website, or in response to a customer inquiry. To reiterate: in *one* of those three ways.

This much is clear already—the standard will lead to changes on the Japanese whisky scene. Many producers are making efforts to align products in their portfolio with the newly established standard. An example is Sakurao Brewery & Distillery (formerly Chugoku Juzo), which started using bulk imported whisky in the 1980s and managed to establish a presence on the Japanese whisky shelves of liquor retailers around the world over the past decade with their Togouchi brand—most certainly not Japanese whisky under the new standard. The company plans to phase out the use of bulk import whisky by 2023 and make all its whiskies JSLMA-standard compliant by then. Many other Japanese whisky producers that have been reliant on whisky imported in bulk from abroad are making similar moves and/or shifting toward transparency and an unambiguous presentation of products that will continue to make use of bulk import whisky.

An area that we will see emerging and developing over the next few years will be that of craft grain distilling. For all but the three major players on the Japanese whisky scene, the lack of access to domestically produced grain whisky is the biggest obstacle to releasing Japanese blended whiskies (as defined by the JSLMA standard). And yet, for most Japanese craft distillers, releasing an entry-level blended whisky is the only way to have a permanently available product on the shelves and to guarantee steady sales. Until further notice, the only option is to import grain whisky in bulk from Scotland, the U.S. or Canada and blend it with in-house produced malt whisky (and/or other malt whisky imported from abroad).

Aware of this conundrum, producers left and right have been trying to address the nonavailability of domestically produced grain whisky in their own ways. Several craft whisky distilleries have, over the past couple of years, been producing grain whisky in relatively small volumes. Kiuchi Shuzo has been experimenting with various grainbills at their Nukada and Yasato distilleries. Sakurao Brewery & Distillery has been producing grain whisky in their hybrid stills and Komasa Jozo has added grain whisky-making facilities to their Hioki distillery, which is used for shochu as well as gin production. These are all examples of fairly limited production and none of it has made it to market yet. That said, word on the street is that in the years to come, we will see a number of dedicated "craft grain distilleries" emerging—especially, it seems, in Hokkaido. It will take half a decade or more for these efforts to shake up the Japanese blended whisky game, but it's a development that is to be welcomed, and a clear indicator of the way in which the JSLMA standard—in spite of it not being enshrined in law—is having a real-world effect.

The new standard also closes the door on shochu and awamori producers, as their licenses expressly prohibit them from using malted grains, which is now a requirement for Japanese whisky under the JSLMA standard. However, it's worth pointing out that most shochu makers are not members of the JSLMA—they have an association of their own—and are therefore not bound by the new whisky standards.

Clearly, the JSLMA standard was set up with the aim of encouraging transparency and making life harder for unscrupulous producers, but some have questioned whether a standard largely modeled after foreign whisky standards is a perfect fit for the Japanese whisky culture. The exclusion of *koji* whisky is a point in case. The use of *koji* has been an integral part of Japanese culture for the past 1,300 years so one would be hard pressed to argue against it being a culturally meaningful practice in Japan.

Whisky making in Japan has always been heavily patterned after whisky production in Scotland (and to a lesser extent, the U.S. and Canada), but after almost a century of Japanese whisky makers leaving the country to learn the ropes abroad and bringing home "the fire," we are now starting to see the beginnings of an influx of foreign talent—both financial and technical—on the Japanese whisky scene. Several new distilleries featured in Part 2 of this book were established by foreign parties and rumors floating around of more to come indicate that this trend is anything but a fad.

The proliferation of craft whisky distilleries in recent years also seems to be eating away at the dictum that "Japanese distillers don't swap stock." One industry figure in favor of stock swapping among Japanese craft distillers is Saburomaru distillery manager and blender Takahiko Inagaki. His thinking was that, as Saburomaru distillery only produces heavily-peated whisky, his company would benefit from having access to different types of spirits from other distilleries in Japan. But the reverse is true, too. For other Japanese craft distillers, having some heavily-peated Saburomaru spirit maturing in their respective warehouses could come in handy when creating some of their blends or blended malts.

In March 2021, Inagaki showed that he was walking the talk when the first-ever collaborative releases of Japanese whisky went on sale. Saburomaru distillery had swapped some of their heavily-peated aged malt whisky for some lightly-peated aged malt whisky from Nagahama distillery and the respective companies then went on to create two types of blended malt whisky each: one a Japanese blended malt, the other a so-called "world blended malt," using malt whisky imported in bulk from Scotland in addition to the two Japanese malts. Saburomaru launched its bottlings under the banner "Far East of Peat" (700 and 7,000 bottles, respectively), whereas Nagahama distillery labeled theirs "Inazuma" ("lightning bolt" in Japanese; 700 and 6,000 bottles, respectively). These products may have been the first collaborative Japanese whisky releases, but it wasn't the first case of collaboration between craft whisky distillers in Japan.

Unbeknownst to other whisky producers in Japan, Venture Whisky (Ichiro's Malt) and Hombo Shuzo (Mars Whisky) had actually swapped some stock in 2015. In their case, new-make spirit was exchanged and was then filled into wood and aged by the receiving party. After a little over five years, each company created a blended malt incorporating the stock they had received from the other party. Ichiro's Malt Double Distilleries 2021 Chichibu x Komagatake (53.5%abv, 10,200 bottles) and Mars Whisky Malt Duo Komagatake x Chichibu 2021 (54%abv, 10,918 bottles) went on sale in Japan toward the end of April 2021 and whisky enthusiasts were clearly enamored with the results as much as with the ethos.

As important as these two collaborative release projects are—and a handful of similar projects have come to fruition since—they remain somewhat anecdotal in the larger scheme of things. Since then, however, a structurally much more ambitious project has been launched: T&T Toyama, the first independent bottler of Japanese whisky (see sidebar). Again, the volume involved may be relatively small, but as the saying goes: great oaks from little acorns grow.

A century into whisky making in Japan, winds of change are blowing through the landscape. What the next hundred years will bring, no one can predict. One thing's for sure, though: if the journey is even half as wild as that detailed in the previous pages, we're in for a thrill. The saga continues . . .

T&T Toyama
The First Independent Bottler of Japanese Whisky

It has been mentioned quite a few times in these pages that Japanese whisky distilleries don't sell or swap stock. Yet, as with all things seemingly set in stone, the possibility that change might just be around the corner cannot be discounted.

In 2021, Takahiko Inagaki of Saburomaru distillery and Tadaaki Shimono, founder of independent online whisky retailer Maltoyama, decided to try and do the impossible: establish a company dedicated to aging and bottling whisky from various distilleries in Japan. They called their enterprise T&T Toyama, in reference to their first names and the prefecture where they are based. In the spring of 2021, Inagaki and Shimono managed to raise close to 40.5 million yen through a successful crowdfunding campaign. This allowed them to develop their plans and go ahead with the construction of a dedicated aging warehouse in Inami, in Nanto city.

T&T Toyama is built on the Gordon & Macphail model, with new-make being purchased from distilleries and filled into carefully selected wood. This isn't just marketing speak. Inami is well known for its extensive woodcarving district, and T&T Toyama are working closely with an independent cooperage (Sanshiro), a mere five-minute drive from the warehouse site.

Prototype bottlings

Up until the launch of T&T Toyama, the idea of purchasing new-make from distilleries in Japan to be aged by a third party would have been declared pie-in-the-sky by anyone familiar with industry practice there. The options were limited and even if you were mad enough to try and if you did manage to find the proverbial exception to the rule, that would still only have given you spirit from one distillery—not exactly a workable business model as an independent bottler. The proliferation of craft whisky distilleries in Japan over the past couple of years, established by existing liquor producers (shochu producers, for the most part), has changed that. Asked if, without a precedent in Japan, it was difficult to find distillers willing to supply T&T Toyama with new-make, Shimono relates that "it was fairly easy once we sat down and explained the nature of our project to them. With the exception of one, the distilleries we approached were all very new distilleries, and they understood where we were coming from. We also had the framework in place, with Takahiko being a distillery manager himself and myself having been involved in whisky retail for the past 10 years. So it wasn't like this was a project of a couple of shady figures coming out of the woodwork."

Inagaki and Shimono visited craft whisky distillers across Japan to taste new-make, quality being of prime importance. By the summer of 2021, they had supply agreements with six distilleries. Aside from Eigashima distillery, all the others are fairly new kids on the block: Sakurao, Kanosuke, Ontake, Osuzuyama and Saburomaru. (The latter has a longer history on paper but is essentially a new distillery in an old shell.) The volume purchased from each distillery varies, based on how much or how little they can spare. By the summer of 2022, T&T Toyama had also managed to source some Japanese rum new-make (from the Iejima Distillery in Okinawa) to age under their wings. The idea is to let the spirit develop in directions it may not / cannot go at the original distilleries themselves: a different aging environment, different wood policies and the different sensibilities of the people watching over the maturation. "What we want to do as independent bottlers," Shimono says, "is to offer a perspective on these single malts and rums that differs from that of the distillery where the new-make comes from."

The Inami aging warehouse was completed in the spring of 2022. Here, too, the founders were looking to break new ground. Rather than go for a steel-framed construction of the sort typically used for large-scale aging warehouses, they were keen to use CLT—i.e. cross-laminated timber, first developed and used in Germany and Austria in the 1990s. Prior to construction, tests were run and the results were as anticipated: high thermal insulation and excellent humidity control (in tandem, creating a stable maturation environment). Another benefit, not insignificant in Japan, is that a CLT construction tends to have a higher earthquake resistance. The wood used in the construction of the Inami warehouse was all locally sourced: 283 trees

Prototype bottlings in the warehouse

from Nanto city and 102 cypress trees from Toyama prefecture. The roof is of the double-skin metal type. Sensors have been installed in the warehouse to allow for close monitoring of the aging environment.

At the moment, only half of the warehouse has been fitted with racks. This will suffice for a few years. When the need arises, the other half will also be fitted with racks. The total capacity is around 5,000 casks (barrels and hogs-heads). There is also a small dunnage area at the front of the warehouse, and a tasting corner.

The first release is slated for 2025, and the aim is to present all T&T Toyama releases as single-cask bottlings at cask strength. The labels on the prototype bottles—not for sale but used for events and tasting purposes—feature the Japanese iris. "We've called this 'Breath of Japan,'" Shimono points out, "which is a somewhat clumsy translation of the Japanese word *ibuki*, a sign of something new and fresh. The Japanese iris is considered a lucky charm, but its Japanese name, *shoubu*, is also a word that carries the connotation of 'battle' or 'contest.'"

It's not unlikely that others will be inspired by the example of T&T Toyama to follow in their footsteps. The Japanese whisky landscape has changed dramatically over the past decade, so who is to say that it's inconceivable to think of a future in which new-make and/or maturing stock from distilleries left and right leaves the nest to continue its journey in new and unexpected ways under someone else's wings. Never say never . . .

Part 2

THE STILLS: JAPANESE DISTILLERIES PRESENT & PAST

The little street that takes most visitors from Yamazaki station to the distillery

Yamazaki Distillery, Hakushu Distillery, Chita Distillery & Osumi Distillery

(Beam Suntory Inc.)

YAMAZAKI DISTILLERY

Yamazaki is an area steeped in history. In 1582, it was the site of the famous Battle of Yamazaki. Centuries later, Yamazaki, conveniently located between Kyoto and Osaka, became the birthplace of Japanese whisky. It was there, at the foot of Mt. Tenno and across from Mt. Otoko, that Shinjiro Torii decided to build the first whisky distillery in Japan.

Torii had received advice from a certain Dr. Moore, a brewing authority in Scotland, that the most important factors in building a distillery were the natural environment and the quality of the water. When Torii hit upon Yamazaki, he felt it ticked all the right boxes as far as "natural environment" was concerned: gently rolling hills, beautiful bamboo forests and a damp climate. At Yamazaki, three rivers—the Katsura, Uji and Kizu—merge, and because of the differences in water temperature between the three, as well as the topography of the area, mist and fog were common occurrences. (I write "was" because the climate has changed somewhat since Torii scouted the location; nowadays, there are only one or two foggy days a month on average.) In any case, at the time, those seemed like ideal, almost Scottish, conditions in which to age whisky. Just one question remained: would the water be good?

The area had long been famous for its exquisite water. It was mentioned in the Manyoshu, the oldest anthology of Japanese poetry, and

legendary tea master Sen no Rikyu had a tea ceremony room built there (the Tai-an) for Hideyoshi Toyotomi (a feudal lord who helped complete the unification of Japan in the sixteenth century) and prepared tea with the water of Yamazaki. Pretty good credentials, but Torii wasn't taking any risks. He sent the samples to Scotland and waited for Dr. Moore's verdict. The good doctor was impressed and the rest is history, as they say.

The construction of Yamazaki distillery began in late 1923 and was completed the following year. The first spirit ran off the pot stills on November 11, 1924 at 11:11 a.m. The pre-war layout was pretty much that of a typical Scottish highland distillery.

During World War II, Yamazaki distillery remained untouched but as a precaution, the casks were evacuated to a tunnel in the gorge. According to the people at Suntory, "These malt whiskies unexpectedly matured well enough to become essential key components of future whiskies."

The distillery has been reconfigured and expanded over the years, first in 1957 and most recently in 2013. In terms of expansion, the limits seem to have been reached, as the town around the distillery has also grown. The distillery is now part of the town. Interestingly, a public road runs through the middle of the site. In the morning and late afternoon, it's not uncommon to see kids walking through the distillery!

Yamazaki Distillery

Mash tun:	2 stainless steel, lauter (100kl, 25kl)
Washbacks:	12 stainless steel (40–90kl)
	8 wooden (Oregon pine, 20-25kl)
Pot stills:	8 pairs
	direct heating (gas) for wash stills, indirect heating (steam) for spirit stills
	lyne arms mostly descending
	shell-and-tube condensers for all but wash still No. 3 and No. 5 (worm tubs)

Malting took place at the distillery up until the early 1970s, but those days are long gone, just like in the Scottish whisky industry. Floor malting was carried out until 1969, with peat imported from Scotland, and mechanical malting from 1969 to 1972. Specialized companies, so-called "maltsters," now take care of that stage of the process. At the time of writing, all barley used by Suntory for whisky production is imported from the U.K. At their beer factories, some domestic barley is used because the financial return is quasi instantaneous. For whisky, which relies on years of maturation and is at the mercy of the whims of the market, the increased cost of using domestic barley (up to five times more expensive than using imported) makes that too risky a proposition.

A range of peating levels is used at Yamazaki distillery. This pursuit of variety at all stages of production will become a familiar trope in what follows. Distillation of heavily peated malt, which tends to be around 40ppm, usually takes place at the end of the year.

Water is taken from bores on the premises. For the mashing,

Shinjiro Torii (right) gives Prince Naruhiko Higashikuni a tour of the distillery (1940)

Two junior high students on their way back home walking through the distillery complex

two stainless steel lauter tuns are used—one big (17.6 tons/16 metric tons), one small (4.5 tons/4 metric tons)—and the filtering of the mash is done slowly to produce a wort that is as clear as possible. Then, the wort is transferred to one of 20 washbacks.

Up until 1988, all the washbacks were constructed from stainless steel. Photographs seem to suggest that wooden washbacks were used in the early days of the distillery, but there are no records to corroborate that. During the 1988 refurbishment of the distillery, the decision was made to go half and half and to also install some wooden washbacks. At the moment, eight of the washbacks used are Oregon pine; the other twelve are stainless steel.

Fermentation in progress at Yamazaki Distillery

One of the original Yamazaki pot stills with the statues of Shinjiro Torii (sitting) and Keizo Saji

Various types of yeast are used in the fermentation process. This includes both distillers and brewers yeast, and most of the strains are proprietary. The standard fermentation time is three days.

The variety at this stage of the process, i.e., the wash, is already quite staggering: various types of barley with varied peating levels, mashed and then fermented with different types of yeast (sometimes in combination) in either wood or stainless steel. In the stillhouse, that diversity gets an exponential boost.

Yamazaki distillery started out with one pair of stills. These were crafted by Watanabe Copper & Ironworks in Osaka and carried by steamship up the Yodo River to the distillery. They were used until 1958 and then decommissioned. The original spirit still can still be seen at the distillery, as it has become a little outdoor monument near the visitor center. Touching the rough, oxidized surface of the hand-hammered still, with the nearby statues of Shinjiro Torii and Keizo Saji gazing into the distance, one can almost feel history.

In 1958, four new pot stills were installed. Over the years, the number of stills has increased, to the present number of 16. Stills are used for between 20 and 30 years. The thickness of the copper is checked every year and when stills become worn out, they are replaced, but not necessarily with new ones of the same size and shape. Some old stills are turned into little monuments on the distillery grounds and a few lucky ones get a new life elsewhere.

Suntory used to put their company logo (which has changed over the years) on the stills, so looking at the logo, one had an idea of when they were installed. In recent years, they have stopped doing this. In 2006, three pairs were replaced. Two pairs of stills were added in 2013. These could not be accommodated in the actual stillhouse so they cleaned out a blending lab nearby and converted it to fit the four additions. The most recent change in the actual stillhouse was in 2022, when Wash Still No. 1 was replaced. (It used to be of the straight type; the new still has a bulge.)

The current set-up is as follows:

YAMAZAKI

year of installation		type	size	lyne-arm orientation	year of installation		type	size	lyne-arm orientation
WASH STILLS					**SPIRIT STILLS**				
2013	No. 8	straight	M	upward	2013	No. 8	bulge	M	downward
2013	No. 7	straight	M	downward	2013	No. 7	straight	M	downward
1989	No. 6	bulge	L	downward (slightly)	1989	No. 6	bulge	M+	downward (slightly)
1989	No. 5	straight	L	downward (sharply)	1989	No. 5	bulge	M+	downward (slightly)
2006	No. 4	straight	M+	downward	2006	No. 4	straight	M-	downward (slightly)
2001	No. 3	straight	M	downward (sharply)	2001	No. 3	straight	S	downward (slightly)
2006	No. 2	bulge	M+	downward	2006	No. 2	bulge	M-	downward
2022	No. 1	bulge	S	downward (very sharply)	2006	No. 1	straight	M-	downward

all wash stills direct-fired (gas), all spirit stills indirect-fired (steam)
all shell-and-tube condensers except wash still 3 and 5 (wormtubs)

The wash stills are direct-fired (gas) so you can often hear the gentle high-frequency buzz generated by the rummagers (rotating copper chains that prevent charring) inside the stills while walking through the stillhouse, especially now that all the stills are pretty much in use non-stop. The spirit stills are indirectly heated by means of steam coils or percolators. All stills are fitted with shell-and-tube condensers, except Wash Stills no. 3 and no. 5, which have worm tubs. Basically, the stills are used in pairs, but the piping can be adjusted to facilitate other combinations.

Yamazaki Distillery in 1929, clockwise from upper left: the malt store with parcels of 'Golden Melon' barley; the malting floor; the mash tun and washbacks; the stillhouse

The first casks used at Yamazaki distillery were ex-sherry casks, imported from the U.K. In fact, the first ever cask filled is still at the distillery. It no longer contains any whisky, but it's interesting for historical reasons. Like a palimpsest, traces of its origin can be seen on the cask head. Underneath the white paint, it says "Lacave & Co., Cadiz," which was an old bodega in Jerez, Spain.

Torii was keen to also make casks in-house but at the time, there was no tradition of cask making in Japan. There were people around, though, who knew how to make watertight wooden vessels: tub makers. In 1934, Torii hired a tubmaker by the name of Gennojo Tateyama, who became the first cooper at Yamazaki distillery. Tateyama taught himself how to make casks by studying imported casks. In the same way that some musicians train themselves by listening to recordings, Tateyama developed his own techniques and his own tools to make casks. He passed his skills on to his son, Noboru, who in turn passed them on to his son, Ryuichi, who became manager of Suntory's Ohmi cooperage.

Ohmi Aging Cellar

Most of the spirit produced at Suntory's distilleries is taken to the so-called Ohmi Aging Cellar, about 43 miles/70km northwest of Yamazaki distillery, near Lake Biwa. The name is slightly misleading because it's a multi-warehouse complex and it's not exactly a "cellar." Ohmi Aging Cellar was built in 1972 and, over the years, more and more warehouses have been added. The most recent one—with a capacity of 140,000 casks—was built in 2022. In the late 1980s, the cooperage at Yamazaki was moved to Ohmi. The Ohmi cooperage specializes in puncheons, whereas the Hakushu cooperage focuses on hogsheads. There is no longer a cooperage at the Yamazaki distillery.

There are a few old-style warehouses with casks stacked three high and a few racked warehouses at Yamazaki distillery, but only about 10 percent of the spirit produced there is matured on site. The bulk is taken away by tanker trucks and matured at the Ohmi complex or at Hakushu distillery. Similarly, there is some Hakushu malt and Chita grain whisky maturing at Yamazaki distillery. Obviously, there are differences in climate between the three maturation locations but there are also pragmatic reasons for splitting the stock up. The warehouses at Hakushu are racked and set up for barrels and hogsheads, the smaller cask types. The average temperature at Hakushu is lower, so a high spirit/wood contact ratio works better, hence the smaller casks. Temperatures at Yamazaki are higher, so the preference there is for bigger casks, puncheons and butts. This has practical implications: a sherry butt doesn't fit in the racks at Hakushu, so sherried Hakushu is matured at one of the other locations, where the set-up allows for that. An added benefit of splitting the stock from three distilleries (Yamazaki, Hakushu and Chita) between three locations (Yamazaki, Hakushi and Ohmi Aging Cellar) is that a major disaster (which is always a possibility in earthquake-prone Japan) or an accident won't result in the complete loss of a distillery's stock. In 2022, Suntory had a combined storage capacity of around 1.7 million casks across its three aging locations.

Facing page, clockwise from upper left: one of the stillmen at Yamazaki Distillery checking the distillate as it runs off the still; distillation in progress; the first cask filled at Yamazaki Distillery; the spirit safe with all stills running; a view of the wash still side of the stillhouse at Yamazaki Distillery

貯蔵庫
Warehouse

Wood Management at Suntory

Suntory is very particular about the wood used to mature its whiskies in. Reluctant to be at the mercy of inconsistencies in supply and quality, they've implemented strategies that allow them to monitor the different steps of the process, from tree to cask.

In terms of ex-bourbon wood, they've got nothing to worry about, especially since the company became *Beam* Suntory in 2014 (my emphasis). Ex-bourbon wood includes barrels (diameter 25.5 inches/65cm, length 34 inches/86cm, capacity 180 liters) as well as hogsheads (28 inches/72cm, 32 inches/82cm, 230 liters), which are made using staves from barrels that have been disassembled.

Puncheons (38 inches/96cm, 42 inches/107cm, 480 liters) are made from scratch in-house, at the Ohmi Cooperage. These are made out of American white oak, which is bought directly in the U.S. and left to air-dry for a minimum of three years.

Sherry casks are exclusively made out of Spanish oak. The people at Suntory strongly believe that it's not so much the previous contents (in this case, sherry) as the type of oak used for the cask that contributes most of the flavors we associate with "sherried whiskies." The Suntory people go through great lengths to get top-notch sherry butts (35 inches/89cm, 50 inches/128cm, 480 liters). First, they travel to the north of Spain to select the trees. Once the logs are cut, the wood is air-dried for three years. Then, it's coopered and seasoned with Oloroso sherry in Jerez for at least three years. Finally, the casks are sent to Japan and filled with whisky. It's a lengthy process, but the people at Suntory believe it's worth the trouble. They've been making their own sherry casks like this for over 30 years and several of their sherried expressions have been singled out as "best in the world" by various high-profile whisky commentators, so they must be doing something right.

Mizunara is a Suntory specialty and an important element of several of their single malt expressions and premium blends. Japanese oak grows slowly, is scarce and therefore expensive, so only a few hundred casks a year can be made. Suntory has access to forests in Hokkaido but sometimes logging rights are suspended for extended periods of time to allow the forest to regenerate. When that's the case, mizunara wood is bought at public auctions.

In addition to those five types, Suntory also uses ex-wine and ex-*umeshu* (plum liqueur) casks. Suntory owns Chateau Lagrange in the Medoc, so access to ex-wine casks is not a problem. The red berry notes in the Yamazaki Distiller's Reserve, for example, come from the use of such casks. The use of ex-*umeshu* casks was driven by the desire to create a malt component that would contribute a distinctive plum note to a blend (e.g., Hibiki 12), but not derived from ex-sherry wood. Since Suntory also makes *umeshu*, they came up with the idea of aging that in ex-Yamazaki casks, and then using the casks afterwards to refill with whisky for a secondary maturation. That's what's called killing two birds with one stone. All of the whisky finished in ex-*umeshu* casks goes into blends. The only chance to try it in isolation was the 2008 release Yamazaki Plum Liqueur Cask Finish. It was limited to 3,000 bottles and restricted to the bar trade.

Wood is a precious resource so casks are refilled multiple times. It's one of the blenders' tasks to determine when a cask is too fatigued to stay in circulation. When casks are retired, they are turned into furniture, flooring, garden containers and so on.

Facing page: One of the Yamazaki warehouses; Maturation in progress

In the Suntory warehouses, casks have a lifespan of 50 to 70 years. Given an average maturation time of around 10 years, that means they can be reused five times. The oldest cask (not the oldest *whisky* in the cask, but the oldest *oak vessel* still used for the maturation of whisky) dates from September 1954. This now contains whisky distilled in 2008. When that liquid is removed, the cask will most likely be retired. The oldest *whisky* still maturing at Yamazaki is from the 1950s.

Blenders also monitor the development of the stock. With well over a million casks spread over the three warehousing locations and only six blenders to follow the progress of the maturation of those casks, it's clear they have to be methodical. When the whisky maturing is young, random samples are taken from each lot of casks, and lots are checked every three to four years. Above 12 years old, each and every cask is sampled.

The oldest cask still used for maturation at Yamazaki Distillery: the engraving at the bottom shows [Showa] 29, which is 1954; the whisky maturing in it now was distilled in 2008

HAKUSHU DISTILLERY

Fifty years after Shinjiro Torii had started building Japan's first whisky distillery, Keizo Saji, the second president of Suntory, took Torii's dream a big step further. In order to expand the company's palette of malt whisky components, the decision was made to build a second distillery in a very different environment. The site picked, after many years of searching, was a vast forest area at the foot of Mt. Kaikomagatake in the Southern Alps.

Hakushu distillery is located at a high altitude (2,323 feet/708m, as opposed to Yamazaki's 82 feet/25m). The climate is cooler than in Yamazaki, with average temperatures about 9°F/5°C lower throughout the year, but the difference in temperature between the daily highs and lows is much bigger, especially in the summer.

In order to protect the rich natural environment, Suntory acquired a 204 square-acre/825,000 square-meter piece of land. About 83 percent of the site is undeveloped and part of it includes a wild bird sanctuary. According to Suntory, "wild birds are very sensitive to changes in the quality of a region's water and therefore a good barometer." Hakushu distillery is literally part of the forest and the people at Suntory go out of their way to keep it as pristine as possible.

Hakushu has had a very interesting development as a distillery. The original distillery, which was completed in February 1973, is known as "Hakushu 1" and was equipped with six pairs of stills. In 1977, capacity was doubled and a building was added, known as "Hakushu 2." The new building also had six pairs of stills. At the time, it was a mammoth distillery—in fact, the biggest in the world—with 4 mash tuns, 44 stainless steel washbacks and 24 pot stills. In 1981, a new distillery was built

Hakushu, "the forest distillery"

Hakushu 1 and its retired stills

across from Hakushu 1 and 2. From June 1988, "Hakushu 3" was referred to as "Hakushu East." Production at Hakushu West (i.e., Hakushu 1 and 2) was terminated shortly after Hakushu East was built, so when we talk about Hakushu distillery now, we are referring to Hakushu East.

People often wonder what motivated Suntory to give up on a working distillery with 24 pot stills and build a new one across the road. The expense involved was considerable, but comparing the respective stillhouses, it's not too hard to understand the motivation. The stills at Hakushu West were all the same size and huge: 30kl wash stills and 20kl spirit stills. Not only that, they all had the same lantern shape and all had descending lyne arms. Basically, the distillery was set up to make lots of malt whisky of the same type. The bulk of this was destined for Suntory Old, their workhorse blend.

Looking at the stillhouse at Hakushu East, one sees smaller stills and a wide variety of sizes, shapes and lyne-arm orientations. Clearly, Suntory had realized two things by 1981: 1) that in distillation, one cannot simply supersize the equipment and expect the result to be "more of the same," and 2) that, rather than having a huge amount of one type of spirit, it was more interesting to produce a variety of types.

Hakushu 2 is mostly gone. Hakushu 1 is still there, although it is not open to the public. Save for a missing neck on wash still no. 4, it is pretty much like it was in 1973. There's something almost forlorn about those impressive dull-copper stills cloaked in silence, across the road from the next generation, all shiny and hot, working round the clock.

Hakushu Distillery (Malt)

Mash tun:	1 stainless steel, lauter (130kl)
Washbacks:	18 wooden (Oregon pine, 75kl)
Pot stills:	8 pairs
	direct heating (gas) except Spirit Stills Nos. 2, 7 and 8 (indirect)
	lyne arms, mostly descending
	shell-and-tube condensers for all but Wash Still No. 3 (worm tub)

The water used to make whisky at Hakushu distillery originates as snowmelt from Mt. Kaikomagatake. It seeps down through the granite strata of the area where it is naturally filtered by the crystals in the granite. This results in soft water with a crisp and refreshing taste. Millions of people in Japan are familiar with the taste of this water. Suntory has been bottling it at their Tennensui Hakushu Plant, very near the distillery, since 2003. It's by far the most popular bottled mineral water in Japan.

At the foot of Mt. Kaikomagatake, the Ojira and Jingu rivers form an alluvial fan of white sand. The name Hakushu (which translates as "white sandbar") refers to this geological feature. The water of the Ojira River is considered to be one of Japan's 100 most exceptional sources of water.

Just like at the Yamazaki distillery, all of the malted barley used at Hakushu is imported from the U.K. A similar range of peating levels can be found here. The mashing process is essentially the same. One batch at Hakushu consists of 10–18t of malted barley. At Hakushu West, all the washbacks were made of stainless steel. When the new Hakushu East complex was built, they switched to wooden washbacks, unlike at Yamazaki, where stainless steel and wooden are used side by side. Most of the washbacks date from 1981 (12 of the 18). Two were installed in 2011, and a further four in 2012. Like at Yamazaki, both distillers and brewers yeast are used, and the standard fermentation time is three days.

Distillation takes place seven days a week, around the clock, with a short break during the summer for maintenance. Hakushu East operated with six pairs of stills until 2014, when two new pairs were added to the stillhouse. Just like at Yamazaki, stills are replaced from time to time. The set-up at the time of writing is shown on page 139.

Interestingly, the tendency is towards smaller stills. The oldest ones (the original 1981 ones) are the biggest ones, whereas the newer ones are generally much smaller. At the old Hakushu West complex, all stills were indirect-fired, by steam coils. At Hakushu East, all wash stills and all but three of the spirit stills are direct-fired. Direct firing contributes to the formation of certain flavor compounds. These were considered to be desirable when Hakushu was rethought in 1981, hence the radical change on that front.

Like at Yamazaki, the stills are usually used in pairs (i.e., Wash Still No. 1 with Spirit Still No. 1, etc.) but other permutations are possible. They are used in equal measure, that is to say, without giving priority to certain pairs over others. All stills are fitted with shell-and-tube condensers, except Wash Still No. 3, which is fitted with a worm tub.

As explained above, not all spirit matured at Hakushu is matured on site. Some of it is, but some is taken to either Yamazaki distillery or the Ohmi Aging Cellar complex by tanker for maturation. Suntory used to have another warehouse location, in Yatsugatake, not far from Hakushu distillery. Constructed in 1983, at the height of whisky consumption in Japan, Yatsugatake Aging Cellar consisted of seven warehouses. They were demolished in 2008, at the all-time lowest point of whisky's popularity.

At Hakushu distillery, there are 18 warehouses. All of these are racked and fairly big, but in terms of warehouse size, there's a bit of variety. As said before, the warehouses are set up for barrels and hogsheads. Large casks such as butts, puncheons and mizunara casks don't fit in the racks, so those are matured elsewhere. Unlike at Yamazaki distillery, there's a small cooperage on site.

A view from the "kiln pagoda"

HAKUSHU

year of installation	type	size	lyne-arm orientation	year of installation	type	size	lyne-arm orientation
WASH STILLS				**SPIRIT STILLS**			
2014 No. 8	straight	S	downward (minimally)	2014 No. 8	straight	S	downward (minimally)
2014 No. 7	straight	M	downward (slightly)	2014 No. 7	straight	M	downward (slightly)
1981 No. 6	lantern	LL	downward	1981 No. 6	lantern	M+	upward (sharply)
1981 No. 5	lantern	LL	downward	1981 No. 5	lantern	M+	upward (sharply)
2005 No. 4	straight	M	downward	2005 No. 4	straight	S	downward
2001 No. 3	straight	M	downward (sharply)	2001 No. 3	straight	S	downward
1981 No. 2	lantern	LL	downward	1998 No. 2	straight	SS	downward
1998 No. 1	straight	M	downward (very sharply)	1998 No. 1	straight	SS	downward

all direct-fired (gas) except spirit stills 2, 7 and 8 indirect-fired (steam)
all shell-and-tube condensers except wash still 3 (worm tub)

A staff member at Hakushu Distillery drawing a sample from one of the washbacks

The stillhouse at Hakushu distillery

The new kids on the block: spirit stills no. 7 and 8

Clockwise from top left: detail of one of the washbacks installed in 1994; inside one of the warehouses at Hakushu Distillery; fermentation in progress

CHITA DISTILLERY

SunGrain—as Chita Distillery was known, before the name was officially changed in April 2019—was set up in 1972 with joint investment from Suntory and Zen-Noh (the National Federation of Agricultural Cooperative Associations). The distillery started producing in 1973. In 1977, a second plant was added to the site. In 1985, the production scope was expanded to also include spirits other than grain whisky.

The main raw material at Chita distillery is corn. The corn is mixed with water and heated in a pressurized continuous cooking tube. After bringing the temperature down to about 149°F/65°C, water-slurried malted six-row barley is added. The unfiltered wort is fermented for three to four days before being distilled to at least 94%abv. The continuous distillation process involves the use of four columns in different combinations. A heavy grain spirit is produced by using two columns; a medium-type spirit by using three, and a clean type by using all four. There are no maturation facilities on site.

Coinciding with the 50th anniversary of the distillery, Suntory invested 10 billion yen into expanding output capacity and variety of styles—the largest investment since its establishment. In addition to a mill, biomass boiler, and cooker and fermentation tanks, a brand-new Coffey-type continuous still was installed. Full-scale operation using the new equipment started in July 2022.

Chita distillery is not open to the public. Aside from health and safety issues, this also has to do with maintaining image. For people used to visiting malt distilleries—picturesque, surrounded by nature, with wood and copper everywhere—the silver, hissing behemoth that is Chita would come as a bit of a shock.

A cask holding Chita grain whisky distilled in 1993

HAKUSHU GRAIN DISTILLERY

In December 2010, Suntory set up a grain whisky facility on the Hakushu site. Following a testing period of a little over two years, grain whisky production officially started in May 2013. The official opening coincided with the 40th anniversary of Hakushu distillery.

The Hakushu grain whisky facility is much smaller than Chita distillery (about one-tenth the size, at the time it was established) and serves an altogether different purpose. Being smaller, the facility lends itself to experimentation and the exploration of variation. Different mashbills and yeast strains can be used, and spirit can be drawn off at different strengths (between 60% and 94%abv). The idea is the same as at the malt distillery next door: create variation in flavor.

Hakushu grain distillery is equipped with a hammer mill, a cooker (these were originally used to make shochu at Hakushu), six stainless steel fermentation tanks and a two-column continuous still. The analyzer has 18 trays and the rectifier has 40. The facility is not open to the public.

I have had the pleasure of trying new-make from Hakushu grain distillery side by side with a sample from Chita distillery and the difference is like night and day. The Hakushu grain new-make has a distinct *katsuobushi* (dried bonito flakes) note. The quality is top-notch and that is part of the idea, of course: having access to top-quality grain whisky for the purpose of perfecting high-end blends.

The continuous still at the Hakushu grain whisky facility

OSUMI DISTILLERY

Osumi Distillery is Suntory's fourth whisky distillery. It was very much under the radar until April 2020, when the fourth installment in Suntory's series "The Essence of Suntory Whisky" was released. One of the two releases was a rice whisky, distilled at Osumi distillery, and that's when the public realized Suntory actually had a fourth whisky distillery in Japan.

The distillery is located on the Osumi Peninsula, which makes up the eastern half of Kagoshima prefecture. It was established by Osumi Shuzo Co., Ltd. in 2004, for the purpose of making sweet potato shochu. Production started in 2005.

In September 2014, the company was acquired by Suntory and production was expanded to also include barley shochu. Suntory launched its flagship *honkaku* shochu brand, The Osumi, in 2019.

What the public didn't know, until the release of the aforementioned "Essence of Suntory" expressions, is that Suntory had acquired a whisky license for the plant in April 2016 and that the production of rice whisky—made without koji—started soon after. The rice whisky is produced using the shochu equipment: a cooker, stainless steel fermenters, and 4 stainless steel stills (operated at atmospheric pressure).

Suntory hasn't disclosed what its plans are, if any, for Osumi Distillery in the near future.

EXPRESSIONS

On March 14, 1984, Suntory launched the first widely available single malt whisky in Japan, Yamazaki Pure Malt Whisky. The pretext was the 60th anniversary of the distillery. Rather than come up with a new special grade blend to mark the occasion, Keizo Saji felt the time had come to usher in the single malt era. Initially, Yamazaki Pure Malt didn't carry an age statement. From 1986, the label said "12 Years Old."

A little note about the nomenclature for those interested in old bottles—and by all means, if you ever have the chance to try an older Yamazaki (or Hakushu) bottling, don't hesitate. Initially, Yamazaki and Hakushu were labeled as "pure malt" whiskies. From 2004, Suntory changed that to "single malt" whisky. There is even a transitional period (2002–2003), where labels showed "pure malt whisky" in big type, and underneath the age statement "single malt" in smaller type. To be clear, all of these were technically single malt whiskies. To make matters even

Sample library at Yamazaki Distillery

more confusing, Suntory also had products that were labeled as "pure malts" and were technically "pure malts" or "blended malts" as we would call them now (i.e., vattings of malt from more than one distillery). An example would be the Suntory Pure Malt Whisky 7yo, released in 1985, which came in two versions: one with a black label featuring a drawing of Yamazaki distillery, the other with a white label showing Hakushu distillery. These were, in fact, vattings of malt from both distilleries, but with the former heavier on the Yamazaki, and the latter containing proportionally more Hakushu. In the case of these two bottlings, the term "pure malt" was correct. There are other examples, as well (e.g., the Hokuto bottlings). As far as pre-2004 Suntory malts are concerned, there is only one way to figure out whether they are single or blended ("pure" in the old nomenclature) malts and that is by doing research.

In 1985, the marketing department at Suntory wanted to add a Hakushu single malt to their lineup. This was exactly 12 years after the distillery started producing, so there was no malt older than that in the warehouses to compose the vatting. The blenders insisted it was too early and the plan was shelved until 1994. At that time, whisky sales had been declining for a decade, and the marketing department wanted an easy-to-drink single malt. Again, the blenders put their foot down. They insisted it needed to have more character. Fortunately for us now, they got their way and "smoke" became a keynote of the entire Hakushu single malt range.

The single malt chart on page 148 shows the expansion of the Yamazaki and Hakushu range. The Hakushu single malt has always stood in the shadow of its older sibling, The Yamazaki. In fact, for over a decade and a half, Hakushu was difficult to sell. Up until 2011, overall sales of The Hakushu were one-seventh of the volume of that of The Yamazaki. In 2012, its figures shot up but this was only a reflection of the general increased demand for high-end Japanese whiskies.

Discussing all the special and limited editions of Hakushu and Yamazaki, not to mention the single casks, would be a book in itself. Starting in 1997, with Yamazaki Sherry Wood 1982, Suntory has made wood expressions of their single malts available on a more or less regular basis. This includes the Bourbon Barrel, Puncheon, Sherry Cask/ Spanish Oak, Mizunara and Bordeaux Wine Cask limited editions. Since 2009 and 2013 respectively, there are also occasional annual Heavily Peated editions of Hakushu and Yamazaki.

In 2015, sales of Suntory's single malts were down for the first time since they started making them, but this was intentional. The company was concerned about continuity, and was putting the brakes on its single malt brands to make sure there was enough stock for the future.

The current Yamazaki single malt core range

Sales of the Hakushu 12 were halted in June 2018, but the much-loved expression was brought back—albeit in limited quantities—on March 30, 2021.

Both Hakushu and Yamazaki distillery have been producing at full capacity since 2010. That means: seven days a week, 330 days a year, around the clock. At some point in the near future, there should be ample mature stock to adequately satisfy demand.

Noteworthy was the release of The Yamazaki 55yo (46%abv, 200btls) in early 2020. Originally priced at 3.3 million yen (including tax), it has since gone on to fetch roughly 25 times that at auction. (The hammer price on June 14, 2022 at Sotheby's in New York was $600,000.)

Of more interest to the drinkers among us is a fascinating series Suntory launched under the banner "The Essence of Suntory Whisky" in February 2018. Designed to showcase the company's ongoing creative research, each release consists of two or three different bottlings (500ml) that spotlight an unusual aspect of production. The labels feature artwork by graphic calligrapher Tansetsu Ogino. The table below lists the editions released so far.

THE ESSENCE OF SUNTORY WHISKY

Release	Date	Distillery	Theme	Age	ABV
1st	27.02.2018	Yamazaki	Peated Malt	12yo	49%
		Hakushu	Rye Type	4yo	57%
		Chita	Wine Cask 4 Years Finish	16yo	49%
2nd	26.02.2019	Yamazaki	Spanish Oak	9yo	56%
		Yamazaki	Montilla Wine Cask	9yo	55%
		Yamazaki	Refill Sherry Cask	10yo	53%
3rd	29.10.2019	[Blended Whisky]	Clean Type (aged in cedar-head casks)	NAS	48%
		[Blended Whisky]	Rich Type (aged in cedar-head casks)	NAS	48%
4th	28.04.2020	Osumi	Rice Whisky	NAS	56%
		Chita	Sakura Cask Finish Blend	[12yo]	50%
5th	31.08.2021	Yamazaki	Golden Promise	[11yo]	53%
		Yamazaki	Islay Peated Malt	[11yo]	54%

Sadly, Suntory is no longer releasing single cask expressions. In the past, the Scotch Malt Whisky Society branch in Japan managed to get a few casks bottled. The quality of these has been superb across the board, so it may pay to look out for distillery codes 119 (Yamazaki) and 120 (Hakushu). Suntory's malt distilleries were listed in 2003; Chita was added and assigned the code G13 in 2014. The same year, The Chita became a core brand for Suntory. Up until then, the grain distillery wasn't spoken of much and the only product around was a slightly expensive NAS Chita Tokusei, which came in a satin glass bottle. Technically speaking, this was the first single grain whisky released in Japan (it came out in 2000). You had to look very carefully to find it, though. In 2014, The Chita—with a new formula and a new look—stepped in to take the pressure off the single malt brands at home. It's now the most visible non-blended whisky in the Suntory portfolio at home.

A much-sought-after limited edition

Meet the Blender:

Shinji Fukuyo

Suntory, Whisky Blending & Planning Department
Senior General Manager,
Chief Blender, Executive Officer

1984	Joined Suntory–worked at Hakushu Distillery
1992	Moved to Whisky Blending Department at Yamazaki Distillery and has since been crafting Suntory whiskies as a blender
1996	Attended Heriot-Watt University in Edinburgh, Scotland
	Dispatched to Morrison Bowmore Distillers, Glasgow
2002	Returned to Japan
2009	Became Chief Blender

Which aspects of the whisky-making process are you involved in?
As chief blender, I am responsible for maintaining a consistent quality across the entire Suntory whisky portfolio currently on the market as well as developing new products. In order to achieve that, I am also in charge of improving the quality of unblended (meaning whisky that will become part of a blended product, not product whisky as such) malt and grain whisky and developing new unblended malt and grain whisky, as well as proposing distilling volumes and types of raw materials (i.e., types of malted barley, yeast, casks and so on) to use for the coming years. Managing the team that looks after the quality and quantity of our whisky stock is also an important task.

What is the structure of the blending department at Suntory?
There are five blenders, including myself. Our blending division also has whisky researchers who work closely with the blenders on whisky development. A hard-handed attitude is necessary to achieve difficult goals, but the atmosphere in the blending department is very friendly and everyone is happy with their job.

What was the first product you were in charge of developing?
I do not quite remember, but the last product I was in charge of just before became a chief blender was the Yamazaki 1984.

In a nutshell, what is the path for a new whisky release from conception to glass?
There is no single answer to this question. Some discoveries are made during the daily tasting, while others may be the result of inspiration that comes in the course of developing a new product. An example of the former is Hakushu Distiller's Reserve (NAS). After finding a young, lightly peated whisky with a hint of mint and grapefruit—just like Hakushu—I wanted to make that into a new product. Hibiki Japanese Harmony would be an example of

the latter. In order to blend a beautiful NAS Hibiki, I felt it was of paramount importance to think through what Hibiki was. If I were to put it into words, it would probably be expressed as a rich, estery aroma and a fine balance. Choosing the whiskies to blend became much easier after building this image. A rich, estery aroma does not necessarily imply a long maturation. Grain whisky in particular, even if it's young, has the potential to become part of a Hibiki if one chooses the right type, cask and storage conditions. After choosing malt whisky based on the same concept, all we had to do was try out all kinds of blends.

For a blender in Japan, are there aspects of the job that are different compared with blenders in Scotland?
Blenders in Scotland usually blend whiskies from many distilleries, not just their own. We, however, start from distilling our own unblended whiskies. We can decide what type of whisky to distill depending on the blending plans. Being able to make whisky from a blender's point of view is a salient characteristic of Japanese whisky making.

In your opinion, what's most rewarding about being chief blender?
Seeing people being fascinated and surprised by our products, making new discoveries in unblended whiskies, and encountering blends beyond our expectations.

What is the hardest part about being chief blender?
As the final person in charge of the quality of whisky, there are certain things that a chief blender must stick to. For example, the whiskies created at Yamazaki and Hakushu distilleries must always have a "Suntory quality." Brands such as Yamazaki, Hakushu and Hibiki have their own individual uniqueness, so when we develop new products, it is important that they conform to the uniqueness of the brand. It is the chief blender's responsibility to make sure the whiskies remain stable, both in quality and quantity. The most difficult part is that all decisions have to be made by relying on your own senses.

In what way does being a blender affect your daily life?
Avoiding food with a strong flavor or scent during the weekdays, maintaining an orderly life and always keeping an eye on my health. Experiencing art, nature, sports, etc. and meeting people from around the globe to develop my sensitivity.

In your opinion, what are the qualities needed to be a good blender?
A continuing interest in and a big heart for whisky.

What is the most important lesson you learned on your way to becoming chief blender?
To always do my utmost best in any and all endeavors; to make sure to constantly review my choices, i.e., to assess whether they are the best ones or not. Not doing so would keep me from sleeping!

Yoichi Distillery in the winter

Yoichi Distillery & Miyagikyo Distillery
(Nikka/Asahi Breweries, Ltd.)

In March 1934, Masataka Taketsuru left Kotobukiya Co. Ltd. Three months later, on July 2, he set up his own company, Dai Nippon Kaju Co., Ltd. (The Great Japan Juice Co.). He was clearly not one to waste time.

Taketsuru had always considered Hokkaido to be the ideal place in Japan for whisky making because it was similar in many ways to the Scotland he knew from his studies. It didn't take him long to find a suitable location. A local entrepreneur who had branched out into the land reclamation business offered Taketsuru a sizeable plot of land near the mouth of the Yoichi River at a good price. By October, distillery buildings had been erected on the plot of land.

Initially, apple products (juice and cider) were made at Yoichi. The idea was that producing something that could be sold almost immediately (juice) would make it possible to invest in a product that would take years to leave the factory (whisky). The plan was good in theory, but it was still a struggle. In 1935, the first apple juice was sold, but most of the product was sent back to the factory because its cloudy appearance turned consumers off. Taketsuru then came up with the idea of distilling the returned apple juice, turning it into apple brandy. More cash was injected into the company and this allowed Taketsuru to order a pot still (yes, just one) from Watanabe Copper & Ironworks in Osaka, the same company that had made the original pot stills used at Yamazaki distillery.

The company got their license to produce whisky and brandy on August 26, 1936 and fired up the still straight away. Because money was very tight, this single still was used for both the first and second distillation. Whisky production at Yoichi started in the fall of 1936.

Yoichi Distillery basking in the sun

Yoichi distillery was also the company headquarters from 1936 until 1952, when the name was changed to Nikka Whisky Distilling Co., Ltd. and the seat of the company was moved to Tokyo. The tiny building that served as the original head office is still part of the Yoichi distillery complex. It's next to the wash house and, although it's no longer used, Nikka wants to keep it to remind its staff and visitors of the humble origins of the company.

Nowadays, Yoichi distillery is used exclusively to produce malt whisky. The apple side of the business was phased out at Yoichi in 1945. From 1960, it was taken up again but at a new site in Aomori prefecture, the Hirosaki plant. Apple juice, wine, cider and syrup are still being produced there.

The original Yoichi pot still

Yoichi Distillery

Mash tun:	stainless steel, rake and plow (50kl)
Washbacks:	10 stainless steel (one 40kl, the others 20–28kl), temperature controlled
Pot stills:	4 wash stills (2x10kl, 2x7kl); 2 spirit stills (10kl, 13kl)
	direct heating (coal) for wash stills, direct heating (coal) and indirect heating (steam) for spirit stills
	with descending lyne arms and worm tubs

Taketsuru wanted to make "a whisky with the taste of the wind" (*kaze no aji no whisky*). He valued the climate and natural features of the north, and it's not difficult to see why he chose Yoichi as the location for his first distillery. Just half a mile/1 km from the sea and surrounded by mountains on three sides, the setting is not unlike what one finds in the Scottish highlands.

The distillery as it is now is almost like a little village. All steps of the whisky-making process take place in separate buildings near the main entrance. Most of these are old stone buildings of the type one sees in the nearby town of Otaru. In fact, when such old buildings in Otaru are torn down, Nikka buys up the stones whenever possible in case they are needed for refurbishment or in the event of a natural disaster.

Yoichi Distillery in the early days with the original head office of the company on the left

The kiln tower

Immediately beyond the production facilities lies a big park with 20-odd warehouses, a small cooperage, some historical buildings— among them, the former residence of Taketsuru (which was moved from the countryside nearby to the distillery grounds)—and facilities for visitors. It may look like a distillery theme park but it is very much a working distillery.

The building that first catches the eye as one enters the main gate is the kiln tower. Malting took place on site until 1974. Peat was taken from the nearby Ishikari Mire, located in the lower reaches of the Ishikari River. This is, in fact, the largest peatland complex in Japan. The specifics of the ecosystem—the bog vegetation (mostly cereal grasses), the topography and the causes of mire degradation—give Ishikari peat a character that is distinct from the kinds of peat used in Scotland.

As barley requirements grew, the cost of malting on site became too high, so malted barley was purchased from different sources around the world and the use of Ishikara peat ceased. Nowadays, all malted barley is imported from Scotland. Non-peated, lightly-peated (5–15ppm) and heavily-peated (more than 20ppm) malt is used. Obviously, the peat used is from Scottish peat bogs. The bulk of the production at Yoichi distillery is lightly peated. The end of the year, from September on, is usually reserved for heavily peated malt.

Water is taken from the Yoichi River. For one mash, 5.5 to 6.5 tons/5 to 6 metric tons of malted barley is used. This results in around 25kl

or wort. There are 10 stainless steel washbacks for the fermentation. Distillers yeast is dissolved in water and then added to the washbacks. The standard fermentation time is three days. All washbacks are constructed from stainless steel and fitted with water jackets to control the fermentation temperature. The stopper on the water jackets is set to 90.5°F/32.5°C. Before the switch to stainless steel, which took place in the late 1980s, the washbacks were epoxy-coated iron tanks. According to the staff, wooden washbacks were never used at Yoichi distillery.

The stillhouse is one of the big attractions at Yoichi. This has to do with the fact that the pot stills are still direct-heated using coal. Every seven to eight minutes, a worker will shovel some into the furnace underneath each still. They will also adjust the temperature by raking the burning coal in ways only they understand. As the people at Nikka like to say, "It requires highly skilled craftsmen."

In Scotland, this method was used up until the 1970s. After that, most distilleries converted from direct coal to indirect steam heating. The last distillery to make the switch was Glendronach, in 2006. The advantages are obvious: steam gives you easier temperature control, is much less labor intensive, and more environmentally friendly. However, as is usually the case and certainly in distilling, a gain here and there means a loss somewhere else. Most old-timers at distilleries in Scotland maintain that the conversion from direct firing with coal to indirect firing with steam resulted in a change in the character of the spirit produced.

The Yoichi River near the distillery

A stillman at Yoichi Distillery throwing coal on the fire

Nikka believes that direct heating with coal plays an essential role in creating the "boldness and toasty burnt flavor" of the Yoichi distillate. In 2003, the decision was made to install a special filter to reduce the environmental impact of coal heating. The cost involved was a staggering 100 million yen. Leading up to this, there were voices in the company advocating the switch to indirect heating, as it would have been cheaper to replace all the stills than to install the filter. Nikka knew that doing so was bound to change the "Yoichi spirit," so they decided to look for the money, install the filter and stick with coal.

There are four wash stills and two spirit stills. They have slightly different shapes but all have straight heads, descending lyne arms and traditional worm-tub condensers. This configuration allows heavier elements to pass into the spirit. Miyagikyo distillery is different on all three counts, which explains the lighter character of the spirit produced there.

All Yoichi spirit is matured on site. Filling strength is 63%abv. At the time of writing, there were 29 warehouses. There used to be 28 and as an inside joke, Bar Hatta in nearby Otaru designated itself "No. 29," on account of its wide selection of Nikka whiskies. However, in 2021, a new state-of-the-art racked warehouse was built on the distillery grounds and that became the actual No. 29. The new warehouse—the first to be

Facing page, clockwise from top left: the four wash stills; the filling store; one of the warehouses at Yoichi Distillery; a cask being recharred at the Yoichi cooperage

built there since 1989—has a capacity of 7,000 casks. Most warehouses are of the dunnage type. "No. 10" is the most photogenic and often features in advertisements and commercials.

There's a small cooperage on site. For the most part, the coopers take care of remaking and recharring casks. Since the mid-1980s, casks are charred rather than just toasted. Virgin oak is used quite a bit to mature the spirit made at Yoichi. Around 1990, Nikka started using virgin oak casks, mostly butts. Virgin oak tends to have a strong impact on the spirit in a very short time. It's not uncommon for whisky to be in virgin oak for a decade or two at Yoichi distillery and yet, when it comes out, it will not be the equivalent of oversteeped tea. In fact, some of the best Yoichi single cask bottlings are from 20-year-old or older virgin oak butts. The theory is that the distillate is robust enough to stand up to the power of virgin oak.

Virgin butts are a specialty of Nikka's Tochigi cooperage. That's also where the marrying takes place. Until 1996, bottling was done at Yoichi distillery. Now, almost all of Nikka's whiskies are bottled at the Kashiwa plant, in Chiba prefecture.

Inside Warehouse No. 10

NISHINOMIYA DISTILLERY (DEMOLISHED)

Unlike in Scotland, where the base of blended whisky was (and still is) grain whisky, in Japan, blended whisky was made using neutral spirits or "blending alcohol," as it was commonly called. Masataka Taketsuru had always wanted to create blended whisky in the Scottish tradition, but the post-war years weren't conducive to attempting something that ambitious.

In the early 1960s, Taketsuru felt that it was necessary for whisky makers in Japan to up their game. As drinkers were becoming more discriminating, making whisky that was "all right" wasn't good enough anymore. Taketsuru felt that proper grain whisky was key in this respect. He didn't have to worry about malt whisky (Yoichi distillery was taking care of that) but without proper grain whisky, he was convinced, Japanese blends "would always lose to Scottish ones." The only obstacle, and it was a formidable one, was money.

The capital needed to set up a grain distillery was enormous. Taketsuru didn't have the funds to do so, but fortunately, someone stepped in who understood the importance of grain whisky at that point in the development of Japanese whisky. The first president of Asahi Bakushu (now Asahi Breweries), Tamesaburo Yamamoto agreed to fully fund the enterprise. In November 1962, he established Asahi Shuzo Co., Ltd., to facilitate Taketsuru's grain whisky project.

In 1962 and 1963, Taketsuru traveled to Glasgow to prepare the project. He ordered a Coffey still from Blairs, Ltd., which was delivered the following year. By August 1964, the grain distillery—built on the east side of Asahi's Nishinomiya site—was ready. Nobody knew how to operate a Coffey still in Japan at the time, so Taketsuru invited some experts from Scotland to come and train the Nikka staff. The Scottish people stayed for three months but the Japanese staff found it difficult to get their head around the process, and it took them a while to really master the process. Grain whisky production at Nishinomiya began in earnest in October 1964.

A year later, Taketsuru was thrilled to present the first "authentic whisky" made in Japan: a blend of malt and grain whisky. In September 1965, Black Nikka (1st grade, 42%abv, 720ml) was launched. In those days, most half-decent whiskies were priced at around 1,000 yen. In fact, the fierce sales competition of the mid-1960s became known as the "One Thousand Yen War" (*sen-yen senso*). Even though the production method of Black Nikka was superior, and certainly more costly, the decision was made to price it at 1,000 yen too—talk about giving the competition a run for their money!

Sales were good and Nikka began to incorporate grain whisky into other products. It soon became clear that more volume was needed. Yamamoto and Taketsuru couldn't have anticipated this when they embarked on the grain whisky project a few years earlier. A second Coffey still, 1.5 times the size of the first one, was ordered from Blairs. By the time it was added to the Nishinomiya distillery, Yamamoto (1893–1966) had passed away. The second Coffey still was fired up in October 1967. In November 1968, Nikka and Asahi Shuzo merged. From then on, the Coffey stills worked for Nikka only.

MIYAGIKYO DISTILLERY (MALT)

Thirty years after setting up his own company, Masataka Taketsuru initiated a project to set up a second malt distillery. His goal was to be able to create more complex blends by expanding the range of malt whiskies available to him. In Scotland, that would simply have involved swapping stock with other companies. In Japan, the only way to go about that was to set up a new distillery in a different environment.

Miyagikyo Distillery

The Nikka River where Masataka Taketsuru first tasted the water

Nikka employees started scouting the north of the main island in 1964. This time, it took a little longer to find a suitable location. Masataka's adoptive son, Takeshi Taketsuru, was in charge of the project. On May 12, 1967, Takeshi took Masataka to some candidate sites near Sendai, in Miyagi prefecture. The plan was to visit the sites on the list and then decide. The first location on his list was a foggy glen enclosed by mountains and sandwiched between two rivers. When Taketsuru arrived at the first candidate site, he sat down near the river and asked for some whisky. As luck would have it, someone had a mini bottle of Black Nikka on them. Masataka took a glass and scooped some water out of the river to make himself a *mizuwari* (2 parts water to 1 part whisky). He loved the taste of it and loved the water. The river happened to be called Nikkawa (Nikka River). Masataka felt this was *go-en*, a Japanese concept usually translated as "good luck," but it implies something beyond the accidental, a connection or relationship with karmic overtones. Masataka wouldn't move and they never made it to the other sites on Takeshi's list. The decision was made there and then: the second distillery would be built on that site.

Construction started in 1968 and was completed in May of the following year. Taketsuru wanted to keep the natural undulation of the terrain and as much of the natural surroundings (the trees, in particular) as possible. Because of those considerations, the distillery was built to fit the terrain, as a complex of separate buildings. Aware of the impact the distillery would have on the scenery, Taketsuru decided to go with red brick construction and opted for underground power lines, which is the exception rather than the rule in Japan.

In September 1972, a new blend was launched. This was the first blend to incorporate malt whisky made at the new distillery, in addition to malt whisky made at Yoichi distillery and Coffey grain whisky. With Northland (2nd grade, 39%abv, 720ml), Taketsuru finally realized his ambition to craft a blended whisky the way it was done in Scotland. Not only that, it was the first Japanese blended whisky created in the Scottish tradition, by combining malt whisky from various distilleries with grain whisky.

Taketsuru had registered the Northland trademark in 1939. He didn't expect to live to see his dream realized. In Scotland, blended whisky was the result of a 400-year development. Japan had just started making whisky. Taketsuru was 40 years old when he founded Yoichi distillery. He knew how much blood, sweat and tears (not to mention money) it took to set up a distillery. Building a second one seemed like a tall order. Thirty-three years after registering the Northland trademark, Taketsuru managed to make his dream a reality. It must have been a very emotional moment.

Sendai distillery, as it was called then, was expanded in September 1976 with the addition of two new pairs of stills. These were exactly the same shape as the original two pairs, but 1.5 times the size. That meant a big boost in capacity. The distillery was also computerized during the 1976 expansion.

In 2001, the name of the distillery was changed to Miyagikyo Distillery. That's the name we will use in what follows, regardless of the era under discussion. Grain whisky, gin and neutral spirits are also produced on site. Bottling took place until 2004. Nowadays, only the locally available, special blended whisky Date and the distillery exclusives are bottled at Miyagikyo.

Miyagikyo Distillery (Malt)

Mash tun:	2 stainless steel, lauter
Washbacks:	22 stainless steel (11x33kl, 11x48kl), temperature controlled
Pot stills:	4 pairs (wash stills 2x16kl, 2x24kl; spirit stills 2x12kl, 2x18kl)
	indirect heating (steam)
	with ascending lyne arms and shell-and-tube condensers

Miyagikyo distillery is a beautiful example of a factory coexisting with nature. It's tucked away between two rivers, the Hirosegawa and Nikkawa, and you don't see it until you get off the Sakunami highway and cross the bridge over the Hirosegawa. It's not uncommon to be greeted by a wild monkey sitting on the edge of the bridge.

As far as malt production is concerned, there are two production lines: Miyagikyo A, which corresponds to the original two pairs of stills, and Miyagikyo B, which corresponds to the two pairs added during the 1976 expansion. As said, B is 1.5 times the size as A, so the numbers reflect that. One batch of malted barley on the A line is 6.5 tons/6 metric tons; on the B line, it's 10 tons/9 metric tons. The rest of the production process is calibrated following the same ratio.

A local resident greeting visitors to Miyagikyo Distillery

The kiln tower

Just like at Yoichi distillery, different peating levels are used. The figures are the same, but at Miyagikyo distillery the focus is more on non-peated and lightly-peated malt. In the early days, floor malting was done at the distillery for a short period (from 1969 to 1975). The peat used at the time was the same as the peat used at Yoichi, Ishikari peat. Since then, all malted barley used for whisky making is imported. From the mid-1970s to the mid-1980s, a lot of Australian barley was used. These days, most of the barley comes from Scotland.

Water is drawn from a point near the Nikkawa River. Clear wort is pumped into temperature-controlled, stainless steel washbacks (33kl for the A line, 48kl for the B line of production). Various types of yeast are used (mostly distillers yeast) and the fermentation time is three days. So far, the process is very similar to that at Yoichi distillery. In the stillhouse, however, things are very different.

The pot stills at Miyagikyo distillery are much larger than those at Yoichi. The necks are very tall, which means more copper contact. The stills at Yoichi have straight heads, but those at Miyagikyo have boil balls (i.e., a bulge), which means more reflux. The lyne arms at Yoichi are descending, whereas those at Miyagikyo are upward sloping, which again means more reflux. The stills at Miyagikyo are steam-heated, allowing for a slower distillation at lower temperatures than heating with direct coal fire. It's a familiar tune by now: more copper contact and more reflux. The condensers at Miyagikyo are shell-and-tube, which—we'll say it one last time—increases the copper contact compared to the worm tubs as found at Yoichi distillery. All of the above contribute to the softer, lighter character of the Miyagikyo spirit.

All spirit made at Miyagikyo distillery is matured on site. Up until 1986, new-make used to be filled into wood at 65%abv. Since then, the standard filling strength is 63%. There are 26 warehouses on site, which include two across the Nikkawa River accessed via a private bridge built by Nikka. Some of the warehouses are of the dunnage type, others are racked. A few have been converted into facilities for visitors. There's still whisky distilled during the inaugural year maturing in wood; one of those casks filled in 1969 was used for The Nikka 40, which was released in 2014. Just like at Yoichi Distillery, though slightly bigger, there is a cooperage on site.

MIYAGIKYO DISTILLERY (GRAIN)

In the wake of the 1989 changes to the liquor tax law, sales dropped considerably, so Nikka decided to restructure their operations. The bottling side of the Nishinomiya plant was closed in April 1992 and moved to the Kashiwa plant. In June 1997, the decision was made to move the grain whisky equipment to a more convenient location. The obvious candidate was Miyagikyo distillery. In May 1998, Nikka started moving the equipment. The final day of grain whisky making at Nishinomiya distillery was October 26, 1998. Shortly after, the land was sold to Asahi Breweries.

By August 1999, the move to Miyagikyo distillery had been completed. It was a long and arduous process, and quite expensive, around 32 billion yen. Since September 1999, the Coffey stills have been in continuous use there. You can't miss the Coffey stillhouse—it's the tallest red brick building on the premises, located to the right of the old kiln.

The main ingredient in the Coffey grain whisky made at Miyagikyo is maize imported from the U.S. To this, a small amount of malted two-row barley is added. The maize is mixed with water and heated in a pressure cooker. After the temperature has been lowered to 149°F/65°C, milled malted barley is added. Using a belt press, the solids are separated from the liquid, and the liquid is fermented. The wash is then distilled to about 94%abv. After being reduced to 63%abv, the spirit is filled into wood and left to mature.

The stillhouse

At some point in the 1970s, Nikka came up with the idea of distilling malted barley in their Coffey stills. This is sold as a stand-alone product (Nikka Coffey Malt Whisky) since 2014. It's also a key component in their All Malt. Between categories, this would be a problem in Scotland where the word "malt" isn't allowed on a label unless the whisky is made by batch distillation in pot stills. Japan doesn't need to worry about the Scotch Whisky Regulations, so they don't lose any sleep over labeling.

Miyagikyo Coffey still

EXPRESSIONS

Nikka released their first single malt expression in November 1984: Single Malt Hokkaido 12yo (43%abv). Obviously, this was distilled at Yoichi. A few months earlier, Suntory had launched their first single malt. Clearly, the time was right. Whisky consumption in Japan was at an all-time high and the two oldest distilleries in the country were paving the way for the "single malt era."

By 2008, Nikka had built up a beautiful core range of single malts from their respective distilleries, which included a NAS and a 10, 12 and 15-year-old from both, as well as a 20-year-old from Yoichi. In 2015, they stunned the whisky community at home and abroad by announcing their decision to discontinue the entire range by the end of August and replace it with two newly developed NAS expressions (45%abv) on September 1. This is now referred to as "The Nikka Shock," and a shock it was. They tried to soften the blow by also releasing two limited-edition variations, a Yoichi Heavily Peated and a Miyagikyo Sherry Cask (3,000 bottles each, 48%abv), but they were gone in a flash so not much consolation there. Other variations—invariably NAS—have followed since. The table below shows details of the releases to date.

NIKKA SINGLE MALT LIMITED EDITIONS (SINCE 2015)

Released	Distillery	Expression	ABV (%)	Outturn (btls)
9.2015	Yoichi	Heavily Peated Limited Edition	48	3,000
	Miyagikyo	Sherry Cask Limited Edition	48	3,000
9.2017	Yoichi	Moscatel Wood Finish	46	1,500
	Miyagikyo		46	1,500
11.2017	Yoichi	Rum Wood Finish	46	3,500
	Miyagikyo		46	3,500
9.2018	Yoichi	Manzanilla Wood Finish	48	4,000
	Miyagikyo		48	4,000
10.2018	Yoichi	Sherry Wood Finish	46	4,000
	Miyagikyo		46	4,000
10.2018	Yoichi	Bourbon Wood Finish	46	4,000
	Miyagikyo		46	4,000
3.2019	Yoichi	Limited Edition 2019	48	700
	Miyagikyo		48	700
3.2020	Yoichi	Apple Wood Brandy Finish	47	6,700
	Miyagikyo		47	6,450
9.2021		Nikka Discovery Vol.1		
	Yoichi	Non-Peated	48	10,000
	Miyagikyo	Peated	48	10,000
4.2022	Yoichi	Grande (Japan Travel Retail)	48	NA
	Miyagikyo		48	NA

For now, the only Nikka single malts permanently on the shelves of liquor stores are the two new NAS expressions. The company has been working hard to try and catch up with demand. In 2019, expansion plans for both distilleries were revealed that should result in an increase in production of about 20%. Its distilleries have been operating at full capacity since 2020. Nikka estimates it can resolve its stock shortages by 2030.

Japanese whisky enthusiasts felt a spark of hope in the summer of 2022 when Nikka announced it would be releasing its first age-statement single malt since 2015, a Yoichi 10-year-old (45%abv). It's not

From left to right: the mash house, the kiln tower and the Coffey stillhouse

exactly "a return of the Yoichi 10," as some have interpreted it, because the formula is different. It's a new expression. It's also not a permanent release (for the time being). Limited to 9,000 bottles per year, the new Yoichi 10 first went on sale in Hokkaido at the end of July 2022. The rest of Japan had to wait until November, with export markets following soon after. There's not enough to go around yet, but it's a sign the tide may be turning—slowly but surely.

In terms of single cask releases, there used to be regular treats. From 1998 to 2014, there was a handful of single cask bottlings every year for the Japanese market. There were also separate annual bottlings for Nikka's distributor in Europe, La Maison du Whisky. Up until 2014, the two distillery shops also carried special single cask bottlings. These came in smaller bottles (500ml) and in a range of ages in five-year increments: 5, 10, 15, 20 and 25 years old. We didn't know how spoiled we were until stocks of mature whisky in the warehouses became too tight and the single cask program was put on hold.

The only hope of getting hold of single cask bottlings now is via the Scotch Malt Whisky Society. Yoichi was added to the Society's list in July 2002 as distillery no. 116; Miyagikyo appeared on the register two years later, in June 2004, as distillery no. 124. It requires considerable

The new Yoichi NAS expression with the old single malt range behind it

The new Miyagikyo NAS expression with the old single malt range behind it

effort on the part of the Society's Japan chapter to make these bottlings happen, so there's never going to be an avalanche of them but they're worth the wait. The Society Nikka bottlings are nothing short of stunning and some are absolutely sublime. The last time we were treated to SMWS bottlings from the Nikka stable was 2015, so it's been a while, but hope springs eternal.

On the grain whisky front, Nikka released their first offering in November 2007: Single Coffey Malt 12yo (55%abv). This was a one-off release, limited to 3,027 bottles, and was from the "Nishinomiya era." The current, permanently available grain lineup consists of Nikka Coffey Grain Whisky and Nikka Coffey Malt Whisky (both bottled at 45%abv). Interestingly, both of these were launched in Europe first (in September 2012 and January 2014, respectively) and then rolled out in Japan and other selected markets a few months after. Bartenders seem to be quite fond of the subtly novel flavors these products bring to their libations.

Nikka also used to release occasional single cask Coffey grain and Coffey malt bottlings alongside their Yoichi and Miyagikyo selections (see above). In 2015, the first Coffey grain (G11) and Coffey malt (G12) casks were bottled for the Scotch Malt Whisky Society.

Meet the Blender:
Tadashi Sakuma

Nikka, Blending & Planning Department, Former Chief Blender

April 1982	Yoichi Distillery, Planning and Quality Control
April 1987	Head Office, Raw Material Procurement and Stock Control
June 1994	London Representative Office, Management of Foreign Subsidiary Distilleries
January 2001	Head Office, Manager of Raw Material Procurement and Stock Control
April 2010	Tochigi Plant (Warehousing, Blending and Coopering) Plant Manager
April 2012	Appointed as Chief Blender
March 2020	Retired as Senior Chief Blender
March 2022	Appointed as Advisor

Which aspects of the whisky-making process are you involved in?
My responsibilities as chief blender are in three main areas: 1) maintaining consistency of quality across the Nikka whisky range and where possible improving the quality in the long term; 2) selecting the contents of new products; and 3) anticipating future needs and laying down stocks in function of those needs—this also includes developing new types of stock for maturation.

What is the structure of the blending department at Nikka?
The blending department consists of 8 people: 4 blenders, 1 shochu blender, 2 people in charge of analysis and myself.

What was the first product you were in charge of developing?
The first completely new product I developed was The Nikka 40, a limited-edition release created to mark the 80th anniversary of the founding of our company.

In a nutshell, what is the path for a new whisky release from conception to glass?
It does happen that the blender comes up with a specific idea, but in general the impetus comes from the marketing department. They usually come up with a concept for a new product and lead the development. Various parameters such as target audience, flavor profile and price point are set, and then a decision is made as to which blender is put in charge of the creation of the new product. The blender in charge doesn't work in isolation, of course. The other members of the blending department also give advice and provide feedback in the course of the development of the new product. For limited-edition products, the final result of the blending process (once approved) gets bottled as is. With core products, surveys are carried out to gauge sensory response and the flavor profile of the blend may be slightly tweaked, if so desired.

In your opinion, what's most rewarding about being chief blender?
Getting feedback from customers about how much they enjoy Nikka whiskies.

What is the hardest part about being a chief blender?
The job comes with a huge responsibility. The chief blender has to assure all materials coming in and going out of the company are of the highest quality. He's not just shaping the present but also the future. On the other hand, this is not a solo effort. The responsibility is shared with other members of the team and other departments in the company.

In your opinion, what are the qualities needed to be a good blender?
Having a profound commitment to the continuous improvement of the products under your wings.

What is the most important lesson you learned on your way to becoming chief blender?
If you are looking in the right direction and work with long-term vision, the quality of the whisky will improve. It's not good to make changes based on short-term strategies. That's what I believe.

Fuji Gotemba Distillery emblem

Mt. Fuji Distillery
(Kirin Distillery Co., Ltd.)

Built near the foot of Japan's iconic snow-peaked cone, it's hard to beat Fuji Gotemba distillery's picture-postcard location. Just 7.5 miles/12 km from the base of Mt. Fuji, the distillery was constructed to have as low an impact on the surrounding natural environment as possible. Today 45 percent of the distillery site is forest. At an altitude of 2,034 feet/620 meters and with an average yearly temperature of 55.5°F/13°C, the conditions are perfect for making whisky.

Unique in Japanese whisky history, Mt. Fuji Distillery was the result of a multinational joint venture. In August 1972, the Kirin Brewery Co., Ltd. (Japan) got together with J.E. Seagram and Sons, Inc. (U.S.) and Chivas Brothers (U.K.) and set up Kirin-Seagram Co., Ltd. Kirin owned 50 percent, Seagram 45 percent and Chivas Brothers 5 percent. Combining Seagram's expertise in the field of grain whisky with Chivas's experience in the field of malt whisky, the idea was to establish a comprehensive whisky manufacturing plant where everything—from malt and grain whisky distilling to blending and bottling—could be done on one site.

Construction of the distillery was completed in November 1973 and, after running tests in mini pot stills, the full-size stills were fired up. There is still some stock from those first weeks of production maturing in the warehouses on site.

In 2000, Seagram started selling off its beverage assets worldwide, bringing to an end its 143-year spirits empire. Kirin bought back Seagram's shares in Kirin-Seagram Co. Ltd. and also acquired Four Roses in Kentucky. Kirin-Seagram Co. Ltd. was renamed Kirin Distillery Co. Ltd. in July 2002 and is now wholly owned by Kirin. Until the spring of 2020, this distillery was known as Fuji-Gotemba Distillery.

It is still referred to as such in Japanese, but to bolster international brand recognition, Kirin decided to officially change the distillery name, when used abroad, to Mt. Fuji Distillery. It will be referred to as such in what follows.

In February 2019, Kirin announced that it would be investing 8 billion yen over the next couple of years to increase production volume and diversity at Mt. Fuji Distillery. As part of that expansion, four wooden washbacks and two new sets of pot stills (for malt whisky production) were installed. These came into operation in July 2021. Storing capacity was increased by one-fifth.

The Malt Distillery

Mash tun:	stainless steel, semi-lauter (45kl)
Washbacks:	2 stainless steel (80kl), with temperature control
	4 Douglas fir (80kl)
Pot stills:	3 pairs (details below)

It's a truism that water is a key component of whisky making. The "mother water" at Mt. Fuji Distillery is taken from three bores on site that tap into underground streams 328 feet/100 meters deep. Analysis has shown that the water used today fell on Mt. Fuji as snow 50 years ago. That's how long it takes for the water to filter through the hardened lava.

Malted barley—non-peated and lightly peated—is imported from Scotland. For one mash, 6.25 tons/5,700kg of malted barley are used. This results in about 30kl of clear wort. Until the summer of 2021, fermentation took place in stainless steel, temperature-controlled wash-backs. In the spring of 2021, four wooden washbacks made of Douglas fir (imported from Vancouver, Canada) were installed. These have been used since, but two of the stainless steel washbacks remain in use for malt whisky production. Washbacks are filled with two batches (60kl) and the fermentation time is 92 hours. Various types of distillers yeast from the Seagram stable as well as ale yeast are used—with ongoing experimentation in that department.

When the distillery was founded, there were two sets of pot stills (one pair 27kl and 17kl capacity; the other pair 25kl and 16kl). These

The distillery with Mt. Fuji in the background

huge stills were said to be modeled after those at Strathisla distillery in Scotland, which was owned by Chivas Brothers and is still a key component in the Chivas Regal blend. The two sets seemed to have identical wash and spirit stills, which was not exactly true. Whereas the respective parts from the floor up were identical in shape, the bottom parts (the actual pots under the floor of the stillhouse) were different in size—one deeper, the other less so. As time went by, only the bigger pair was used and the other pair retired. (The retired spirit still, as an object, became part of the distillery tour.)

Master Distiller Osamu Igura in the stillroom

During the 2021 expansion, two new, smaller pairs of pot stills—made, like the original ones, by Miyake Industries—were installed. At the moment, the set-up is as follows:

OLD PAIR, VERY LARGE (Miyake)	NEW PAIR 1, SMALL (Miyake)	NEW PAIR 2, SMALL (Miyake)
1 wash still (lantern type; 27kl)	1 wash still (squat with short neck; lantern type; 4kl)	1 still (tall neck; lantern type; 4kl)
1 spirit still (bulge type; 17kl)	1 spirit still (lean with tall neck; lantern type; 3.2kl)	1 still (tall neck; straight type; 4kl)
both indirect heated, with ascending lyne arms and shell-and-tube condensers	both indirect heated, with slightly descending lyne arms and shell-and-tube condensers	both indirect heated, with slightly descending lyne arms and shell-and-tube condensers
		used interchangeably as wash and spirit still

With three pairs of stills in operation—and, in the case of "New Pair 2," the option of switching between stills for the first and second distillation—it became possible to produce a wider variety of malt whisky distillates. The overall goal at Mt. Fuji Distillery is to produce a spirit that is "clean and estery."

The Grain Distillery

Cooker:	stainless steel
Fermenters:	6 stainless steel, with temperature control (80kl)
	4 stainless steel, with temperature control (120kl)
	plus 1 beer well
Stills:	3 units, used in various configurations: 1 multi-column still (5 columns), including beer column with 26 trays
	1 kettle (60kl)
	1 doubler (11kl)

The grain whisky facility at Mt. Fuji Distillery is compact. It is set up so that, by using the equipment in a modular way, three types of grain whisky can be produced: light, medium and heavy.

Ninety-five percent of the mash bill is corn (non-GMO, imported from the U.S.). The remaining 5 percent is malted barley. One batch consists of 10.6 tons/9.6 metric tons of corn and .5 ton/.5 metric ton of malted barley. For the heavy-type grain whisky, a small amount of rye is added to the mash. This is imported from Canada or Europe. Fermentation time is three days at 91.4°F/33°C.

Light-type grain whisky is made using a standard multi-column still. Batch-light (medium-type) grain whisky is produced by going from the beer column to the kettle and then to the rectifying column. This process is used by very few distilleries around the world. Just like the light-type, the batch-light type is distilled to a very high abv (94%) but it leaves a bit more flavor in the spirit. The heavy-type is produced in the same way that most bourbon is made nowadays, i.e., going from the beer column to the doubler.

Fig. 10 Mt. Fuji Distillery Grain Whisky Distillation Equipment

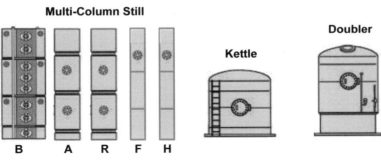

Multi-Column Still

Kettle

Doubler

B   A   R   F   H

B = beer column
A = aldehyde column (purifier)
R = rectifying column
F = fusel oil column
H = heads column

Since the processes involved are fairly complex, for our purposes, the following diagrams probably say more than lengthy paragraphs would.

The three types of grain whisky have been made since the distillery started production, but up until recently, most of the grain whisky produced was of the light-type. However, since receiving accolades for their batch-distilled grain whisky—Blender's Choice and Small Batch

25yo, both of which are of the medium type—the distillery has increased production of the medium and heavy type.

In addition to the mash bill and distillation process, the filling strength and maturation regime have also been calibrated for the desired style of grain whisky. Details change over time as tweaks and adjustments are made, but in 2016, the various elements in play were as detailed in the chart on page 186.

Fig. 11 Grain Whisky Light Type Distillation

Fig. 12 Grain Whisky Batch-Light ("medium") Type Distillation

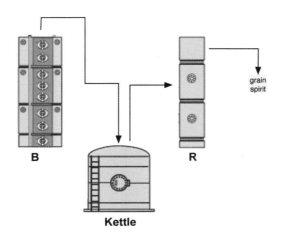

Facing page: Column stills; Master Distiller Osamu Igura checking one of the column stills

Fig. 13 Grain Whisky Heavy Type Distillation

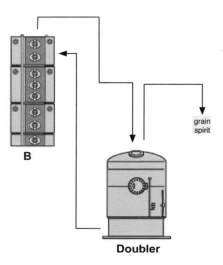

B

grain
spirit

Doubler

Grain Whisky Types—Production Methods

	Light	Batch-Light (Medium)	Heavy
mashbill	corn (90 percent) + malted barley		corn + malted barley + rye
distillation type	continuous	batch	continuous
stills	multi-column	beer still ➙ kettle ➙ rectifying column	beer still ➙ doubler
distillation strength	94%abv		68%abv
filling strength	62.5%abv		55.5%abv
maturation	mostly refill ex-bourbon casks	first in 1st fill ex-bourbon casks, then transferred to refill casks, if needed	mainly in virgin oak barrels, also some 1st fill ex-bourbon casks

WAREHOUSING

All spirit, both malt and grain, produced at Mt. Fuji Distillery is matured on site. With the exception of Warehouse #7, which was built as part of the recent expansion, all other warehouses are set up for barrels only (180-liter casks of the type used in the bourbon industry), as almost all of the spirit produced at Mt. Fuji Distillery is filled into barrels. These warehouses (#1–6) are huge, automated racked warehouses, holding between 35,000 and 50,000 casks each.

This sort of focus on a single cask type is very unusual in the Japanese whisky industry, where diversity is pursued in most departments of production. At Mt. Fuji Distillery, the ideal of a "clean and estery" whisky motivated the decision to limit maturation to 180-liter American white oak barrels, as these were found to be most effective in terms of ester formation.

A similar explanation is behind the unusually low filling strength at Mt. Fuji Distillery. In the early days, Seagram ran tests in collaboration with Kirin and found that 50.5%abv led to the best results as far as the desired whisky profile was concerned. Ever since, that has been the default filling strength for malt new-make at the distillery.

Most of the casks used are ex-Four Roses barrels. That's not a surprise, of course. New-make is filled into fresh ex-bourbon barrels, i.e. first fill, for the most part, but they are also reusing some casks for second and third fills. Their batch-light grain whisky, for example, is transferred to such refill casks after spending a period in first-fill ex-bourbon wood.

From the mid-2010s, some other casks types started appearing, on a very occasional basis, at the distillery, e.g. sherry butts, mizunara casks and wine casks. (Kirin owns Chateau Mercian, so ex-wine wood was an obvious candidate for secondary maturation purposes.) Because these casks literally don't fit in the warehouses—being too big for the racks—they were kept in the filling store. During the expansion that was remedied and now there is a completely new warehouse (#7) that can accommodate a variety of sizes, including puncheons, hogsheads and wine barriques. It is much smaller in comparison with the others, though, with a capacity of "only" 5,000 casks. There is no cooperage on site, only basic facilities for repairing casks.

Inventory survey usually takes place in the first half of the year. Casks are sampled regularly from three years onwards. With thousands

Warehouse manager Hiroaki Yoshikawa at work

Barrel filling in progress

of casks maturing, a system has been devised in which three random casks are chosen from one lot (roughly 250 casks). These samples are taken from different levels in the warehouse. This is necessary because the casks are stacked 18 to 20 high and casks at the top of the racks will mature faster than those down below. The variations are very slight, though, since the warehouses are single-story and designed to have a consistent temperature throughout the buildings. According to master blender Jota Tanaka, the maturation peak for Mt. Fuji malt whisky is generally between 12 and 18 years old, depending on the location of casks in the warehouse and other, more mysterious, factors. But as he often says, "Age is just a number, maturity is a matter of character."

Casks from the first year of production

EXPRESSIONS

Kirin waited more than 30 years to release its first single malt. In February 2004, without much fanfare, The Fuji Gotemba Single Malt 18yo was launched alongside its grain sibling The Fuji Gotemba Single Grain 15yo (both bottled at 43%abv). These were available from the distillery shop and from a handful of retailers who had bought a few bottles there.

In September 2005, Kirin presented its new brand Fujisanroku ("At the Foot of Mt. Fuji") with an entry-level NAS blend (Tarujuku 50°) and another 18-year-old single malt (Fujisanroku 18yo, 43%abv). For the next few years, there was a bit of confusion. The distillery had two different 18-year-old single malts but their prices were very different, the new one being twice as expensive as the one launched the year before. Apparently, this was because the recipe of the generally available (newer) release contained malt up to 24 years old.

Fujisanroku 18yo

The single malts never sold huge volume but that wasn't the reason they were there. It was more to have a little twinkle at the top end of the portfolio. The more reasonably priced 18-year-old (The Fuji Gotemba 18yo) was phased out towards the end of 2008, but the 15-year-old single grain remained available for a few more years at the distillery shop.

In February 2015, a new Small Batch 17yo Single Malt and Small Batch 25yo (46%abv) were created. These were only available through the online shop and at the distillery. They were priced higher than anything coming out of Mt. Fuji Distillery until then—save for the 27-year-old single cask grain released to commemorate the distillery's 40th anniversary in 2013—but the climate was such that this wasn't an obstacle. The craze for Japanese whisky made prices almost irrelevant. Word quickly spread that these were superb whiskies, so people did what they had to do to get their hands on a bottle or two.

Two Blender's Choice bottlings

What people didn't know when these limited edition pairs were released was that, after 10 years in the market, Kirin was pulling Fujisanroku 18yo off the shelves. In the wake of the highball boom and with demand for Japanese whisky increasing by the day, there just wasn't enough stock to keep it going long term. In May 2015, it was officially discontinued.

In March 2016, the Small Batch 25yo Single Grain was named the "World's Best Single Grain Whisky" at the World Whiskies Awards (WWA) in London. It repeated this feat at the 2017 and 2019 WWA.

In March 2019, Kirin discontinued its Fujisanroku 50° because of stock shortages. A year later, a new flagship brand, Fuji, and a new entry-level expression (Riku, 50%abv) was announced. A preview of the Fuji brand had been given in February of that year, with the release of a Fuji Single Grain Whiskey Aged 30 Years (46%abv; note the spelling, with "e"). This limited edition went on to win not only a trophy at the International Spirits Challenge 2020 but also "World's Best Single Grain Whisky" again at the 2020 WWA.

Riku went on sale in May 2020, but was revamped in April 2022—both the formula (a little richer) and the label (a little less austere). Fuji Single Grain Whiskey (no-age-statement) was released in April 2020. In June 2022, the brand was joined by two expressions in the single blended category (i.e. all malt and grain whisky components distilled at one and the same distillery). A generally available Fuji Single Blended Japanese Whisky (no-age-statement, 43%abv; note the spelling, without "e") and a limited edition expression dubbed 2022 Masterpiece (50%abv, 1,000btls).

Until very recently, Kirin's whiskies were not available outside Japan. The company had always maintained that it wanted to build a solid customer base at home before looking towards markets abroad. Having picked up some high-profile awards at international whisky competitions, the knocks on the door were getting louder. In 2016, Kirin sent its first shipment of whisky overseas: a few hundred cases destined for France. In 2020, exports to France resumed. In 2021, Kirin started exporting to the U.S. for the first time, and the year after, China and Australia were added to their list of export markets.

Kirin reported a massive 40 percent increase in the sales volume of their domestic whiskies during the first half of 2022. This bodes well for the future, ahead of Mt. Fuji Distillery's 50th anniversary in 2023.

Meet the Blender:
Jota Tanaka

Kirin Distillery Co. Ltd., Kirin Whisky, Master Blender

1988	Joined Kirin Brewery Co., Ltd.
1989–1994	Worked as oenologist at Raymond Vineyard & Cellar, Napa Valley, California; Graduate Studies at University of California, Davis
1995	Kirin-Seagram (Japan)—Product Development and Quality Control, Brand Marketing for wine; then Product Development for whisky and ready-to-drink products
2002–2009	Four Roses Distillery, Kentucky—Director of Quality and Production Planning; in charge of production planning and product development of bourbon
2009	Kirin Brewery (Japan), Research and Development; whisky blending
2010	Master Blender

Which aspects of the whisky-making process are you involved in?
I would say the whole process from start to finish. My main focus is in the following areas: 1) product development, i.e., concept work and flavor profiling—"creating new flavors" would be a more poetic way of putting it; 2) production planning of new malt and grain whiskies based on long-term forecasts; 3) quality management, i.e., working on blend formulas with the aim of continuous improvement; and 4) brand building, i.e., promotion and educational activities to increase the understanding of the specificity of

What is the structure of the blending department at Kirin?
We are part of the marketing department at Kirin. The blending team consists of two blenders and myself.

In a nutshell, what is the path for a new whisky release from conception to glass?
Usually, at other companies, the concept for a new product tends to come from the marketing department. At Kirin, however, the blenders are part of the marketing department, so we are involved in the development of a new product right from the start and follow it all the way through from conception to realization. Quite often, it also happens that we come up with a concept and lead the development. In a nutshell, this is how it works: first, we work on the concept; then, we translate it into technical elements; next, we choose the components that will go into the blend and the way to go about creating the blend; then we make a test blend and check to what extent the test blend coincides with the original concept; then, the other people in the marketing department evaluate the blend; if everyone's happy with it, we make a candidate blend; then, we do a market survey to get feedback on the product, and if that is good, we go ahead with production and bottle it.

In your opinion, what's most rewarding about being chief blender?
As far as blending is concerned, bringing out the different characters of each spirit and creating a good blend is a source of great happiness. Integrating somewhat "naughty" blending components—component whiskies that are difficult to work with—to add depth and a glamorous character to a blend is a challenge I like. When those "naughty" elements tie everything together and transform the blend into something really delicious, I am so happy I get goose bumps. However, nothing makes me happier than seeing the smiles on customers' faces and receiving compliments from them about how much they enjoy our whiskies.

What is the hardest part about being a chief blender?
Fulfilling my responsibility to meet customers' expectations in the current climate of growing demand for our whisky is the hardest part. We are now in a situation where demand for our whisky is far greater than what can be produced. We are doing our best to respond to customers' expectations by managing the quality and quantity of our whisky inventory.

In what way does being a blender affect your daily life?
I think that unless you experience the multitude of culinary delights in this world, you can't make tasty whisky. I am always hungry for smells and flavors. Likewise, when I am in nature, I enjoy sniffing flowers, herbs, mush-

rooms, etc., tasting them if possible and expressing their characteristics in my own words. This is second nature for me. I don't have to force myself to do it. It comes naturally. Needless to say, prior to the sensory evaluation of whisky I try not to have foods and drinks that get in the way.

In your opinion, what are the qualities needed to be a good blender?
Good sensory evaluation skills are a basic requirement, of course—"a good sense," one might say—but passion for whisky blending and brand building are of key importance, too.

What is the most important lesson you learned on your way to becoming chief blender?
Making whisky is a team effort and we always have to think long term. The malt and grain components we use today were produced and laid down by our seniors at Kirin in the recent and not-so-recent past. They poured their hearts and souls into making the whisky maturing in the warehouses now. It is our duty as a team to produce malt and grain spirit with the generation that comes after us in mind and to do so with the same dedication and passion that they brought to the enterprise and create products in which people can "taste" their passion.

Mars Shinshu Distillery & Mars Tsunuki Distillery
(Hombo Shuzo)

The Hombo family traces its business history back to 1872, when they founded a cotton processing company in Kagoshima. The company entered the liquor field in 1909, when it was granted a license to make shochu, and over the next fifty years, Hombo Shuzo expanded its portfolio to include mirin, sake, neutral spirits, *umeshu* (plum liqueur), sweet fruit wine and various others types of liquor. The company has also been active in the field of forestation and forestland management since the late 1920s.

Hombo Shuzo's whisky history started in 1949 when they got their whisky license. For the first 10 years, they concocted "whisky" in pretty much the same way that most companies did, i.e., by blending "components" that may or may not have included malt whisky into a liquid with a flavor resembling that of whisky. In 1960, they decided to get serious and set up a proper malt whisky distillery. Hombo Shuzo had just annexed The Fuji Wine Co., Ltd., which came with some nice real estate in Yamanashi, Japan's prime wine-producing region. They figured it would be an ideal site to make whisky and they had just the right person to make it happen, too.

Kiichiro Iwai worked for Hombo as an advisor at the time because of his expertise in continuous distillation, which they put to good use in their shochu operations. He wasn't exactly a beginner when it came to whisky making, either. Forty years earlier, Iwai was working for Settsu Shuzo, where he had a certain individual by the name of Masataka Taketsuru working under him. When Taketsuru came back from his

Facing page: Mars Shinshu in the winter

Kiichiro Iwai

study trip to Scotland, he submitted his report—the now famous "Taketsuru Notebook"—to Iwai. When Hombo Shuzo asked Iwai to help set up a malt distillery in Yamanashi four decades later, he knew exactly what he needed from his library: that little notebook. Iwai designed the stills based on Taketsuru's observations and calibrated the distillation process to get a heavy type of spirit, Taketsuru-style.

Throughout the 1960s, the wine business—run from the same site in Yamanashi—was booming. Whisky sales, on the other hand, were nothing to write home about. In 1969, they decided to call it a day and close the distillery. Towards the end of the 1970s, with whisky becoming increasingly popular in Japan, they decided to give it another try. By then, the Yamanashi site was used exclusively for wine making, so they had to look for a new location. As an interim solution, they decided to produce some malt whisky at one of their production sites in Kagoshima. The original pot stills were still in Yamanashi, in storage, so they used two tiny (500-liter) copper pot stills (until 1984) in Kagoshima. The unusual pot stills are now at the Mars Tsunuki Distillery. One is still being used to make spirits.

By 1985, Hombo Shuzo had acquired a new site in Shinshu (Nagano prefecture), at the foot of Mt. Komagatake. The original Iwai pot stills were moved from Yamanashi to the new site, but this time the company decided to aim for a lighter type of distillate, more suited to the Japanese palate. The *ji-whisky* boom was in full swing (see page 70 for more on this) and the timing seemed right. Unfortunately, things were about to get worse, again. The tax reform of 1989 hit smaller producers like Hombo Shuzo very hard. Their whisky workhorse, Mars 2nd grade blended whisky (1.8 liters), jumped up in price from ¥1,600 to ¥3,300 in retail, whereas Scotch whisky prices were coming down. Competing under the new tax system became increasingly hard.

The tiny spirit still used at Kagoshima Distillery

The warehouse at the Shinshu factory, as it was called then, was filling up fast but very little whisky was leaving. In 1992, there was no more room for casks and Hombo Shuzo decided that enough was enough.

For the next 19 years, no whisky production took place at the Shinshu factory. The pot stills were occasionally used to distill brandy, but that was about it. That doesn't mean the site was dead. Shortly after beer regulations in Japan were changed in favor of small-scale production, a microbrewery was set up next to the mothballed distillery. Minami-Shinshu Beer (est. 1996) was the first craft brewery in Nagano.

After 2008, courtesy of the highball boom, Mars noticed demand for their whisky was increasing. The pre-1992 stock had served them well for the past 15 years but it was clear that it wasn't going to last forever. Mr. Hombo asked his staff to check what the warehouse situation was like and they got a bit of a shock. In less than 10 years, they'd be staring at the walls, and that was without figuring in rising demand.

In 2010, Hombo Shuzo started dusting off the distillery. There was nobody in Shinshu anymore who knew how to make whisky, but there were people around who were familiar with the first half of the process . . . those making beer next door at Minami-Shinshu Brewery. They grabbed Koki Takehira and flew over the former master distiller, Kenji Taniguchi (who had become managing director of Hombo by then) to fill him in on the second part of the process. In 2011, after a bit of repair work, the stills were fired up and spirit began to flow again after almost two decades.

The stills themselves were clearly running on their last legs, though, and after three seasons, the decision was made to replace them with brand-new ones. Since the legacy of Kiichiro Iwai is so important to Hombo—the company *and* the family (Iwai's daughter married the youngest son of the founder of the company)—they asked Miyake Industries to build exact replicas. These were installed in November 2014, and the original Iwai stills dating back to 1960 became a monument outside the distillery.

Mars Shinshu Distillery

Mash tun:	stainless steel, lauter (5.5kl)
Washbacks:	3 Oregon pine (7kl)
	3 stainless steel, with temperature control
Pot stills:	1 pair (wash still 6kl; spirit still 8kl), Miyake indirect heating (steam percolators)
	with descending lyne arms, shell-and-tube condenser for wash still, worm tub for spirit still

Mars Shinshu Distillery is located in the village of Miyada, in Nagano prefecture, at an altitude of 2,618 feet/798 meters. It's surrounded by the Central Alps and the Southern Alps, whose mountain lines are incorporated into the bottle design currently used for its single malt expressions .

When the distillery first restarted production, whisky was only produced for 6 months a year—during the colder half of the year. Over the years, production volume was increased little by little, and since 2020, the distillery has been active all year round, except for a two-week maintenance period, typically in mid-August. Up to and including the 2019–2020 season, production took place in the original stillhouse. During that season, however, a brand-new production-building-plus-warehouse (under the same roof) was constructed on site. This was part of a 1.8 billion yen investment by the company to increase production by 10 percent and to double storage capacity. But we are getting ahead of ourselves.

When production resumed at Mars Shinshu in 2011, after a 19-year hiatus, the decision was made to start with a clean slate. Through trial and error, the staff figured out what worked best and discovered what

Top: The entrance to the distillery; below: Inside the new stillhouse

the right character of the (new) Mars Shinshu spirit might be. Variation was explored in all departments, starting with the malted barley, all of which was (and still is) imported from the U.K.

Until the end of the 2018–2019 season, four peating levels were used: non-peated, lightly peated (3.5ppm), heavily peated (20ppm) and super heavily peated (50ppm), as they were referred to within the company. From the following season, however, this was simplified to two types: non-peated and 50ppm.

A view from the top of Yakushima Denshogura

Former distillery manager Koki Takehira checking the spirit flowing off the still

Since 2020, a small amount of locally-grown barley (i.e. in Miyada village) has been distilled at the distillery. For this, the two-row barley varietal Koharu Nijo is used. This is a varietal, developed in Japan in 2009, with a higher cold and snow mold tolerance than other two-row varietals. Distillation takes place the year after harvesting, usually in March. The first year, just 1.8t was distilled. In 2021, there was 7.5t at hand, and in 2022, double that amount. According to the staff at the distillery, the local barley yields a spirit with a sweeter flavor and a stronger, more fragrant aroma.

For the mashing, water is taken from 394 feet/120 meters underground. The standard "three-waters" system (with the third water recycled for the next batch) is used during the mashing process. One batch used to be 1t but after its sister distillery Mars Tsunuki (see below) moved to a 1.1t system, Mars Shinshu followed suit. In mid-2020, when production was moved to the new distillery building, the original semi-lauter mash tun (7.2kl, dating from 1985) was retired and replaced with a new state-of-the-art Miyake full-lauter tun. Its last day of work was June 6, 2020.

In the fermentation department, there has been quite a bit of change as well. Originally, when the distillery resumed production, 5 cast-iron washbacks were used. These dated from the 1960s and were transferred from Yamanashi Distillery. By the early 2010s, the washbacks

View from the riverside

were pretty beat up and rusty. In addition, they were anything but user-friendly. The daily cleaning routine involved climbing into the washback using a ladder. As the opening at the top was very narrow, only people with a low BMI were eligible for this dubious honor. In late August 2018, three Oregon pine washbacks (7kl capacity) were installed next to the cast-iron ones. Two years later, when the new production building was ready, the cast-iron washbacks were retired along with the old mash tun. Only the wooden washbacks were moved to the new building, where they were joined by 3 brand-new stainless-steel fermenters with water jackets, manufactured by Miyake Industries.

Initially, three types of yeast were used—Scottish distillers yeast, slant yeast dating back to the first year of production at Mars Shinshu (1985), and ale yeast from their brewery next door. This was also stream-lined recently and now distillers yeast is the default type. The fermentation time used to be three days, but in 2016, it was increased to 4 days to promote the development of a more estery profile.

The new pot stills were installed in November 2014 and are replicas of the 1960 Iwai stills with three minor modifications: the joints (to make it possible to replace parts of the pot still after wear and tear instead of having to replace the entire still), small windows in the neck of the wash still (to be able to better monitor the first distillation) and a switch from steam coils to percolators. When they were moved to the new production building, in mid-2020, the "man door" on both stills was changed to a transparent, glass one (like the ones at Tsunuki Distillery), so that visitors could see inside the stills.

An unusual feature of the still set-up at Mars Shinshu is that the spirit still is bigger than the wash still. Until mid-2018, three runs from the wash still were combined and put into the spirit still for the second distillation. After the wooden washbacks were installed, this was changed to two wash runs for one spirit run.

The play of variables then continues with the maturation process, but at Hombo Shuzo they take this further than at most places. Not only do they use a variety of wood types and cask sizes, they also experiment with different climatic conditions. Most of the spirit produced at Mars Shinshu is matured on site, but some spirit is sent to Tsunuki Distillery in Kagoshima and some to Yakushima Island, where Hombo Shuzo has a shochu distillery, for maturation there.

The chart below illustrates the differences in climate. The island of Yakushima is particularly extreme. The annual precipitation there is one of the highest in the world and the locals often say it rains "400 days a year." Lots of tests are being run by filling casks of the same type and size with the same kind of spirit at the same time at those different locations. It will be interesting to see how the spirit distilled at Mars Shinshu develops in those very different environments.

	Mars Shinshu Distillery	Mars Tsunuki Distillery	Yakushima Aging Cellar
altitude	2,618ft/798m	187ft/57m	164ft/50m
distance from sea	62 mi/100km	4.5 mi/7km	.6 mi/1km
temperature range	5°F–91°F -15°C–33°C	28.5°F–97°F -2°C–36°C	41°F–95°F 5°C–35°C
average temperature	50°F/10°C	64.5°F/18°C	66°F/19°C
humidity	65%–67%	70%–72%	74%–76%
precipitation	55in/1,400mm/year	90.5in/2,300mm/year	169in/4,300mm/year
pressure	920hPa	1,016hPa	1,015hPa

Retired casks outside Mars Shinshu

At Mars Shinshu Distillery, there are four warehouses—all racked—with a combined capacity of 4,500 casks. Most of the wood used is ex-bourbon, with ex-sherry a distant second, but there is a wide variety of other cask types in the warehouses, too.

Towards the end of 2015, Hombo Shuzo surprised friend and foe by announcing that the company was planning to set up a second whisky distillery at their Tsunuki Kishogura site in Kagoshima. This is the Hombo family's home base, so it's not just another location. There's a lot of history involved. The company was born there in 1872, and the current president was born next door and grew up there, so it's a bit like bringing the spirit home. The first distillation (wash run) took place on October 27, 2016. The first spirit run was done the following day.

Setting up a second distillery wasn't merely a matter of increasing production volume. If that had been the primary goal, the company could have made arrangements to distill in Shinshu all year round in shifts. Instead, the company wanted a spirit with a totally different character, produced in a totally different environment. Reducing the environment to a central, iconic image, if that of Mars Shinshu is the majestic mountains, that of Tsunuki is Sakurajima, the nearby active volcano.

Inside Warehouse No.1 at Tsunuki Distillery

Mars Tsunuki Distillery

Mash tun:	stainless steel, lauter (5kl)
Washbacks:	5 stainless steel (7.9kl)
Pot stills:	1 pair (wash still 5.8kl; spirit still 3.3kl), Miyake
	indirect heating (steam percolators)
	both with descending lyne arms and worm tubs
	1 hybrid still (400l)

Tsunuki Distillery is located in Minami-Satsuma city. It's quite remote and a bit of a trek to get to, but there's a top-notch visitor center so plenty of whisky enthusiasts are more than happy to make the effort.

The distillery may be new, but the place itself is steeped in history. Tsunuki is the place where Hombo Shuzo's spirits business was started and the former home of Tsunekichi Hombo, the second president of the company, is right next door. (It has been transformed into the so-called Hojo, hands down the most beautiful visitor center/bar/café attached to a distillery in Japan.) But the connection is not just a historic and emotional one. It was and still is a very vital one: for over a hundred years shochu has been made in Tsunuki. The new distillery sits where one of the warehouses (for shochu maturation) and a bottling line used to be.

It's clear that the visitor experience was an integral part of the planning, both large-scale and in the details. Entering the distillery building, the visitor goes up the stairs to a central area on the second floor where all processes can be observed from behind glass: the mashing, the fermentation and the distillation. This doesn't include the milling but watching a malt mill in action is about as exciting as watching paint dry, so that's not a great loss.

The technical mastermind at Tsunuki Distillery is Tatsuro Kusano. Kusano studied at Kagoshima University and joined Hombo Shuzo in April 2013. He spent three years at Mars Shinshu, learning the ropes from then-master distiller Koki Takehira there, before he was transferred to Kagoshima in the summer of 2016 to oversee the construction of Tsunuki Distillery. (He was 27 at the time.) Kusano has been in charge of production ever since.

Facing page, clockwise from top left: Part of the old continuous still; one of the old stone Tsunuki warehouses; the garden of the ancestral home; the stone warehouses seen from across the little river; the columns of the continuous still

The production volume and seasonal structure is roughly the same as at its sister distillery, Mars Shinshu. Kusano is very R&D driven, though, so there tends to be much more variation in the details, much more experimentation and much more tweaking and adjusting at Tsunuki Distillery.

The first season (2016–2017), 180t of malted barley was processed. At the time, one batch was 1t, so 180 mashes. Just like at Mars Shinshu, malted barley with four different peating-levels was used: non-peated, lightly peated (3.5ppm), heavily peated (20ppm) and super-heavily peated (50ppm). The first season, the emphasis was on lightly-peated barley (80t processed). The second season, production was increased to 230t and the emphasis shifted to non-peated barley (90t). During the second season, batch size was increased to 1.1t. This was done in preparation for one of Kusano's many projects: using specialty malts (e.g. caramelized and roasted malts). The thinking was: 100kg of specialty malt could be added to the regular mashbill to create flavor accents. And that's what happened from the next season (2018–2019). Even when no specialty malts are used, the batch size is 1.1t now.

Just like at Mars Shinshu, the system with four peating levels was abandoned from mid-2019. The focus now is on non-peated and 50ppm, but occasionally malted barley peated to 80ppm is used. Sometimes, new-make is blended before it is filled into casks. For example, by blending 0ppm new-make and 50ppm new-make at the right ratio, it's possible to create a 5ppm new-make. Since 2020, Tsunuki has also used a small amount of local barley. The first time, during the 2020–2021 season, 6t were distilled.

Mashing takes place in a state-of-the-art mash tun, manufactured by Miyake Industries. It is fitted

Bust of Tsunekichi Hombo, the 2nd president of the company, in the garden of the ancestral home next to Tsuneki Distillery

with a sight glass, which comes in handy for someone as obsessively focused on the minutiae of the whisky-making process as Kusano. The water used is the same as that used for shochu making: soft spring water from Mt. Kurata behind the distillery premises.

The first two seasons, a "two-waters" system was used, i.e. starting each mash with clean water. The third season, a 3kl tank was installed, to make it possible to move to a "three-waters" system. According to Kusano, this had a

A cask that used to contain Kagoshima whisky, refilled with rice shochu in 2005

marked influence on the quality of the wort. With peated production, in particular, the difference was pronounced. Kusano adjusts various other parameters—the milling ratios, the mashing temperatures, the speed, etc.,—in function of the various types of spirit he is looking for. This is not the sort of distillery where parameters are fixed and set in stone—far from it. Everything is continuously recalibrated with the purpose of creating as much variety as possible.

That applies to the fermentation process, too. The climate in Kagoshima is quite hot, so the choice was made to go with stainless steel fermenters that could be temperature-controlled. The fermentation time at Mars Tsunuki is 4 days. The first season, the same three yeast types as those used at Mars Shinshu were used. The second season, in Kusano's words, was "all about exploring the fermentation process." Various types of beer yeast and shochu yeast were tried out in combination with distillers yeast. That season, Kusano also focused on increasing the secondary lactic fermentation in a variety of ways. Careful temperature control over the course of the four-day fermentation period was one. Another was a process inspired by shochu making. This involves taking a bucket of wash from the "fifth fermenter" (i.e. the one ready for distillation) and adding the contents of the bucket to the "first fermenter" (i.e. the one being filled with fresh wort that day).

The next step is distillation. The stillhouse is dominated by two pot stills made by Miyake Industries. Both have straight heads, descending lyne arms (10° more downward than at Mars Shinshu) and both are fitted

Tsunuki Distillery under construction with a new lick of paint on the old continuous still tower

with a worm tub condenser, which is the exception rather than the rule at most distilleries nowadays where shell-in-tube condensers are used for the most part. With the latter, there is much more copper contact, resulting in a light and clean spirit. At Tsunuki Distillery, the goal was to create a heavier spirit, hence the more traditional worm tubs. There is also a 400l hybrid still and a small 500l copper pot still (which was used at Kagoshima Factory to make whisky until 1984) in the stillhouse, but these are not used to make whisky at present.

At the moment, the distillation time is about 7 hours, for both stills, but again various parameters—such as distillation speed, the width of the cut, etc.—are varied in function of the desired spirit character. "At the start of the second season," Kusano relates, "I slowed down the distillation speed considerably, both for the first and second distillation. This seems to fly in the face of using worm tub condensers, which are aimed at creating a heavier spirit, but we are using this approach to get a rich, yet clean spirit."

The so-called man doors of the pot stills are made out of glass, making it possible to see inside the stills when they are in operation. Speaking of which: whereas the wash still is cleaned every day, after distillation, the spirit still isn't. It's cleaned very infrequently, but Kusano assures me this isn't laziness on their part. It's all about the aroma of the accumulated residue and oils—think vegemite plus clay. "If we were to clean the spirit still, the spirit would become lighter. We want a more robust spirit and we also want the accumulated residue to become an aromatic part of the spirit." I can't imagine any of the staff complaining about the no-cleaning policy for the spirit still.

One batch results in about 500l of new make at 64%abv, so at filling strength (60%abv) that is about three barrels per batch. The maturation policy at Mars Tsunuki is about 50 percent ex-bourbon barrels; the other 50 percent is made up of ex-sherry casks—butts, hogsheads and puncheons—virgin American white oak casks . . . and things they find left and right: ex-rum casks, ex-brandy casks, ex-Laphroaig casks, etc.

As with Mars Shinshu, the new-make is aged on site, but a portion is sent to its sister distillery and to the Yakushima Aging Cellar for maturation there. At Mars Tsunuki, there are five warehouses for the maturation of whisky. Three of these are historical stone warehouses; the others are new, racked warehouses. The total maturation capacity on site is currently a little under 7,000 casks.

The angels' share at Tsunuki is 6–7 percent (for a barrel), which is high. (At Mars Shinshu, it's about 3 percent.) Because of the high temperatures, Kusano feels larger cask sizes tend to work better for aging whisky at Tsunuki, at least long-term. For a while, the staff at the distillery had been trying to get hold of hogsheads but this cask type is not so common in Japan. In 2021, they managed to acquire a hooper from the cooperage at Satsuma Shuzo. Going forward, the plan was to try and put together some hogsheads in-house. In recent years, they have also been using more second-fill casks, little by little. As Kusano says, "it's all about striking a balance between the short term and the long term."

SUPER ALOSPAS STILL

Mars Tsunuki distillery is the only place in Japan where you can see a Super Alospas still. It was installed in 1956 and was used to make neutral spirits until 1974. It occupies a seven-story tower that is about 26m high. The tower was renovated and repainted when Tsunuki distillery was constructed. You can't climb up the tower, but you can see up through glass windows in the ceiling when standing inside at ground level. There are also some informative bilingual panels explaining the intricacies of the Super Alospas still as well as other aspects of Hombo Shuzo's history.

A bird's-eye view of the first Aging Cellar

YAKUSHIMA AGING CELLAR

Since 1960, Hombo Shuzo has been making shochu in a small, traditional distillery on the island of Yakushima. Yakushima is situated about
60km south from the southern tip of Kagoshima prefecture. It's the last
ecosystem dominated by Japanese cedar and one-fifth of the island
is registered as a UNESCO World Heritage Site. The island's ancient
forest served as the inspiration for the landscapes in Hayao Miyazaki's
animated movie *Princess Mononoke* (Studio Ghibli, 1997).

A few years after whisky production at Mars Shinshu was resumed,
the idea was floated to age some of the spirit at the Yakushima
Denshogura. The "Yakushima Aging" project at Hombo Shuzo started
in 2014. Initially, there were only a handful of casks and they were
stowed at the back of a warehouse full of bottling supplies. In July 2016,
some unused lodgings behind the shochu distillery were torn down and
a small dunnage-style warehouse was built, with a capacity of around
400 casks. The inside was clad with local cedar, obviously not the
protected 1,000+-year-old type, but replanted cedar that's about 100
years old.

In 2021, a second warehouse of the same type but twice the size
was built behind Warehouse No. 1. At present, the total maturation
capacity is 1,200 casks. At the time of writing, there were a little under

400 casks maturing on site—80 percent ex-bourbon barrels, the rest ex-sherry and ex-port casks. The oldest Shinshu vintage maturing on Yakushima is 2014. The first Tsunuki shipment arrived in March 2017.

The conditions on Yakushima are rather extreme. In the winter, the temperature in the warehouse drops to about 10°C, but the humidity can be around 50%. In the summer, it's not uncommon for temperatures to reach 38°C—and the humidity to soar to 85%—in the warehouse. The angels' share is around 8%.

Originally, the company felt that heavily-peated spirit would best express the dramatic natural conditions of the island, but after observing the development of the spirit aging at Yakushima Aging Cellar for a couple of years, most of the staff seemed to prefer the non-peated spirit. In a way, without the peat, the natural conditions can "enter" the whisky more easily.

Tatsuro Kusano agrees, but his take is slightly different. "I feel that the climate on Yakushima drives out the good qualities of the heavy peat. They kind of evaporate into thin air, if that makes sense, so I've come to see non-peated or lightly-peated spirit as more suited to the maturation conditions of Yakushima."

Between 2017 and 2021, Hombo Shuzo released four "Single Malt Komagatake Yakushima Aging" expressions. (There was no release in the year 2018.) These were all single malts, the whisky having been distilled at Mars Shinshu distillery. Once the Tsunuki spirit started to come of age, a new possibility suggested itself: creating a blended malt.

Inside the Aging Cellar #1

And lo and behold, in June 2022, the company announced its new Yakushima-aged blended-malt whisky brand, Mars The Y.A. The higher outturn (12,000btls for edition #01) will make it possible to also promote this brand in key export markets.

EXPRESSIONS

In the late 1990s, Hombo Shuzo released its first proper single malts. They started with Maltage Satsuma 12yo (released in 1996, in a glass decanter) and continued two years later with another three releases in a ceramic decanter of the same shape: Maltage Satsuma 15yo, Maltage Komagatake 10yo and Maltage Komagatake Sherry Cask 10yo. The Satsuma and Komagatake releases—distilled in Kagoshima and Nagano (Shinshu) respectively—were never meant to be standards. They came and went, and that was it.

The Maltage quartet was followed by a succession of one-offs in a bewildering variety of bottle shapes and sizes over the next decade. At a time when Japanese whisky was getting the cold shoulder, the folks at Hombo Shuzo tried everything and then some to flog their wares, including doing single-cask bottlings diluted to 43%abv. By the time Japanese whisky had become a hot category again, they only had malt in the warehouses that was two decades old and over, and very little at that—not exactly a great foundation to build a single malt range on.

Miyake staff working on the swan neck of one of the Tsunuki pot stills

They fired up the stills again in 2011, and when the spirit from that first season of production had become whisky three years later, launched Komagatake The Revival 2011 (58%abv, 6,000btls). Since then, the company has kept fans happy with regular limited editions and occasional single cask releases. The single malt expressions coming out of Mars Shinshu are all bottled under the Komagatake brand.

The oldest bottlings from the "ancient regime" at Mars Shinshu are 30-year-old expressions. A trio of bottlings, all from the 1986 vintage, was released in 2016. This was made up of an American White Oak expression (a vatting of four casks, 61%abv, 1,137btls) and two expressions matured in ex-sherry wood (the same vatting of two casks, but one was reduced to 48%abv, 619btls, whereas the other was bottled at vatting strength, 53%, 163btls).

The first release of Mars whisky made after the 19-year hiatus

Noteworthy is the so-called Mars Malt Le Papillon Takahide Komatsu Edition released in October 2021. This was a bottling of a single American White Oak cask filled in 1990 (#1043, 30yo). Limited to 365 bottles, each had a unique label featuring a butterfly native to Japan made by Rinpa-style artist Takahide Komatsu. The current president of Hombo Shuzo is a keen amateur lepidopterist and this edition is, in fact, part of an ongoing Papillon series (since 2016). The other releases in the Papillon series—fifteen, at the time of writing—are all either single casks or what-they-refer-to-as "double casks" (i.e. vattings of two casks) of malt whisky distilled at either Mars Shinshu or Mars Tsunuki.

The first single malt release out of Tsunuki dropped on April 27, 2020. Highly anticipated after a series of in-progress bottlings for the Hojo (i.e. the Tsunuki Distillery visitor center) during the first three years, Tsunuki The First (59%abv, 9,948btls) was well-received by whisky enthusiasts in Japan and abroad. It was followed by a peatier expression simple called Tsunuki Peated (50%abv, 14,830btls) in January 2021. Just like with Mars Shinshu, there are regular limited-edition bottlings as well as occasional single-cask bottlings for retailers or bars at home and abroad.

Making Whisky by Serendipity: Mars Maltage 3+25

In late 2012-early 2013, I had the pleasure of being on the Japanese panel for the World Whiskies Awards for the first time. As always, everything was judged blind but for the most part, one could make educated guesses as to what the liquid at hand was. There was one particular whisky in the "blended malt" category that blew me and my fellow judges away, but it was a total mystery. Nobody had any clue as to what it could be. We even thought someone had slipped in a 1970s Benriach as a prank. The mystery whisky made it through the two rounds in Japan and then it was off to London for the final round, where it would be judged blind against the best from the rest of the world in the same category. On March 21, 2013, when the "World's Best Blended Malt" was announced, we discovered what the mystery whisky was: Mars Maltage 3+25.

The "3+25" refers to the age. To understand why they called it that, rather than "28yo," have a quick look at Hombo Shuzo's whisky history as outlined above. When they moved their whisky operations from Kagoshima to Shinshu, rather than move the maturing stock as it was (as casks with whisky in them), they poured all the liquid into a tanker and transported the empty casks separately. In Shinshu, they refilled the same casks with the vatted liquid and left the whisky to further mature. Two decades and a half later, those casks were vatted again and bottled as "3+25," shorthand for three years of maturation in Kagoshima followed by 25 years of maturation in Shinshu. That didn't make it a "blended malt," of course, as maturation location is irrelevant to the definition of the category (i.e., a blend of single malt whiskies from different distilleries). To understand why it really was a blended malt whisky, we have to go even further back in time.

When Hombo Shuzo moved its whisky business from Yamanashi to Kagoshima, they had done exactly the same thing and transported the liquid and the casks separately before refilling them. So, when all the whisky maturing in Kagoshima was moved to Shinshu in 1985, there was in fact a small portion of malt from the Yamanashi days involved, making it, technically, a "blended malt."

Two days before the awards ceremony in London, I happened to be at Mars Shinshu Distillery and one of the things on the agenda that day was the bottling of the last remaining 3+25 liquid. Two days before being crowned the best blended malt in the world, the last 2,500 bottles were being filled and because serendipity had created the whisky, there simply wasn't any way to make more of it or recreate it.

The irony wasn't lost on the people at Hombo, but they took it well. Having recently restarted their whisky operations at Mars Shinshu after a 19-year hiatus, they came up with the fabulous idea to create a reverse "3+25"—that is to say, to send whisky distilled in Shinshu and matured there for three years to one of their warehouses in Kagoshima for a 25-year slumber. I, for one, hope to be around to try that side by side with the "original" 3+25.

Eigashima Distillery
(Eigashima Shuzo)

As far as location is concerned, it's hard to beat Eigashima Distillery. In fact, there's no other distillery location in Japan that's as pleasant year round in terms of climate as the small fishing village of Eigashima. The distillery is right by the Inland Sea, on the Akashi Strait, and benefits from a mild maritime climate. It enjoys high average temperatures and a low average rainfall.

In 1888, Hyokichi Urabe merged some of the sake makers in the Eigashima area and established Eigashima Shuzo Co., Ltd. In 1919, a production plant for shochu, mirin, whisky and brandy was completed and sales started. The company was granted a license to manufacture whisky (as well as brandy and other spirits) on September 8, 1919. On paper, that would make it the oldest whisky producer in Japan. As often, the reality is slightly more complex.

How exactly whisky was "made" at Eigashima up until the early '60s—and we know it was from old bottle labels—is anyone's guess. The company has very scant records relating to whisky production. Initially, it's likely that shochu equipment and methods were harnessed to create something approximating the amber nectar. What we do know is that until 1961—when malt whisky was made in-house for the first time—an allospas still was used to make neutral spirit and that this was then turned into whisky with the help of flavorings and colorings.

Facing page: View of the Inland Sea from the distillery grounds

Eigashima Shuzo in the early days

All things considered, it's probably best we don't know too much about what went into those "whiskies" from the early days. It's highly unlikely the present-day whisky drinker would recognize them as such.

In 1961, two small copper pot stills were installed and proper malt whisky production began in earnest. All of this malt whisky was destined for their blends, so there is no telling what the distillate was like. According to the staff at the distillery, the first pot stills were used until about 1970. (They can still be seen—blue-green from decades spent outdoors—from a window on the ground floor of the current whisky production building.)

In 1981, as whisky consumption in Japan was soaring to previously unseen heights, the decision was made to build a new distillery on site. White Oak Distillery, as it was known then, was completed in May 1984 and malt whisky production resumed with new equipment . . . but not everything was brand-new. The company didn't order brand-new pot stills from Miyake Industries. Instead, they reused the top part of two stills that were previously used by Silver Whisky Distillery in Nara and fitted them with new bottom parts. Silver Whisky is one of those distilleries lost in the mists of time. Apparently, a fire destroyed their premises in 1963 and shortly after, the company disappeared from the scene. Once in a blue moon, a Silver Whisky bottle shows up at auction, but to say they're rare as hen's teeth is an understatement. Interestingly, even though the new stills were much larger, the shape was very similar to that of the old 1961 stills.

In 2018, it was time for another "changing of the guard" in the distillery building. The 1984 pot stills had reached the end of their working life, but just like before, a bit of history was kept alive. New upper parts (shoulder + swan neck + condenser) were ordered from Miyake Industries, but the bottom parts of the respective pots (including the heating mechanism) were still in decent working order and therefore kept in place. The last time the old configuration was used was on November 6–7, 2018 (wash run and spirit run, respectively)—the end of the 2018 whisky season. In February of the following year, the old top parts of the twin pots were removed and new replicas were installed. (Nothing gets thrown out, so the old top parts are now on display in front of the distillery building.) The "new" wash and spirit still were used for the first time at the start of the 2019 whisky season, i.e. on March 28 and 29, 2019, respectively. In early 2020, a new mash tun and a new *shubo* (yeast starter) tank were installed.

In the summer of 2019, the name of the distillery was officially changed from White Oak Distillery—which was seen as having become a bit nondescript on the global whisky stage—to Eigashima Distillery. That is the name we will use in what follows, regardless of the era under discussion.

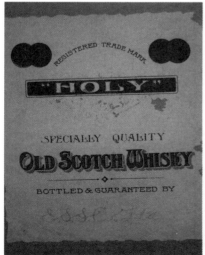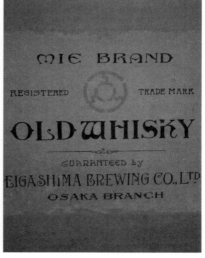

Old Eigashima whisky labels

The Distillery

Mash tun: stainless steel, mash tun and lauter tun (5kl)

Washbacks: 3 stainless steel (10kl), with temperature control

Pot stills: 1 pair (wash still 4.5kl; spirit still 3kl), Miyake

                     indirect heating (steam coils)

                     with descending lyne arms and shell-and-tube condensers

Eigashima Distillery used to be a part-time whisky distillery. During the colder half of the year (September–March), the staff would be busy making sake. After that, they would move on to barley shochu (April–May), then to whisky making (June–July), before taking a break in August, and going back to sake production. Over the past decade, the whisky-making season has been extended incrementally, but since the different types of liquor are produced by the same group of people, more time for one product means less time for another.

Up until 2013, 44 tons/40 metric tons of malted barley was used per season, one ton per batch. By 2016, Eigashima had doubled its whisky production and cut out the shochu season altogether. During the 2017 season, 110 tons/100 metric tons of malted barley were processed and production spanned 7 months. Fast forward to 2021 and the distillery was at 160t for the season. At the time of writing, the whisky season ran from mid-March to the end of November, with a three-week maintenance/rest period from the end of July until mid-August. In 2022, the distillery processed a record 200t of malted barley. Currently, there are 6 people working in production.

Per batch, 1t of malted barley is processed. The milling ratios tend to be a bit higher on the husks (3:6:1) than the textbook ratios, but this helps to create a clearer wort according to the staff at the distillery. The malted

The old Eigashima pot stills

Top: Eigashima Distillery; below: The second pair of pot stills in front of the distillery building

barley is imported from the U.K. but the specs have changed slightly over the years. Prior to 2014, the malted barley was lightly peated, in the region of 3.5 to 5ppm. In 2014, the peating level was dialed up to 10ppm and that was the new standard up to and including the 2017 season. Then, the consensus was that the focus on peated malt exclusively was not the best strategy long term. In 2018, three types of peating levels

Inside Eigashima Distillery

were explored: 0ppm, 10ppm and 50ppm. The feeling after that season was that the 10ppm had become somewhat redundant and from the 2019 season onwards, just two types of malted barley were used: mainly non-peated and some heavily-peated (50ppm). During the most recent season (2022), the latter accounted for 10 percent of production.

Water is taken from a bore on site. The same water is used for their sake, and seeing as water quality is of the utmost importance there, it's clear there's nothing to worry about on that front. The distillery is equipped with a stainless steel mash tun and a lauter tun and a "three-waters" system is used, but not in the habitual sense. The first and second water yield about 3,400 liters of wort. The third water (1,200 liters) is added to the *shubo* tank. This is the yeast preparation tank, which always contains 300 liters before the 1,200 liters of the third water are added along with the yeast. So, in effect, the *shubo* tank contains 1,500 liters and one-fifth is always kept in it, for continuity (a bit like a sourdough starter). Four-fifths of the 1,500 liters in the tank are sent to the washback the following day along with the first and second water of

The fermentation takes place in stainless steel washbacks. These are fitted with a sensor and when the temperature reaches 30°C, a shower function is engaged and water trickles down from the top of the washbacks along the exterior. Distillers yeast is used, but since mid-2021, it's a mix of two types of distillers yeast (Pinnacle and Lallemand). Apparently, this brings out the best flavor profile further down the line. The fermentation time used to be 48 hours, but in recent years, this has been dialed up to 66 hours (with longer fermentations, up to 90 hours, over the weekend).

According to company president Mikio Hiraishi, the plan is to add a wooden washback (Douglas fir) to the setup in April 2023 and to bring that into the production cycle from May onwards. The fermentation

Inside one of the warehouses

time would then be extended so that the wash can spend its last day in the wooden vessel before being charged to the wash still.

As explained above, the pot stills are new from the shoulders up. These are identical in shape and size to the old top parts, but the man doors on both stills were changed to glass (a recent trend in Japan, thanks to Miyake Industries) and the wash still got a sight glass. The wash still is charged with 4,600 liters. The first distillation takes about five and a half hours and results in around 1,700 liters of low wines. The second distillation takes about 7 hours, and the result is around 550 liters of new-make at about 70%abv. This is then dilluted to 63.5%abv before it is filled into wood.

In recent years, the cut has changed somewhat. The cut to feints used to be at 60%abv (for non-peated production), but in 2021, the middle cut was made a little tighter and the cut to feints moved to 65%abv. On the peated front (50ppm), the cut used to be at 58%abv (i.e. from 2018 onwards), but in 2022, two different cut points were implemented. For half of the 20t heavily-peated malted barley used that season, the cut was made at 65%abv; for the other half, it was made at 62%abv. What may seem like a small numerical difference actually results in a pronounced difference in terms of distillate character: the former a little cleaner; the latter smokier but heavier and therefore better suited for longer maturation.

All stock is matured on site in old warehouses. Currently, four of those are used for whisky maturation. The priority is ex-sherry wood. About 60 percent of production is filled into ex-sherry casks (a mix of real bodega casks and seasoned casks). Only about 100 bourbon barrels are filled each year. There are also some red and white wine casks from the company's winery (Charmant Winery) in Yamanashi. These are used mainly for finishing purposes.

Casks are kept on or close to the ground and even when racks are used, they are typically stowed three-high at most. The angels' share is 2–5 percent for sherry casks and 5 percent for bourbon barrels, but in the latter case, it can go up to 8 percent. It's not uncommon for one-fifth of a barrel's contents to be gone after three years of maturation on site.

At the time of writing, there were about 1,500 casks in the warehouses. The bulk of this is 5 years old and under. The oldest stock was 14 years old (just one cask). The second oldest was 11 years old (a mere four casks). From 9 years down, the stock situation was more comfortable.

Eigashima Shuzo has come a long way since they got their whisky license, a little over a century ago. Currently, the majority of their bottom line comes from whisky sales. Quality comes first now, and continuing R&D is the order of the day. One new project involves the use of locally grown barley. At the end of May 2022, 20t of barley harvested in the Yahata district of the neighboring city of Kakogawa were earmarked for use at the distillery. This barley is of the six-row Shunrai varietal and, once malted, the staff at Eigashima Distillery are expecting to be able to distill 16–18 batches, likely in June/July 2023. There are records at the company indicating that domestic barley was used in 1961 but it is unlikely that this was barley from Hyogo prefecture, so all in all, it's fair to say this is the first time barley from the distillery's home prefecture is used for the production of whisky.

EXPRESSIONS

Eigashima Shuzo's focus, as far as whisky is concerned, has always been on reasonably-priced, easy-drinking blended whiskies (1st and 2nd grade whiskies in the pre-1989 tax classification, "cheap blends" as we would call them now) for the home market. The company entered the single malt arena very late and very hesitantly, somewhat puzzled that people were interested in trying what they considered to be merely a component of whisky. It wasn't a strategic decision and it definitely wasn't backed up by a long-term vision, at the time.

Their first single malt was an 8-year-old launched in September 2007 (40%abv, 4,500 bottles), under the new brand name of Akashi to set it apart from their White Oak blended range. Branding was minimal. Bottled in apothecary-style 500ml bottles with a very basic label and sold through unusual channels (which included a major convenience store chain), it was a case of product and presentation being strangely at odds with each other. It took more than two years to sell the entire outturn of that first release.

By 2010, it had become apparent that they couldn't supply more 8-year-old, so instead they launched a 5-year-old (45%abv) with the intention of making this their flagship single malt. Towards the end of the year, they added a somewhat premium 12-year-old (2,000 bottles) to their lineup. A few historically significant cask-strength (albeit not single cask) private bottlings also date from these years: a 5-year-old (2004/2009, 59%abv, 100 bottles) for Bar Zoetrope's 4th anniversary, and a double set selected by and bottled for yours truly made up of a 5-year-old (2005/2010, 59%abv, 102 bottles) and a 12-year-old (1997/2010, 59%, 102 bottles). The 12-year-old was the oldest stock in the warehouse at the time of bottling.

A little bit of the 12-year-old stock (matured in Spanish oak ex-sherry casks) was kept back and transferred to other casks to create a 14-year-old expression launched in two batches in 2012 (the first finished in an ex-white wine cask for a year and a half, the second moved to an American oak ex-sherry cask for a year and a half, and then finished for half a year in an ex-white wine cask), and a 15-year-old expression in 2013 (finished for two years and a half in a *konara* cask). Not only was the oldest stock gone by then, they were also struggling to find enough liquid in the warehouse for their standard 5-year-old single malt. In August 2012, they decided to give up on the idea of a 5-year-old flagship malt and switch to a no-age-statement expression (46%abv, non-chill-filtered and non-colored). That's been on the shelves ever since (black label), together with a NAS blended whisky also called Akashi but sporting a white label.

Enthusiasts are kept happy with occasional single cask releases for various trade customers since 2013. Worth singling out is cask #118171, which was bottled in the summer of 2022 (63%abv, 667 bottles). This held distillate from 2018 (and was refilled after bottling with 2022 distillate). The cask is rather special. It's entirely made out of Japanese chestnut (*kuri*). Casks with heads made of Japanese chestnut (and other types of wood) can be spotted at many craft distilleries in Japan. (The independent Ariake Cooperage is the main supplier of these sorts of casks.) A cask entirely made from Japanese chestnut is a rarity, though, and at Eigashima Distillery, they just had one specimen. That the use of wood types other than oak is not just pursued for the sake of novelty is exemplified by cask #118171. The wood drives the distillate almost in the direction of a liqueur, but the balance in the case of this single-cask bottling is absolutely superb. It is well worth seeking out.

Recently, the staff at Eigashima have become more aware of the fact that, while releasing single-cask bottlings does manage to quench the thirst for variety among whisky enthusiasts to a certain extent, it does make it more difficult to reach a wider section of the drinking populace. The plan going forward is to also create expressions with a larger outturn by vatting a judicious selection of aged stocks.

Facing page: A chestnut cask

Chichibu shrine

Chichibu Distillery
(Venture Whisky)

Ichiro Akuto is a man of vision. Just four years after being forced to sell his family's liquor business and witnessing the dismantling of his grandfather's Hanyu distillery, he was back with a brand-new distillery of his own. To set up this new venture, he returned to his roots and the roots of his family: the village of Chichibu, about an hour and a half northwest of Tokyo, in Saitama prefecture.

In preparation, Ichiro visited as many distilleries as he could, especially small ones like Kilchoman, Edradour, Benromach, Daftmill, Penderyn, Cornish Cyder Farm and The Somerset Cider Brandy Co. He also spent some time working at Karuizawa distillery (in 2006) and Benriach distillery (in 2007). That was the fun part of getting ready to set up a new distillery. The less fun part was persuading people (banks, landowners, even his own family) that there was a future in the project. One has to keep in mind that Ichiro was trying to sell this dream at the end of a spectacular 25-year decline in whisky consumption in Japan, prior to any indication that things were about to change.

Ichiro felt that there was a place in the market for a whisky made on a small scale with painstaking attention to detail. At the time, it was a daring proposition. Construction started in 2007, the whisky license came in early 2008 and in February, the first spirit ran off the stills. Ichiro and his team haven't looked back since.

In 2019, Ichiro established a second distillery in Chichibu, referred to as "Chichibu II" (see page 367 for more on this). This has impacted the workflow at the original Chichibu distillery somewhat, as will become clear in what follows.

The Distillery

Mash tun:	stainless steel (2.4kl)
Washbacks:	8 mizunara (3.2kl)
Pot stills:	1 pair (wash still 2kl; spirit still 2kl), Forsyths indirect heating (steam coils)
	both with descending lyne arm and shell-and-tube condensers

The majority of the production at Chichibu distillery is non-peated. Every year, for a month or two before the summer maintenance season, some heavily peated (50+ppm) malt is distilled. Pre-2019, the bulk of the non-peated malted barley used at Chichibu distillery was imported from Crisp Malting in Norfolk, England, with a small amount imported from Germany. The peated malt is imported from the northeast of Scotland. On the peated front, nothing changed post-2019, but on the non-peated front the decision was made—once production at Chichibu II was in full swing—to concentrate on domestic (though not necessarily local) barley at the original Chichibu distillery. During the 2021–2022 season, domestic barley accounted for a staggering 70 percent of production at Chichibu.

Right from the start, it was Ichiro's intention to supplement the imported barley, as much as logistically and financially possible, with locally grown barley. "Local" can be a bit of an elastic concept, but in the case of Chichibu, it can mean as close as five minutes from the distillery site. In the beginning, Ichiro persuaded some of the farmers in the area to plant 'Optic,' which was the most commonly used barley variety in brewing and distilling at the time, but it didn't seem to be suited to the Saitama environment and climate. He has since switched to local varieties, like Sai-no-hoshi.

Since 2008, Ichiro and some of his team have made regular visits to their malting company in Norfolk to work on their floor malting skills. The malting floor at Chichibu distillery has a capacity of three tons, but there's only one steep tank with a one-ton capacity, so they are somewhat limited in that respect. Even though the distillery needs are tiny compared with the big distilleries in Japan, it will never be feasible to use locally grown barley exclusively. It's about five times as costly as importing malted barley from Europe. The first local barley vintage at Chichibu was 2011.

The water used at the distillery is supplied by the city and comes from the nearby Arakawa River. For one mash, 882 pounds/400kg of malted barley are used, resulting in about 2,000 liters of wort. Like most of the production processes at Chichibu, mashing is very much hands on. There are no rakes in the tiny mash tun, so stirring and measuring volume is done manually by whomever is in charge of the mash that day. This sort of human contact with the materials-in-transformation is one of the things that characterizes Chichibu distillery and makes it a "craft" distillery in the real sense of the word.

Unique in the world of whisky, the fermentation takes place in washbacks made of mizunara. When the distillery was opened, there were five; now, there are eight. The washbacks proved to be difficult to "tame." The first four days of use, an extra 22 pounds/10kg of yeast had to be added to counteract the tannins in the wood. They're also costly, hard to clean and sanitize and prone to leaking, but Ichiro feels they're worth the trouble because naturally occurring lactic acid bacteria and other microorganisms in the wood contribute to flavor formation in their own mysterious way.

Distillers yeast, originally from Scotland but propagated in Japan, is used and the fermentation time is close to 100 hours. It used to be between 62 and 80 hours but after the 2015 summer maintenance

Chichibu Distillery

Among the mizunara washbacks

season, Ichiro extended the fermentation time to encourage the work of lactic acid bacteria in the fermenting mash. Late lactic fermentation can add fruity and estery notes, as well as a sweet, buttery aroma to the spirit. After Chichibu II came up to speed, Ichiro was able to extend the fermentation time even further, to 5 days. When there was only one distillery, on some days, two batches were done, so there was not enough leeway. Once Chichibu II went in production, only one batch per day was done at the original distillery and it became possible to extend the fermentation time to encourage an even fruitier flavor profile.

Before being transferred to one of the washbacks, the wort is cooled to about 68°F/20°C. Wood is a good insulator, but due to variations in climate and the lack of temperature control, maintaining consistency as far as fermentation is concerned is a bit of a challenge. This is seen as a good thing: more variety! In the summer, for example, the wort contains more alcohol (about 2 percent more) because hot weather makes the yeast happier.

The stills

Like everything else in the main distillery building, the pot stills are very compact. Squat with short necks and downward lyne arms, they've been designed to produce a rich and heavy spirit. In the early stages of planning, Ichiro thought about reusing the old Hanyu pot stills. However, the copper on those stills was fairly thin, and it soon became clear that ordering new ones wasn't going to cost all that much more versus having the old Hanyu stills repaired and installed. There were more fundamental reasons, too, to purchase them new. At Hanyu distillery, 1,764 pounds/800kg of malted barley was used for one batch. Ichiro felt this was too much and wanted to scale it back. Most importantly, he felt that all the equipment that would influence the quality of the product (the mill, mash tun, washbacks and pot stills) had to be brand new.

Originally, Ichiro wanted to install worm tubs, but condensers of that type require a good supply of water, which can be a bit of an issue in the hot summers at Chichibu, so the decision was made to use shell-and tube condensers, which are used at most whisky distilleries around

Sparging in progress at Chichibu distillery

the world. The cut is made by nosing and tasting the spirit, not by numbers—again, a very hands-on process. The result is about 200 liters of spirit, which is very little compared with what comes off the stills at other distilleries in Japan.

Around 25 distillation batches are accumulated in a tank—which smooths out minor variations—before being diluted to 63.5% and filled into wood.

It's fair to say that Ichiro has more fun with wood than anyone else in the whisky business in Japan. The variety in terms of wood types, cask sizes and previous contents is mind-boggling. There's one warehouse on the main site, and four more a five-minute walk from the distillery, where the cooperage, the blending lab and the bottling hall are. All of these warehouses are of the dunnage type. There is another dunnage warehouse (#6) and a large racked warehouse (#7) next to Chichibu II Distillery.

That may seem like a lot of warehouses for a distillery that only produces about 53,000 liters of pure alcohol (equivalent to 400 barrels) per year and has been in operation for just a decade and a half, but there's more than just Chichibu maturing in the warehouses there. What's left of the old Hanyu and Kawasaki stock as well as imported grain and malt whisky for Ichiro's blends is also kept there. Up until early 2015, the Chichibu warehouses also provided a temporary home for the remaining Karuizawa stock.

About half of the spirit produced at Chichibu is filled into ex-bourbon barrels. The other half goes into a wide variety of casks: ex-sherry (both American and Spanish oak), ex-wine (both domestic and foreign), ex-port, ex-madeira, ex-cognac and mizunara (both first-fill and refill). Once in a while, Ichiro gets his hands on some more unusual cooperage, such as ex-rum, ex-tequila and ex-grappa casks.

In the beginning, just after the distillery had been set up, it was hard to get hold of good-quality casks. Suppliers abroad obviously didn't know who Ichiro was and what he was doing at his tiny distillery in Japan. As far as ex-bourbon wood was concerned, he could only get hold of barrels from Heaven Hill. Ichiro's approach to this problem was the same as the approach he took to selling the old Hanyu stock when very few people knew about its merits: to go out and talk to the people. He regularly travels to the U.S. and Spain to visit cooperages and dis-tilleries/bodegas there. It's all about getting to know the people behind the operations and building up a relationship of trust with them. At the same time, Ichiro feels that every visit is an opportunity to learn more about the craft of whisky making. In that sense, it's like killing two birds with one stone: you get smarter and you get hold of the good stuff.

Ichiro has also been using ex-beer barrels to mature or finish his whiskies. Local craft brewers were interested in barrel-aging some of their suds but they couldn't get their hands on casks. The big compa-nies didn't want their casks to leave the house and the smaller whisky makers had a hard time as it was getting hold of good cooperage for their own products. Some of the brewers came knocking on Ichiro's door and he immediately felt there was an opportunity there for both parties involved. Rather than give or sell them his ex-Chichibu casks, he lent them out so that, once they had been used to age the beers and returned to the distillery, he could refill them with new Chichibu spirit or use them for secondary maturation purposes. It was a win-win for everyone: the brewers had access to good-quality casks and Ichiro had a new "color" to play with in his wood block puzzle. Ex-IPA casks seem to mesh particularly well with the Chichibu spirit. "I feel there's a kinship between IPA and malt whisky," Ichiro relates. "Of course, both are made using barley, but there's a certain fruitiness to good IPAs that you also find in some malt whiskies."

Sometimes cooperation is the way to go, but a bit of DIY from time to time doesn't hurt either. There's plenty of that going on at Chichibu as far as wood management is concerned. In 2008, Ichiro and his staff started training with Mitsuo Saito, the former master cooper of Maru-S Cooperage. When, in 2013, Saito decided to retire and close shop, Ichiro bought all the equipment and had it moved to Chichibu. Since 2014, the distillery has a fully functional cooperage of its own, located next to the blending lab.

Some of the work at the cooperage involves modifying casks in original ways, making "designer casks," if you like. One example of this is the *chibidaru*, Chichibu's original quarter-cask. For this, they take a standard ex-bourbon barrel, cut off the section between the quarter hoop and the head at either end, and close the now-shortened barrel with new heads. A *chibidaru* holds about 130 liters and because there is more wood contact, it speeds up the maturation process. Originally, all *chibidaru* at Chichibu were made out of American white oak (being modified bourbon barrels), but there are also a few *chibidaru* made out of mizunara slumbering in the warehouses. In recent years, however, the *chibidaru* type has been used much less.

Other designer casks being made at the Chichibu cooperage include hybrid types, like casks made out of American white oak but fitted with mizunara or red oak heads. They were conceived as prag-matic solutions to problems but turned out to be successful experi-ments. Red oak is very porous, so making an entire cask out of red oak is a risky proposition. Mizunara, on the other hand, is scarce and expensive. Using these types of oak for the heads only made it possible to integrate some of the unique flavors they bring to the whisky mat-uration process without having to worry too much about the cost or risk involved.

ADVENTURES IN MIZUNARA

Ichiro is particularly keen on mizunara. He fell in love with the wood from the first time he tried a whisky matured in Japanese oak. But it's a precious and expensive natural resource, so getting hold of mizunara casks for his whiskies was a bit of a headache during the early years.

A few years into production, Ichiro decided to go straight to the source—that is to say, to Asahikawa in Hokkaido, home to the largest hardwood log auction in Japan—and to take matters into his own hands.

"I went to Hokkaido to purchase mizunara wood for the first time in 2010," Ichiro relates. "I went just once that year, but after that, we started to go regularly. The mizunara logs are sold in the wintertime,

Ichiro Akuto and staff at a hardwood auction in Hokkaido

between December and March. Since 2011, we've been going four times a year, on average." The logs are sold by blind auction. Each session consists of three days: two days to inspect the logs and one day when the actual bidding takes place. With around 5,000 logs to be sold on that one day, "it's not like Sotheby's," Ichiro explains. "People interested in a log submit their bid blind and the highest bidder wins. It all happens very quickly. Within 15 seconds of a log being called, the winner is announced. Based on that information, we can modify our bid for the next log we're interested in. Obviously, in the course of the day, prices tend to go up. Sometimes we get lucky, especially when a certain big whisky producer starting with S isn't around. Then, we can buy the wood we want very easily."

The mizunara auction is extremely competitive. Whisky producers aren't the only ones interested in purchasing wood, but they are at a disadvantage compared with high-end furniture makers and the like because they can't afford to compromise. They need the best and therefore most expensive wood. When Ichiro inspects the logs, he's looking for a number of things: "Of course, we have to avoid wood with defects, but it also has to be as straight as possible, have the proper diameter (i.e. between 40 and 60cm) and be tight-grained."

Buying wood is one thing; making casks, another. Initially, Ichiro had his logs cut into staves in Hokkaido, where they were then air-dried for about 3 years. Where these staves were going to be made into casks

Ichiro among the mizunara logs outside the cooperage

was still up in the air at the time. However, in the summer of 2013, it became clear that Ichiro would soon be able to take full control of the tree-to-cask process. At the age of 86, Mitsuo Saito felt it was time to hang up his hat. Ichiro purchased all the equipment and set up his own cooperage—a bold move for such a small-scale operation. It wasn't until October 2016, however, that the first mizunara cask entirely made in-house was completed: cask #6818.

It was a long journey to get to that point. The wood for cask #6818 had been bought in early 2011. Half a year later, the logs had been cut into staves in Hokkaido and left to air-dry for 2 years. Then, the staves had been moved to Chichibu where they were patiently waiting to be put to good use. The two young coopers at the distillery, Masashi Watanabe and Kenta Nagae, started by making two mizunara hogsheads. Mizunara has fewer tyloses—the balloon-like swellings that fill the vertical-running vessels of a tree—than American or European oak and is therefore much harder to use for watertight cooperage. When the coopers at Chichibu Distillery tested their first two casks, both turned out to leak all over the place. Rather than have two leakers, they moved staves around until they had one good cask—the "survivor," as they affectionately call it. Cask #6818 was filled with non-peated Chichibu spirit and moved to Warehouse 1, with cask #3826—the first cask made in-house at Chichibu—in the row behind it.

Clearly, though, this wasn't going to be workable in the long term: making two casks and ending up with one good one at best. Some coopers in Japan tackle the leaking issue by painting the outside of their mizunara casks with *kakishibu* (the fermented tannin juice of unripe, astringent persimmons), which was traditionally used in Japan to waterproof umbrellas, wrapping paper and so on. Ichiro has always been skeptical about this "solution." "It may be completely natural, but casks need to be able to breathe so just painting the outside to stop them from leaking may solve one problem but create another. To me, it sounds a bit like painting the outside of a cask with paraffin or something like that." Never one to cut corners or go for half-baked solutions, Ichiro was keen to work out a structural solution.

The problem with the staves used during the first attempts at making mizunara casks in-house was that they had been sawn rather than split. With wood rich in tyloses—e.g. American white oak—this is not a problem, as it can be sawn in a number of planes and still be impermeable, but more porous wood like mizunara demands to be split in specific planes following the vessels running through the wood if it is to be watertight. "Very straight wood can be cut by saw and left up in Hokkaido to air-dry," Ichiro points out, "but the poorer-quality logs we

Lines indicating the splits to be made

have to deal with ourselves, so they are moved to Chichibu. Most of those logs are a little bit twisted, so if you saw them into staves, you cut through the vessels in the wood and the casks will leak. However, if we split these logs by axe, we can make watertight casks out of them. For hogsheads, we need staves that are about 1m long, so we can take 1m portions that are relatively straight out of these 'imperfect' logs."

With just two coopers to take care of all the work on site, splitting logs manually would be a bit wearying. Ichiro and his staff came up with the idea of attaching an axe to one of the hoop-press machines at the cooperage and have since been using that to split logs into staves. "Once we started using those staves, we had no leaks on the outside whatsoever. We just observed some small leaks on the chime of certain staves, but those are easy to fix. We just put a small wooden nail in the wood and the leaking stops. Progress," Ichiro says with a smile.

Most of the mizunara casks made at Chichibu distillery are hogsheads. "There is an independent cooperage in Japan where we can buy mizunara puncheons if we need to," Ichiro clarifies, "but if we want mizunara hogsheads, well, we have to do it ourselves, so that's why we are focusing on that." Hogsheads are a bit harder to make, because mizunara staves are slightly thicker than normal (38mm) and hogsheads staves are by definition shorter than puncheon staves, so they can crack more easily when bent into shape. "If it were easy, we wouldn't have to do it," Ichiro says. "Then anyone could do it, and we could just pay *them* to do it."

The reason for doing as much as possible in-house is not just to be self-sufficient, but to have complete control over the quality of all stages of the whisky-making process. Ichiro had purchased mizunara casks from an independent cooperage in Japan before, but wasn't entirely satisfied with the quality. He noticed the grain wasn't as tight as he wanted it to be. Tighter-grained staves typically release and integrate their flavors and aromas more slowly into the whisky maturing so they are better for extended aging. This is because tight-grain barrels release a greater quantity of wood aromatics, whereas open-grained barrels tend to release a larger amount of tannins.

Traceability is important to Ichiro, too. All logs and staves are marked with a number, and he tries to make casks from one or a very limited number of logs as much as possible. "It's still early days, of course," Ichiro says, "but using these numbers, we can trace the wood back to the place where it grew and the part of the tree it came from."

Log splitting in progress

Staves and traceability

For Ichiro and his staff, the mindset seems to be that there is always a new adventure beckoning, a new challenge to take on. The next dream project was trying to secure local mizunara. "You can find mizunara trees in forests in Chichibu above 1,000m altitude," Ichiro points out. "We're not allowed to cut down trees in the national parks, but it *is* possible to purchase mizunara wood from privately-owned forests in the mountains around here." It took almost three years of exploring the mountains in Chichibu but the persistence paid off: in May 2018, Ichiro finally managed to get hold of some Chichibu-grown mizunara—enough to make a dozen casks further down the road, if lucky. The cost involved must be astronomical. "Oh yes," Ichiro says, "it is much, much more expensive than sourcing mizunara in Hokkaido, and that's expensive enough as it is, but there's no point in calculating the cost. This is a kind of R&D." Spirit was filled into Chichibu mizunara for the first time in 2019. At the time of writing, a total of 10 casks had been filled: seven with spirit distilled from local barley; three with spirit distilled from barley imported from the U.K. (all of it, non-peated).

Little by little, though, it does become possible to scale things up. Whereas initially the coopers would only be able to make a handful of mizunara casks from scratch, at the time of writing, the cooperage produces about 200 mizunara casks a year and about the same number of bourbon hogsheads. Meanwhile, they are also kept busy repairing casks.

Ichiro always takes the long-term view and is rarely swayed by pragmatic objections if he feels something is worth doing. Point in case: the mizunara trees he and his staff have planted outside the distillery. Those should be ready to be made into casks in 200 years or so.

Top: Ichiro inspecting a stave; bottom: Mizunara (left) and American white oak (right)

Raising the barrel

EXPRESSIONS

In terms of releases, Chichibu has been a paradigm changer. It started selling distillate aged for just a few months (Chichibu Newborn) the same year it fired up the stills. Almost all of the Chichibu single malt is sold in the form of single-cask bottlings. There are hundreds of those and counting. The prices they command on the secondary market are staggering, considering most of them are under ten years old.

The closest Chichibu comes to having "standard expressions" are the limited editions listed in the chart on page 252. Those used to be generally available with about 30 percent set aside for export. In recent years, the outturn tends to be split evenly between the domestic market and foreign markets. Getting your hands on one of those bottles has become a struggle, too. In Japan, they basically sell out the day they are released. Abroad, the situation is not much better.

The First Ten was a milestone. Released in November 2020, it was a vatting of 26 casks, mainly first-bourbon, but also with some mizunara and ex-sherry casks in the mix. A small portion of peated whisky was incorporated to help lift the flavors.

Top: Cooper Masashi Watanabe with his first cask; bottom: Samples taken while "making the cut"

Chichibu The First (2011); Chichibu On The Way (2013) and Chibidaru (2014)

EXPRESSION	VINTAGE / RELEASED IN	ABV	# BOTTLES (700ml)
The First	2008/2011	61.8%	7,400
The Floor Malted	2009/2012	50.5%	8,800
The Peated	2009/2012	50.5%	5,000
Port Pipe	2009/2013	54.5%	4,200
Chibidaru	2009/2013	53.5%	3,900
On The Way	/2013	58.5%	9,900
The Peated	2010/2013	53.5%	6,700
Chibidaru	2010/2014	53.5%	6,200
The Peated CS	2011/2015	62.5%	5,980
On The Way	/2015	55.5%	10,700
The Peated 2016	2012/2016	54.5%	6,350
IPA Cask Finish	/2017	57.5%	6,700
The Peated 10th Anniv.	2013/2018	55.5%	11,500
On The Way 2019	/2019	51.5%	11,000
The First Ten	/2020	50.5%	5,000
The Peated 2022	/2022	53.0%	11,000

An American in Chichibu

Japanese whisky distilleries are notoriously closed when it comes to giving people an insight into the nitty-gritty of their operations. Internships are unheard of. Unsurprisingly, Chichibu is the proverbial exception. Ichiro is happy to welcome beginning distillers and give them the chance to learn in the same way that he learned when he was starting out, namely, hands on. In March 2015, Ryan Friesen—at the time, head distiller of Blinking Owl Distillery in Santa Ana, California; since January 2022, in the same role at The Connacht Distillery in Mayo, Ireland—had the chance to spend some time at Chichibu distillery. For eight days, he was part of the team there. His observations as an outsider who became an insider for a week, written at our request, capture the ethos of the distillery and reveal what makes it such a special place.

Ichiro has command of all the basic prerequisites to being a good distiller. He understands the whole product stream from grain to consumer. His quality control is consistent, with every fermentation and every distillation tested for metrics he has arrived at through what I would imagine are his own technical experiences and personal preferences.

The distillery is clean. It seems like that should go without saying, but it doesn't always and it's worth noting. Staff takes specific care to manage housekeeping during the day.

Ichiro spent the extra money to have the distillery hard-piped. Again, this isn't always the case. In fact, in my experience in the U.S. craft scene, it's rather rare that a distiller has the ability to hard-pipe. It's an upfront expense that pays off in labor savings, consistency, and sanitation.

Doing a Scotch malt-style mash is an exercise in control: temperature control, water flow control, timing and sensory determination. The mashmen are all trained on the same procedures and metrics, and while Ichiro only uses a few varieties of malt, he appears to know how to get the most out of his starch conversions.

Chichibu uses closed-top oak vats for fermentation, which add complexity to the fermentation along with difficulty in maintaining regular fermentations. The mashmen seem to have a pretty intuitive understanding of their fermentation tanks, being that each one has unique characteristics due to the nature and variability of oak. Different vats present different qualities and Ichiro's staff knows which ones to use for which product. Very little is left to chance at the distillery.

Even though the distillery is located in a somewhat remote location, resources are nonetheless precious. Ichiro has efficient boilers, good water practices, and uses hot spent effluent from the morning stripping run to preheat subsequent runs—big time and cost savings for energy consumption.

As with the added expense of having a QC [quality control] lab and hard-piping the distillery, Ichiro is one of the very few small craft distillers anywhere that I know of who has two coopers on staff. They are studying under a lifelong now retired cooper and not only manage the warehouses but also repair the barrel inventory and make new casks from scratch. Having a cooper on staff puts Ichiro into a category of small distillers not common outside of Scotland, if even there.

The dedication to the cut was the second most impressive thing I observed during my stay at Chichibu distillery. Ichiro himself starts every morning providing notes to the stillmen on the previous day's runs. Ichiro's palate holds the secret to the flavor of Ichiro's Malt, but it's no mystery why he is able to make good choices repeatedly. The daily tasting notes are shared with staff and there is a conversation about when the cut was made and why. Though I don't speak a word of Japanese, I was present during the morning notes and was able to understand the importance that is placed on the cut, and the care Ichiro puts into communicating his notes to the stillmen who actually make the cut at the spirit locker. To get those samples for Ichiro's morning routine, the cuts are monitored with almost fanatical precision. Stillmen take samples starting slowly, and increasingly in rapid succession as each run nears the cut point. Time and temperature notes are taken and the appropriate samples surrounding the actual cut are saved for further tastings. This process is a study in how a distiller is able to develop his or her palate and reproduce a consistent product on a regular basis.

The final piece of my experience, and the one that impressed me the most, wasn't technical, but rather cultural. I don't mean the differences in Japanese and Western or American culture, but the culture Ichiro has created at the distillery. Getting buy-in to what you are trying to accomplish is one of the most difficult and important pieces of running any organization, and Ichiro manages to pull it off. Everyone at Chichibu distillery, from the ladies in the bottling room, to the brand ambassador, to the mashmen and stillmen, has the same goal: making quality spirit. And Ichiro supports the people who work for him not just by giving them a job, but by inspiring them to love whisky and the process by which it is created.

Venture Whisky is a growing company with a young staff. It's hard to get a job at the distillery, but once you are there, if you pay attention and work hard, there is opportunity to learn the trade and grow with the company. I was fortunate enough to join Ichiro and his staff at a couple of tasting sessions accompanied by a nice dinner. Each staff member is invited to participate and everyone takes it seriously, even though it's still a good time. The group does blind tastings and takes notes and shares their experience of the lineup. It's an undervalued exercise, at least in distilleries I've visited, and I hope to replicate the model at home. But it's more than buying his staff dinner and drinks. The staff works hard and long hours. It's a reciprocal relationship. Veteran staff members sometimes even get to travel and learn more about malting or coopering, etc. All of this internal culture is transferred into the spirit itself, and I think it shows. The buy-in Ichiro gets, at least from this outsider's perspective, isn't fostered to help Ichiro sell more whisky, it's there to help everyone at Chichibu distillery make better whisky.

Ryan Friesen
December 2015

Okayama Distillery
(Miyashita Shuzo Co., Ltd.)

Miyashita Shuzo is a multitasking liquor producer based in Okayama City that entered the whisky field in the wake of the highball boom. Doing so wasn't an earth-shattering development. The brewing and distilling know-how and much of the infrastructure necessary to make whisky was already on hand. It was just a matter of taking a few extra steps.

Founded in 1915 as a sake brewery, Miyashita Shuzo expanded its operations to include shochu making in 1983, before becoming one of the pioneers in Japanese craft beer following the relaxation of brewery license regulations in 1994. In 2003, they started single-distilling some of their hoppy beer in a shochu still. They filled this into American white oak and kept a close watch on it. Encouraged by the way in which it was developing, they started thinking about producing whisky, the idea being they could launch a new product to celebrate the company's 100th anniversary in 2015.

Miyashita acquired a license to make whisky in 2011 and they immediately went to work, using the equipment that was already in place. Mashing and fermentation was done in the equipment used for beer making; distillation was carried out under low pressure (i.e., low temperature) in their stainless steel shochu still by running it twice.

Whisky distillation and stainless steel are awkward bedfellows, so when 2015 came and went and no product was launched, the assumption was things hadn't turned out quite as expected on the whisky front. Doppo Beer Spirits, released in 2013 after 10 years in wood, was a hit, but distilling hoppy beer and making whisky were clearly

Facing page: The hybrid still at Okayama Distillery

two different things. The staff at Miyashita must have realized this, too, because by July 2015, a brand-new copper hybrid still, manufactured by Arnold Holstein, had been installed on the premises. It's been used for whisky making (as well as gin and vodka production) ever since.

Originally, the hybrid still was housed in a somewhat cramped room in the beer brewery. By mid-2017, a stylish new visitor center/restaurant/shop had been constructed on the premises (Doppo Kan) and a tiny stand-alone stillhouse was built.

The Distillery

Mash tun:	stainless steel, mash tun and lauter tun (1.5kl)
Washbacks:	4 stainless steel (4kl), with temperature control
Stills:	2011-7.2015 stainless steel still (1kl)
	7.2015 hybrid still (1.5kl), Holstein

With more sunny days and fewer rainy days than most other prefectures, Okayama is known as the "Land of Sunshine" (*hare no kuni*). It's also a traditional barley-growing region. In spite of the considerable extra expense, Okayama distillery is keen on using local barley. They source a variety known as 'Sky Golden' from farmers in the region, then send it to a malting company in Tochigi (a bit of a trek at 466 miles/750 km) and then send it back to Okayama. All in all, this makes using Okayama barley roughly five times as expensive as using imported barley. Since they can't source enough locally, half of their malted barley is imported from Germany. No other distillery in Japan comes even close to this in terms of domestic barley use. (One of Miyashita's mottos is "think globally, act locally" and they clearly walk the talk.)

The underground water used runs 328 feet/100 meters under the Asahi riverbed and is similar to the famous Omachi no Reisen water, which runs near the distillery and is included by the Ministry of Environment on its list of "Japan's 100 Remarkable Waters." For one batch, 375kg of malted barley is used. The bulk of the production is non-peated. Occasionally, medium-peated (20ppm) malt is used.

Milling, mashing and fermentation takes place in the beer brewery. In 2019, a new Schulz mash tun and lauter tun was installed. This made it possible to increase whisky production slightly, from 7klpa to 10klpa per year—still a tiny volume, even by craft whisky standards.

Fermentation is temperature controlled (at 68°F/20°C) and unusually long (seven days). Ale yeast and sake yeast are used. The wash is then double-distilled in the hybrid still. Receiver strength is very high, at around 80%abv. This is then brought down to 60% before the new-make is filled into casks and matured in a racked warehouse on site.

A variety of cask types is used. This includes the usual suspects —ex-sherry and ex-bourbon—as well as ex-brandy and virgin oak mizunara casks. The distillery also uses hybrid casks—for example, casks with oak staves but heads made from cedar, sakura or Japanese chestnut (*kuri*) wood.

EXPRESSIONS

The first Single Malt Okayama was released in 2017 and since then a handful of bottlings have been produced. Unfortunately, the distillery's offerings are almost never seen in the wild. The company occasionally drip-feeds some—typically 30 bottles—via its online store (and always via ballot). Even at bars in Japan, it is rarely seen.

In July 2019, a vatting of whisky matured in three different cask types (brandy, sherry and mizunara) was released under the name Triple Cask (43%abv). This expression was well received and picked up a couple of prestigious awards abroad. Other notable releases include Sherry Cask Debut (58%abv), a single-cask bottling for posh department store Takashimaya, released in the fall of 2019 and Sakura Cask Debut (43%abv), released in March 2021 in 200ml bottles to make it (marginally) more available.

In late 2021, a set of three bottles was released as the Okayama Collection 2021. Consisting of a Japanese Cedar Cask Strength, a Chestnut Cask Strength and a Bourbon Cask-Strength (3, 4 and 5 years old, respectively and all bottled at 60%abv), only 30 sets were made available by ballot at a whopping 220,000 yen per set. In the same vein, there was also a 5yo Mizunara Cask Strength, bottled exclusively for Takashimaya.

岡山

OKAYAMA

JAPANESE
SINGLE MALT WHISKY

岡山県木「桃」

岡山

OKAYAMA

JAPANESE
SINGLE MALT WHISKY
40% alc./vol. ウイスキー
700ml

岡山県木「桃」

Nukada Distillery
(Kiuchi Shuzo)

Nukada Distillery is the most under-the-radar whisky distillery in Japan. Even among die-hard whisky fans in Japan, chances are the name will not ring a bell. Mention "Hitachino Nest," however, and people will know exactly who you're talking about. Hitachino Nest is the beer brand of Kiuchi Shuzo. Its iconic owl logo is a familiar sight at craft beer bars in Japan, but it also has a big presence abroad, particularly in the U.S. where Hitachino Nest is almost synonymous with "Japanese craft beer."

Kiuchi Shuzo was established in 1823 by Gihei Kiuchi, the headman of Konosu village in Ibaraki prefecture. Under the first seven generations, it was a traditional sake company like many others in the country. Under the eighth generation (current CEO Toshiyuki Kiuchi and his brother Yoichi) the scope of the company's liquor production was widened and things got exciting. In 1996, they launched a beer division. It made business sense to do so after lawmakers had opened up the beer industry to small-scale producers. Sake brewing is traditionally limited to the winter season, whereas beer's peak season is summer.

In 2003, a distillation facility was set up to aid with recycling and to reduce waste. The first product made was shochu distilled from sake lees. In 2008, the main beer brewery was moved to the Nukada site, located about 2.5 miles/4km from the original sake brewery. A larger brewhouse was built on the premises in 2011. The company also has a vineyard next to the brewery.

Kiuchi Shuzo started making whisky in 2016, but Toshiyuki Kiuchi insists that this was not in response to the Japanese whisky boom.

Facing page: The hybrid still at Nukada Distillery

The original Kiuchi brewery site

His plans to make whisky go back more than a decade, when Japanese whisky was in a slump. To understand his motivation, we have to rewind the clock even further, to 1900. In that year, a farmer by the name of Ushigoro Kaneko created the first Japanese variety of beer barley by crossing Shikoku (a Japanese landrace strain used for noodle making) with Golden Melon (a two-row barley variety originating in Northern Europe). Kaneko was pleased with the result and named his new barley Kaneko Golden. It became popular in Japan before the World War II, but after the war the government consolidated the beer industry and encouraged a switch to barley varieties that were more economical to grow. Further losing ground to cheaper barley imported from abroad, Kaneko Golden disappeared in the 1960s. In 2004, Toshiyuki Kiuchi obtained 16 seedlings from the Department of Agricultural History and started a revival project in cooperation with the local association of young farmers. The 2009 harvest yielded enough to start brewing again with Kaneko Golden and to put a product on the market (Hitachino Nest Nipponia).

In the course of working on the Kaneko Golden revival project, there was quite a bit of "junk barley," as Toshiyuki Kiuchi calls it. Some

Hitachino Nippponia

of the barley wasn't suitable for beer making because of the high protein content, which can cause a beer to throw a haze, reduce mash efficiency, decrease a beer's stability and drive up the total processing costs. Kiuchi's thinking was that there was one way to stop this "junk barley" from going to waste and that was to distill it. Kiuchi was a whisky fan and had visited Scotland many times, so it didn't take him long to realize that there was an opportunity to make something good out of a bad situation: turning the "junk barley" into whisky. The heavy investment in a bigger brewhouse on the Nukada site delayed the start of the whisky project for several years. In 2015, a corner of the second floor of the packaging warehouse was turned into a compact distillery. Finally, they were ready to start making whisky.

The Distillery

Mash tun:	stainless steel, lauter (at the beer brewery)
Washback:	1 stainless steel (12kl)
Still:	1 hybrid still (1kl)
	indirect heating (steam)

The first distillation at Nukada Distillery took place on February 10, 2016. After the very first batch, which was a regular whisky mash, some old beer stock was distilled. Kiuchi's spirits license also covers distilled beer. They already have a product in the market that falls under this category, Kiuchi no Shizuku. This is made from their white ale, which is distilled once (in their shochu still, not the new hybrid whisky still) and matured for one month in oak barrels with the addition of coriander, hops and orange peel before more white ale is added. This is distilled again, matured for a further six months and then bottled at 43%abv.

After the initial period of distilling of old beer stock, whisky making was resumed. What follows relates to the latter, not the former.

The first step of the whisky-making process, the mashing, invariably takes place at the brewery. Initially, the malted barley used was mostly German two-row barley. For some of the earlier mashes, Japanese-grown raw wheat was used. After a while, the staff at Nukada Distillery started using Sachiho Golden, a Japanese malting barley cultivar released in 2005 and grown in Tochigi prefecture.

Two mashes of around 4.5kl are done in a row and transferred to a large 12kl tank near the distillery, where the mash is left to ferment for around three days. In general, dry distillers yeast is used. According to Toshiyuki Kiuchi, their Belgian ale yeast was used for some batches. This contributes a subtle smoky flavor to the spirit. Kiuchi feels this is an interesting take on "smoky whisky." Rather than using peated barley, the smoky note is created during the fermentation.

After fermentation, the wash is sent to three holding tanks at the distillery (roughly 1.4kl each) that act as a queue. Then it goes into the still. The distillation equipment was designed by the team at Kiuchi and manufactured in China to their specifications. The still is of the hybrid type, i.e. a pot still with a column attached to it. These sorts of stills were quite popular at craft distilleries in the U.S., but in Japan, Nukada Distillery was among the first to use this type. The pot still has a 1kl capacity but is only filled to about 700 liters for each distillation so that the wash doesn't touch the top of the pot or get into the lyne arm.

The first year of production, whisky was produced by single-distilling the wash, using the pot in conjunction with the column. In 2017, the staff switched to double distillation. During both runs, the column is skipped. (The cynics among us may wonder why the column is there then—the answer is: it's used when making gin.) After a few wash runs, the combined low wines are redistilled in the same pot.

In terms of maturation, the net is cast wide and experimentation is the order of the day. Toshiyuki Kiuchi has a soft spot for sherried whiskies—Macallan in particular—so quite a bit of the new-make has been filled into sherry butts. Oak casks fitted with heads made from other wood types (sakura, i.e. Japanese cherry wood, for example) have been used, too.

The output at Nukada Distillery is tiny and whisky is made very infrequently. The annual production volume varies but usually no more than 7.2klpa is produced, and

some years considerably less. When Kiuchi Shuzo decided to establish a much larger stand-alone whisky distillery near Mt. Tsukuba (see the chapter on Yasato Distillery for that story), the attention shifted to that project and since 2019, very little has happened on the whisky front at Nukada Distillery. (They're still busy distilling beer and making gin there, though.)

At the time of writing, no whisky had been produced since February 2021. The distillery still has its whisky license, though, so never say never.

EXPRESSIONS

Atypically for the new wave of Japanese craft distilleries, Kiuchi Shuzo has resisted the temptation (or need) to release new-make or "new-born" whisky in their first few years.

On April 1, 2019—and no, this wasn't an April Fool's joke—a limited edition canned highball (9%abv) was released. The whisky used was both malt and grain distilled at Nukada distillery, aged in ex-sherry and ex-wine casks for 3 years.

In the spring of 2022, Kiuchi Shuzo launched its Hinomaru Whisky brand. The products released so far have all been blends of whisky distilled at Nukada and Yasato distillery, but maybe one day, whisky enthusiasts will get the chance to try some Nukada whisky on its own.

Facing page: A cask fitted with sakura heads and sample indicating the impact after a mere 18 months; above: Various types of Nukada whisky (unreleased, for tasting purposes only)

The home of Sasanokawa Shuzo

Asaka Distillery
(Sasanokawa Shuzo)

Sasanokawa Shuzo, founded in 1765, is a liquor producer based in Koriyama, Fukushima. Sake and shochu are their bread and butter, but even though the name may not ring a bell among fans of the amber nectar, they're not exactly new to the whisky game.

Immediately after World War II, the scarcity of rice threw a bit of a wrench in the works at many a sake brewery. At the same time, the Allied occupation of Japan meant there was huge demand for whisky from the Americans and Brits. The people at Sasanokawa put two and two together and applied for a whisky-making license in 1945, which was granted the next year. They immediately got to work and, quality being irrelevant at that point, made do with what they could put their hands on and what they could concoct. Surplus industrial alcohol from the war effort was colored, flavored and mixed with other types of booze in ways we wouldn't want to know too much about today. Their field was the lowest grade of blended whisky (3rd grade, which became 2nd grade in 1953), meaning malt whisky as a component was not a necessity from a legal point of view.

As the economy recovered, so did people's palates. Sasanokawa wanted to up their game and, among other things, tried their hand at making their own malt whisky in makeshift stills. In the 1960s, apparently they put a still together by taking the bottom of an enamel tank and fitting it with a stainless steel swan neck. Sales weren't always great throughout the '60s and '70s but the structure of the company kept their whisky business alive during the hard times. Sake making took up 200 days of the year, so rather than having the staff while away the remaining 150 days, they were kept busy making whisky.

In the 1980s, there was another DIY attempt. This time around, the bottom of the still was made out of stainless steel and the top from copper. Mercifully, that still only lasted about five years. While it's hard to imagine what sort of spirit would have come off this sort of equipment, they did well enough to become one of the three big players of the 1980s *ji-whisky* boom (together with Hombo Shuzo in the west and Toa Shuzo in the east; see page 70 for more on this). Serendipity may have played a bit of a role in this, though.

The brand-new Asaka Distillery logo

In 1980, someone at Sasanokawa had the clever idea of importing whisky in casks from Scotland. They weren't primarily interested in the whisky. It was the wood they were after. Someone did the math and came to the conclusion that it was cheaper to buy casks from Scotland with whisky in them than to buy new casks. Initially, 60 casks were ordered. The whisky in them was mixed with Sasanokawa's homemade malt whisky and then returned to wood. In 1981, there was a spike in sales. Coincidence? Hard to tell. One thing is for sure, from this point on, imported Scotch malt whisky started playing a major role in their blending operations. The missing piece of the puzzle—the blending alcohol—was produced in-house and distilled from molasses to 96%abv in a continuous still.

Towards the end of the 1980s, the whisky situation was starting to look grim in Japan. Sasanokawa slowly dialed down their whisky production but they had enough stock maturing in the warehouses to keep their whiskies on the shelves of liquor stores over the next couple of decades. Other producers weren't that lucky. Toa Shuzo was sold in 2004 but the new owners weren't interested in the whisky part of the business (Hanyu). Sasanokawa played a crucial role in helping Ichiro Akuto save the Hanyu stock by providing warehousing facilities for the remaining 400 casks from 2004 until 2008, by which time Ichiro had built his own distillery in Chichibu. At Sasanokawa, only ex-bourbon barrels were used for maturation up until that point, so when Ichiro came

The distillery building

with his hogsheads, puncheons and sherry butts, something needed to be done about the racks. Up until this day, you can still see how some of the racks in the Sasanokawa warehouse were modified to fit the Hanyu casks.

With demand for Japanese whisky at an all-time hysteric high but supply pretty low, Sasanokawa decided to set up a proper malt whisky distillery in 2015, the 250th anniversary of the company. No DIY stills this time—thankfully.

The Distillery

Mash tun:	stainless steel (1.7kl), semi-lauter
Washbacks:	5 Oregon pine (3kl)
Stills:	1 pair (wash still 2kl, spirit still 1kl), Miyake
	indirect heating (steam percolators)
	both with descending lyne arms and shell-and-tube condensers

Top: The pot stills, still wrapped in plastic; bottom: Wash run in progress

Sasanokawa looked into ordering pot stills from Forsyths in Scotland but quickly discovered there was a four-year wait. Domestic maker Miyake could get the job done in less than a year, so that proved to be an easy, though not necessarily cheaper, decision. By December 2015, the two small pot stills had been installed in a vacant warehouse that had been retooled as a compact distillery. All processes prior to maturation, from milling to distillation, take place under one roof.

Nobody at Sasonokawa had any actual whisky-making experience, so the three people assigned to whisky production spent two weeks training at Chichibu Distillery in March 2016. Test distillations were carried out during the summer of 2016 (May to September). October of that year saw the official start of whisky making at Asaka Distillery.

Asaka is a small distillery. Yearly production volume is around 50,000lpa. Malted barley is imported from the U.K. and the bulk of production is non-peated. The last month of each season (which accounts for about 10% of the total production volume) is set aside for heavily-peated (50ppm) production.

Per batch, 400kg of malted barley is used. For the mashing, only 2 waters are used. For the first three seasons, fermentation took place in enamel-coated steel tanks of the type used in sake production. In mid-2019, these were replaced with 5 Orgeon pine washbacks. The default yeast type used is distillers yeast, but experiments with other types of yeast (e.g. sake yeast) have been run over the years. The fermentation time is 90 hours.

Top: Making the cut; bottom: Mashwoman Minami Sakakura stirring the yeast in

Distillation takes place in small twin pots (2kl and 1kl, respectively) with downward lyne arms and shell-and-tube condensers. This results in about 200l of new-make at around 71%abv per batch. This is proofed down to 63.5%abv and then filled into a variety of casks for maturation in racked warehouses on site.

EXPRESSIONS

When they entered the whisky field, in the late 1940s, Sasanokawa decided to market their products under the brand name Cherry. This may seem like an odd choice—and customers actually wondered if the whisky was made from cherries—but it's not totally random. The company used to be called Yamazakura Shuzo, which translates as "mountain" (yama) plus "cherry tree/blossom" (sakura). Hoping to contribute to a return to traditional Japanese beauty after the war years, the company settled on the image of the cherry blossom but wanted something that sounded hip, hence, "Cherry Whisky." Prior to setting up Asaka Distillery, Sasanokawa added a slightly more premium range of blends and so-called "pure malts" (i.e. blended malts) to its whisky lineup and for this they reverted to the Japanese Yamazakura. The Asaka single malt expressions are also bottled under this brand name.

The first single malt expression (Asaka The First, 1,500btls) was released in December 2019. A year later, the distillery showed its peaty side for the first time with Asaka The First Peated (2,000btls). Like its predecessor, this was aged for 3 years in first-fill ex-bourbon barrels and bottled at 50%abv. The peated expression was also awarded World's Best Label Design at the 2022 World Whiskies Awards. And the company went home with another high-profile award at the same competition: their Yamazakura Sherry Wood Reserve (a vatting of malt whisky produced at Asaka distillery and malt whisky made by an undisclosed craft whisky producer in Japan; 50%abv, 440btls) won World's Best Blended Malt. As so often in the world of Japanese whisky, by the time the awards were announced, both products were no longer available.

Hard graft, art & craft

The *kamidana* ("shelf for the Gods") at Saburomaru Distillery

Saburomaru Distillery
(Wakatsuru Shuzo)

Wakatsuru Shuzo traces its history back to 1862, when a sake brewery was established in the town of Tonami, in Toyama prefecture. The area is well known for its top-quality rice and what has been described as silky, pure water, so making sake there was a no-brainer. In May 1925, Kotaro Inagaki became the second president of the company. Kotaro was an enterprising fellow. It was under him that the company would start to expand its operations to include cider, port wine and whisky.

In 1939, rice supplies came under government control. By 1942, rice and other staple foods (wheat, barley and rye) were monopolized by the government. For sake brewers, this was obviously a serious problem. After the end of the Pacific War, many sake breweries looked into making other types of liquor to remain solvent. Wakatsuru Shuzo was one of those companies.

In September 1947, Kotaro Inagaki established the Wakatsuru Fermentation Research Centre. The initial research focused on using sunchoke (Jerusalem artichoke) to produce alcohol. A shochu production license was obtained in February 1949, and research continued during the years that followed. In July 1952, the company acquired a whisky and port wine production license. The first "whisky"—don't ask how it was made, you don't want to know—was launched the following year under the brand name Sunshine. The public was asked to come up with a name and they settled on "Sunshine Whisky," to symbolize a new start after the war: "Let's make the sun rise again in Japan, which lost everything during the war, with this spirit that is made from water, air and sunshine," a document from the time proclaims.

On May 11, 1953, a fire broke out in the alcohol plant, destroying almost all of the facilities. Undeterred, Kotaro Inagaki reconstructed the brewery/distillery and in September of the same year, he installed a type of state-of-the-art continuous still imported from France known as an "allospas." In 1959, it was moved to the northern end of the site. This still was used to make whisky until the late 1980s.

It's easy to get the wrong idea about the scale of Wakatsuru's whisky operation. It was very minor indeed. In the early 1960s, they were selling just 140 bottles (1.8l) a year. Even at the height of whisky consumption in Japan (1983)—which coincided with the *ji-whisky* boom, of which they were an exponent; see page 70 for more—only 3,000 bottles of Sunshine found their way to the consumer in a year. Sales were very sluggish, so there was more whisky maturing in the warehouse than there was leaving the company. Because of this, the malt whisky that was used in the blends became progressively older. In the 1980s, some of the whisky being mixed in had been aged for 20 years, which was unheard of in those days, certainly for bottom-shelf whiskies. In spite of that, Sunshine had a reputation for being "nose-bendingly wild."

The renovated distillery building

The Distillery

Mash tun:	stainless steel, lauter (1t)
Washbacks:	4 enamel-coated steel (6.6kl), temperature control
	2 Douglas fir (6kl)
Still:	1 pair (wash still and spirit still 3kl), Oigo Works
	both with descending lyne arms and shell-and-tube condensers
	wash still parallel direct steam injection and indirect heating (percolators), spirit still indirect heating (percolators)

Around 1990, a whisky distillery was set up in the currently used building (which dates from the early 1920s). In 2016, Takahiko Inagaki—representing the fifth generation of the family to play a leading role in the business—decided to breathe new life into the whisky side of the business. In his late twenties at the time, Takahiko had a new vision for the distillery, the only whisky distillery in the Hokuriku region. What he had inherited, though, was makeshift equipment in a rickety old two-story wooden building. Clearly, a lot of work needed to be done. Takahiko Inagaki initiated a refurbishment program through crowdfunding and, with the support of 463 people, managed to raise over 39 million yen.

I had the pleasure of visiting the distillery in the summer of 2016, i.e. prior to the refurbishment. To say that it was unusual is an understatement. At the time, the whisky-making process started on the upper floor, where the staff manually dumped one ton of milled malted barley into the mash tun—resulting in a thick cloud of "flour dust." The wort was then transferred to one of six enamel-coated stainless-steel tanks where ale yeast was added. After three days' fermentation, the wash was transferred to an alumite pot still and distilled once, after which the low wines were put back into the same still and distilled for a second time. The spirit was then filled into heavily-charred ex-bourbon casks at 63.5%abv and moved to a warehouse next to the distillery building. Interestingly, sake lees were also temporarily kept in this air-conditioned warehouse so the smell that pervaded the air was not your typical whisky-warehouse aroma. At the time of my visit in 2016, annual

The mash tun

production was around 2,000 liters—barely enough to fill 10 barrels—and there were 60 casks in the warehouse, which was the entire inventory from over five decades of whisky making.

Since the crowdfunding campaign, a lot has changed at Saburomaru Distillery. Takahiko Inagaki's approach has been to improve something or other each year, so rather than walking through the production process in sequence, we'll take a look at how things have changed year on year since 2017.

Initially, the focus was on restoring the building. Within the company, there was a discussion to dismantle it, but some were reluctant to do so as its architecture was considered to be of historic value. By July 2017, the building had been completely restored and opened to the public.

Whisky production at the company has traditionally been a summer activity, when there was no work to be done—and, importantly, no water needed—for sake production. The first couple of whisky-making seasons after the renovation spanned 3–4 months (June to September). This has gradually been expanded, and now Saburomaru distillery is in operation for a little over 6 months. During the 2021 season, 160 mashes were done. For 2022, the target was 200 mashes. In the large scheme of things, this is still small-scale but for Saburomaru distillery it represents an enormous growth in a relatively short period of time.

The other big project for 2017 was bringing copper into the distillation process. The old 1kl alumite pot still was fitted with a new copper neck and a copper condenser. In this condition, it was used for two seasons (2017–2018)—not a perfect solution, but a step in the right direction, nonetheless.

In 2018, the mashing was addressed. The old mash tun was a DIY affair. It had been made in-house by remodeling a rice immersion tank used for sake-making in the late-'50s and early-'60s. It was far from efficient—both in terms of labor efficiency and quality of the wort produced—and progress was well overdue. In May 2018, a brand-new computer-controlled mash tun manufactured by Miyake Industries was installed and the quality of the wort improved dramatically. The old one was kept on the premises so that visitors could see what life was like before.

The new Miyake mash tun is a stainless-steel full-lauter tun, and the first one—in Japan, at least—with a pinwheel masher. The exterior of the mash tun was finished using Takaoka copper. Two waters are used for the mashing—the first 63.5°C, the second 79°C—resulting in 5kl of clear wort.

The new warehouse on site, almost like Islay

Takahiko Inagaki (left) with two members of his team and the Zemon pot stills

In 2019, Saburomaru Distillery went the whole hog and decided to replace its single remodeled pot still with new twin pots. The distillery is located near the city of Takaoka, which happens to be the biggest production center of copperware in Japan, with a history going back 400 years. Takahiko felt it made sense to make the stills locally, even though Takaoka copperware involves casting rather than hammering. Pot stills being fairly large, Takahiko reached out to Oigo Works, a local company that specializes in the production of temple bells and the only company capable of creating large-scale bells up to 50 tons. He figured the challenge of making the world's first cast copper pot stills would be right up their alley.

"The alloy used in casting consists of 90% copper and 8% tin," Takahiko explains, "so we did some research in collaboration with a local university to see what the effects on the character of the spirit would be." He had three tiny stills built, each the size of a whisky bottle: one in stainless steel, one cast from the alloy, and one hammered from copper sheets. These were tested with a stainless-steel condenser and a copper condenser, and a sensory analysis was carried out on the resulting spirit. "As expected, stainless steel was a big no—much too

Inside Oigo Works

sulphury—but, comparing the spirit made using the other two stills, both in combination with the copper condenser, we discovered that the cast still actually resulted in a slightly less feinty and meaty spirit compared with the hammered copper still."

The rest is history, as they say. Oigo Works created the stills in about 6 months' time. I had the pleasure of visiting the factory shortly after the stills had been completed. "Because you're not dealing with bells, where sound is a consideration," general manager Shohei Oigo explained, "for a pot still, you can just make molds for one half of the still, cast twice and then put the two halves together." Imagine a chocolatier making a big Easter egg and you'll get the picture. This is also the reason why both the wash and the spirit still are identical.

There are certain advantages to using cast stills. According to Shohei Oigo, "the walls are about twice as thick as those of sheet-hammered copper stills—about 12mm at the thickest points, disregarding the bottom which is 40mm, so they are very durable and have high heat retention, so they are very energy efficient. Parts can easily be replaced in case of wear and tear, as we have the molds anyway. And dreaming out loud, you could easily make different parts and interchange them

—for example, a different type of head, or an upward lyne arm—and create different types of spirit that way."

"We wanted a rich spirit, so we went for a shallow lantern head and a short downward lyne arm," Takahiko relates. "One batch is split in half, so we charge the wash still with 2.5kl of wash. The low wines of 3 wash still runs combined with the heads and tails of the previous second distillation go into the spirit still and that results in about 800l of new make. During the first distillation, we want to recover a lot of flavor compounds so we use parallel direct steam injection and indirect steam heating. For the second distillation, we only use indirect steam and distill slowly to refine the desired character of the spirit."

The first distillation using the new so-called Zemon stills took place on June 20, 2019. Comparing the distillate made in the Zemon stills— "Zemon" is the local nickname for Oigo Works—with that made in the hybrid alumite-copper still used the previous two seasons, the difference is clear: the Zemon new make is much more chiseled, estery and complex.

The other project for 2019 was the construction of a large racked warehouse—with room for about 1,200 casks—on the premises. Like elsewhere on the site, it's a mix of old and new. The roof of what used to be a beverage warehouse was kept and new walls were built. The exterior features stark white walls with the distiller's name in big black capitals—a bit like on Islay and not coincidentally so. Interestingly, the roof is fitted with a water system to keep the temperature down in summer.

In 2020, the fermentation was addressed. Up until 2016, ale yeast was used for the fermentation. From 2017 onwards, ale yeast was used in conjunction with distillers yeast and the fermentation time was increased from 3 to 4 days. The fermentation took place in old enamel-coated open-top sake tanks that had been fitted with a system that allowed water to trickle down the exterior. For the first day, the water system would be used to keep the temperature under 33°C and a switcher used to control the foaming. Looking to dial up the lactic fermentation, a single Douglas fir washback was installed in the summer of 2020. The initial fermentation still took place in enamel tanks, but for the final 24 hours, the wash was moved to the wooden washback. In March 2022, one more Douglas fir washback was added and from that season onwards the fermentation regime for each batch was 2 days in enamel and 2 days in wood.

The two wooden washbacks

One of the fermenters (with the shower function engaged)

The other project for 2020 focused on the raw material used, the malted barley. Saburomaru distillery is unique in Japan in its exclusive focus on heavily-peated whisky production. Until 2020, the malted barley imported from Scotland was of the mainland type (50ppm). In 2020, the distillery managed to source some malted barley smoked with Islay peat (45ppm). That year, production was split half-and-half between the mainland peat type and the Islay peat type.

Also in 2020, a very small amount of locally grown (i.e. in Toyama prefecture) barley was used. To malt the barley, the facilities of nearby Unazuki Beer were used. This barley was, of course, non-peated. It was used at the distillery for some limited production with the local barley providing an accent of sorts. The mashbill used was 95% of the usual heavily-peated barley and 5% of the local Toyama barley. From 2021, the distillery also started using some super-heavily-peated barley (80ppm). That year also marked the first year that production was limited to Islay-peated barley exclusively. The idea was to do so henceforth, but the vagaries of the global supply chain during the pandemic made it impossible to stick to that plan in 2022. At the start of the 2022 season (in May of that year), the malted barley imported from abroad hadn't arrived yet, so 10 mashes using domestically-sourced non-peated barley were done. It was also necessary to use some mainland-peated barley (50ppm) again, in addition to Islay-peated barley (45ppm and 86ppm). Preparations have been made to ensure a steady supply of Islay-peated barley from 2023 onwards.

In 2023, the "upgrade" project on the agenda was the removal of one of the enamel tanks—three being plenty now that there are two wooden washbacks as well. This will free up space to install a hot liquor tank and switch to the textbook "three waters" system for the mashing. With peated production, the third water has a marked impact on the phenol content of the wort, so again, it will be interesting to see how this will affect the profile of the Saburomaru new-make.

The changes, year on year, can be a bit difficult to keep track of. The diagram below may help.

SABUROMARU TECHNICAL OVERVIEW

YEAR	MALT	MASH TUN	WASHBACKS	YEAST	FERM. TIME	STILL(S)
2016		modified sake tank		ale yeast	3 days	alumite
2017	50PPM		enamel			modified alumite
2018						
2019				ale yeast + distillers yeast	4 days	
2020	50PPM Islay 45PPM	Miyake lauter tun				
2021	Islay 45PPM Islay 80PPM		enamel + wood			Zemon
2022	0PPM 50PPM Islay 45PPM Islay 86PPM					

In terms of the wood used for maturation, the regime at Saburomaru is around 80 percent ex-bourbon, 10 percent ex-sherry and 10 percent "other." The latter category includes ex-bourbon caks fitted with local mizunara heads. The distillery has been working with a woodworker in the nearby town of Inami since October 2018 to get some casks modified with/made from Toyama-grown mizunara. There is never going to be huge number of those, but it's all part and parcel of connecting with the local community and the resources at hand. Since June 2022, the cooperage also specializes in creating hogsheads from ex-bourbon barrels with new American white oak/mizunara heads.

The filling strength at Saburomaru distillery is 60.5%abv and most of the production is aged on site: the bulk in the large racked warehouse constructed in 2019 and some—sherry butts, in particular—in the actual distillery building (which is much hotter for most of the year and therefore a better maturation environment for the large-sized casks, according to the staff). Some casks are aged at the T&T Toyama Aging Warehouse in Inami.

EXPRESSIONS

Wakatsuru Shuzo has always been synonymous with the cheap blended whisky Sunshine. In 2013, a limited edition 20-year-old single malt was released in a porcelain decanter. This was followed in 2015 by a 1990 (25-year-old) limited edition, again in a porcelain decanter. Most people didn't know what to make of these very pricey Sunshine whiskies, so in 2016, the decision was made to create a new brand for Wakatsuru's single malt expressions and to bottle them under the Saburomaru banner.

The first Saburomaru release—a 55-year-old—was launched on June 21, 2016. At the time, Saburomaru 1960 (47%abv, 155 bottles) was the oldest single malt Japanese whisky ever bottled. It was distilled in May 1960 in the old allospas still. (Technically, this wouldn't be considered a single malt whisky in Scotland, since it was distilled in a continuous still. In Japan, this doesn't matter.) The casks used were ex-red wine casks from Yamanashi from the days when Wakatsuru Shuzo dabbled in port wine.

The first single malt from the post-2016 era was released in November 2020. This release also introduced the theme under which the distillery is planning to release its single malts henceforth: the 22 cards of the Arcana Major in the tarot. Since these are numbered from 0 to 21, the first release was Saburomaru 0 The Fool (48%abv, 2,000btls). This was a vatting of spirit distilled during the first season—when they were "starting from zero," in a way—and was entirely matured in ex-bourbon barrels. There was also a more-limited cask-strength edition (63%abv, 200btls).

The year after, the follow-up came out: Saburomaru I The Magician. This was a vatting of spirit distilled during the 2018 season, using the new mash tun, and aged in ex-bourbon wood. Again, there was a regular release (48%abv, 3,000btls) and a cask-strength one (63%abv, 360btls). In July 2022, a special single cask edition of The Magician was released for the famous "avant-guard regional cuisine" restaurant L'évo in Toyama (60%abv, 208btls). Appropriately given the restaurant's ethos, it was a cask fitted with heads made from local mizunara.

Saburomaru I The Magician single cask

Saburomaru 1960

The east coast of Hokkaido near the distillery

Akkeshi Distillery
(Kenten Jitsugyo Co., Ltd.)

Akkeshi Distillery was established by Tokyo-based import/export firm Kenten Jitsugyo. Keiichi Toita, the CEO of the company, is a longtime whisky aficionado with a penchant for Islay malts. In the wake of the highball boom in Japan, Toita was keen to add Japanese whisky to his export portfolio, but it was getting harder to source. There was less of it around and more and more people eager to get their hands on the little that was available. Toita figured there was only one surefire way to get hold of quality whisky in that sort of climate: make it yourself.

In 2010, he started thinking in earnest about setting up a whisky distillery and began looking for potential sites. Toita couldn't imagine his distillery being anywhere other than Hokkaido. Similar in climate and terrain to his beloved Islay, he felt this was the ideal place to craft his own whisky. Since there was already a distillery on the west coast (Yoichi), Toita focused on the east coast of the island.

It wasn't long before he came across the town of Akkeshi, about 30 miles/50km east of Kushiro. Near the sea, surrounded by beautiful wetlands and with an abundance of peat, Akkeshi ticked all the right boxes. On top of that, Akkeshi is famous for a local delicacy that goes hand in glove with peated whisky: oysters. In 2010, Toita approached the mayor of the town. In 2014, the town agreed to lease the land (located about a mile/2km from the sea, as the crow flies) and approved the construction of the distillery. Construction began in October 2015 and continued all through the harsh winter months. By July 2016, the main distillery building was equipment ready. Production started in October of that year. The first distilling season was a very short one. Unlike most distilleries, which close for maintenance during the hot summer months,

Akkeshi stops producing during the winter. Temperatures can drop to 4°F/-20°C, which makes it challenging to run a distillery, to say the least. Therefore, the maintenance season at Akkeshi distillery runs from the end of December to the middle of March. The second season started in the spring of 2017.

The Distillery

Mash tun:	stainless steel, semi-lauter (1t)
Washbacks:	6 stainless steel (5kl)
Pot stills:	1 pair (wash still 5kl; spirit still 3.6kl), Forsyths indirect heating (steam coils)
	both with descending lyne arms and shell-and-tube condensers

Akkeshi Distillery is one of the hardest distilleries to get into—literally. Distillery manager Katsuyuki Tatsuzaki comes from a dairy background and he runs his distillery with the sort of protocols in place that he was used to when he worked in dairy production. Cleanliness is next to godliness, as they say. Only on rare occasions are visitors—press or industry people—allowed inside the actual production building. Most of the time, they have to content themselves with looking from the outside in, through a window on a raised platform.

Most of the equipment at Akkeshi Distillery was made by Forsyths in Scotland. Per batch, 1t of malted barley is used. The first year (2016), 80 percent of the barley used was non-peated, but the following year, peated production was increased. At the time of writing, it was split half/half between heavily-peated (50ppm) and non-peated barley. Mashing takes place in a semi-lauter mash tun with a copper canopy. Water is taken from the Homakai River, in the upstream reaches of the Oboro River (which flows behind the distillery).

For the fermentation, six closed stainless steel washbacks without temperature control are used. The yeast used is distillers yeast and the fermentation time is 5 days. For the distillation, twin pots are used. These

The stills a few days after they were installed

were ordered from Forsyths in 2014. There was a four-year lead time when the order was placed, but the Akkeshi team got lucky and their stills and other equipment were delivered by August 2016. The stills (5kl and 3.6kl, respectively) are pear-shaped, like those at Lagavulin's distillery on Islay. They are fitted with descending lyne arms and shell-and-tube condensers. The Akkeshi spirit is on the heavier side of the spectrum. It is filled into wood at 63.5%abv.

Unusually, there was whisky maturing on site before there was a distillery. In October 2013, a small test maturation warehouse was built. New-make purchased from and filled into casks at two Japanese distilleries—Araside (code speak for Chichibu) and Eigashima—was transferred to Akkeshi so that the team could gauge the effect of the climate on the maturation process. The temperature range throughout the year is very wide. In the summer, temperatures rarely exceed 77°F/25°C, but in the winter they can drop to -4°F/-20°C, which is about 18°F/10°C lower than average temperatures at Yoichi distillery in the winter.

The team at Akkeshi distillery is continuing their investigations into the effect of microclimate and location on the maturation process to this day. Initially, the spirit was aged in a small dunnage-style ware-

Top: Locals drying konbu (kelp); bottom: Akkeshi oysters

house on site. That quickly filled up, so in 2017, another warehouse was built across the road, also of the dunnage type. In early 2018, a third warehouse—racked, this time—was built adjacent to the sea, and in the spring of 2020, a fourth (also racked) warehouse was built on a hill overlooking Akkeshi Bay. They have even used a kelp hut to mature two barrels. In the summer of 2021, the company started trial aging in Furano, in the center of Hokkaido, about 260km from the distillery.

Akkeshi Distillery also has an ongoing project, which they have dubbed the Akkeshi All-Star project. The ultimate goal with this project is to create a whisky that is 100% Akkeshi. That means: barley grown in

The Oboro River near the distillery

Akkeshi, smoked with peat harvested in Akkeshi and matured in wood from mizunara trees felled in Akkeshi.

The project got underway in 2018. In the summer of that same year, the team started using local barley, two-row Ryofu barley from Furano. This was then filled into called casks made from Hokkaido-grown (albeit not in Akkeshi) mizunara. The next step was using barley grown in Akkeshi and wood felled there. In the spring of 2019, the company managed to source some Akkeshi-grown mizunara, which was then air dried in preparation for coopering. They also distilled some more Hokkaido-grown barley at the time. In the summer of 2019, the first Akkeshi-grown barley was harvested (about 10t). This was then sent off to a malting company and distilled the year after. The first coming together of Akkeshi-barley distillate and Akkeshi-grown mizunara took place in the summer of 2020. The company is continuing to work with farmers in Akkeshi to ensure a yearly supply, however small in the large scheme of things, of local barley.

The third phase of the Akkeshi All-Star project involves local peat. There are peat beds (around and literally under the distillery) extending down from 6.5 to 164 feet/2m to 50m deep, so there's certainly no shortage there. But to get from access to peat to actually distilling barley smoked with local peat is not an easy jump. Peat can only be harvested when the bogs are not frozen. In April of 2020, the team at Akkeshi harvested its first load of local peat (5t). This was then dried so it could be used to smoke Akkeshi barley harvested in the summer of the year after. To do so, the company set up a small drum-malting facility on site.

Sampling the mizunara puncheon in the test maturation warehouse

In terms of volume, the Akkeshi All-Star project is a tiny side project, but it's one the team feels very strongly about in spite of the considerable effort (not to mention cost). It will be interesting to see what sort of flavor profiles the distillery will manage to unlock with this project.

EXPRESSIONS

Between February 2018 and August 2019, the distillery released four different "Foundations" bottlings in small 200ml bottlings. This made it possible for whisky aficionados to share the distillery's journey in those early years.

The first single malt was released—also in 200m bottles—in February 2020. It was a vatting of whisky produced during the first (short) season and matured in bourbon, red wine, sherry and mizunara casks (bottled

at 55%av). This first single malt release was called Sarorunkamuy—the word used in the Ainu language for the red-crowned crane. The area around the distillery is a mating area for the red-crowned crane (*tancho*), which Akkeshi Distillery has integrated in its logo. The red-crowned crane is considered a symbol of fidelity, good luck and longevity in Japan, three important qualities for a whisky distillery.

In October 2020, the company started a new series called the 24 Solar Terms Series—a reference to the 24 "small seasons" (*sekki*) of the traditional Japanese calendar. Henceforth, the offerings were all in full-sized 700ml bottles. At the time of writing, four editions had been released. So far, the odd-numbered releases have been single malts and the even-numbered ones blended whiskies (using grain whisky imported from abroad).

Two of the old Karuizawa pot stills in
the warehouse at Shizuoka Distillery

Shizuoka Distillery
(Gaia Flow Distilling)

Shizuoka Distillery is one of two new distilleries built from the ground up in 2016. As is the case with the other one, Akkeshi Distillery (see page 293), it was the first foray into liquor production for the company involved.

Shizuoka Distillery is the brainchild of Gaia Flow founder Taiko Nakamura. Nakamura had been an aficionado of quality liquor since his college days. He'd familiarized himself with various types of liquor and had a keen interest in the production process of whisky, wine and sake. His desire to enter the field of whisky production was sparked by his experience of touring Islay (and Jura) in June 2012. The four-day trip was Nakamura's first visit to Scotland. The final distillery visit on that trip was to Kilchoman, which was (at the time) the youngest distillery on Islay. Kilchoman had managed to build a solid reputation in a few years' time, so Nakamura's mental image of the distillery was one of automation and efficiency. He was surprised to find that, in reality, it was a small farm distillery with a small warehouse and a small team running things. Sitting in the garden at Kilchoman Distillery, Nakamura realized that this wasn't unlike the approach to the production of sake at many *kura* in Japan. With this, the seeds were planted in his mind to try and set up a whisky distillery of his own in Japan along similar hands-on, small-scale DIY lines.

Back home after his trip, Nakamura started wondering who he could approach for advice. At the time, there was only one man who had managed to pull off the sort of thing he had in mind in Japan: Ichiro Akuto. Nakamura made contact with Akuto at the first Osaka Whisky Festival,

The Tamagawa River in front of the distillery

visited Chichibu Distillery, got tons of advice and started drawing up a business plan. The crucial difference with the situation at Chichibu was that, unlike Ichiro, Nakamura didn't have stocks from a previous distillery venture (Hanyu) and a brand (Ichiro's Malt) to rely on in building a new distillery from scratch. To get a foot in the door of the spirits industry in Japan, Nakamura decided to set up a liquor import company, or rather to reconfigure the company he had set up in January of the same year. He kept the name, Gaia Flow, and business structure but completely changed the focus of the company from renewable energy to importer of fine liquors. The bigger goal was, of course, to set up a distillery of his own as soon as possible. Nakamura still remembers how, upon visiting the local tax office and informing the staff there of his plan to make whisky in Shizuoka, they looked at him in utter disbelief.

Over the next four years, Nakamura visited over 170 distilleries, breweries, and wineries at home and abroad. The search for a good site for his own distillery was on, too. Although his hope was to set up shop in his hometown of Shizuoka, he thought the prospect of that happening was unlikely. Shizuoka city is a relatively mountainous area and what little land there is for construction is usually very expensive. Undeterred, Nakamura looked at other parts of Shizuoka prefecture as well as sites in the neighboring prefectures of Yamanashi and Nagano. Time was passing. One of the things Ichiro had impressed upon

Nakamura was that it wasn't a smart strategy to set up a distillery one step at a time. According to Ichiro, it was necessary to do things parallel. In other words, rather than do A, then B and then C, do A, B and C concurrently, even when B and C are dependent in some way on A.

In May 2014, Nakamura put in an order for two pot stills with Forsyths in Scotland. He hadn't found a site yet, but there was a lead time of two years for the stills and he remembered Ichiro's words. A month later, Nakamura found his site, in the Tamakawa area of . . . Shizuoka city! In the 1990s, a side-hill cut had made some level land in the area available. The land was owned by Shizuoka city and in the course of the following decades, many ideas had been thrown up for the use of the land but none of these came to anything. Unbeknownst to Nakamura, the city official in charge of the land was a whisky fan himself. He had carried out in-depth research on Chichibu distillery and had even harbored hopes that the land could be used to build a small whisky distillery. When Nakamura enquired about the land, it seemed like destiny had come knocking. It was almost like the land had been laying in wait all those years for two people's vision for its future to come together.

Two old Karuizawa stills in Warehouse No.1

Taiko Nakamura with the active ex-Karuizawa still

Shortly after finding the land and getting permission from the authorities to establish a whisky distillery there, Nakamura set up Gaia Flow Distilling. In terms of distillery design, Nakamura wanted something simple but modern. He asked the Shizuoka-based architect bureau West Coast Design (led by Derrek Buston) to come up with some ideas and when he saw the plans, he immediately felt they were on the same wavelength.

In 2015, Nakamura purchased the old Karuizawa Distillery equipment at a public auction organized by the city of Miyota for a little over 5 million yen. Karuizawa Distillery was going to be demolished (which eventually happened, in February 2016), so the equipment had to go. It was clear that most of it was not going to be of much use, since the distillery had been mothballed since 2000. The washbacks were rotten and the mash tun was completely rusted but some of the equipment was still in good enough condition. Of the four Karuizawa pot stills, the newest one (fixed and with a new heating system installed) got a new life at Shizuoka Distillery. Another key piece of equipment from Karuizawa that is reused at Shizuoka Distillery is the Porteus malt mill. According to the last Karuizawa malt master, Osami Uchibori, the mill (which was installed at Karuizawa Distillery in 1989 and was far from busy during the final years of production there) was worth four times the hammer price of the entire equipment. A bargain indeed! A few other pieces of Karuizawa equipment (the destoner and a hoops press machine) would also come in handy at Shizuoka Distillery. Some historically important pieces of equipment from Karuizawa Distillery that have outlived their usefulness (like the other pot stills) are on display in Warehouse 1.

Nakamura received his whisky license in September 2016 and production began the following month. The first cask-filling took place in December of that year.

The Distillery

Mash tun:	stainless steel, lauter tun (5kl)
Washbacks:	4 Oregon pine (8kl)
	6 Shizuoka cedar (8kl)
Stills:	1 wash still (referred to as "K," 3.5kl), ex-Karuizawa, indirect heating (steam percolators); with horizontal lyne arm
	1 wash still (referred to as "W," 6kl), Forsyths, hybrid heating system: indirect (steam) and direct (wood-fired); with slightly upward lyne arm
	1 spirit still (referred to as "S," 3.6kl), Forsyths, indirect heating (steam coils); with downward lyne arm
	all with shell-and-tube condensers

Top: The production building; bottom: The tasting room with the Forsyths stills in the background.

Shizuoka distillery sits on a 5-square-acre/20,000-square-meter site right beside a tributary of the Abe River. It's surrounded by small green tea farms and beautiful forested mountains with plenty of wildlife (monkeys, deer, wild boar and the like). The climate is very mild all year round. Even in the winter, it's relatively warm, with temperatures rarely dropping below freezing.

The main distillery building is ingeniously designed. Inspired by Karuizawa Distillery, everything from milling to filling (the barley and casks, respectively) takes place under one roof, but in different "rooms." Airflow can be controlled by opening various shutters in the building. Another thing that's carefully considered is the way in which the landscape outside is visible from various points in the distillery building. What is most impressive, and unique among Japanese whisky distilleries, is the fact that the "visitor experience" is integrated into the design of the distillery. The distillery opened for tours—by appointment only, though—in December 2018. Visitors can walk through the building and see the different stages of the whisky-making process without being in the way. At the end of the tour, they end up in a tasting room on the second floor where, overlooking the stillhouse, they are able to sample whiskies seated at a long *hinoki* (Japanese cypress) counter. The tasting room is designed for the "selfie age." When guests take a picture of themselves sipping a whisky there, they are doing so against the backdrop of the stillhouse. Nakamura and West Coast Design deserve to be applauded for taking this into account. At most other distilleries in Japan, the visitor experience is a mere afterthought.

Per batch, 1t of malted barley is processed. The source of the malted barley can vary quite a bit. "We've used malt imported from England, France, Germany, Canada and Australia in the past. We also use quite a bit of domestic barley," Nakamura points out, "and even a small amount of locally-grown barley." (See below for more about this.) The bulk of production is non-peated. In the spring, for a short period of time, malt peated at around 40ppm is used. "The first season, we did our peated production before the silent season (which runs from the beginning of August until the end of September)," Taiko explains, "but we found summertime to be less than ideal for distilling peated malt, so we changed to spring."

The mill room is quite a colorful affair: a red Porteus mill, a green destoner (both from the old Karuizawa Distillery) and a brand-new orange grist bin. "The green can be seen as standing for green tea and the orange for Shizuoka's signature fruit, *mikan*," Nakamura jokingly says. A Porteus mill at a distillery may be nothing to write home about if you're in Scotland, but in Japan they are rare as hen's teeth. In fact, this is the only specimen you're likely to encounter in the wild, as the other two—at Yamazaki and Hakushu Distillery—are hidden from the public eye.

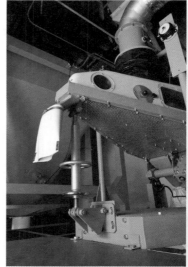

Next door to the milling room is the mash tun. This is a one-ton full lauter tun made by Miyake Industries. "It's a piece of art," Nakamura says, "and as such, I asked the company to put their name on the glass manway. That was a first for them, so the lettering is a bit wonky." Maintenance was a

Top: The destoner and the grist bin; bottom: The old Karuizawa Porteus mill

major consideration in having this piece of equipment made in Japan rather than by Forsyths in Scotland (which was commissioned to make the pot stills).

Water is drawn from a bore on the property tapping into the underground river table. It's moderately soft at 69ppm, which on the water hardness scale falls between Yamazaki Distillery (slightly softer) and Chichibu Distillery (slightly harder). Because there is no hot liquor tank at the distillery, only two waters are used: the first 4kl at 64°C, the second 2kl split in half as far as temperature is concerned (75–80°C for the first thousand, 85–90°C for the second thousand liters). This results in about 5,200l of clear wort, which is then sent to the tun room.

The tun (or fermentation) room is very spacious. When production started at Shizuoka Distillery in late 2016, the four 8kl Oregon pine

The tun room

washbacks looked a bit forlorn in the large tun room, but that was forward planning on Nakamura's part. In February 2017, a washback made of Shizuoka cedar was added. In 2018, three more of the same type were added, and in 2020, another pair was added.

The fermentation time at Shizuoka Distillery is 3–5 days and the default yeast used is dry distillers yeast. According to Nakamura, there is a clear difference between the Oregon pine wash and the cedar wash, particularly during the lactic fermentation. "At the moment, we get more esters from the Oregon pine washbacks, but it's unfair to compare as the cedar washbacks are relatively new and there are still lots of tannins in play," he explains. "It will be a few years before both types of washbacks are in a similar sort of condition and then we can make a fair comparison."

The next place to geek out is the stillroom, which is an interesting mix of old and new. There is one pair of stills (6k and 3.5kl, respectively), made brand new by Forsyths, both with a bulge—"because I happen to like whiskies distilled in stills with a bulge," Nakamura says. The wash still is the only direct wood-fired still in operation at a whisky distillery in the world, with the possible exception of George Washington's Distillery at Mount Vernon in Virginia, but that is a seasonally operated, historical recreation of an early 19th-century distillery with a very small still. Local thinned wood—cedar and cypress—is used to fire the wash still at Shizuoka distillery. The wash still is heated using a combination of indirect heat (steam) and direct heat until the wash boils. Once it starts boiling, the steam system is cut off and only direct fire is applied. The spirit still is steam-heated.

Then, there's a third beast: a pot still that clearly has decades of heavy toil behind it. You've guessed it: this is one of the old Karuizawa stills—the one that was in the best shape—dating from 1975. Miyake prepared it for an active life again, after 16 years of idleness. It's equipped with two little side glasses now and the heating system was changed from steam coils to percolators. "We use this one for the first distillation," Nakamura explains. "In general, we use the Forsyths wash still in conjunction with the spirit still three times a week, and the Karuizawa wash still in conjunction with the spirit still two times a week. We don't mix the low wines, because that difference in character is what we are after." The middle cut is 75%abv to 64% for non-peated malt; for peated runs, they take it down to 60%abv.

With three stills, there's one more mathematical possibility, of course: triple distillation. "No plans at all in that direction," Nakamura says, "although we have done some accidental 2.5 distillation." Something he picked up at the Springbank Whisky School, perhaps? "Not at all. It was simply a case of human error and correcting that error without letting anything go to waste. While doing some of the early batches, we noticed that the abv of the low wines was about the same as the abv of the wash itself. It didn't take us long to figure out what had happened. After rinsing the low wines receiver, someone had forgotten to drain the water. To remedy that, we redistilled those diluted low wines again in the wash still and then did a spirit run, and vatted the new make from that reluctant triple distillation with spirit obtained using standard double distillation, hence 2.5. We did about 20 batches like that, and the flavor is quite different so that will be a rarity when it is bottled and released one day."

The spirit is filled into wood at 63.8% abv and then begins its long slumber in one of three warehouses on site, one dunnage and two racked. The dunnage warehouse also houses the other Karuizawa stills, as a historical display, and the hoops press machine from the cooperage at Karuizawa Distillery. In terms of wood policy, there is clear bias towards ex-bourbon wood. "I happen to prefer the flavor of bourbon-matured whiskies," Nakamura admits, "so most of our spirit is aged in ex-bourbon barrels." The remainder is matured in ex-wine or ex-sherry casks.

"At Shizuoka Distillery, we aim to make whisky that expresses the terroir of Shizuoka," Nakamura relates. "In 2017, a local farmer started growing some barley for us and a year later, we did a 100% local batch, using local barley as well as local yeast. Until now, barley hasn't been cultivated all that much in Shizuoka, but with the cooperation of the prefecture's public research institutes, agricultural cooperatives and farmers, the yield is increasing year by year." During the 2021–2022 season, the amount of local barley used at the distillery exceeded 10 percent of the annual production—a significant amount for a small craft producer.

As mentioned above, there is also something stirring in the fermentation department. "Over 30 years ago," Nakamura explains, "the Industrial Research Institute of Shizuoka prefecture developed a sake brewers yeast that helped in producing excellent *ginjo* sake, and Shizuoka became known as "the Kingdom of Ginjo Sake." Recently, there has been an explosion of craft beer breweries in the prefecture, so a special yeast strain for beer and whisky production (named NMZ-0688) was developed by the Institute, which was released in the spring of 2019. We used that local yeast for that one batch mentioned earlier." The Institute has been working on a second yeast strain to ferment barley maltose since then, and Shizuoka Distillery is closely following their progress in this area.

So what is the impact on the actual flavor of the whisky? It's early days but what Nakamura can tell us about the flavor of the new-make produced with barley, water and yeast from Shizuoka is that it has "a mild yet deep taste. People often say that folks from Shizuoka tend to be calm, collected and unfussy and the spirit gives off that impression, too."

The final piece of the puzzle is locally harvested wood for the maturation. "We're working on making casks from Shizuoka mizunara," Nakamura reveals. "The project is still in its infancy but we have tremendous support from the local forestry organizations, so it's just a matter of time."

EXPRESSIONS

Shizuoka Distillery released its first single malt on December 19, 2020. It was called Prologue K—K for Karuizawa. Until June 2017, when the Forsyths pair of pots was ready to be fired up, Nakamura was using the old Karuizawa still for both the wash and the spirit run. Prologue K is a vatting of that type of spirit, distilled using imported as well as domestic malted barley and entirely matured in first-fill ex-bourbon barrels (55.5%abv, 5,000btls).

The follow-up, Prologue W (same abv and outturn) was released in June 2021. This was a vatting of spirit distilled using the wood-fired still, using non-peated and peated malted barley imported from Scotland as well as domestically sourced barley and beer barley from Germany. It was aged in a mix of cask types (first-fill bourbon barrels, first-fill quarter casks and virgin oak casks).

November 2021 saw the release of Contact S (again, same abv and outturn)—a vatting of whiskies of the K and W types, matured in a variety of cask types.

"The idea is to release three types of products—W, K and S—every year under the Single Malt Shizuoka brand," Nakamura clarifies. "The core item is S. W and K, on the other hand, will explore different specifications, each time. Single cask whiskies will be released, too, by independent bottlers such as Blackadder and Asta Morris, with whom we have good relationships."

It is also worth mentioning that, since 2017, Shizuoka Distillery has been running a private cask program—the only distillery in Japan to do so on a consistent basis.

The first cask filled

Three Blackadder releases

Nagahama Distillery
(Nagahama Roman Beer Co., Ltd.)

Nagahama Distillery was publicly unveiled the day after the first edition of this book went to press. There was just enough time to include it as a pinpoint on the map at the back of the book, but that was all. It is fitting, therefore, to open the post-2016 distillery section with this quaint little distillery.

Located in the picturesque town of the same name in Shiga prefecture, Nagahama Distillery was the smallest distillery in the country when it first fired up its stills in November 2016. But there are a few things—other than the size—that set Nagahama Distillery apart from other distilleries in Japan.

The first thing that is striking about Nagahama Distillery is how quickly it was set it up. Whereas most companies take years to get from the planning stage to the reality of an actual distillery ready for production, it took the company behind Nagahama Distillery a little over 7 months. It helped that they didn't have to start from scratch. Nagahama Distillery is, in fact, an extension of Nagahama Roman Brewery (with the emphasis on the second syllable, as in "romantic"). The brewery was set up in 1996 as a brewpub, and the first half of the whisky-making process—mashing and fermentation—takes place in the equipment used for beer-making. For the second half of the process—distillation—a small "stillroom" was created behind the bar counter. A glass wall was put in so anyone visiting the restaurant can see the distillery in operation.

The distillery in the winter

Distillery manager Takashi Kiyoi connecting a pot with its condenser

Looking at the stillhouse, very few people would suspect that the inspiration for Nagahama Distillery came from Scotland, but that is where the idea for the project was born. The inspiration didn't come from any of the iconic, well-known, traditional Scottish distilleries, but from the (at the time) new wave of small-scale distilleries. In November 2015, a small team from Liquor Mountain (the parent company of Nagahama Roman Beer) visited a number of new distilleries in Scotland, among them Strathearn and Eden Mill, with the intention of looking into the quality of their products and the possibility of distributing their whiskies in Japan in the future. What they saw impressed them, but it wasn't until they returned to Scotland in April 2016 that they considered setting up a whisky-making operation of their own in Japan along similar lines.

Strathearn Distillery started producing whisky in October 2013 and, at the time, it was the smallest distillery in Scotland. The pot stills used at Strathearn are tiny (1kl and 500l, respectively) and not of the type generally used in Scotland. They are fitted with alembic heads and are of the type traditionally used for making calvados, cognac or pisco. Made by Hoga Stills in Portugal, they are favored by many smaller craft distillers, particularly in the U.S. The small alembic stills are cheaper than traditional pot stills and faster to get delivered. Whereas at Forsyths, the leading maker of pot stills in Scotland, you would find yourself on a waiting list for a couple of years, Hoga Stills can get your stills made and delivered in a matter of months. The approach and setup at Strathearn Distillery inspired the people at Eden Mill, a brewery that expanded into a distillery. They ordered similar alembic stills from Hoga Stills and started making whisky in November 2014. Eden Mill was the first combined brewery/distillery in Scotland so it isn't hard to see why the Liquor Mountain team felt inspired by their experiences visiting these two distilleries. They had a brewery of their own in Nagahama city, so an extension of that operation into the field of whisky suggested itself, especially given the unquenchable thirst for Japanese whisky, both at home and abroad.

In July 2016, work on setting up a whisky distillery within the Nagahama Roman Brewery premises began in earnest. Pot stills of the same type and size as those used at Strathearn were ordered from Hoga Stills. Unlike other distilleries-in-progress, the whole project was kept under wraps, so it came as a big surprise when the distillery was officially announced to the public via social media on November 1, 2016. The Hoga stills arrived in Nagahama on November 10 and the first distillation took place a week later (November 16–17).

Initially, Nagahama Distillery was equipped with two Hoga stills (1kl and 500l, respectively). In the spring of 2018, the small spirit still was removed and two stills identical to the 1kl still were added. If the distillery wants to produce more in the future, they will have to relocate as three is indeed a crowd as far as this stillroom is concerned. There is no room for further expansion at the present site, which is in fact a restored rice warehouse dating back the Edo period.

The Distillery

Mash tun:	stainless steel + lauter tun (2kl, used by the brewery)
Washbacks:	6 stainless steel (2kl; in general, 4 used for whisky production, 2 for beer brewing)
Stills:	2 wash (1kl) and 1 spirit (1kl) still, alembic-type, Hoga indirect heating (steam coils)
	shell-and-tube condensers

The official motto of the Nagahama Distillery team is One Batch, One Barrel (*ichi-jo ichi-taru*). This refers to the fact that one batch produces enough spirit to fill one barrel, give or take. The obvious advantage here is versatility and the freedom to experiment to your heart's content. And they do plenty of that at Nagahama Distillery. You'd be forgiven for thinking their motto was "Try Everything."

Per batch, 425kg of malted barley is processed. The bulk of the barley used is imported from Germany and Scotland. The barley used spans the entire spectrum from non-peated to heavily-peated, and the staff have experimented with specialty malts (used for beer making), as well. The first batch ever distilled at Nagahama Distillery was non-peated with a small proportion of peated barley added. Until mid-2021, production was about 50/50 peated/non-peated. After that, non-peated barley was prioritized. Since 2020, the distillery has occasionally worked with local barley, grown in Shiga prefecture, but the amounts involved are tiny, by necessity.

The mashing takes place in the tun used for beer making. The wort is clarified using a whirlpool technique. One batch results in 1.9kl of wort. This is then sent to one of six stainless-steel fermenters on the second floor of the same building. Again, the fermenters are part of the original brewery setup. Once the wort is pumped up to a fermenter, distillers yeast is added. The fermentation time is 72 hours.

After the fermentation has run its course, the wash is pumped down to the stillhouse. Everything is very hands-on at Nagahama Distillery, so the staff literally have to connect a hose pipe to the bottom of the fermenter on the second floor and lower it down straight into the spirit still on the first floor . . . all manually. The same applies to removing the draff from the mash tun. This is done by hand and is a laborious process.

The draff is picked up by farmers from the area, who use it as fertilizer to grow crops that will end up on the menu of the restaurant a few months down the line. Talk about closing the circle.

As mentioned above, the pot stills are of the alembic type, fitted with a large head in order to promote reflux, which is meant to produce a cleaner spirit.

With the initial 2-still setup, half of the wash (800l, at the time) was distilled in the morning and the remaining half in the afternoon. For the second distillation, a similar procedure was used. In the morning, 400l of low wines were distilled, and then, in the afternoon, another 400l of low wines. At the end of the process, one batch resulted in about 200l of new-make at around 68%abv.

A year into production, it became clear that there was room to improve the efficiency of the distillation process and increase production at the same time. In the spring of 2018, the small spirit still was removed and two new 1kl Hoga stills were installed. With the 3-still set-up, it was possible to streamline the distillation process somewhat. Henceforth, the wash was stilled split in two halves (two times 950l), but now there were 2 wash stills and a spirit still twice the size of the old one. Efficiency aside, the new setup also made it possible for the distillery to process two batches a day.

Before filling into wood, the new-make is reduced to 59%abv. The first spirit produced at Nagahama Distillery was filled into a mizunara hogshead. Since then, the distillery has tried any and all types of casks.

Mashing in progress

It would be hard to think of a type they haven't filled into, so I won't bore you with examples.

Due to space constraints, maturation takes place off-site. Since 2021, the company has diversified its aging locations and now there are four distinct locations.

In 2021, the company started renting the premises of a local school (Nanao Elementary School), 8km northeast of the distillery, at the foot of a mountain. The school was closed in 2018 and is now used as Nagahama Distillery's "Azai Factory." I am not aware of any other place in the world where whisky is aged in a school building. At Azai Factory, the casks are everywhere, stored dunnage-style in classrooms, the teachers' room and even the former principal's office. The school's science room is now used as a blending lab. It's quite a surreal sight. The distillery's other main aging site is further up in the mountains and is actually a disused tunnel. The tunnel was closed in 2006 and Nagahama Distillery has been renting it since 2018. About 300m in length, it is cool inside all year round, creating a more gentle aging environment. Casks are also stored dunnage-style here.

Since 2021, the distillery has also been aging a small number of casks on island locations: one very near and technically part of Nagahama city (Chikubu Island), the other about as far away as you can get without leaving Japan (Okinawa). Chikubu Island is a tiny island in the northern part of Lake Biwa, about 12km northwest of the distillery. It's called the "Island of the Gods" because of its historically significant Buddhist temple and Shinto shrine and is considered to be a "power spot" in Japan.

Nagahama Distillery's parent company is Liquor Mountain, a liquor retailer with stores scattered all over Japan, so getting the whisky to market was not a challenge, at all. They've made consumers part of the distillery's journey right from the start. Five hundred bottles of non-peated new-make were made available to consumers in the spring of 2017. In those early days, the company also offered a special DIY-maturation kit, consisting of a 1-liter mini-barrel made out of American White Oak and a bottle of new-make to fill your mini-barrel with.

Nagahama Distillery released its first single malt expressions in May 2020: a mizunara cask (batch #0002), a bourbon cask (batch #0007) and an Oloroso sherry cask (batch #0149). Over 30 other expressions have been released since, all single-cask and bottled at cask strength. By definition, these releases are all highly limited—a few hundred bottles, typically—and gone in a flash. At the time of writing, the distillery was planning to work on single malt releases with a higher outturn by vatting multiple batches. Perhaps, this will make it possible for the consumer to start discerning a house-style.

One of the very first releases: some new-make and a mini barrel to age the spirit at home

Inside the warehouse

Kaikyo Distillery
(Akashi Sake Brewery / Marussia Beverages)

Kaikyo Distillery was established by Akashi Sake Brewery on their premises in the historic port city of Akashi, in Hyogo prefecture, but is wholly owned by Marussia Beverages, an international producer and distributor of wines, sake and spirits.

Akashi Sake Brewery traces its history back to 1856. Initially, the focus was on soy sauce making. In 1917, the company entered the field of liquor production and, in the course of the following decades, the staff was kept busy manufacturing *mirin*, liqueurs, synthetic sake (used as cooking sake, for the most part), *korui shochu*, so-called "brewer's alcohol" (neutral spirit used in the production of certain types of sake) and so on. In 1980, the production of soy sauce was discontinued.

The current president of Akashi Sake Brewery, representing the fourth generation, is Kimio Yonezawa. He was born in 1960, which also marks the year the company started producing authentic sake. After graduating from university and having worked at another company for 9 years, Kimio returned home and joined the family business. At the time (1992), the company's sales focus was on the lower end of the market— in other words: low margins and lots of competition.

More often than not, the company's fortunes depended on the whims of the market and competing against producers who had the economies of scale was become increasingly difficult as the years rolled by. Eventually, Kimio Yonezawa decided to ditch the sake-in-cartons market and to focus on the higher end: *ginjo* and *daiginjo* sake. However, the problem with that strategy was that the brand had to be built from the ground up and this turned out to be more challenging than anticipated.

In 2005, Yonezawa started looking abroad for answers. With the help of two experienced marketeers, he managed to get some key accounts in the U.K. after a few years. Again, there were ups and downs, but eventually Akashi Sake Brewery's portfolio was taken on by Eaux de Vie, Ltd., a specialist spirits distribution business established by Neil Mathieson in 1984.

In 2010, Eaux de Vie was acquired by Marussia Beverages and the name changed to Marussia Beverages UK Ltd. In 2013, Neil Mathieson suggested a new project to Kimio Yonezawa: whisky making. Two years later, the wheels were set in motion, and in May 2017, Kaikyo Distillery— named after the Akashi Strait (in Japanese: Akashi Kaikyo)—got its whisky production license.

The distillery officially opened to the public on August 24, 2022.

The Distillery

Mash tun:	stainless steel, semi-lauter, with a copper canopy
Washbacks:	2 stainless steel (4kl), without temperature control
	1 stainless steel sake tank, with temperature control
	1 wooden (6kl)
Stills:	1 pair (wash still 3.5kl, spirit still 2.3kl), Forsyths indirect heating (steam)
	both with ascending lyne arms and shell-and-tube condensers

It's somewhat of an understatement to say that it took a while for Kaikyo Distillery to get into its stride. In fact, it took nearly five years.

In November 2016, the team at Akashi Sake Brewery took delivery of a single copper still (2.3kl) and a lone stainless-steel tank, both made by Forsyths. The tank turned out to be too tall for the building, so they cut it in half and ended up with two fermenters by fitting one half with a new bottom and the other half with a new top. Production started in the fall of 2017. There was no mill and no mash tun at the distillery, so malt extract was used during that initial phase.

Half a year into production, a Japanese whisky legend (who shall go unnamed) dropped by and told the staff in no uncertain terms that this was not the way forward. Kimio Yonezawa took the constructive criticism to heart and came up with a different interim solution: having the wort prepared by a nearby craft beer brewery and getting that transported to the distillery site for fermentation and distillation. This system was used from mid-February 2019.

In 2020, the distillery was expanded and brand-new twin buildings were erected on site: a stillhouse (left, when facing the structure) and a visitor center (right). Both feature a glass façade. If you happen to be traveling on the Sanyo Main Line, either coming from Kobe or from Himeji, you can look right into the stillhouse from the train, provided you know when to look.

In February 2020, a mash tun and one more copper still arrived, but the COVID-19 pandemic made it impossible for the team at Forsyths to take care of all the wiring at the time. It wasn't until April 2022 that a technical crew from Forsyths could come over to finalize the setup and that production in the near-complete distillery could begin. I write "near-complete" because there is still no mill on the premises. The malted barley is delivered to the distillery as grist. The plan is to purchase a mill in 2023.

The description of the production process below captures the state of the distillery in mid-2022.

The mashing and fermentation process takes place in a small building adjacent to the sake brewery. Malted barley is imported from Scotland and, for the time being, is all non-peated. Kimio Yonezawa's initial goal is to create a benchmark whisky, so rather than throwing stuff at the wall and seeing what sticks, his approach is to refine one recipe until the desired quality is achieved.

Per batch, 700kg of malted barley is processed. As mentioned above, this arrives at the distillery as grist. The mashing takes place in a stainless steel, semi-lauter tun with a copper canopy using the textbook "three waters" system.

The wort (3.5kl) is then sent to one of the washbacks and distillers yeast is added. Here, things get interesting. As described above, there are two stainless steel washbacks (the large Forsyths tank, cut in half) without temperature control. There is also a sake-making tank with a water jacket to control the temperature. In early September 2022, a wooden washback was added to the kit. In effect, there are three different environments for the fermentation now: stainless without temperature control, stainless with temperature control and wooden. The idea,

Inside the stillhouse

according to Kimio Yonezawa, is to try out the various environments and see which type produces the best results.

During the 2022 season, 4 batches were processed per week. Because the staff have the weekend off, that means two batches have shorter fermentation times (3 days), and the other two batches have longer fermentation times (4 days). From 2023 onwards, the idea is to produce every day of the week and settle on one fermentation time.

Until 2020, there was only one still and this was used for both the wash and the spirit run. The arrival of its big brother in April 2022 made it possible to streamline the process. Both stills—the new (wash) still and the old (now: spirit) still—occupy center stage in the brand-new still-house. They both have a bulge and, according to Neil Mathieson, "they have been designed with tall necks, in relation to the bowl, to produce a lighter and fruitier spirit which will age well but show light, floral and malty notes at a younger age."

The stock is matured dunnage-style in a warehouse off-site, about a kilometer and a half west of the distillery, near Akashi station. In addition to ex-bourbon and ex-sherry wood, quite a lot of mizunara is used. Some ex-umeshu casks are used, too. (In addition to whisky and sake, the company also makes gin and liqueurs at the distillery site. The casks used to age their umeshu are reused for whisky maturation/finishing purposes.)

Two Hatozaki releases

EXPRESSIONS

Kaikyo Distillery has not yet released any single malt expressions, and there are no works-in-progress for sale either (no new-make or minimally-aged spirit), so we will have to wait a bit longer to get a feel for the distillery character.

Since late 2018, however, the company has been releasing blended malt and blended whiskies under the Hatozaki brand, named after the nearby lighthouse of the same name. (This is, in fact, the oldest stone lighthouse in Japan, built in 1657.) The malt/grain components of the Hatozaki whiskies have been imported from Scotland and North America but aged and blended in Akashi.

The Hatozaki expressions are available in Europe and in the U.S., but not (yet?) in Japan.

The stills

Kurayoshi Distillery
(Matsui Shuzo)

Matsui Shuzo is based in the city of Kurayoshi, in Tottori prefecture, and traces its history back to 1910, through its acquisition of sake and shochu producer Ogino Shuzo. Sake brewing was discontinued and the main focus of the company became the production of authentic shochu (dried sweet potato shochu, in particular). That is, until whisky beckoned.

Interestingly, Matsui Shuzo entered the Japanese whisky scene in 2016 as a brand rather than a distillery, with age-statement releases of "Japanese pure malt whisky" at a time when age-statement Japanese whisky had become rare as hen's teeth. The company had acquired a whisky license in April 2015 and seeing as it didn't have any actual distilling capacity until late 2017, it was clear to the savvy whisky enthusiast that the liquid in the bottles must have been imported in bulk from abroad.

A bewildering plethora of brands and expressions followed, but in 2017, actual in-house distillation began. This happened away from the public eye, and because of the lack of transparency (and the lax regulations governing whisky labeling in Japan), it was very unclear, post-2017, what exactly the provenance of the liquid in the bottles was. This remains the case, but an aggressive sales strategy has given Matsui Shuzo's various whisky brands a strong presence on the shelves of liquor outlets (including duty free) around the world, creating the impression of a vibrant Japanese whisky brand (the ambiguity as to whether this means "Japanese' + 'whisky brand" / "Japanese whisky" + "brand" strategically built in). At the time of writing, Matsui Shuzo's whiskies are sold in over 60 countries.

The distillery building

The Distillery

Mash tun:	stainless steel semi-lauter tun
Washbacks:	enamel-coated steel tanks (6.7kl)
Pot stills:	1 pair (wash still 5kl, spirit still 3kl), made in China
	indirect heating (steam)
	both with near-horizontal lyne arms and shell-and-tube condensers
	also equipped with 3 alembic-type stills (1kl)

Unsurprisingly, details of production at Kurayoshi Distillery are scant. For the fermentation, enamel-coated steel tanks of the type used in sake production are used. Initially, three 1kl Hoga alembic-type stills were used for distillation. In the fall of 2018, two larger pot stills (3kl and 5kl, respectively) were installed and whisky production was shifted to those twin pots.

In the fall of 2018, Kurayoshi Distillery started working with a local farmer, and the following year, a small amount of that local two-row barley was distilled. Experiments with floor-malting on site were undertaken, but the process was judged to be too laborious and costly.

Malt whisky distilled at Kurayoshi Distillery is bottled under The Matsui brand name. The range consists of three no-age-statement expressions: The Peated, The Mizunara Cask and The Sakura Cask, each with a variety of label designs, in function of the market targeted.

Kanosuke Distillery & Hioki Distillery

(Komasa Jozo Co., Ltd.)

Up until 2015, whisky-making in Kyushu was nothing more than a little blip in Japanese whisky history—a distant memory. Seven years later, there are seven active malt distilleries on the island, with the highest concentration in Kagoshima prefecture. Kanosuke Distillery is the second distillery that makes up the unofficial Kagoshima Triangle—the first and third, chronologically, being Mars Tsunuki and Ontake Distilleries. And just like the other points of the triangle, it was established by a company with a strong background in shochu making, Komasa Jozo.

Komasa Jozo was founded in 1883 by Ichisuke Komasa. The company received its license under the Liquor Tax Act in 1905 and quickly established itself as one of the leading shochu makers in Kagoshima. From 1953, under its second president, Kanosuke Komasa, the company worked hard to broaden the appeal of shochu nationwide. Two years earlier, the company had started to develop a novel product, a rice shochu aged in oak casks of the type used for whisky maturation. After six years of maturation, the new product Mellowed Kozuru was launched (1957). The rest is history, as they say. It appealed to discerning drinkers and is still the flagship shochu of the company now, more than 60 years later.

The idea to establish a whisky distillery was born in 2015. After more than 130 years of making shochu, the people at Komasa Jozo felt the time was right to take on a new challenge. The project was spearheaded by Yoshitsugu Komasa, who represents the fourth generation of the family to play a leading role in the company. Yoshitsugu Komasa

Inside one of the warehouses

entered the company in 2003 and worked in various areas of production. He also worked to raise the profile of shochu among the Japanese community abroad, at izakayas and other Japanese-style eateries.

Cask-aging is an area in which Komasa Jozo has built up great expertise over the last 60 years, but the stringent regulations applying to shochu-making—especially with regards to the color of the bottled product, which has to be light and cannot exceed a certain (low) absorbance value—make it difficult to push the envelope a lot in that particular area. In the field of whisky, those constraints don't apply so it made a lot of sense to them to expand their liquor operations in that direction.

The first and most formidable obstacle was acquiring a whisky license. Since Komasa Jozo didn't have an old whisky license that they could simply transfer to a new location, they had to apply for a brand-new one. In shochu-dominated Kagoshima, this is anything but easy and it took considerable effort to sway the people at the local Tax Office. In 2016, the company submitted its application and a little under a year later, when all the equipment was in place, the license finally came through.

As the location for the new distillery, they picked some vacant land the company owned next to the three warehouses where their shochu is matured. The location itself is stunning. A stone's throw—about 100m to be precise—from the East China Sea, the piece of land borders on Fukiage beach, which is considered to be the longest beach in Japan, stretching over 47km from north to south, and is known for its beautiful white sand.

The location also holds special significance for the company and the Komasa family. Kanosuke Komasa had a vision to build a brand home for Mellowed Kozuru on the plot of land and there are even some images showing the intended plans for the plot dating from 1982. Kanosuke Komasa passed away so nothing came of the plans, and the question remained what to do with the plot of land . . . until the idea was had to build a whisky distillery and then everything fell into place. It's also worth mentioning that Miyama, the small town near the distillery, is well known as the birthplace of Satsuma pottery, so there's a history of craft and creative work in the area around the distillery going back several hundreds of years.

In setting up the actual distillery, the staff at Komasa Jozo were fortunate to be able to get advice from Hombo Shuzo who, at the time, were also in the process of setting up a new distillery in their home prefecture

A bird's-eye view of the distillery

of Kagoshima. In fact, Tsunuki Distillery is just a 40-minute drive south along the same road that Kanosuke Distillery sits on, Route 270. In the field of shochu, the two companies may be rivals, but as far as whisky is concerned Hombo Shuzo has over 60 years of experience so their advice was most welcome.

Komasa Jozo also looked abroad for inspiration and expertise. Together with two other staff members from the shochu distillery, Yoshitsugu Komasa went to Scotland to get his hands dirty making whisky there. They attended the Whisky School at Strathearn Distillery in May 2016. It was just one week and the scale of operations was very different—Strathearn is one of Scotland's smallest distilleries with a 300kg mash, as opposed to Kanosuke's 1-ton mash—but it was an invaluable experience, according to Yoshitsugu Komasa.

While in Scotland, the team also visited various distilleries on Islay, Skye and in Speyside. They were particularly inspired by the compact design and layout of Ballindalloch Distillery, a relatively new distillery located in Speyside that started operating in September 2014. In terms of scale, Ballindalloch was identical to what the team from Komasa Jozo had in mind for Kanosuke Distillery, i.e., a 1-ton mash per batch. For the other distillery specs, the inspiration came from in-house, drawing on the company's shochu expertise. The worm tub condensers—also the type used in the production of shochu—are an example of this.

For the equipment itself, the company chose to go with Miyake Industries, who were also contracted by Hombo Shuzo to provide the equipment for Tsunuki Distillery. Construction of the distillery buildings began in March 2017. The equipment was installed later during the summer and the whisky license was granted in November. Production officially started on November 13. On April 28, 2018, the distillery was officially opened to the public. To commemorate the opening of the distillery's visitor center, the first official release coming out of Kanosuke distillery was launched that day: a baby bottle (200ml) of new make.

On September 8, 2021, Kanosuke Distillery announced that Diageo had purchased a minority stake in its operations through drinks accelerator Distill Ventures. Further details have not been made available since, but the investment is bound to result in a significant expansion, increase of production and wider exposure for Kanosuke Distillery in the near future.

Kanosuke Distillery (Malt)

Mash tun:	stainless steel (6kl), lauter tun
Washbacks:	10 stainless steel (7kl), with temperature control
Stills:	3 pot stills: wash still (6kl), spirit still no.1 (3kl), spirit still no.2 (1.6kl)
	indirect heating (steam percolators)
	with horizontal (no.1), descending (no.2) and ascending (no.3) lyne arms, respectively; all with worm tubs

The distillery is U-shaped with one building (when facing the distillery, the building on the left) the production area and the other, parallel building (on the right) for warehousing. The two buildings are connected by a reception area/distillery shop.

Per batch, 1t of malted barley is used. The milling ratios tend to be 2:6:2 (husks:grits:flour). Most of the malted barley used at the distillery is imported from the U.K. The bulk of the production is non-peated. Occasionally, heavily-peated malt (50ppm) is used. During the 2021–2022 season, this amounted to about 15 percent of the total production. Sometimes, mixed mashes (non-peated barley mixed with peated barley) are done, too.

Clear wort

A small amount of local Kyushu barley is used, too. It's traditional practice for sweet potato farmers in the area to rotate crops to avoid losing yield and quality. To replenish the soil, sweet potato is alternated with barley. Komasa Jozo uses the barley grown by the farmers to make barley shochu—which is produced using unmalted barley. Taking this a step further by getting a small portion of the barley malted for whisky making was an obvious path to go down, though the cost involved is considerable. During the 2021–2022 season, just 3t of local Kyushu barley was used. Though the yield is low—the wort tends to be cloudy and the wash doesn't get beyond 6.6%abv—the flavor is good, according to the team at the distillery.

The spacious wooden-floored mash/fermentation room houses the mash tun and the washbacks. The 6kl mash tun is exactly the same as the one used down the road, at Tsunuki Distillery. Only two waters—rather than the traditional three—are used in the mashing process: the first at 65°C and the second at 80°C. One ton of malted barley results in around 5.5kl of wort. This is then transferred to one of the stainless-steel washbacks. Initially, the distillery did one batch per day, seven days a week, and made do with five washbacks. In July 2022, five more washbacks were added, so that production could be increased. Starting in November 2022, the distillery moved to a two-shift system,

Yoshitsugu Komasa with the stills

making it possible to do two batches per day. This allowed the distillery to increase their annual production volume by about 70 percent.

The washbacks are equipped with jackets to control the temperature of the fermentation. The first two days, the temperature inside is kept at 32°C. On day three, it's increased to 35°C. Distillers yeast is used in conjunction with brewers yeast and the fermentation time is 96 hours. During the first year of production, some trials with shochu yeast and wine yeast were run, but the fermentations didn't progress well, so those routes were abandoned.

To enhance the fermentation, the distillery has adapted a process used in sake and shochu making known as *kumikake* (i.e., the recirculation of liquid while making the fermentation starter). In the case of whisky production at Kanosuke, what happens is that a small amount of wash at the end of the fermentation process (at the start of day 5) is added to the washback containing wash that is two days younger, when it is ascertained that the wash in the latter washback is in the right condition to receive that small portion of older wash. The amount that is recirculated and what exactly constitutes "the right condition" are company secrets. Distillers yeast dies out within approximately 48 hours, so in essence, this process is carried out to enhance the secondary lactic fermentation and bring out fruitier flavors. (A similar process is used at Mars Tsunuki Distillery, though the specifics vary, of course.)

Next to the mash/fermentation room is the stillroom. The unusual set-up of three copper pot stills of different shape and size was driven by a desire to produce a variety of distillates with a distinct individuality. At the company's shochu distillery, seven stills are used—big and small, stainless and wooden—but unlike shochu, whisky is double distilled, so in effect, with fewer stills you can obtain comparably more variety. The left still has a 6kl capacity and a horizontal lyne arm; the middle still has a 3kl capacity and a downward lyne arm (at an 80° angle) so there is not so much reflux; the right still is the smallest one, with a capacity of 1.6kl. It also has a different shape—lantern-shaped—and an upward lyne arm (at a 100° angle) so there is lots of reflux during the distillation process. The left still is exclusively used as a wash still and the right one is exclusively used as a spirit still, but the middle one can be used for either. So, in terms of first and second distillation, the options are: left+middle, middle+right, and left+right. In actuality, the left+middle combination is the one used most often, and the small still is not used very frequently. There simply aren't enough spirit receiver tanks to wildly diversify.

Vatting different distillate types before filling into wood further opens up the field of possibilities—so, for example, you can have a cask that contains distillate that has been produced using all three stills (without having been triple distilled).

The spirit is filled into wood at 59.8%abv. In addition to the usual ex-bourbon and ex-sherry casks, the distillery uses a lot of recharred ex-Mellow Kozuru puncheons. These are 450l casks that previously held Mellowed Kozuru. Typically, rice shochu is filled into these casks at 44%abv and left to mature for about half a year, after which the liquid is transferred to a tank. The casks are then refilled with new rice shochu and left for six months. This process continues until, after about 10 years, the casks are exhausted. They are then sent to Ariake Cooperage where they are re-charred before being sent back to the distillery to be filled with new-make spirit or to be used for finishing. Other cask types used in recent years include virgin oak casks, various types of wine casks and barrels that have been loaned to craft brewers and then sent back to be refilled with whisky at Kanosuke Distillery. Each year, the distillery fills about half a dozen mizunara casks. The first 30 casks filled were ex-Oloroso sherry casks, so cask #1 is of that type.

The building parallel to the production building has a small warehouse that holds about 220 barrels. Shutters can be opened to let air from the sea in. Next door from Kanosuke distillery are three big warehouses, two of which were built in 1985 and a third one in 1993, for the purpose of aging Mellowed Kozuru. Two of these are now used to mature whisky. Combined they can hold about 2,000 casks. Sitting in earth up to the waist, these warehouses provide the ideal conditions for maturation: damp and cool, even in the summer. The angels' share is between 6 and 9 percent.

Kanosuke Distillery is one of the few Japanese distilleries happy to welcome visitors. There is no better place to contemplate the distillery's bright future (or anything else, for that matter) than the Mellow Bar on the second floor of the central building. Sitting at the counter—a beautiful 11m-long slab of African cherry wood—with a spectacular view of Fukiage beach and the East China Sea beyond, sipping a whisky or three, vinyl playing in the background, is an absolute joy for the senses.

Between 2018 and 2020, various New Born expressions (aged for less than 3 years) were bottled. The first single malt expression was released on June 16, 2021—Kanosuke 2021 First Edition (58%abv)—followed by the Second Edition (57%abv) on November 12. The following year, the nomenclature was changed and what was, in effect, the third edition was labeled as Kanosuke 2022 Limited Edition (59%abv, released June 15, 2022). A few single cask bottlings for retailers and whisky festivals have been released so far and there is also an ongoing series of distillery-exclusive bottlings (200ml) and an ongoing Artist Edition series.

The first releases

HIOKI DISTILLERY (GRAIN)

When Yoshitsugu Komasa decided to take his company into the field of whisky production, he was keen to make not only malt whisky but also grain whisky. Doing so would enable the company to make its own blended whisky without relying on bulk imports of grain whisky from abroad—in other words, produce a true Japanese blended whisky—which is rare for a craft producer in Japan.

In 2020, a grain whisky license was acquired for the company's existing Hioki Distillery, a 10-minute drive from Kanosuke Distillery, and production could begin in earnest. Hioki Distillery is the company's main manufacturing plant. All shochu as well as their shochu-based gin is made there. Sweet potato shochu is produced during the latter half of the year. During the winter, the distillery focuses on barley and rice shochu production. This left the off-season, spring and early summer, for grain whisky making.

Getting the distillery ready for this new adventure required minimal efforts and funds. All that was needed was a portable mill and a hoist crane to move materials around. All other equipment needed was already there.

The grain whisky made at Hioki Distillery is batch-distilled and made entirely from barley. One batch is 6t, so considerably larger than at the malt whisky distillery. The mashbill consists of 90 percent (unmalted) naked two-row barley and 10 percent dehulled malted barley. The latter is milled, added to the mashing vessel and yeast is added. The former is steeped, steamed, cooled and sent to a fermentation tank outside. The malted barley mash (+yeast) is added and the mixture is left to ferment for 5 days, resulting in a slurry with an abv of 14%.

The wash slurry is then double distilled in stainless steel shochu stills. For this, two 6kl stills are used that can switch between vacuum and atmospheric distillation. For grain whisky production, vacuum distillation is used. (There are various other types of stills at Hioki Distillery, including a rare horizontal shochu still and a wooden still, but these are not used for grain whisky production.) The resulting spirit is then filled into wood and aged.

The stills used to make grain whisky

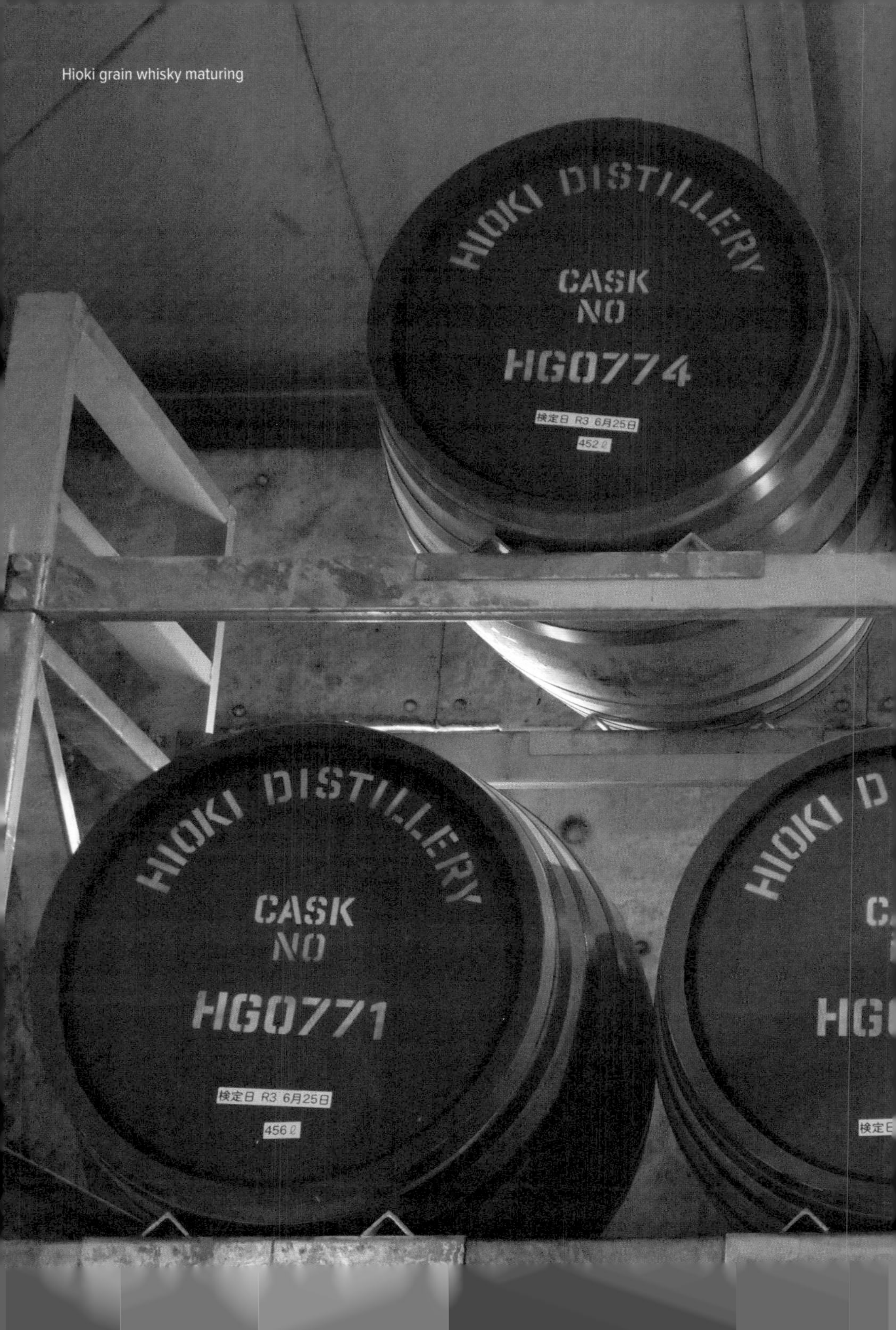

Hioki grain whisky maturing

HIOKI DISTILLERY

CASK
NO

HG0775

検定日 R3 6月25日
455ℓ

HIOKI DISTILLERY

CASK
NO

HG0776

検定日 R3 6月25日
455ℓ

HIOKI DISTILLERY

CASK
NO

HG0773

検定日 R3 6月25日
449ℓ

Sakurao Distillery
(Sakurao Brewery & Distillery Co., Ltd.)

As is so often the case with new craft whisky distilleries in Japan, the distillery may be new but the company behind it is not exactly a new kid on the block. Chugoku Jozo was established in October 1918 as a limited partnership and incorporated in 1938. Apparently, in September of that year, whisky "production" started. Exactly how is lost in the mists of time. From 1963 onwards, the company produced and sold a variety of products, including shochu, sake, mirin, liqueurs and whisky. One of the company's claims to fame is that it was the first to release sake sold in cartons, Hakosake Ichidai (1967). They were also well known for their Daruma shochu.

Up until the liquor-tax change of 1989, Chugoku Jozo's field was second-grade whisky, bottled at the lowest legally-allowed abv (37%), mostly in 1.8l bottles. Their flagship whisky was Glory, which in the early '80s apparently consisted of a vatting of 6+yo Scotch malt whisky imported in bulk, 10+yo in-house-produced malt whisky and 6+yo "grain spirits" (whatever that may have been). In 1989, in-house whisky distilling was suspended, and henceforth, the company sourced all components for their whisky products abroad.

In 2003, the company launched a 17-year-old blended whisky under the name Togouchi. In the course of the next decade and a half, this brand grew into a range of expressions from NAS (no age statement) to 18yo. The malt and grain whisky components for this range were imported from abroad. Some expressions also used neutral spirit, which was made in Japan.

A retired pot still used to make malt whisky at Chugoku Jozo in the distant past

Bits and pieces of Chugoku Jozo's whisky history are still around left and right when you look around their headquarters in Hatsukaichi, but everything is shrouded in mystery. There is a display of old labels, including whisky labels, but who knows what those whiskies tasted like? There is also an old copper pot still standing outside. This probably dates from the late '50s/early '60s and—so we are told—was used to make malt whisky in-house until about 1980, but how and up until when nobody seems to know. No records survive and there is nothing on the pot still that can help us date it, either—not even the name of the manufacturer.

Relics of times past in bottled form are still around, too. There is a Special Very Rare Old "Glory" Blended Malt Whisky "distilled and bottled by the oldest distiller in Hiroshima," so the label says, "guaranteed fully matured in wood and certified by chemical analysis." Another bottle looks even older: Heart Brand, The Finest Old Scotch Whisky, and underneath in small font "Made in Japan." Those were the days . . .

To celebrate the 100th anniversary of the company, Chugoku Jozo decided it was time to restart in-house whisky production with a clean slate and Sakurao Distillery was established on site. (In March 2021, the company name was officially changed to Sakurao Brewery & Distillery Co., Ltd.)

The Malt Distillery

Mash tun:	stainless steel, semi-lauter (5kl)
Washbacks:	3 stainless steel (5.7kl), with temperature control
Stills:	1 pot still (5kl), Holstein (in use from 2020) with descending lyne arm
	1 hybrid still (1.5kl), Holstein (in use from 2018)
	both indirect heating and with stainless steel condensers

Sakurao Distillery is used for the production of gin, whisky and liqueurs. Whisky production started in mid-January 2018 and all steps of the malt whisky-making process from milling to distillation were carried out in one and the same raven-black newly constructed building. In order to ramp up production and to allow for the production of grain whisky, the distillery was expanded between September 2019 and early January 2020. Two buildings were added in the same raven-black color. (Both the exterior and interior are black—the official color of Sakurao, according to the staff.) In addition to the original building (which became Distillery Building #1), there is a Distillery Building #2 (used for the milling, mashing and fermentation of grain whisky—everything except for distillation, which takes place in Building #1). Next to Distillery Building #2 is maturation Warehouse #1. The whisky/gin side of the company's operations occupies the west side of the company's site. The east side is used for the production of sake. In the middle, there is a bottling facility.

Inside Distillery Building #1, a Buhler four-roller mill is used to grind the barley. One batch at Sakurao distillery consists of 1t malted barley, which takes the mill about an hour to process. Since September 2021, usually 2 batches are processed per day. Malted barley is imported from Scotland. About half of the production is non-peated. The other half is medium-peated (20ppm).

The mash tun, made by Bavarian Breweries & Distillers, is a simple affair with two mixing arms and a CIP system. The water for the mashing is spring water from the Ozegawa River. The first of the two waters goes in at between 63°C and 65°C, and the second water at 75°C. For the mashing, less water than normal is used and only about 4.5kl of wort is extracted.

From there, the wort is sent to one of three stainless steel washbacks, also made by Bavarian B&D. The washbacks have a capacity of around 5.7kl, but aren't filled all the way to the top. Distillers yeast is used and the fermentation time is 72 hours. The washbacks are equipped with jackets to keep the temperature stable. Once the temperature inside the washbacks reaches 30°C, the jackets are used to stop the temperature from rising beyond that point. At the end of the process, the wash has an abv of about 9%.

On to the distillation then, but here things get quite complicated. Until the end of 2019, there was only one still—an Arnold Holstein hybrid still consisting of a pot and a column with 6 plates—and the procedure was as follows. Because the pot only had a capacity of 1.5kl and one washback yielded about 3 times as much, the wash from one washback was divided into three batches. On day 1, a first distillation of about 1.5kl of wash took place in the morning and another in the afternoon. By the end of day 1, two-thirds of the washback had been distilled once. The remaining third was distilled the following day in the morning, and then

The first Holstein still installed at the distillery

in the afternoon the combined low wines from those three sub-batches were filled into the pot to be distilled a second time. So, in effect, it took two days to complete a double distillation of one washback and this system was used twice a week. For the first distillations, each of which took about 4 hours, only the pot still part was used. In other words, the vapor went straight from the top of the pot still into the condenser (which is made of stainless steel). For the second distillation, which took around 6 hours, the pot still was used in conjunction with the column: i.e. the vapor was sent from the top of the pot to the bottom of the column, through which it rose before it was condensed. It was a complex system, but it produced the sort of spirit they were after: sweet and accessible. The non-peated new make was clean and light with biscuit and cereal notes, and the peated new make was equally approachable, with more of a floral profile and a hint of *konbu*.

The system may have produced good results, but efficient it was not. And so, when the distillery was expanded in late 2019, the deci-

Two Chugoku Jozo whiskies from the dark ages

sion was made to add another, much larger Holstein still (albeit without column). With the new setup, the double distillation process became more straightforward. Now, the new Holstein lantern-type still is used for the first distillation of one entire batch, and the old Holstein still with column and all six plates is used for the second distillation. Again, there is a slight twist, however. Whereas normally, the heads and tails of the previous batch's second distillation are charged to the spirit still together with the low wines from the current batch, at Sakurao Distillery, the heads and tails of the previous batch are added to the first run (i.e. the wash still) of the current batch. This is done for practical reasons (because the small Holstein still doesn't quite have the requisite capacity to follow the orthodox way of doing things), but again, it produces results. Both stills have propeller-like agitators inside. At Sakurao, the agitator is used for the second distillation, which according to the staff, helps create the sort of spirit they are after: light and estery, with an almost Irish whisky-style profile.

Receiver strength is around 65%abv, which is reduced to 60%abv before being filled into wood. The first three casks filled at Sakurao Distillery were 450l ex-sherry casks (one Oloroso, the two others PX). In terms of maturation policy, the focus is on ex-bourbon and ex-sherry wood but various other cask types are tried out, too.

The distillery ages its spirit in two locations: in Warehouse #1 on-site (when bottled, this single malt is released under the Sakurao brand) and at the Togouchi Sandankyo Warehouse, about 30km northwest, as the crow flies, from the distillery (when bottled, this single malt is released as Togouchi). The climatic conditions of the two sites are markedly different. The distillery itself is located right by the Seto Inland Sea and the warm winds from the Inland Sea and the cold winds from the mountains cause a large temperature difference throughout the year—resulting in a faster maturation. Warehouse #1 has a capacity of 4,000–4,500 barrels and is hybrid dunnage/palletized. The malt whisky is matured dunnage-style (stacked 4 high) and the grain whisky palletized (stacked 5 high). The Togouchi Sandankyo warehouse location, on the other hand, comes with a bit of a story.

Togouchi is a town located in the Nishi-Chugoku Sanshi Quasi-National Park, which was merged with two other towns into what is now Akiota city. In the 1970s, Japanese National Railways began construction of a line intended to connect Kabe station with Hamada station on the Sanin Main Line. The project was abandoned in 1980, but a couple of decades later, Chugoku Jozo started using some of the tunnels built as part of that project to mature their casks of bulk import whisky—hence the Togouchi brand, mentioned earlier in this chapter. "The tunnels are very long—around 400m—and the temperature in the tunnels is a stable 15°C all year round," master distiller Taihei Yamamoto explains, "with a humidity of around 80%, so the maturation is much slower than at our distillery site." The tunnel warehouse has a capacity of around 4,000 casks. At the time of writing, about 1,000 casks were stored there.

July 1, 2021 saw the first release of the company's own single malt whisky, which was in fact a double release to spotlight the two different maturation locations: Single Malt Sakurao 1st Release Cask Strength (54%abv) and Single Malt Togouchi 1st Release Cask Strength (52%abv). A follow-up to both, albeit at 43%abv, was released on June 6, 2022, together with a limited-edition third expression, Sakurao Sherry Cask Stillman's Selection (50%abv).

THE GRAIN DISTILLERY

Ahead of the release of the distillery's first single malt bottlings, Sakurao B&D announced its intention to move away from reliance on bulk imports in order to make all their whisky products compliant with the regulations announced by the Japan Spirits & Liqueur Makers Association in February 2021. This was a bold move from a producer that had been relying on whisky imported in bulk from abroad for decades for its bottled whiskies. On the single malt front, they were on the right track post-2018, of course. But when the company said *all* whisky products, they also meant blended whiskies released henceforth, and for that you need grain whisky . . . which is not really available on the open market in Japan. They had, of course, considered that problem.

When the distillery was expanded, batch distillation of grain whisky was part of the plan. To make this possible, a hammer mill and a unique contraption for distillation were added to the setup. Grain whisky production began in early 2020. The mashbill is made up of 90 percent domestic pearled barley (of the type used in shochu making) and 10 percent malted barley, imported from abroad. After milling, mashing and fermentation, they end up with 4.5kl, about the same as the wash yielded by one batch of malt whisky production.

Until mid-2022, a single still was used for the distillation process and the procedure was similar to that used for malt production pre-2020 (when they were using a single still, as well). There were some tweaks, though. For starters, the equipment was one of a kind: a stainless steel shochu still with a 6-plate copper rectifier attached to it. The first distillation took place in the still (without the column) at vacuum pressure. The combined low wines from three such distillations were then charged to the same still and distilled for the second time, but this time at atmospheric pressure and with the use of the rectifier to boost the abv level.

In mid-2022, a new stainless steel still was added to the setup (without column) and, as was the case with the streamlining of the malt whisky production process described above, it made the grain whisky production process more efficient. The new 4.5kl stainless steel still is used for the first distillation and is run at vacuum pressure. The hybrid contraption that was already there is used for the second distillation at atmospheric pressure and with the column. The grain new make is about 83%abv. It will be interesting to see how the grain whisky made in this way will develop as it matures over the years to come.

Yuza Distillery
(Kinryu Co., Ltd.)

Most new distilleries come with a compelling story—a gripping epiphany, a serendipitous meeting, a lifelong ambition finally realized, a seemingly impossible dream nurtured into reality, a dead past resurrected . . . anything to grab the attention of the market. In the case of Yuza Distillery, there was nothing of the kind. It was a simple matter of survival.

Kinryu, the company behind Yuza Distillery, was founded in 1950 in Sakata city in Yamagata prefecture. It was a joint venture funded by nine local sake producers, initially to make neutral spirit (which is added to most sake to improve the taste and/or inexpensively increase volume, depending on who you ask). Over time, Kinryu started making and selling so-called *korui shochu* (shochu made in a continuous still)—in the case of Kinryu, from molasses, for the most part. Kinryu is the only specialized shochu maker in Yamagata and the bulk of what they make is sold in their home prefecture. Overall consumption of shochu in Japan has been on the decline for decades. In the case of Yamagata prefecture, there's an even more alarming downward curve in play: over the next three decades, the population of Yamagata is expected to fall by over 30 percent, twice as hard as the national average, which is bad enough. There was no need for a crystal ball at Kinryu. They knew they had to do something if they valued the survival of their company. "We knew," company president Masaharu Sasaki relates, "the time to act was now—while there was still time—rather than twenty years later, when it would be too late."

New-make and its habitat for the coming years

The distillery in the fall

Unsurprisingly, they turned to whisky in search of a brighter future. "We started thinking about entering the field of whisky in 2016," Sasaki continues, "but we didn't want to rush into anything. Speaking with small-scale producers like Sasanokawa Shuzo, Venture Whisky and Gaia Flow made it clear that whisky is not just a field that is reserved for the big companies. The more we looked around and the more we spoke with craft producers in Japan, the more we realized this was the right path for us." After a trip to Scotland and a visit to Forsyths in February 2017, the wheels were set in motion.

The Kinryu team spent a year looking for a suitable location and had a list of ten candidate sites. The one they finally settled on, in Yuza city at the foot of Mt. Chokai, ticked all the boxes. Mt. Chokai has the highest precipitation of any mountain in Japan, so there's an abundance of good quality spring water—which explains the huge patchwork of rice fields in the area. "We need around 22kl of water per hour for our operations, but we can easily get over 50kl/h here, so we're assured of both quality and quantity," Sasaki explains. The scenic beauty of the area was another consideration. The shape of Mt. Chokai changes depending on the angle it is viewed from. Looking through the large windows of the stillhouse, the twin peaks stand out beautifully—which is shown in the distillery logo, too. Movie buffs may be familiar with the view, as the Academy Award-winning movie *Okuribito* (Departures, 2008) features an iconic scene filmed very near where the distillery was built.

Of course, practical considerations were important, too. There was a road with good access for trucks. It was also possible to discharge the pot ale and spent lees (the latter after removing toxic levels of copper) directly into the local sewer system.

For the equipment, Kinryu decided to go with the Scottish company Forsyths rather than with their Japanese colleagues at Miyake Industries—again, a matter of pragmatism. "Miyake is aimed at pros," Sasaki explains. "They come in, install the equipment and leave. They expect you to already be familiar with how to operate the equipment. Forsyths was a better fit for us, because they teach you how to work the equipment and offer tremendous support to beginning whisky distillers." The pot stills arrived at Sakata port on June 29, 2018 and were moved inside the distillery building two days later. After that, the team from Forsyths spent three hot summer months (July–September) getting the distillery ready. On September 27, the local tax office granted Yuza Distillery its whisky-making license.

The Distillery

Mash tun:	stainless steel (5kl), semi-lauter tun
Washbacks:	4 Douglas fir (7.4kl)
Stills:	1 pair (wash still 5kl, spirit still 3.4kl), Forsyths
	indirect heating (steam)
	both with downward lyne arms and shell-and-tube condensers

The first official distillation took place on November 4–5, 2018. To run the distillery, Sasaki had assembled a trio of absolute beginners: mashwoman Shione Okada, stillwoman Miho Saito and warehouseman Koji Sato. At the time, Okada and Saito were fresh out of university. Sato was in his early '30s and had left his job in banking to pursue his dream of making whisky. "I didn't want to bring in an expert or a veteran," Sasaki explains, "because then it becomes that person's distillery. I wanted to start from zero, with young, motivated people and put our own stamp on things."

The vision of the distillery team is encapsulated in an acronym they came up with: TLAS. It doesn't exactly roll off the tongue, but other

The distillery team

configurations of the same letters would have been a bit unfortunate. T stands for Tiny. The land is 4,550 square meters but the distillery occupies just 620 square meters. The L . . . we'll come back to later. The A stands for Authentic. "Even though sake consumption is on the decline, those who make sake using traditional brewing methods remain," Sasaki explains. "Our thinking is the same with respect to whisky-making, which means: traditional Scottish distilling practice albeit with a Japanese mindset."

Theset up and processes are textbook Scottish. The barley used is imported from Scotland, too. The house style is non-peated and one batch is 1t. The mashing takes place in a 5kl mash tun and follows the standard "three waters" procedure: the first 3,750l at 63.5°C, the second 1,750l at 76°C and the third (which is used for the next batch) 3,210l at 86°C.

For the fermentation, there are five Douglas fir washbacks, made in Japan—in fact, by the same company that made the washbacks for Chichibu Distillery. Distillers yeast is used and the fermentation time is 90 hours. Then, it's on to the distillation. The wash still is 5kl and has a

Cask #13 being rolled to its resting place

straight head—inspired by Macallan, apparently. The spirit still is 3.4kl and has a boil ball—inspired by Glendronach, it seems. Both stills are equipped with downward lyne arms and shell-and-tube condensers. The spirit aimed for is a rich yet clean spirit.

The maturation regime is classic, through and through: 63.5% filling strength, primarily ex-bourbon casks supplied by Speyside Cooperage and two dunnage warehouses. Even the filling store occupying the corner of Warehouse 1 is retro: no fancy state-of-the-art filling pumps here, but an old-fashioned platform scale to weigh the casks before and after they're filled. Just the way it was done 50 years ago in Scotland. The first cask filling took place on November 6, 2018. The climate in Yuza city is very different from Scotland but Sasaki feels they got the better deal. "We've got a temperature difference of 40°C in the course of a year—from -5°C in the winter to 36°C in summer—so we're expecting our whisky to mature faster. A 5yo Yuza would be like an 8yo Scotch."

This brings us to the S, for Supreme. "We're focusing on single malt exclusively," Sasaki explains. "We don't have the scale or the skills to compete with other companies in the blends market. Also, quality is what we are after, so we're not going to release anything premature. Sake makers in this prefecture routinely take the highest awards at competitions domestically and abroad, so they made it clear to us they were supportive as long as we kept the flag of the region flying high—which we aim to do."

And finally: L—for Lovely. "It's very dark here during the winter months," Sasaki points out. "People wear dark clothes, eyes cast down as they walk, leaning into the wind. I want Yuza Distillery to be an element of brightness, of loveliness if you like, in this landscape. So that, when people see the bright white walls of our distillery with the phonebox red doors and window frames, they get the feeling there's something different—something special happening here."

In February 2022, the distillery presented its first single malt release: YUZA First Edition 2022, matured entirely in ex-bourbon barrels (61%abv; limited to 8,500 bottles). A one-off release of YUZA Asahimachi Wine Barrel Aged Whisky (in baby bottles of 180ml) came out in August 2022. Because of the Yamagata collaborative nature of the project—whisky from Yuza aged for 3 years in ex-red wine casks from Asahimachi Wine—this release was limited to retail outlets in the home prefecture of the producers.

Stillwoman Miho Saito preparing for the middle cut

Top: Stillwoman Miho Saito turning down the heat on the wash still; bottom: Mashwoman Shione Okada

Tamba Distillery
(Kizakura Co., Ltd.)

Tamba Distillery is located in Tamba-Sasayama, a historical city in the eastern-central part of Hyogo. It is located at 300m altitude, in an inland basin surrounded by mountains on all sides and blessed with a sub-tropical climate.

Tamba Distillery is owned by Kizakura Co., Ltd., a liquor producer founded in 1925 and based in the Fushimi district of Kyoto city. Kizakura is famous for its sake and the cheeky *kappa* character it created to promote its brand in 1955 is famous throughout Japan to this day. (*Kappa* are amphibious supernatural spirits said to inhabit the ponds and rivers of Japan.) Its *kappa* character has been featured in rather naughty (think: lots of nudity) animated TV commercials since 1957.

In 1974, the company built a sake factory in Tamba-Sasayama—also well-known as a sake-producing area—to increase production volume. In 2004, a *honkaku* shochu production license was obtained for the Tamba factory.

In 1995, Kizakura was the first liquor producer in Kyoto to enter the craft beer field. One lucrative field that had remained unexplored was whisky. In 2018, the company remedied that by obtaining a whisky production license for its Tamba factory.

Tamba 1st Edition

The Distillery

Washbacks: 2 enamel-coated tanks

1 stainless steel tank (4kl)

Stills: 1 stainless steel still with copper plate inserted (used until October 2021)

1 pair of copper pots (wash still 2.5kl, spirit still 2kl), Forsyths (used from November 2021)

indirect heating

slightly ascending and descending lyne arms, resp., both with shell-and-tube condensers

Per batch, 1.5t malted barley is used and both peated and non-peated barley is used. Interestingly, the first part of the whisky-making process takes place off-site. Looking to make the most of the famed Fushimi-water—renowned for its purity, softness and flavor in the sake business—the company does the milling and mashing at its Fushimi factory. The wort (about 8kl per batch) is then transported to the distillery, an hour-and-a-half away, by truck.

The fermentation takes place in two enamel-coated open-top tanks of the type used in sake production. The distillery uses a variety of yeasts (including distillers yeast, sake yeast and brewers yeast).

Starting in 2018, until the fall of 2021, distillation took place in a stainless steel still of the type used in shochu making, albeit fitted with a copper plate inside. In October 2021, two copper pots made by Forsyths were installed: a 2.5kl wash still with a straight head and slightly ascending lyne arm, and a 2kl spirit still with a bulge and a slightly descending lyne arm—both with shell-and-tube condensers. These twin pots have been used for whisky production since November of that year. According to the company, the spirit character aimed for is soft, gentle and light.

Maturation takes place in a dunnage-style warehouse on site, with a capacity of around 500 casks. Ex-bourbon, ex-sherry and virgin oak are the most-used cask types, for the time being.

On April 1, 2022, the first single malt, Kizakura Whisky Tamba 1st Edition, was released (47%abv). This contained whisky made using the stainless steel still and was a vatting of spirit matured in ex-bourbon and virgin oak casks. It was limited to a mere 600 bottles and available to the on-trade (bars, restaurants, etc.) only. At the same time, the company released a more widely available product, Sakura Chronos (47%abv), a blend of malt whisky imported from Scotland and in-house-produced malt whisky.

It's worth noting that, on January 18, 2021, Kizakura obtained another whisky license—this time, for their Misugura factory in Kyoto city. This seems to indicate that the company has ambitious plans on the whisky front.

●

Ichiro Akuto in the stillhouse

Chichibu II
(Venture Whisky)

The demand for Ichiro's Malt vastly outstrips supply. It's a nice problem to have, but a problem nonetheless. Being the sort of person who is always way ahead of the curve—before anyone else even sees a curve—Ichiro Akuto decided to do something about this state of affairs: by making more . . . at a brand-new, second distillery. "Production is so small at Chichibu Distillery," Ichiro explains, "even working in two shifts, we can only make about 320lpa a day, which is a little over two barrels. In 2014, I started thinking about building a second distillery." Two years later, he decided to get serious and got in touch with Forsyths, who had supplied the equipment for his first distillery.

Unlike Suntory, Nikka and even Hombo Shuzo, who built their second distilleries in locations that were very different in character from the environment of their first distilleries, Ichiro wanted to stay in his hometown of Chichibu. "It wasn't easy to find land," Ichiro says. "I looked at many sites for my second distillery, but I just couldn't find the right one." He eventually found it a stone's throw from his first one. All it takes to reach it is a two-minute drive. "The plot was part of a parcel of land that was leased to a local company that makes parts for car manufacturers and so on," Ichiro explains, "but the president of the company loves whisky—in fact, he is a private cask owner at Chichibu Distillery—so we managed to arrange to take over the lease of the 15,000m² of unused land next to their factory."

Construction began in April of 2018. A little over a year later, the distillery was ready for production. The first spirit (test production) came off the stills on July 9, 2019 and the first cask (an ex-bourbon hogshead) was filled on July 26. The distillery was in full swing after the traditional summer break.

The Distillery

Mash tun:	stainless steel (10kl), semi-lauter
Washbacks:	5 French oak (5kl)
Stills:	1 pair (wash still 10kl, spirit still 6.5kl), Forsyths
	both direct-fired (natural gas)
	both with downward lyne arms and shell-and-tube condensers

Ichiro has an inquisitive mind, but he knows there's no point in varying all parameters, so there are quite a few features of the new distillery that are the same as at Chichibu I. What's markedly different is the scale. "The new distillery is five times as big as the first one, so the annual production volume is around 260,000lpa, and that's working in just one shift, which we are planning on doing for the first couple of years," Ichiro points out.

On the barley front, things are a little different. With two distilleries active, Ichiro decided to use the original (first) distillery for the distillation of domestically sourced malted barley mainly (non-peated) and for heavily-peated barley (50ppm, imported from Scotland). At Chichibu II, there is a bit of non-peated production, but most of the malted barley processed is medium (20–30ppm) or lightly (10ppm) peated. At Chichibu II, one batch is 2t and the mill is similar to that used at Chichibu I, an Alan Ruddock mill but twice the size.

The water is the same as that used at Chichibu I. The mash tun—stainless steel with a copper canopy—is obviously a different beast. No more hand-stirring the mash at the second distillery with the new semi-lauter tun, although the process is still closely monitored. Asked about the long, vertical sideglass on the mash tun, Ichiro says: "that was my request, as I want to be able to check the grain bed and the filtration process." Obsessive? Maybe a little.

For the fermentation process, Ichiro stuck with wooden vessels, but with a twist. "I wanted to use Japanese oak, just like at Chichibu I, but it's extremely difficult to get mizunara staves of this size, so I decided to go for French oak, instead. I had visited Taransaud Cooperage in France a number of times and found their wooden tanks to be very good so I commissioned them to make the washbacks for the new distillery."

Ichiro checking the washbacks during the construction phase

The stills and a basket of yeast being "warmed up" for use between them

Above: The gate to the distillery; below: The first cask filled, a hogshead

At the moment, there are 5 washbacks (15kl capacity with 10kl of wort going in), but there's room for a few more. "When we move to a two-shift system," Ichiro explains, "we'll add three more." As far as the yeast is concerned, Ichiro is sticking with his proprietary strain.

In the stillhouse, we have a déjà vu. The stills are much bigger, of course (10kl and 6.5kl, resp.), but they look eerily similar to those of Chichibu I. "They are the same shape," Ichiro smiles, "and even the lyne-arm angle is the same (12° downward, if you need to know)." But appearances can be deceptive. Unlike at Chichibu I, where the stills are indirect-heated, both the wash still and the spirit still at the new distillery are direct-fired. "It's a very traditional way," Ichiro says, "and this has a big impact on the character of the spirit. It produces a more robust, a more complex spirit."

Direct heating makes the distillation process harder to control. "That's for sure," Ichiro says, "but that's why we're doing it. We're no longer novices. At the first distillery, we learned how to make whisky. Now, we're experienced, so we're ready for this." Demonstrating the temperature control and the way in which the perfectly aligned pairs of sight glasses on the front and back with the natural backlight make it easy to monitor and control the first distillation, it's clear Ichiro has given this some thought.

The first distillation takes 6–7 hours, and the second distillation takes 5–6 hours. The cut points are similar to those at Chichibu I. "Just like at Chichibu I," Ichiro goes on, "the cut is made by nosing and tasting, not by numbers." As always, the human element is important. "I know that distilleries can be operated by computers these days, but I want people working here to know exactly what is happening every single moment during each phase of the whisky-making process."

Increased production means increased storage space, but Ichiro has got that covered, too. A new dunnage warehouse (#6) was built right next to the Chichibu II distillery building. That was of the same capacity as the other dunnage warehouses at the annex site (about 3,000 casks). In 2020, construction of a much larger (18,000-cask capacity) warehouse began, in front of #6. That one (#7), a state-of-the-art racked warehouse, has been in use since February 2021.

At the time of writing, no whisky produced at Chichibu II has been released yet.

The first Osuzu Malt release

OSUZU MALT

OSUZUYAMA DISTILLERY

JAPANESE WHISKY

ESTABLISHED 1998

DISTILLED IN MIYAZAKI, JAPAN.
HANDCRAFTED FROM LOCALLY GROWN BARLEY,
USING THE BOX MALTING METHOD.

NEW MAKE

VOLUME 200ml

ALCOHOL 59%

JAPANESE WHISKY

OSUZU MALT

NEW MAKE

HANDCRAFTED FROM LOCALLY
GROWN BARLEY, USING THE BOX
MALTING METHOD

尾鈴山蒸留所
シングルモルトウイスキー

alc.59% / vol.200ml

Osuzuyama Distillery
(Kuroki Honten Co., Ltd.)

Kuroki Honten is one of the most iconic shochu producers in Japan. Founded in 1885 in Miyazaki prefecture, the company is most famous for its barrel-aged barley shochu Hyakunen no Kodoku (literally, "One Hundred Years of Solitude," named after the novel by Gabriel García Márquez). The company is currently run by 5th generation president Shinsaku Kuroki, who started a new chapter in the company's history by taking it into the fields of gin and whisky.

Osuzuyama Distillery was established by Kuroki Honten in 1998 as a shochu distillery. The distillery takes its name from the Osuzu Mountain massif, where it is located. Whisky production started on November 1, 2019.

According to the company, the pristine water was the main attraction of the site, and with an annual rainfall of 3,000ml, there is certainly plenty of it available. Water for production is taken close to the source in the upper streams of Osuzu Mountain. The company's goal, with all the distilled spirits they produce, is to create something "that is uniquely ours, that can only be achieved on this land." That's not empty rhetoric. All ingredients—be it potatoes, barley or rice—are sourced locally (in the Kyushu region) and the company also has its own farm (Yomigaeru Daichi no Kai). The company's entire supply of barley comes from their own farm. For whisky production, the malting itself is done in-house (in a greenhouse, in fact) using a specially developed technique involving small boxes, which Kuroki has dubbed "box malting" (a tongue-in-cheek reference to the "floor malting" technique traditionally used in Scotland).

The Distillery

Mash tun:	stainless steel (4kl)
Washbacks:	15 open-top cedar
Stills:	2 stainless steel shochu stills, hybrid heating system (steam injection/direct heating)
	1 copper pot still (2kl), Miyake
	indirect heating (steam)
	with descending lyne arm and shell-and-tube condenser
	1 small copper pot still (400l) for gin and spirits, Miyake

Per batch, 800kg of malted barley is processed. The milling ratios are 3:5:2 (husks:grits:flour), the bigger husk percentage creating a better filter bed and a clearer wort. Mashing takes place in a 4kl stainless steel tun, manufactured by Miyake Industries. For the fermentation, 15 fermenters made of *Obi sugi* (a type of cedar tree from Miyazaki prefecture, traditionally used in shipbuilding throughout Japan) are used. These are also used for shochu production. The distillation process is rather unique. For the first distillation, two stainless-steel shochu stills are used. For the second distillation, a copper pot still made by Miyake Industries is used. This still has a straight head, a descending lyne arm and is fitted with a shell-and-tube condenser. There is also a small 400l copper still (also made by Miyake) for the production of gin and other spirits.

The distillery has released some Osuzu Malt New Make (unaged) and Osuzu Malt New Born bottlings (aged for 18 months and 27 months, released in 2021 and 2022, respectively) that have shown great promise.

Yatogi Falls in Osuzu Prefectural Natural Park

The warehouse and Sakurajima in the background

The Ontake Distillery
(Nishi Shuzo)

The Ontake Distillery was established by liquor producer Nishi Shuzo in 2019 and is part of a golf course they own, Kagoshima Golf Resort. Nishi Shuzo traces its history back to 1845 and is best known for its sweet potato shochu. The company's Hozan lineup is highly regarded among aficionados of sweet potato shochu and they also produce a sweet potato shochu aged in sherry casks (Tenshi no Yuwake—literally "angels' temptation," a reference to the so-called angels' share).

Ontake is the formal name for the active volcano just east of central Kagoshima city that constitutes Sakurajima. As one might expect, the distillery isn't actually located there. The distillery took the name because of the fabulous view of Ontake it offers from the distillery site, a 20-minute drive southwest from downtown Kagoshima city, up into the mountains.

The Ontake Distillery is one of the most spotless distilleries you'll find in Japan (or anywhere in the world, for that matter). It is also one of the most beautifully designed, sparing no expense, and is integrated in the actual golf course. The water from the condensers flows into a pond separating the production building from the warehouse, and turns into a creek at the 18th hole.

The equipment was manufactured by Miyake Industries and production started in December 2019. The distillery operates seven days a week and each day a 1t-batch of malted barley is processed. For the time being, only non-peated malted barley is used. Mashing takes place in a 4.7kl lauter tun and the aim is a clear wort. For the fermentation, five 6.6kl stainless steel washbacks fitted with water jackets and switchers are used. The yeast used is a proprietary strain and the fermentation

time is 5 days. Distillation takes place in two copper pot stills (6kl and 3kl capacity, resp.), both with ascending lyne arms. Both distillations are done very slowly and the cut is made by nosing and tasting. The spirit still has a boil ball and the aim is to collect a clean spirit.

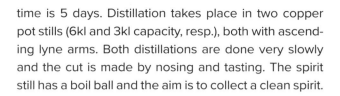

The Distillery

Mash tun:	stainless steel, lauter tun (1t)
Washbacks:	5 stainless steel, with water jackets
Pot stills:	1 pair (wash still 6kl, spirit still 3kl), Miyake
	indirect heating (steam)
	both with upward lyne arms and shell-and-tube condensers

There is one racked warehouse on site, which is underground for the most part and therefore cool all year round. The angels' share is a mere 1 percent (for the first year of maturation). Most of the production is aged in real (i.e. non-seasoned) ex-Oloroso butts, of the type the company has a good supply of for their Tenshi no Yuwake shochu. The distillery is also using ex-Pinot Noir casks, sourced from the winery it owns in New Zealand (Urlar, acquired in 2018). A single malt release is planned as soon as the spirit maturing reaches 3 years of age.

The Ontake Distillery is one of the few Japanese distilleries that runs an Owner's Cask program. The casks offered are sherry butts and therefore pricy, but owning a cask comes with benefits involving the use of the golf course and clubhouse built thereon. The Owner's Cask program was started in early 2020, so we can expect to see quite a few private bottlings in a few years' time.

The stills

The gate to the distillery

Hikari Distillery
(Hikari Distillery Ltd.)

Walking through the gates of Hikari Distillery, you would think you were in a picturesque part of the Low Countries. Two imposing blackish-grey twin buildings with stepped-gable façades typical of 17th-century Dutch and Flemish architecture face the visitor, and to the left, in contrasting white, a stately country house seems to be plucked straight out of rural Flanders. And yet, it's a distillery and it's located in the Japanese countryside, about an hour north of Tokyo. Closer to the twin buildings, the top of the wrought-iron inner gate connecting the twin buildings confirms that this is a distillery after all but the motto "Dum Spiro Spero" seems to be another nod to Old Europe. Not so quickly, though. "*Dum Spiro Spero*—'While I breathe, I hope' in Latin—was the motto of the Kingdom of Sarawak," relates distillery founder and CEO Eric Chhoa, "and that's the state within Malaysia on the northern coast of Borneo where I'm from. As for the architectural style, I just happen to have a soft spot for the sort of historic buildings you see in cities like Antwerp, Bruges and Amsterdam."

Hikari Distillery is somewhat unusual in many regards. It's the first foreign-owned licensed whisky distillery in Japan. One might have expected the team at the distillery to make a big song and dance of this, but something else that sets this enterprise apart from its peers—certainly in Japan—is that they are shunning the spotlight as much as possible: no press releases, no grand openings, no new-make bottled, no 7-month aged works-in-progress released, no private casks sold and no visitors, please. Even though Chhoa has enough business acumen to know that, often, no PR is the best PR, the distillery's low-key stance

Not quite Flanders, but close...

is pragmatic rather than strategic. "We weren't sure how our enterprise would be perceived by the Japanese whisky community, so rather than be distracted by that, we decided to focus on the task at hand, which is to create a top-quality, distinctive single malt whisky. Also, we have a very small team here." In addition to Chhoa, who literally lives at the distillery during the week and is very much a hands-on CEO, there's Masao Okuzawa, mashman, stillman, warehouseman and jack-of-all-trades, and Emi Ueno, who takes care of administration. And that's it: essentially, a trio operation.

Exactly how and why a Malaysian businessman in his late '50s ended up making whisky in the Japanese countryside is a long story. The short version is that Eric Chhoa discovered Scotch whisky in his early '30s in New York City and quickly developed a fondness for it. By that time, after periods studying in Japan and in the U.S. and working in investment banking for a couple of years, he was back in Malaysia and the U.K., running a fiber optic cable and components business. "I spent the past 25 years of my life working in that particular industry," Chhoa relates, "but on business trips, I would often try to make a detour via Scotland. On my fortieth birthday, I decided to set up a distillery." In the course of the next decade, Chhoa sought out opportunities to learn more about the whisky-making process and worked as an apprentice at various distilleries. "The two that stood out for me were St. George's Distillery in Norfolk and Strathearn Distillery in Perthshire—the former because my own distillery ended up being very similar to in size and the latter because everything was done on a very small scale with very little mechanical assistance and lots of elbow grease."

On his fiftieth birthday, Chhoa decided to move his whisky project into overdrive. In 2014, he started looking for a location. Japan was his main focus, but Australia—Tasmania, in particular—was on the table, too. In the end, he settled on Japan. "I had spent many years in Japan, knew the culture very well, and felt this was the right place to build my distillery," Chhoa explains. "There's a strong brewing tradition in Japan and a fastidiousness and commitment to quality that's ingrained in the culture." Chhoa was keen to find a site within a one-hour radius from Tokyo and found a suitable piece of land in Konosu city, in Saitama prefecture, which he purchased in the summer of 2015. "The site has an interesting history. There used to be a minor castle here and, more recently, a silk processing factory. Raw silk would be transported from neighboring Gunma prefecture down the Arakawa River and there was a vibrant silk processing industry in Konosu until faltering demand for silk, the inflow of cheap silk products from overseas and improvements in chemical fibers forced many factories to close their doors. The factory that was on this site was in that unfortunate position, too. Interestingly, it apparently produced silk parachutes for the war effort during World War II. In the 1970s, the factory disappeared and, since then, the land had been unused."

That the site had serious potential for whisky production was suggested by the historical presence of many sake breweries in the area, along the Nakasendo, one of feudal Japan's highways. Water quality is of key importance in sake brewing and an analysis of the local groundwater confirmed that it ticked all the right boxes for whisky-making, too. For the equipment, Chhoa reached out to Forsyths in Scotland. "I wanted a very compact distillery with all the production equipment on skids—sort of like giant Lego blocks—to facilitate implementation as well as to allow for easy reconfiguration, if needed, in the future," he relates. "Keen on exploring new ideas, Richard Forsyth Jr. saw the logic in this and made it happen. The equipment arrived in Japan in November 2019 and we were fortunate enough to be able to get the commissioning done before COVID-19 hit." The first spirit came off the still on February 24, 2020, and the first cask-filling took place on March 11.

The Distillery

Mash tun:	stainless steel, semi-lauter tun (1t)
Washbacks:	6 stainless steel (7.5kl), no temperature control
Pot stills:	1 pair (wash still 5.5kl, spirit still 3.6kl), Forsyths indirect heating (steam)
	both with downward lyne arms and shell-and-tube condensers

Having a distillery is one thing. Finding the right person to actually make whisky is another. Japan is not exactly blessed with a giant pool of skilled whisky-makers, so Eric Chhoa cast his net a bit wider, looking for a local with brewing experience and the right mindset. He struck gold and found Masao Okuzawa, a man in his early '50s from neighboring Ibaraki prefecture who had a wealth of experience in the fields of craft beer, sake and wine production, but who—since working as a bartender in the mid-1980s and discovering Scotch whisky—had always harbored the hope of one day being able to work in whisky production. A few years into production, it's practically impossible to think of the distillery without Okuzawa. He's the *shokunin* there—a word often translated as "artisan" or "craftsman" but, in Japanese, the connotations include a total commitment to one's craft and a journey towards perfection (never attained, of course).

Hikari Distillery's production season runs from the end of October to about mid-June. The rest of the year, it's simply too hot for comfort—fermentation would be compromised and cooling at various stages of the production process would be a serious struggle. Konosu city is next to Kumagaya city, which is the hottest place in summer in Japan, so it gets rather toasty in the production building in the summer.

The distillery takes its water from a borehole on site, drilled to a 120m depth. Batch size is 1t and in an average week, four batches are processed. Malted barley is imported and non-peated for the most part. Occasionally, medium and heavily-peated malt (24ppm and 50ppm, resp.) is used. Mashing takes place in a stainless steel semi-lauter tun with a copper canopy. Then, the wort is sent to one of six stainless steel washbacks (7.5kl capacity) without temperature control. For non-peated production, distillers yeast is used in conjunction with brewers yeast. For peated batches, the team uses distillers yeast only. The standard fermentation time is 90 hours, but the team has experimented with shorter and longer fermentations as well. The wash tends to be around 8.2%abv by the end of the process, but this is then slightly lowered to 7%abv before being sent to the wash still. For the distillation, a 5.5kl lantern-type wash still and a 3.6kl spirit still with a boil ball is used. Both are fairly squat (because of building height restrictions), steam-heated, with descending lyne arms and shell-and-tube condensers. Distillation is unhurried—both first and second 10 hours on average—and the aim is a floral, fruity spirit.

The spirit is filled into wood at 62–63.5%abv and about 85 percent of production ends up in ex-bourbon barrels. Other cask types used so far are ex-Oloroso and ex-Manzanilla butts and ex-barley shochu puncheons. Warehouse No.1 (the left twin building) is dunnage-style with casks stacked four high. Two years into production, that was full (500-odd casks) so construction of a new, much larger warehouse on

The team in front of the stills

Inside Warehouse No.1

site started in October 2021. Warehouse No.2 was completed in March 2022 and has a capacity of around 3,000 casks—good for 6 to 7 years.

The above may give the impression of a fairly run-of-the-mill operation, but there is some decidedly nonstandard production going on at Hikari Distillery as well. "It's important to have some creative freedom," Chhoa points out, "so, from time to time, we explore the unusual and both Masao and I have our own pet projects." One of Chhoa's projects involved Manuka-smoked malt, imported from New Zealand. "We took delivery of 20 tons of Manuka-smoked malt at the end of 2021 and started distilling that in early January 2022." The new-make turned out to be very liquorice-forward with a nice spice kick and gentle wood smoke in the background. "We've filled lots of this into ex-Woodford Reserve Rye casks," Chhoa reveals. "We have a soft spot for these casks and are hoping they will mesh well with the character of the new-make."

Okuzawa's projects—affectionately dubbed "Okuzawa Specials" by the team—push the envelope even more. His first "special" involved three different types of malt (crystal malt, chocolate malt and heavily-peated malt), which were distilled separately, the distillates vatted

together, rested for 10 months in 1,000-liter clay pots (which had previously been used for resting barley shochu) before being filled into Japanese chestnut casks. The plan is to finish them later in casks fitted with *sakura* (Japanese cherry wood) heads. For his second "special," Okuzawa distilled rye and wheat malt—again, resting the distillate in the clay pots for 10 months before filling it into ex-bourbon wood. Okuzawa has also ventured into making small-batch grain whisky, double-distilling a mashbill consisting of 65 percent malted barley and 35 percent Yamada Nishiki rice (famous for its use in high-quality sake brewing). "It's a very expensive kind of grain whisky," Okuzawa muses, "but we are keen to try out grain types other than malted barley."

There's something refreshing about the self-contained approach of the team at Hikari Distillery. There's no hobnobbing with fellow whisky-makers in Japan and the team is in no hurry to release their first whisky. When the whisky is ready, Chhoa is planning to export 90 percent of it—mainly to the UK, mainland Europe, Hong Kong and Singapore. The projected volume is a mere 60,000 bottles a year, so there won't be much left for the domestic market.

Yasato Distillery
(Kiuchi Shuzo)

Kiuchi Shuzo entered the field of whisky in 2016. That story can be found earlier in this book, in the Nukada Distillery chapter. In 2019, it became clear that the company had more ambitious plans on the whisky front, when word leaked that they were in the process of setting up a much bigger, stand-alone whisky distillery in the town of Ishioka, near Mt. Tsukuba. Those familiar with the Kiuchi brothers—Toshiyuki and Yoichi—knew that this was not going to be an enterprise modeled after Scottish practice.

"We are looking to create a genuinely new kind of whisky, not a copy of Scottish whisky," Toshiyuki asserts. "Most craft whisky distilleries in Japan are set up as copies of Scottish distilleries. To a certain extent, I see parallels with the craft beer movement that took off in Japan twenty years ago. Most craft brewers then were copying the German style. We were one of the first to enter the field of craft brewing after the government relaxed regulations governing micro-brewing in 1996, but right from the start, we set out to create our own style of beer." It's not hard to see why the Kiuchi brothers would have a similar vision for their whisky. At the time of writing, the Hitachino Nest beer brand with its familiar owl-logo is available in over 40 countries and is the most widely recognized Japanese craft beer worldwide. Clearly, they are doing something right.

The idea to set up a stand-alone distillery took root in early 2018. "We started scouting for locations in 2016, and initially we focused on

The stillroom

abandoned schools," Toshiyuki relates, "but the buildings we came across were in very poor condition and not really suitable for the purpose of making whisky. Then, we found this building in the Yasato district of Ishioka, which was designed by a famous local architect and was used as a community center. It was a little smaller than we would have liked, but we worked around that. The building was 50 years old and had been damaged by earthquakes, so we completely renovated it. In retrospect, it probably would have been cheaper to tear it down and build a new structure from the ground up."

In what may seem like another irrational move, the distillery kit was sourced from many different companies around the world. There is reason to this madness, though. "We are beginners in the field of whisky," Toshiyuki explains, "so we want to try lots of things and find a direction, find our way. If we had ordered all distillery equipment from one place—say Forsyths in Scotland—we would be constrained in our thinking by that particular setup and we would be making whisky in that particular style, following Scottish practice. But, we have engineers in-house, and we have know-how from sake brewing and beer brewing, so we designed the distillery ourselves and sourced the equipment from companies around the world that, in most cases, we already had a relationship with."

The Distillery

Mash tun:	stainless steel, mash tun and lauter tun
Washbacks:	2 mixed oak (8.4kl), with temperature control
	2 French acacia (8.4kl), with temperature control
	4 stainless steel (17.6kl), with temperature control
Stills:	1 pair (wash still 12kl, spirit still 7.5kl), Forsyths indirect heating (steam)
	with descending lyne arms and shell-and-tube condensers
	1 hybrid still (4kl), Ziemann, with 3 columns and gin basket

Late summer at Yasato distillery

The distillery is set up so that both malt and grain whisky can be produced (the latter using batch distillation rather than continuous distillation). At the time of writing, malt whisky accounted for 80–90 percent of production. The malted barley used is non-peated for the most part. Occasionally, some lightly or medium-peated barley is used. (Extremes of flavor don't seem to be of interest to Kiuchi Shuzo. The brewery doesn't have a ridiculously hoppy beer in its portfolio, either.)

About 10–20 percent of the annual production is grain whisky. Two types of mashbill are used for this: one consisting of rice bran (the byproduct of rice polishing for sake production) and malted barley in equal measure; the other is made up of wheat (grown in Ibaraki) and malted barley, again in equal measure. The latter mashbill is used more often, as the amount of rice bran available is rather limited. At Yasato distillery, grain whisky production is considerably more expensive than malt whisky production.

Toshiyuki Kiuchi checking the spirit

The grain store is set up so that different types of grain can be handled with equal ease. There are two bag stations—which can contain the same type of grain or a different type each—and there is also a separate small feed, and in all three cases, the grain can either go through the four-roll Alan Ruddock mill and into the hopper, or be directed straight into the hopper.

The grist hopper has a capacity of 1.6t, but standard batch size at Yasato distillery (for both malt and grain whisky production) is 1t, which results in around 5kl of wort. In the mash room, there are two tuns: a mash tun, made by Ziemann Holvrieka and fitted with a Steeles masher made by Briggs, and a lauter tun, made by Briggs. The mash tun has a steam jacket, so it can be used as a cooker to accommodate the different gelatinization temperatures of various grains. The "first water" phase (1–2 hours) takes place in the mash tun; the "second water" phase (4 hours) in the lauter tun. The aim is a clear wort.

Given the variety of grains used, it's not too much of a gamble to expect a variety of options for the next stage of the production process, too: the fermentation. There are four wooden washbacks indoors, made by the Italian company Garbellotto. These have a capacity of 8.4kl but are only filled to 5kl. Two washbacks are made of mixed oak—Slavonian and French—and two are made of French acacia. Each of the wooden washbacks has a cold plate suspended in the liquid, to keep

The new hybrid still at Yasato distillery

the temperature inside under 30°C. There are also four large stainless steel fermenters outside. These are fitted with jackets to control the temperature, as it gets really hot in the area in the summer. They have a capacity of 17.6kl and are filled with two batches of wort (10kl). Currently, 6 batches are done per week. Four of these go into the wooden fermenters and two go into one of the stainless steel fermenters.

Unsurprisingly, there's more to the story here, too. Kiuchi Shuzo has a long history of using different types of yeast for sake and beer brewing, so there is a separate area for yeast propagation at Yasato distillery, with a tank to boil some wort and five 500l propagation tanks. Toshiyuki Kiuchi and his team are well aware that the fermentation stage is crucial when it comes to flavor development, and they have done a lot of work to fine-tune this stage of the whisky-making process. At the moment, for each batch, two yeast regimes are introduced in succession: the first is adept at creating alcohol, the second at creating complex flavors. The former uses a distillers yeast which is propagated on site. This is introduced when the fermenter is filled. Then, at an undisclosed point in time (towards the end of the distillers yeast's working period), one of two proprietary yeasts (also propagated on-site) is introduced. The total fermentation time is unusually long: 6–7 days. Trials with other types of yeast (beer yeasts, etc.) have also been run.

The stillroom is the only part of Yasato distillery that looks "straight out of Scotland": a 12kl wash still and an 8kl spirit still, with shell-and-tube condensers, made by Forsyths. The team went for a simple shape—straight head and slightly downward lyne arm—because there are already lots of flavor variables to play with prior to the distillation stage. After fermentation, the wash is about 7–8%abv. Two batches are then combined and charged to the wash still. The tail cut of the second distillation is at around 60%abv, in order to capture some of the heavier congeners created by the proprietary yeast strains.

Interestingly, regardless of whether the fermentation was in oak, acacia or stainless steel, all new-make is mixed before it is filled into casks. The aim, again, is to create complexity. The spirit is filled into wood at 63%abv and matured on-site, for the most part. There is a small warehousing area on the ground floor of the actual production building and two larger warehouses next to the production building. The latter two are hybrid types: half-racked, half-palletized. Another large warehouse off-site (though still in Ishioka city) is of the dunnage type.

The first casks filled at Yasato Distillery were ex-bodega sherry casks (i.e. non-seasoned) and ex-bourbon barrels. Currently, most of the new-make is filled into ex-bourbon barrels. According to the team at the distillery, the Yasato malt new-make seems to develop particularly well in casks previously used by the Chattanooga Whiskey Company (Tennessee). This is one of those serendipitous things because the Tennessee distillery's products are not available in Japan and the staff at Yasato distillery has not yet had the chance to try the whisky that the barrels originally held. Other cask types used include ex-rum casks, 30-gallon ex-Koval casks, and a handful of ex-cherry brandy and ex-beer casks (used to age Hitachino Nest's stout beer). By the summer of 2022, nearly 3,000 casks had been filled.

In 2022, a 3-column hybrid still (4kl capacity, made by Ziemann) was added to the stillroom. At the time of writing, the hybrid still was only used for gin production.

Yasato Distillery is located along the so-called Fruits Line between Tsukuba and Kasama. There are various flower parks nearby and the characteristic pottery of the Kasama area is produced further down the road. The distillery is not well served by public transportation, so to (partly) remedy that, a tasting room was opened at Ishioka Station on July 10, 2022. That doesn't mean the company has given up on trying to attract people to the distillery area itself. To spotlight the agricultural bounty of the area, construction work on a café/restaurant, visitor center and shop in front of the distillery began in April 2022.

The same month, Kiuchi Shuzo also unveiled its Hinomaru Whisky brand. Two products have been released so far: Hinomaru Blended New Born 2022 (a teaser of sorts, released in June 2022, limited to 300 bottles and bottled at 48%abv) and Hinomaru 1st Edition (released on July 20, bottled at the same abv but with a much higher, undisclosed outturn). Both are vattings of malt and grain whisky distilled at Nukada and Yasato Distilleries. The 1st Edition was made entirely from grains grown in Ibaraki (Kaneko Golden barley, rice and wheat). Kiuchi Shuzo is gearing up to make more whisky available to the public in 2023, to mark the 200th anniversary of the founding of the company.

At the time of writing, Kiuchi Shuzo was in the process of setting up a new distillery near Yasato, called Ishioka-no-Kura Distillery. This new distillery will also include a floor-and-drum malting facility.

Spirit flowing at Yasato Distillery

Rokkosan Distillery
(Axas Holdings Co., Ltd.)

Rokkosan Distillery is owned by Axas Holdings, a company that imports and sells a variety of goods (cosmetics, household goods, sports/outdoor gear, alcoholic beverages, etc.). Axas Holdings was founded in 2016 and is based in Tokushima city, but the distillery itself is located in Kobe city, near the top of Mt. Rokko.

Mt. Rokko was historically a popular summer mountain resort area and used to be considered the Kansai version of Karuizawa, but following the collapse of the bubble economy in the early 1990s and the 1995 Great Hanshin Earthquake, visitor numbers dropped and the area's popularity quickly waned. A survey carried out by Kobe city in 2016 showed that over 70 percent of corporate retreats were not being adequately maintained and that a large number of said retreats as well as holiday homes were starting to fall into ruin. The same year, the city launched a revitalization project, offering subsidies to companies looking to establish new enterprises in properties sitting idle on Mt. Rokko. Axas Holdings submitted a proposal to establish a small-scale whisky distillery as part of that project, and in 2019, the company publicly announced it would go ahead with its distillery project. The distillery got its license on April 9, 2021 and production started in July of that year.

The distillery occupies a three-story building formerly operated as a recreational facility by a pharmaceutical company. It's located at an altitude of 800m, a short walk from Rokko Sanjo station on the Rokko Cable Line. The distillery is open to the public on Sundays.

The "10 Million Dollar Night View" from Mt. Rokko

The Distillery

Mash tun:	stainless steel, semi-lauter tun (2kl)
Washbacks:	2 stainless steel (2kl)
Still:	1 still, Holstein
	indirect heated (steam)
	with descending lyne arm and shell-in-tube condenser

Rokkosan Distillery is a micro-distillery. The projected annual production volume is a mere 11klpa.

Per batch, 300kg of malted barley is processed. All of this is heavily-peated (50ppm), for the time being. There is no mill on site, so the malt is delivered to the distillery as grist. The mashing takes place in a stainless steel semi-lauter tun made by SK Škrlj (Slovenia). The mineral-rich spring water used is the same as that used in the production of the famed Nada sake.

One batch yields 1,500 liters of wort. After fermentation, the wash is double-distilled in a lantern-shaped Holstein still. Casks are aged on the third floor (i.e. in the attic) of the building.

A commemorative limited release of new-make, Rokkosan THE FIRST (66%abv, 350 bottles, 500ml), went on sale on November 22, 2021. For the time being, the company sells Rokkosan Whisky 12yo and Rokkosan Whisky 12yo Peated, both blended malts made with bulk-imported Scotch and diluted to 42%abv using water from Mt. Rokko.

Not your average distillery exterior

Fuji Hokuroku Distillery
(Ide Jozoten)

Ide Jozoten traces its history back to about 1700 when the production of soy sauce and miso began. The company's home base is located at 850m altitude, on the southern side of Lake Kawaguchi, in what is now Fujikawaguchi city. Towards the end of the Edo period, the Ide family moved into sake production. The 16th generation president, Yogoemon Ide, is credited with that audacious move in 1850 and the company is still the only sake producer in the Fuji-Goko (i.e. the five lakes around Mt. Fuji) region to this day. Water is not an issue—Mt. Fuji's snowmelt is filtered through porous lava layers over 80 years and the quality is second to none—but the area is not suitable for sake rice growing because of the cold climate.

For a few years, the current (21st generation) president—also named Yogoemon Ide—had been thinking of moving into whisky production. He decided to dive in at the toughest of times, right at the start of the COVID-19 pandemic. A tiny distillery was set up next to the historical sake brewery and production began with the first milling on July 14, 2020. Whisky production takes place during the warmer half of the year (from the beginning of April until the end of October) when the staff is not busy with sake brewing.

The garden behind the Ide family's historical residence, located next to the sake brewery

The Distillery

Mash tun:	stainless steel, semi-lauter tun
Washbacks:	2 repurposed enamel-coated steel sake tanks
Pot still:	1 stainless steel still with copper plates in the neck

Fuji Hokuroku Distillery is entirely operated by sake-brewing staff. (The distillery name translates as "at the northern foot of Mt. Fuji.") As novices in the field of whisky, they are committed to a trial-and-error approach to production. Grain types, milling ratios, fermentation times, cut points, etc. are all up for discussion and tweaked until satisfactory results are obtained.

One parameter where variety is not explored is the yeast type. The distillery's exclusive use of sake yeast sets it apart from other craft producers in Japan (some of whom do use sake yeast but not exclusively and/or in conjunction with distillers/brewers yeast). Fermentation takes place in repurposed sake tanks and the fermentation time is 4 days. At the end of the process, the wash is about 7%abv. This is then double distilled in a stainless steel still fitted with copper plates in the neck. The spirit comes off the still, after the second distillation, at an average of 73.5%abv. This is then brought down to 63.5%abv, filled into wood and matured on site. Most of the spirit is filled into ex-bourbon barrels and virgin oak barrels.

The production volume at Fuji Hokuroku Distillery is tiny. The annual output is the equivalent of 40 barrels. The first two seasons, casks were stored somewhat ad hoc on racks in a half-open warehouse. In September 2022, construction of a purpose-built racked warehouse behind the distillery building was completed. This new warehouse has a capacity of around 450 barrels, so they're good for a few years.

A little over a year after production started, the distillery released its first product, Fuji Hokuroku Highball, a canned highball (8%abv). This was available in the Fuji-Goko area and was well received. Pleasant and clean in taste, it was surprising that this sort of quality could be achieved using whisky that was about a year old (and remember, in Japan, that is technically "whisky"). What is most unusual for a small Japanese craft whisky producer is that the blended whisky used in this RTD highball is 100% made in-house. (The grain whisky is made using rice as the main ingredient.)

Two distillery exclusives containing whisky-in-progress

In April 2022, the distillery released Daijukai 2020 1st Original Grain & Malt (45%abv). Again, very young whisky but also completely made in-house and priced on a par with blended whiskies released by other Japanese craft producers (who tend to rely on grain whisky imported in bulk from abroad).

Fuji Hokuroku Distillery plans to release its first single malt expression in the summer of 2023, when the stock laid down in the summer of 2020 reaches 3 years of age.

Kyoto Miyako Distillery
(Kyoto Shuzo)

In spite of a strong social media presence, there is very little actual information about Kyoto Miyako Distillery and the company behind it available. The distillery itself is located in Kyotamba-cho, in central Kyoto prefecture, roughly 60km northwest of Kyoto city. It got its whisky license in July 2020 and the first products were released under the Kyoto Whisky brand in March 2021. As these were blended / "pure malt" whiskies, one has to assume the contents were not distilled in-house (and most likely not in Japan). No single malt has been released so far.

All production takes place under one roof and the equipment includes a small mash tun, some enamel-coated open tanks (of the type used in sake production) used as fermenters and a pair of pot stills—the wash still onion-shaped, the spirit still with a bulge—both with slightly descending lyne arms and shell-and-tube condensers. The fermentation time is unusually short, a mere 60 hours. The spirit aimed for is soft and light. There is also a small alembic-type still, used for the production of gin.

The distillery is located on the Tamba Plateau, surrounded by gently sloping mountains, and according to Kyoto Shuzo, the relatively large daily temperature swings "accelerate the whisky aging." Time will tell.

Kyoto Whisky Aka-Obi, the company's entry-level blended whisky

Ikawa Distillery
(Juzan Co., Ltd.)

Until further notice, Ikawa Distillery is the highest whisky distillery in Japan. Located in a UNESCO Eco Park (Biosphere Reserve) in the Southern Alps at an altitude of 1,200m, it is also one of the most remote distilleries in Japan. It's about a four-hour drive from the center of Shizuoka City, even though it is technically part of that city. The distillery is owned by Juzan Co., Ltd., a wholly-owned subsidiary of Tokushu Tokai Paper Co., Ltd. (which specializes in the manufacturing, processing and sales of paper products). Juzan was established on April 1, 2020, to manage the Ikawa Forest, including the production and sale of alcoholic beverages and the development of entertainment, lodging and other facilities in the forest.

Establishing a distillery in a remote mountainous area is not for the faint-of-heart and there were initial concerns at Juzan about the challenges that lay ahead. The idea was to have the distillery ready for full-scale production by July 2020, but highway damage caused by heavy rain caused considerable delays.

Whisky production eventually began in November 2020. The batch size is 1t and non-peated, medium-peated (30ppm) and heavily-peated (50ppm) malted barley imported from Scotland is used. The equipment includes a 4.7kl mash tun, four stainless steel washbacks (6kl capacity, filled to 5kl) and twin pots (6kl and 3kl capacity, respectively) made by Miyake Industries, both with straight heads, slightly descending lyne arms and fitted with shell-and-tube condensers. Distillers and brewers yeast is used and the fermentation time is 68 hours.

The Miyake stills

The Distillery

Mash tun:	stainless steel (4.7kl)
Washbacks:	4 stainless steel (6kl), with temperature control
Stills:	1 pair (wash still 6kl, spirit still 3kl), Miyake
	indirect heating (steam)
	both with downward lyne arms and shell-and-tube condensers

For the maturation, ex-bourbon and ex-sherry wood is used, but the company also has ambitious plans to make its own barrels using wood types other than oak, harvested from the forests surrounding the distillery. The company's focus is squarely on the single malt whisky category. According to production manager Norikazu Ishihara, the first whisky release—a 5-year-old—is planned for 2026.

The distillery sits along the Oi River and is a part of a scenic area. The company plans to take full advantage of this by fleshing out ecotourism options in the future, including distillery tours and outdoor activities.

Top: Patience, please: whisky slumbering; bottom: Deep in the forests of Shizuoka

Kuju Distillery
(Tsuzaki Trading Co., Ltd.)

Whereas for many of the newer whisky distilleries in Japan, a certain amount of bandwagonism is involved, this is emphatically not the case for Kuju Distillery and the person behind it, Shoji Utoda.

Kuju Distillery is located in the small town of the same name in Oita prefecture. It sits at an altitude of 600m and the area is part of the majestic Kuju Plateau. Founder and CEO Shoji Utoda was born and raised in the area, but left to go to university where he studied agriculture. During his college days he got bitten by the whisky bug. "I went to a bar with some friends from college," Utoda relates, "and had single malt whisky for the first time—it was probably a Glenfiddich—and I really enjoyed the taste of it. In those days, whisky didn't have a particularly positive image in Japan. It was something people drank *mizuwari* (i.e. heavily diluted with water) in copious amounts at watering holes after work. I was rather weak when it came to alcohol, but discovered that I really enjoyed sipping single malt whisky."

In 2000, after three years working as a salaryman, Utoda moved back to Kuju to work at his family's liquor store. He continued his "whisky education" at bars in nearby Oita city and started dreaming of establishing a whisky distillery of his own in his hometown. In the winter of 2004, Utoda met someone who had a similar vision: Ichiro Akuto. "I met Ichiro back when he was trying to sell the first Hanyu he had bottled himself," Utoda-san remembers. "On average, he had to go to ten bars to sell just one bottle. The objections were always the same: it was expensive, it was (too) characterful in flavor, and Scotch was

Kuju Distillery at night

Head distiller Yu Takeishi checking the spirit

better. With the Card series, a little later, it was the same story. He had to go to a hundred bars to sell three cases. Then, slowly, there was more interest from abroad, and later on, also in Tokyo . . . but Kyushu is very different. There's a strong shochu culture here, so when I was trying to sell Ichiro's Malt at my liquor company, the reaction was usually: 'Ichiro, the baseball player?'"

In 2010, Whisky Talk Fukuoka was established by bartender Kazuyuki Higuchi and Tsuzaki Trading handled the logistics of special bottlings for the festival. "In 2011, for the second edition of Whisky Talk Fukuoka, we bottled a Hanyu single cask. We had about 180 bottles, but could only sell one third at the event. It took us a year and a half to sell the rest. For the 2012 edition, a Hanyu puncheon was selected and the outturn was over 400 bottles. We knew we wouldn't be able to sell that much, so we offered half to Number One Drinks who sold the bottles abroad. Even so, it took us a year to sell our allocation. It wasn't until 2013, when we bottled a single cask Chichibu that interest in Japanese whisky had grown to the point where we were able to sell the entire outturn at the event." The tide seemed to be turning. In the same year, Utoda heard that a man by the name of Taiko Nakamura was also keen to build a distillery of his own (that would turn out to be Shizuoka Distillery, a story featured elsewhere in this book) and he felt inspired by the fact that another person who had the same dream as his had emerged in Japan.

In 2015, Utoda got serious about his distillery project and by the end of 2016, he had found and purchased a plot of land. "There was a sake brewery called Kobayakawa Shuzo on this site, but they stopped production in 1989. To me, this was an indication that there must have been a good water supply here, both in terms of quality and quantity. This turned out to be right. We drilled 40m deep, and the abundance of water was such that we could use it for both production and process water." In 2017, Richard Forsyth Jr. visited the site and a rough distillery layout plan was drawn up. In May of the same year, Utoda was allowed—having asked for many years—to do an internship at Chichibu Distillery. (He's been back a few times since.)

To raise money for his venture, Utoda issued corporate bonds to bartenders, liquor retailers and other interested parties. Via word-of-mouth, some investors from abroad also came on board and by 2019, he had managed to assemble enough money to pay for the building and equipment. The container with the distillery equipment arrived at the end of May 2020. This would have been followed by a few weeks' commissioning by the Forsyths staff from Scotland, but the pandemic made that impossible. "We held off until August," Utoda relates, "but it was clear by then that we couldn't wait any longer. We contacted a local engineering company, Hirano Shoten, which has experience working with large shochu and sake makers, and they set up the distillery, with online support from the staff at Forsyths, during the last four months of 2020." The distillery was ready by Christmas and the whisky license came through on January 5, 2021. The first distillation at Kuju Distillery took place on February 20, 2021 and the first middle cut was made on February 27.

The Distillery

Mash tun:	stainless steel, semi-lauter tun (500kg)
Washbacks:	5 Douglas fir (3kl)
Pot stills:	1 pair (wash still 2.5kl, spirit still 1.8kl), Forsyths indirect heating (steam percolators)
	both with downward lyne arms and shell-and-tube condensers

The entire production from milling to filling takes place under one roof, in a very compact building. Aside from Utoda, there are four people working in production. The head distiller is Yu Takeishi, who made a career switch from IT to whisky in 2017, when he was 26 years old.

Per batch, 500kg of malted barley is processed. Initially, three mashes per week were done. By July 2022, this was increased to 7 a week. The distillery operates year round, except for a 3-week maintenance period in August. Two months a year is reserved for peated production (40 and 50ppm). The rest of the year, non-peated malt is used. "We use imported barley for the most part," Takeishi-san explains, "but we have a contract with a farmer in Bungo-Ono city who will supply us with 20t of local barley from 2022 onwards."

The husks:grits:flour ratio is 30:55:15, which is a little heavier on the husks than at most distilleries. Mashing takes place in a semi-lauter tun and the aim is a clear wort. The usual three waters are used (first 2kl at 70°C, then 1.2kl at 80°C and finally 1.6kl at 90°C). Each batch results in about 2.5kl of wort, which is sent to one of five washbacks. Initially, four of the washbacks were repurposed enamel-coated sake tanks with a capacity of 4kl and the fifth one was made from Douglas fir and had a capacity of 3kl. By the end of the summer of 2022, the four sake tanks were replaced with Douglas fir washbacks so, since then, everything is fermented in wooden vessels. Distillers dry yeast is used and the fermentation time is 92 hours, resulting in a wash with an abv of around 8%.

Distillation takes place in a 2.5kl wash still and a 1.8kl spirit still, both with straight heads, slightly descending lyne arms and fitted with shell-and-tube condensers. Takeishi-san made the rough design of the pot stills with the aim of obtaining a fruity and rich spirit. "We went for straight heads because we wanted a flavorful profile," he explains. "We distill slowly, both distillations taking about 6 and a half hours. For the second distillation, we are on foreshots for about 8 minutes and the tail cut is at 63.5%abv. The spirit we obtain is slightly heavier than we had imagined during the design phase but we are happy with it." One batch results in about 320–330 liters of new-make at 60%abv, which is then filled into wood and matured on site. A week's worth of production is about ten barrels.

Most of the production—about 70 percent—is filled into ex-bourbon barrels. The remainder is filled into ex-sherry, ex-brandy, ex-Armagnac, ex-rum and ex-Calvados casks. One year into production, the small dunnage-type warehouse next to the production building was completely full (500-odd casks). At the time of writing, there were plans to build a new, racked warehouse on site with a capacity of 850 to 900 casks.

The first release coming out of Kuju Distillery was Kuju Newborn, non-peated distillate, matured for 7 months in ex-bourbon barrels (200ml, 59%abv, 3,087btls) released in March 2022.

Founder Shoji Utoda in the stillroom

A bottling of Niigata Kameda new make, distilled using Niigata barley

Niigata Kameda Distillery
(Niigata Micro-Distillery LLC)

Niigata Kameda Distillery is located in the city of Niigata, in Niigata prefecture. It is the brainchild of Koji Douda, who is an executive at Otani Co., Ltd., one of the largest manufacturers of personal seals (*hanko*) in Japan.

Douda is originally from Hokkaido and loves a good dram. His favorite tipple was Taketsuru 17, until it became impossible to get hold of. One day, whilst bemoaning the ever-increasing scarcity of Japanese whisky, his wife suggested he make it himself then. A tall order, for sure, but a seed was planted.

In the summer of 2018, Otani participated in the Niigata Innovation Program, organized by the Niigata Branch of Nomura Holdings. In response to the increasing digitization of bureaucracy in Japan (and with the *hanko* destined to become a relic a few years down the road), there was an acutely felt need to diversify at Otani and to consider side businesses with potential outside Japan, as well. The whisky idea came up. To make a long story short: Otani formulated a proposal, got two other Niigata-based companies on board and decided to enter the field of whisky production.

Douda and his wife established Niigata Micro-Distillery LLC in March 2019 and started refurbishing one of the Otani warehouses on a small industrial park 5km from JR Niigata Station. You wouldn't think so by looking at the map, but it is actually the easiest (and probably fastest) accessible distillery from Tokyo. Even though it's 250km as the crow flies, it only takes two hours by *shinkansen* from Tokyo to Niigata Station, and then a 10-minute taxi to the distillery site.

Niigata Kameda Distillery got its whisky license in June 2020, but because of delays caused by the pandemic, production didn't start until February 2021. The first distillation took place on February 9, 2021.

The Distillery

Mash tun:	stainless steel, lauter tun (2kl)
Washbacks:	3 acacia (3.1kl)
	3 stainless steel (3.1kl), with temperature control
Stills:	1 pair (wash still 2kl, spirit still 1.4kl), Forsyths indirect heating (steam)
	both with sharply descending lyne arms and shell-and-tube condensers

Most of the malted barley (both peated and non-peated) is imported from Scotland, but some local Niigata barley is used as well. One batch consists of 400kg. The mashing takes place in a lauter tun manufactured by Ziemann Holvrieka (Germany) using the infusion method and the aim is a clear wort (about 2kl per mash).

For the fermentation, there are 3 washbacks made from acacia by the Italian company Garbellotto as well as 3 stainless steel washbacks. All of these have a capacity of about 3.1kl but are only filled with 2kl of wort. The standard fermentation time is 96 hours, but longer fermentations (up to 120 hours) have been trialed, too. Distillers yeast (sourced from various companies) is used. The staff at the distillery has developed a preference for fermentation in the wooden vessels—to encourage the secondary lactic fermentation—and that is the default method used. When there are no wooden vats available, the stainless steel washbacks are used, but in that case, the wash is transferred to a wooden washback on the morning of the third day so it can continue its secondary fermentation in that environment. There are plans to install three more wooden washbacks—this time, made of oak—in the near future.

Twin pots made by Forsyths are used for the distillation. The wash still (2kl) is of the lantern-type; the spirit still (1.4kl), on the other hand, has a boil ball. Both have sharply descending lyne arms and are fitted with shell-and-tube condensers. The spirit character aimed for is clean and elegant, but with a decent body. Niigata is one of the leading sake-producing prefectures in Japan and consumers tend to prefer the sort of light, fragrant and fruity profile of *ginjo sake*, so Niigata Kameda Distillery is aiming for a similarly fresh, light and estery profile.

The spirit is filled into wood—ex-bourbon, ex-sherry and ex-wine casks, mainly—at 63%abv and matured at various locations in Niigata prefecture. The main warehouse, at the time of writing, was in Yahiko, about 30km southwest of the distillery. Also used is the basement of a hotel in Tainai, about 30km northeast of the distillery. The distillery has also been looking into storing casks in the hull of the Awashima Kisen ferry (which connects the port of Iwafune with Awashima Island, 20km off the coast of the mainland) to investigate the effect of the rocking movement of the ship on the maturation process. In a more pragmatic move, the company is also planning to build a large maturation warehouse on site.

Niigata prefecture has the highest rice crop yield in Japan and its rice is considered to be of superior quality. Niigata Kameda Distillery is planning to take advantage of this by also producing rice whisky in the future. A grain cooker will be added to the distillery kit to facilitate this.

In early 2022, the company released three types of new make in limited quantities: Peated, Non-Peated and Niigata Barley (200ml, 60%). The first single malt release is planned for 2024.

Hanyu Distillery
(Toa Shuzo Co., Ltd.)

The history of Toa Shuzo goes back to 1625, but its history of whisky making, which started in 1946, came to an end in 2004. The details of that story are in the Lost Distilleries section of this book under Hanyu Distillery. So, what explains the presence of a distillery with the same name in this section of the book? It's complicated, as they say.

In 2004, Toa Shuzo was acquired by Hinode Tsusho Co., Ltd (renamed to Hinode Holdings Co., Ltd. in 2019). Hinode Holdings traces its own history back to 1900 and specializes in mirin, cooking wine and sake, cooking sauces and alcoholic beverages. When Hinode acquired Toa Shuzo, whisky was the ugly duckling of the drinks business in Japan. Fast-forward to 2016 and Japanese whisky is all the rage. That year, Toa Shuzo starts importing whisky in bulk again for the purpose of further aging, blending and bottling whisky (for their Golden Horse brand). Fast-forward a bit more and in the fall of 2020, the company announces that it would be reviving malt whisky production at Hanyu Distillery—by necessity, a new Hanyu Distillery since the old one was demolished in 2004 and the remaining equipment, scattered left and right, of mere historical (but technically: scrap) value.

Peated Hanyu new make bottled for crowdfunders

The Distillery

Mash tun:	stainless steel lauter tun (1t)
Washbacks:	5 stainless steel (8kl), with temperature control
Pot stills:	1 pair (wash still 6kl, spirit still 3kl), Miyake indirect heating (steam)
	both with downward lyne arms and shell-and-tube condensers

A brand-new distillery was set up with new equipment provided by Miyake Industries and production resumed in February 2021. The kit consists of a 1t (6kl) lauter tun, five stainless steel temperature-controlled washbacks (8kl capacity) and a pair of steam-heated lantern-shaped pots (6kl and 3kl, resp.), based on the blueprints of the original Hanyu pot stills, with downward lyne arms and fitted with shell-and-tube condensers. The company raised additional funds—destined for the construction of a visitor center and the implementation of distillery tours—via Makuake, a popular Japanese crowdfunding platform in the spring of 2021. With the support of 1,426 backers, a total of over 26 million yen was raised (well over 20 times the targeted amount). A set of two New Pot bottlings (200ml, 60%abv, one distilled using non-peated malt, the other using peated malt) was made available to backers in April 2021, with a further 100 sets sold at the company's online store shortly after. For the time being, that is the only taste of the new Hanyu Distillery.

Non-peated Hanyu new make bottled for crowdfunders

Setouchi Distillery
(Miyake Honten Co., Ltd.)

Setouchi Distillery is the most recent project of Miyake Honten, a well-known sake producer based in Kure city, Hiroshima prefecture.

The company traces its history back to 1856, when it operated under the name Kawachiya. The focus at the time was on the production of mirin, shochu and *shirozake* (a sweet, sake-like liqueur). They started making proper, quality sake in 1902—the same year the city of Kure was officially incorporated.

Kure has a strong industrial and naval heritage—the second-oldest naval dockyard in Japan is located there—and the company benefitted from the naval connection. In the late 1920s, its products became the official military-use sake aboard naval ships and, unwittingly promoted by naval personnel who took the sake home when they were on leave, their flagship brand Sempuku became very popular throughout the country.

Fast-forward to 2020 and Miyake Honten decides to enter the whisky and gin field. Gin production started in 2020. Their whisky license was granted on New Year's Day 2021. Which begs the question: Don't the people at Japan's National Tax Agency ever take a break?

The first release of non-peated Setouchi new-make

The Distillery

Mash tun:	stainless steel, semi-lauter
Washbacks:	4 stainless steel
Still:	1 pair (wash still 1kl, spirit still with column 1kl), DYE (Daeyoo Tech Co. Ltd.)
	indirect heating
	both with descending and slightly ascending lyne arm resp. and shell-and-tube condensers

Setouchi Distillery occupies a nondescript factory building that used to be a bottling hall at Miyake Honten's headquarters. The operation is relatively small. In fact, the mill, mash tun, hot water tank, fermenters and the hybrid still are all lined up against a single wall of the building. In the interest of expediency, all equipment was purchased in China. The distillery was ready for full-scale production on March 30, 2022, when an official inauguration ceremony was held.

Water is taken from a borehole on site (60m deep) that taps into the water table of Mt. Haigamine. Malted barley is imported from Australia and the U.K. Domestic barley is used, too. Production is limited to non-peated barley.

Even by craft whisky standards, the scale of operation is tiny. One batch is a mere 250kg of malted barley. This is milled using a small, two-roll mill. Mashing takes place in a 1kl stainless steel semi-lauter tun, using four waters in succession. Nine hundred liters of wort is sent to one of four fermenters of the type used in beer brewing, and the remainder is used for the next mash.

For the fermentation, a combination of beer yeast—propagated on site—and distillers yeast is used. The fermentation time is 4–5 days. At the end of the process, the wash is 10–11%abv, which is unusually high.

Until mid-September 2022, distillation took place in a 1kl hybrid still, i.e., a pot still (with a bulge) with a column attached to it. Initially, this one still was used for the first and second distillation. In mid-September 2022, a second 1kl pot still was installed (this time with a straight head, and without a column) and from then on the two pot stills were used in tandem: the new one as the wash still and the hybrid one as the spirit still.

Setouchi lemons

Atypically, the team at the distillery has decided to focus on sherry wood (ex-Oloroso) for the maturation process and the plan, going forward, is to release single-cask products for the most part. The filling strength is 63.5%abv.

Setouchi Distillery released some new-make (60%abv, 200ml) in the spring of 2022 to allow enthusiasts to savor the "rough, distinctive flavors" of its spirit. It's still very early days, so it remains to be seen what house style the team is aiming for and what niche they are looking to carve out for themselves in the ever more crowded landscape of Japanese whisky.

Shindo Distillery
(Shinozaki Co., Ltd.)

Shindo Distillery is a brand-new facility built by Shinozaki Co., Ltd. The company was founded in 1922 and is famous for its superb barley shochu. The company's portfolio also includes sake, amazake, gin and the koji-whisky Takamine.

Representing the eighth generation of the family, vice-president Michiaki Shinozaki was keen to respond to the increasing demand for Japanese whisky by building a stand-alone whisky distillery in the company's home base of Asakura city, in Fukuoka prefecture. Construction began in November 2020 and whisky production started in August 2021. Shindo is the name of the land on which the distillery sits, but also refers to the direction (*shindo* in Japanese means "new road"): "the quest for the original." Unlike many new craft whisky-makers in Japan, Michiaki Shinozaki is not interested in learning the ropes from whisky distillers in Japan or abroad. He feels that, given the company's decades of experience in the field of barley shochu production, they're more than capable of forging their own path.

The wash still

The Distillery

Mash tun: stainless steel, semi-lauter tun (1t)

Washbacks: 5 stainless steel, with water jackets (7kl)

Pot stills: 1 pair (wash still 5.8kl, spirit still 3.3kl), Miyake indirect heating (steam)

both with downward lyne arms and shell-and-tube condensers

Per batch, 1t of malted barley is used, and per week, five batches are processed. Since production began in the summer of 2021, many types of malted barley have been used. One month a year is reserved for heavily-peated (50ppm) production. The remainder of the year, non-peated malt is used.

Aside from the mill (Kunzel), all production equipment was manufactured by Miyake Industries. Mashing takes place in a semi-lauter tun, using a complex mashing procedure. In fact, every single aspect of production at Shindo Distillery is tweaked to a degree not often seen at other distilleries, and understandably, the staff is playing their cards close to their chest. One batch yields about 5.8kl of clear wort.

Michiaki Shinozaki in the warehouse

Fermentation takes place in stainless steel washbacks with water jackets. A proprietary process is used for the fermentation. Currently, there are 5 washbacks but there is room and plans to add five more.

After 4–5 days, the wash has an abv of around 7%. Distillation takes place in copper twin pots. The 5.8kl wash still has a straight head; the 3.3kl spirit still is of the lantern type. Both have downward lyne arms and are fitted with shell-and-tube condensers. Again, lots of R&D is under-taken at this stage of the process. According to Michiaki Shinozaki, the "golden time" occurs about 3½ hours into the second distillation when an unmistakable aroma of honey and coconut and a heavy, sweet flavor comes through. This is what they want to capture.

Filling strength is the classic 63.5%, and the wood policy at the time of writing was 70 percent ex-bourbon wood, 20 percent ex-sherry wood and 10 percent "other" (mizunara, ex-rum casks, ex-natural wine casks from New Zealand, etc.) Again, they don't just fill into whatever happens to be at hand. Everything is carefully thought out. The heavily-peated spirit, for example, meshes very well with ex-rum barrels—a combina-tion that brings out a dark chocolate flavor, according to Shinozaki.

There are no plans to release anything as of yet. Knowing the com-pany's commitment to quality of flavor, this is likely to happen when the whisky is ready rather than as dictated by a timeline on paper.

Shindo Distillery in the spring

Niseko Distillery
(Niseko Distillery Co., Ltd.)

The basic premise of the background story—existing sake/shochu producer enters the field of Japanese whisky—may sound a bit old hat by now, but in the case of Niseko Distillery, there is a bit of quirkiness involved, so it's worth telling the story.

The story starts over a decade ago and the figure entering the scene—please picture a snowy scene—is Jiro Nagumo, CEO of Hakkaisan Brewery Co. Ltd., a sake powerhouse founded in 1922 in Minami-Uonuma, at the foot of Mount Hakkai in Niigata. Niigata prefecture benefits from the heaviest snowfall on Japan's main island of Honshu and is known for its top-notch ski resorts. Nagumo's local, Naeba, was once the most famous ski resort in Japan but in the early 2000s, Niseko (on the island of Hokkaido) became the most popular skiing destination in the country, favored by travellers from all over the world for its exceptional powder snow. Keen to figure out how to help revitalize his local ski resort, Nagumo began making regular visits to Niseko. As it happened, he fell under the spell of Niseko himself and, over time, became convinced that Niseko just might be the perfect place to build a whisky distillery. He shared his plans with the locals and found that they were equally keen. The rest is history, as they say.

Nagumo established Niseko Distillery Co., Ltd. as a subsidiary of Hakkaisan Brewery Co. Ltd. on February 25, 2019 and construction started in the spring of 2020. The distillery sits on a 9,990 square meter

The stills

The distillery in the winter

plot leased from the town, located near the Niseko Annupuri International Ski Area. The distillery building was completed on December 21, 2020 and then, little by little, the equipment sourced from various corners of the world was pieced together.

The first whisky distillation took place on March 24–25, 2021 and the first barrel-filling took place in early May of the same year. The distillery also produces Ohoro Gin. Tourism is an important part of the distillery's business plan and the grand opening took place on October 1, 2021.

The Distillery

Mash tun:	stainless steel (1t), lauter tun
Washbacks:	3 Douglas fir (7.5kl)
Stills:	1 pair (wash still 5.5kl, spirit still 3.6kl), Forsyths indirect heating (steam)
	both with horizontal lyne arms and shell-and-tube condensers

The setup is textbook Scottish but with equipment sourced from various corners of the world: a four-roll Bühler mill (from Switzerland), a 1t full-lauter mash tun from SK Škrlj (Slovenia), three Douglas fir washbacks made domestically by Nihon Mokusou Mokkan Co. and a pair of pot stills from Forsyths in Scotland. There is also a 600l Arnold Holstein hybrid still for the production of gin and, possibly, vodka in the future.

The whisky-making process is straight out of Scotland, too. One batch is 1t and the malted barley (non-peated) is imported from the U.K. The wort (5kl) is fermented in Douglas fir washbacks for 4 days. Distillation takes place in twin pots. The wash still is onion-shaped; the spirit still has a bulge. Both have horizontal lyne arms and are fitted with shell-and-tube condensers. The aim is to produce a clean, harmonious spirit that "expresses a balance of flavors."

The new make is filled into wood at 60%abv and matured in a dunnage warehouse on site. Cask-types used so far include virgin American white oak casks coopered in Japan, ex-bourbon, ex-sherry and ex-wine casks. Mizunara is on the wish list. By late August 2022, about 200 casks had been filled.

The distillery's first whisky release is slated for 2024.

Yamaga Distillery
(Yamaga Distillery Co., Ltd.)

Yamaga Distillery is the first whisky distillery in Kumamoto prefecture. It's located in the north of the prefecture, in the city of the same name. Sake has been made there for centuries, which indicates the availability of high-quality water.

The distillery is part of the MCA Holdings group, which was established in 2006 as an offshoot of the Minami-Kyushu Cocoa-Cola Bottling Co., Ltd. MCA Holdings acquired VinEx Yamaga in 2013. VinEx specialized in the manufacturing and sales of spirits and drinking water and moved into *honkaku* shochu production in 2014. In 2021, the business model was transformed, the focus shifted from shochu to whisky production and the name of the company changed to Yamaga Distillery Co., Ltd.

Though the company and the people involved are new to whisky production, there is a family connection. The president of MCA Holdings is Masafumi Hombo—of the Hombo family that owns the Mars Shinshu and Tsunuki Distilleries. The team at Yamaga Distillery received significant technical support from Hombo Shuzo, and a lot of the equipment and processes—and even the design of the distillery itself—is reminiscent of Mars Shinshu and/or Tsunuki.

Yamaga Distillery sits on a 1,258m^2 plot of land, with all production buildings newly constructed. The company received its whisky license on October 29, 2021 and production started the following month. The first distillation took place on November 15, 2021.

The Distillery

Mash tun:	stainless steel, lauter tun (8kl)
Washbacks:	5 stainless steel (6kl), with temperature control
Stills:	1 pair (wash still 6kl, spirit still 3kl), Miyake
	indirect heating (steam)
	both with ascending lyne arms and shell-and-tube condensers

At Yamaga Distillery, all processes from milling to distillation take place under one roof. Visitors are able to observe the whisky-making process from behind glass, just like at Mars Tsunuki and the new Mars Shinshu distillery building. It's quite a modest operation, with only four people working in production. Except for the mill, all equipment was made by Miyake Industries.

The batch size is 1t (occasionally 1.1t) and the barley used is imported from the U.K. Production is non-peated, for the most part. Occasionally, heavily-peated malt (50ppm) is used. For the mashing, groundwater from the Kikuchi River is used and the procedure is textbook Scottish, following the "three-waters" method.

The fermentation takes place in stainless steel washbacks and the fermentation time is 96 hours. For non-peated production, distillers yeast is used in conjunction with ale yeast. (There are two 700l yeast tanks to prepare the ale yeast.) For peated production, distillers yeast only is used.

On the distillation front, a setup facilitating lots of copper contact was engineered. The wash still has a bulge; the spirit still has a straight head. Both are indirect-heated and have ascending lyne arms (100° and 95°, respectively) and shell-and-tube condensers. The resulting new-make is clean and approachable.

The spirit is filled into wood at 60%abv and matured in a warehouse on site. The warehouse has mobile racks and a capacity of around 3,300 casks. The first barrel—an ex-bourbon cask—was filled on December 2, 2021. Since then, the wood used has been primarily ex-bourbon and ex-sherry (both seasoned and ex-bodega). Yamaga benefits from a humid climate with temperatures ranging from -5°C in winter to 40°C in summer—perfect conditions for the swift maturation of whisky, according to the staff at the distillery.

Yamaga is one of the few Japanese distilleries open to the public. Its visitor center opened on April 16, 2022 and a self-guided experience has been designed, along the lines of what you will find at Mars Tsunuki and Shinshu Distilleries. Mini-bottles (200ml) of "Yamaga New Pot" were available at the visitor center in limited quantities.

Top: The stills; below: Yamaga distillery

Kamui Whisky K.K. Distillery
(Kamui Whisky K.K.)

It's hard to put a pin in a more remote location on the map of Japan than Rishiri Island, but sometimes a location chooses you as much as the other way around. For husband-and-wife entrepreneurs Casey Wahl (U.S.) and Miku Hirano (Japan) that's what happened. In 2016, they had planned to visit Rebun Island, off the northwestern tip of Hokkaido. The ferry from Wakkanai stopped at Rishiri Island first, and to make a long story short: they never made it to Rebun Island. The couple fell for the dramatic scenery of Rishiri Island, dominated by its eponymous mountain—referred to as Rishiri-Fuji, on account of its resemblance to Japan's iconic peak—and started thinking about what sort of business they could possibly start in such a remote location. On the ferry back, the whisky distillery idea was born.

In his teens, Wahl had a friend whose family lived on Islay, and he had fallen in love with the Islay landscape. "Rishiri reminded me of Islay," he relates, "the landscapes, the beauty, the ruggedness of the locals. There was something about the Rishiri locals that wasn't Japanese. Of course, they spoke Japanese, but there was a bit of the cowboy, a bit of rule-breaking, a bit of freedom that felt more like Texas than the rule-bound, kept-in-line-through-guilt social construct of Yamato Japan that had me further falling for the place."

Setting up a whisky distillery in Japan is rather challenging. To do so as a foreigner and in a location as remote as Rishiri multiplies the challenges significantly. "It took us several years to get land and build up

Water from 3 different springs with one of the stills in the background

the necessary relationships in Rishiri", Wahl explains. "Rishiri is a complicated and quite-difficult place to do business. There are almost no 'outside' new businesses created. It is incredibly local."

Eventually, the team managed to acquire some land on the west side of the island, near the coast, overlooking the Sea of Japan and Rebun Island. The groundbreaking ceremony took place on July 4, 2021 and exactly one year later, the pot stills arrived. A completion-of-construction ceremony was held on July 17, 2022 and production started in September.

The Distillery

Mash tun:	stainless steel, lauter tun (800l)
Washbacks:	4 stainless steel, with temperature control (700l)
Stills:	1 pair (wash still 750l, spirit still 350l), Vendome indirect heating (steam) both with descending lyne arms and worm tubs

Kamui Whisky K.K. Distillery is the northernmost distillery in Japan. It's named after the locale, but it's an auspicious name for a whisky distillery. It means "sacred water where the gods reside" in the language of the indigenous Ainu.

The distillery building is a compact, one-story wooden affair with an exterior evocative of a fisherman's lodge. The water used is volcanic-filtered over 30 years, coming out in several natural springs around the island, all with different pH levels and attributes. According to Wahl, "Reiho Spring will be used for most of the production, but special barrels will use Kamui and Kanro spring water."

The malted barley used is imported from Scotland, but some Hokkaido malt is used, too. Plans for the future include using local peat. "We have access to several peat bogs and have tested them," Wahl says, "so, in the future, we will do our own peated malt with Rishiri peat."

Per batch, 200kg of malted barley is processed. Fermentation takes place in stainless steel fermenters. The yeast used is distillers yeast and the fermentation time is 4–5 days. In the future, the team is hoping to capture wild yeast on Rishiri and propagate that.

For the distillation, twin pots made by Vendome Copper & Brass Works in Louisville, Kentucky are used. Vendome stills can be found in every nook and cranny of the U.S., but in Japan, this is the first pair made by Vendome. Each still has a bulge, a relatively tall, slender neck and a short, downward lyne arm. Each is fitted with a small worm tub condenser.

It's still very early days, but the spirit aimed for is one that has "subtle layers of flavor and is lightly peated." Interestingly, the team will be filtering its new make before filling it into wood. Dubbed the "Rishiri Filtration Process," it's a bit like the Lincoln Country Process used in Tennessee but using volcanic rock rather than charcoal. "We have developed a special volcanic rock filtering system over a two-and-a-half-year research period with a U.S. university. There are three types of rock on Rishiri Island, from different eruption periods, and each one adds a different flavor when used for filtering."

Once filtered, the spirit is filled into ex-bourbon wood for the most part. Douro wine barrels will be used for secondary maturation purposes. Mizunara sourcing is in progress. The filling strength is 58–60%abv. At the moment, there is one small dunnage-style warehouse on site with a capacity of around 100 casks. This is right by the sea, of course, and the doors are kept open during the day to maximize the maritime influence on the maturation process. A second warehouse will be built in the next couple of years.

The projected production volume for the first year is the legal minimum of 6,000lpa. At the moment, there are just two people working in production and whisky-making will most likely be seasonal rather than all year round. The first winter experience will reveal the limits of the feasible.

Kamui Whisky Distillery with the Sea of Japan in the background

Nozawa Onsen Distillery
(MDMC Co., Ltd.)

Nozawa Onsen is a well-known tourist destination in Nagano prefecture, popular with snow sports, onsen, hiking and biking enthusiasts. What it lacked was a distillery, or so a group of foreign residents thought in 2020. So founding partners David Elsworth, Philip Richards, Bradley de Martino Rosaroll and Ryotaro Yao decided to rectify that (no pun intended). The team found and repurposed an old canning factory a two-minute walk from the main street. A groundbreaking ceremony was held on September 10, 2021 and a little over a year later the distillery was ready.

Isamu (Sam) Yoneda, formerly of Nukada/Yasato Distillery, is the head distiller, which is a perfect fit, since the team is not aiming for a traditional Japanese whisky style (i.e. along Scottish lines), but more of a new-world style with room for various grain types and for thinking outside the box.

One batch is 400kg and, for the time being, non-peated Australian malted barley is used. Other grains—local wheat, buckwheat and rice—will also be used. The distillery is equipped with a hammer mill. For the mashing, a 2.2kl mash cooker (from Carl GmbH) with direct steam injection and a crash-cooling jacket is used in conjunction with a mash filter. Nozawa Onsen Distillery is currently the only Japanese craft distillery using a mash filter, giving flexibility to develop unique flavor profiles.

A close-up of the column

The Distillery

Mash tun:	stainless steel mash cooker (2.2kl) with direct steam injection and a crash-cooling jacket
Washbacks:	4 stainless steel (2.8kl), with temperature control and agitators
Pot stills:	1 pair (wash still 1kl, hybrid still 700l), Carl GmbH
	indirect heating (steam jackets)
	both with downward lyne arms

For the fermentation, stainless steel, temperature-controlled tanks are used. A pair of pots (also made by Carl) is used for the distillation: a 1kl pot still is used for the first distillation and a 700l hybrid still for the second distillation, both of the lantern type and both with downward lyne arms.

The distillery also has a small Knapp Lewer still for gin production (currently, the only Tasmanian-made still in Japan). Gin production started in October 2022 and whisky production began in December 2022.

Facing page: (top) The Carl stills, fresh out of the box; (bottom) Lead distiller Isamu Yoneda with the Knapp Lewer still

Whisky Making in Okinawa

Until fairly recently, Okinawa didn't really figure much in discussions of whisky-making in Japan. That doesn't mean there wasn't any "production" going on, but finding out what really *was* going on has proved to be very difficult.

Liquor producers are more than happy to share the culture of *awamori* with those interested in learning more about the indigenous distilled spirit unique to the islands. Whisky is a different story. Some producers have dabbled in whisky on and off, but they tend to be tight-lipped when asked about the when, what and how. I have done some due diligence on my visits to Okinawa, but my requests for information and/or visits have all been met with a wall of silence. Maybe the future will bring more transparency. In the meantime, the following is meant to chronicle what little we do know.

Helios Shuzo has been "producing" whisky since the early '70s. The company was founded as Taiyou Shuzo in 1961 and initially focused on making rum from local sugarcane. In 1969, the name was changed to Helios Shuzo. The company entered the field of whisky in 1972 and starting selling Highlander Whisky and Helios Whisky, both bottom-shelf products. How exactly those whiskies were made is unclear. In 1999, Helios Shuzo started selling Kamiya Whisky 12yo, exclusively in Taiwan. Again, the provenance of the liquid was unclear.

In 1979, Helios Shuzo started producing *awamori* and towards the end of the 1980s, the company also started cask-aging *awamori*. In 1991, the Kura brand was launched. Initially, this brand featured the company's cask-aged *awamori*, but in recent years, whiskies made with bulk-imported Scotch malt whisky have also been marketed under the Kura brand name.

In the fall of 2016, a ripple of excitement spread through the Japanese whisky community when Helios Shuzo announced the release of Reki Pure Malt Whisky 15yo (40%abv, 200 bottles, 500ml). This was sold, in a rather unorthodox way, through the Lawson convenience store chain. In spite of the (for-the-time) high price (¥8,850 plus tax), it sold out instantly. The story was that the source of the liquid was a lot of 9 casks that had been discovered in one of the warehouses at Helios Shuzo. Apparently, it had been distilled in-house.

The same 15-year-old liquid was used to produce more Reki (non-age-statement, this time) in 2016 and 2017. This time around, however, it was vatted with 80 percent malt whisky imported in bulk from abroad and sold in 180ml bottles, albeit through the same convenience store chain. I am not being facetious in my use of the word "liquid" in this and the previous paragraph. To understand why, we have to fast forward to New Year's Eve 2020.

On that day, Helios Shuzo started selling—what they described as— the first ever release of an Okinawan single malt whisky, Kyoda Cask Strength 2020 (60.9%abv, 1,432 bottles). Atypically, the year refers to the year of release, not the year of distillation. The whisky had been distilled at Helios Shuzo in 2017 using peated malted barley imported from the U.K.

The year after, a single cask single malt expression was released, again on New Year's Eve: Kyoda Single Cask 2021 (cask #4248, 56.8%abv, 556 bottles). This was distillate from 2018 and again made from peated malted barley imported from the U.K.

This brings us back to Reki Pure Malt Whisky 15yo. Even though this was not explicitly stated at the time, the impression among the whisky cognoscenti in Japan was that, since it was purportedly distilled in-house and since it was a malt whisky, it was a single malt whisky. Helios' claim that Kyoda Cask Strength 2020 was the first Okinawan single malt whisky released, of course, invalidates that assumption. But what exactly was Reki 15yo then? We'll probably never know, but at the time it was released, some whisky fans in Japan commented on its "unique flavor," which was described as "smoky shochu." Those who felt the product leaned towards shochu/*awamori* may just have been projecting, of course. Again, we'll never know.

Helios Shuzo is not the only Okinawan producer associated with whisky. In the U.S., the so-called Ryukyu Whisky brand Kujira has gained considerable traction since it was launched in 2018. The range consists of expressions spanning no-age-statement to 31-years old, and the liquid is supplied by three well-known Okinawan liquor producers: Masahiro Shuzo, Shinzato Shuzo and Kumesen Shuzo. These Ryukyu whiskies are in, in fact, barrel-aged *awamori* and because of the use of *koji* in the production process, these products are not categorized as whiskies in Japan or the E.U. (and are, therefore, not available in those markets). Interestingly, both Masahiro Shuzo and Shinzato Shuzo acquired (proper) whisky production licenses in 2020.

Shinzato Shuzo wasted no time in capitalizing on its entry into the brave new world of whisky at home. At the time of writing, the company's Shinzato Whisky (43%abv) is the most visible whisky sold in Okinawa. It's literally everywhere, from liquor stores to supermarkets and even in convenience stores (where it's sold in pocket format, in 200ml bottles, as well as the standard 700ml bottles). As stated on the packaging, the company's goal is to create a new Okinawan whisky: "Not just a delicious whisky, but a whisky that expresses the essence of Okinawa—a whisky that can only be made by an *awamori* maker" (my translation). Shinzato Whisky is made by blending bulk-imported Scotch blended whisky with 13-year-old barrel-aged *awamori*. The vatting is then further aged in heavily-charred virgin oak barrels. The product is bottled without chill-filtration. This is, of course, just one producer's interpretation of what an Okinawan whisky ought to be.

It's highly likely that we will see more companies applying for a whisky production license in Okinawa in the years to come. Part of this has to do with the waning popularity of *awamori*. For the past decade and a half, the shipment volume of *awamori* has decreased year upon year. In 2020, the amount sold was less than half of that in 2004.

Impending changes to the liquor tax situation in Okinawa will prove to be another stimulus to enter the lucrative field of whisky. In 1972, when Okinawa was reverted to Japan from U.S. control, lower taxes were introduced for alcoholic beverages produced and shipped within the prefecture. This was done to help consumers (the liquor tax rate in U.S.-occupied Okinawa was lower than that in the rest of Japan) as well as to promote local industries. Initially, the tax break was a massive 60 percent. This was gradually trimmed in the course of the decades following. Most recently, the alcohol tax rate levied on *awamori* was 35 percent lower in Okinawa than that applied to similar alcoholic beverages produced in mainland Japan. The rate for beer and other alcoholic beverages was 20 percent lower. In 2021, the tax breaks covered liquor produced by 48 Okinawan companies shipped within the prefecture. Towards the end of that year, however, word came that the central government would be phasing out these tax breaks from 2022 onwards. An appeal by *awamori* producers to phase out the tax break over 10 years (to May 2032) was accepted by the government. For other alcoholic beverages produced in Okinawa, the tax relief measures will be phased out by October 2026.

Given these circumstances, it's to be expected that producers who are already skilled in the art of distillation (and aging, to a certain extent) will seek to turn their hand to whisky-making. Time will tell whether the quality will be on par with the whisky produced elsewhere in Japan.

●

Facing page: Helios' Kyoda 2021 release

The Lost Distilleries

Some of the most sought-after Japanese whisky at the moment is from distilleries featured in this chapter. It's the same old story: while they were active, they weren't held in particularly high esteem; after they were gone, people started realizing what was lost . . .

KARUIZAWA DISTILLERY & KAWASAKI DISTILLERY (MERCIAN)

The narrative surrounding the Karuizawa and Kawasaki distilleries is one of the most complex in the history of Japanese whisky. It's also the one with the most twists and turns. During the course of it, we will see no fewer than five distilleries coming and going. Some of these were only around for a few years; others witnessed the ups and downs of the Japanese whisky rollercoaster that was the second half of the twentienth century. None of them exist any longer. The last and most high-profile one, Karuizawa distillery, was leveled to the ground in early 2016. Of all the twists and turns, nothing remains now. The only traces that remain of the dramatic narrative of the rise and fall of these distilleries are liquid in glass and a handful of casks with whisky still maturing in them.

As with most tragedies, there are different lineages involved. The two main lines in this story both start in 1934.

Dry ivy at Karuizawa Distillery in late 2015

THE SANRAKU LINEAGE

In 1934, Chuji Suzuki founded Showa Shuzo to facilitate the production of alcohol (neutral spirits) and synthetic sake. He acquired his license in 1935 and started making alcohol from soybeans. During the Second Sino-Japanese War (1937–1945), Japan struggled with serious rice shortages and this affected the production of sake. Priority was given to rice to feed the army rather than for sake brewing, but people still wanted a drink from time to time, so a creative solution was devised. By diluting authentic sake and then supplementing the alcohol content by adding neutral spirits one could get fairly close to the effect (if not always the taste) of the sake that people knew and loved. This is what's referred to as "synthetic sake" (*sanbai-shu* or *sanzo*). One of the first producers to offer this, Showa Shuzo did relatively well initially.

Showa Shuzo wasn't Suzuki's first foray into business, however. In fact, it was more of a side business. Three years earlier, Chuji had become president of the company his father had founded in 1909, now known as Ajinomoto, which produces seasonings and sweeteners, among other products (it is the world's largest producer of aspartame). Suzuki subscribed to the idea that *"nomen est omen."* He believed that part of the reason for Ajinomoto's success was its name, which translates as "the essence of taste." Being slightly superstitious, he wanted a good name for Showa Shuzo's brand, too. He came up with Sanraku, which pairs the Suzuki family's lucky number (three, or *san*) with the word for comfort, ease and relief, *raku*. Someone had already registered Sanraku as a trademark, but Suzuki simply bought it from the person in question.

As the war went on, production dropped, but as soon as the war was over, things started looking up. In 1946, a shochu distillery (Yashiro Factory) was established in Kyushu. The year after, another factory was set up, this time in Kawasaki. At the Kawasaki Factory, their first whisky was made. How exactly is unknown and maybe that's for the best. Their first product, Sun Luck Whisky, was launched the year the factory was built, so it's very unlikely it was anything like what we would now recognize as "whisky." In any case, whisky making wasn't a priority. It accounted for a mere 0.1 percent of Showa Shuzo's business at that time.

In 1949, the company was renamed Sanraku Shuzo. Management wanted to diversify its portfolio so they branched out into port wine, gin and other types of western liquor. More effort was poured into whisky making, as well. In 1956, they started selling Sun Luck Whisky in 180ml hip flask bottles. In 1958, the Kawasaki factory started making "malt whisky." Again, we'll have to take their word for it, seeing as no details are known about the equipment and processes involved. In 1959, they launched a new product, Sun Luck Gold, and the year after, they added Sun Luck Corrie to their lineup. The former was a dead ringer for Old Parr: same bottle shape, same dark-colored glass and a very similar label style. In dark and dingy bars late at night, more than a few customers must have assumed they were drinking—and paying for—"the good stuff."

Sanraku Shuzo also started promoting their whisky in an unusual way. The company sales staff would visit bars incognito and order Sun Luck Whisky in an ostentatious manner, in the hopes of drawing in other customers who happened to be around. Unlikely as it may seem, they must have had their fair share of luck (no pun intended) with this, as sales weren't too shabby.

By 1961, the limits of whisky production had been reached at the Kawasaki factory, so Sanraku Shuzo started looking for a solution. The idea was to find a site where they could develop both their whisky and wine interests. As far as wine was concerned, the obvious candidate was Yamanashi prefecture, so they looked for a plot of land there and started building as soon as they had found one. However, the same year, Sanraku acquired Nisshin Brewery Co. and wine maker Mercian. Because Mercian had a major reputation in the Japanese wine world, Sanraku felt it didn't make sense to compete with themselves by following through with the wine plans they had in mind for the Yamanashi plant. Instead, they decided to focus on whisky only in Yamanashi. By October 1961, the distillery was ready and malt whisky was being produced.

Things were about to change radically the year after. However, before we move forward, we need to step back in time again and follow the second line in this grand narrative from the beginning.

THE OCEAN LINEAGE

The early 1930s is not a period that's fondly remembered in Japanese history. During the Showa Depression (1930–1932), Japan experienced the deepest economic downturn in modern history. Enormous deflation, extreme rural impoverishment and the rationing of virtually all material industries were the order of the day. On December 13, 1931,

A 1950 advertisement for Ocean Whisky

a new government was sworn in and the catastrophic policies of the previous government were reversed. The economy began to recover in 1932 but in the course of the following years, Japanese politics was gradually overtaken by the military.

It is remarkable that, in that climate, there was room for enterprise in the field of liquor. In the same year that Chuji Suzuki set up Showa Shuzo and Masataka Taketsuru set up Dai Nippon Kaju, an entrepreneur by the name of Kotaro Miyazaki established Daikoku Budoshu. Miyazaki had been one of the shareholders in the Dai Nihon Yamanashi Budoshu Co. This was the first private wine maker in Japan, established in 1877. Production-wise, things were a struggle from the get-go. Lacking the know-how, they just couldn't make it work technically. When the company was dissolved (1886), Miyazaki took over the equipment and set up a new business, Kaisan Winery, with two partners.

The quality of the Kaisan wines improved but sales were a problem. There was no wine-drinking culture in Japan, so no demand for Kaisan's products. Miyazaki opened a sales office (Kaisan Shoten) in Tokyo, but not much changed. In 1890, his partners left and Miyazaki continued on his own. The year after, he adopted an illustration of Daikokuten (the god of wealth and commerce and one of the Seven Lucky Gods) as a trademark for Kaisan Winery. In another case of *"nomen est omen,"* this brand did well and became widely recognized.

In 1934, Miyazaki rethought his business and—inspired by the success of the Daikokuten label—renamed it Daikoku Budoshu. As indicated by the word *budoshu* (literally, grape + alcohol), the focus was still very much on wine and brandy. In fact, Miyazaki was strongly opposed to using the nation's staple (rice and grain) for anything other than eating.

Daikoku Budoshu entered the field of whisky making after WWII. In 1947, Kotaro Miyazaki passed away and his grandson, also named Kotaro Miyazaki, succeeded him as president of the company. It's under Kotaro the younger (as we will call him) that Daikoku Budoshu became a serious whisky producer.

People sometimes point to the 1922 K.M. Sweet Home Whisky as the first whisky associated with the company. It's a particularly appealing story, milked in the company's publicity, because it was made in response to a suggestion made by then Crown Prince Hirohito on a visit to the winery. However, it's fair to assume that this was a whisky in name only. Exactly how it was concocted two years before the first pot stills were installed in Japan (at Kotobukiya, now Yamazaki distillery) is anybody's guess.

In the late 1940s and early 1950s, Daikoku Budoshu produced whisky at their Tokyo factory in Shimo-Ochiai. They were not making malt whisky in-house, but strictly speaking, this wasn't an obstacle. Third-grade whisky could be produced without any malt component in it, but Kotaro the younger was not a fan of that practice. He felt products like Takara Shuzo's Ideal and Tokyo Jozo's Tommy were fake whisky. Keen to get his hands on good-quality malt whisky to use in Daikoku's whisky brand Ocean Whisky, Kotaro the younger got in touch with a business contact up north, Masataka Taketsuru. A deal was worked out whereby neutral spirits made by Daikoku would be swapped for malt whisky distilled at Yoichi. Because of this arrangement, unbeknownst to many fans of old Japanese whisky, early Ocean Whisky bottlings often contain Yoichi malt—a small percentage, but still.

The people at Daikoku Budoshu took advertising very seriously. They even pushed their whisky in publications abroad. The advertisement on the facing page appeared in a popular American weekly news magazine in the summer of 1950. The bottle in the advertisement looks eerily familiar. How the people at Kotobukiya (now Suntory) felt about this Kakubin lookalike we don't know.

In 1952, Daikoku wanted to start producing malt whisky in-house. The company owned a vineyard in Shiojiri in Nagano prefecture, so they sent an employee by the name of Tanaka over to set up a distillery there. On March 5, 1952, Daikoku got their license to make malt whisky. If it wasn't for the account left by Akira Sekine, a young man who joined the company the same month, the story of the trials and tribulations of Shiojiri distillery as well as the early days of Karuizawa distillery would have been lost to time. Much of what follows is taken from his little book *A Page of Making Western Style Liquors*, which has not been translated and is long out of print in Japan.

SETTING UP A MALT DISTILLERY IN THE 1950s: A CASE STUDY

After working in Daikoku Budoshu's test lab for 10 days, the company sent Sekine to the Shiojiri factory and called Tanaka back to Tokyo. From then on, Sekine was in charge of the distillery project.

The distillery setup was basic: a malt mill, a 2-kiloliter (kl) mash tun, a single 2kl washback and one 2.5kl pot still. Water was taken from a bore, 49 feet/15 meters deep, on site. The first mash took place on March 29, 1952. It became apparent quite soon that the distillate was not what they had hoped for. Sekine felt it smelled grassy and vegetal (*aokusai*) and tasted even worse. Back in Tokyo, Tanaka was of the opinion that, after three years in wood, it might improve. Sekine considered this wishful thinking, but complied.

After two months, the well had dried up and whisky making had to be suspended. While they were drilling a deeper water bore, Sekine went back to the lab in Tokyo to analyze the Shiojiri distillate and compare it with new-make from other companies. This confirmed his initial thoughts about the quality of the Shiojiri distillate.

After the grape harvest in the fall of 1952, Sekine found himself back in Shiojiri, ready to give it another try. One of the things that Sekine was concerned about was the level of iron in the groundwater. He suspected this was the culprit of the metallic, dirty taste of the new-make. In order to remove the iron, a zeolite-filter was installed. The last day of whisky making in 1952 was December 15.

Spirit was filled into American white oak barrels and subjected to high-voltage electricity and high-intensity ultrasonic energy to speed up the maturation process. It was clear they were desperately hoping for a miracle.

As soon as they started making whisky again the following year, new problems occurred. The fermentation wasn't going well so Sekine focused on sanitation and changed the yeast but to no avail. In 1954, he noticed the water seemed to be killing the yeast. The decision was made to bring in water from the nearby Naraigawa River. Sometimes, even rainwater was used. The fermentation was improving, so they were clearly on to something, but the quality of the new-make was still suspect.

The waste products from the distillation process were dumped literally in their own backyard. The draff was spread out over the vineyard (much to the chagrin of the neighborhood) and the spent lees were dumped in a hole near the bore. In effect, they were polluting their own water source. After a while, they decided to dump the spent lees into the Naraigawa River just a mile downstream from the distillery. This sort of practice is unimaginable these days, but according to Sekine, other distillers in Japan were solving problems in similarly "creative" ways.

Gradually, the water vein tapped via the deep bore on site dried up. In 1955, different types of yeast were brought in (American whiskey yeast and Copenhagen beer yeast) but there was little progress as far as the resulting distillate was concerned. Sekine felt they had hit the wall and had come to the conclusion that the problems at Shiojiri distillery were structural. To put it in plain language, the place was bad. Sekine and his colleagues saw a possible solution to the problem, however—a radical one—relocating the distillery.

In 1939, Daikoku Budoshu had established a winery in Karuizawa. Karuizawa was once a busy station on the Nakasendo (literally, the Central Mountain Road). This was one of five routes established during the Edo era, and one of two connecting Kyoto with Edo (present-day Tokyo). After the Meiji Restoration, the highway system fell into disuse and the town began a period of decline. In 1886, Alexander Croft Shaw, a Scottish missionary, arrived in Karuizawa and, struck by the similarities with his homeland, built a summer residence there. Many Tokyo residents followed his example, and after a rail link was established in 1888, the town blossomed into a resort town with international flair.

Sekine and his colleagues were convinced Karuizawa would be a much better place to make whisky. Located at the foot of Mt. Asama, the water was good, the site was spacious and there was a way to get rid of waste products there. They wrote a letter to the head office asking for the distillery to be moved there, but the letter never arrived. Tired of waiting for a reply, they decided to make the trek back to Tokyo and plead their case in person. They found the powers-that-be in a good mood and their request was immediately granted.

That was the end of the Shiojiri distillery adventure. Between March 1952 and November 1955, they had produced a total of 230kl of spirit (calculated at 65%abv). It was anything but mature and was very unsatisfying in terms of quality, but since there was no minimum three-year maturation regulation in Japan, it was blended away into 2nd grade whisky.

Wine production at the Karuizawa site was terminated and the whisky license was moved from Shiojiri to Karuizawa. With renewed hope and courage, Sekine and his colleagues relocated to Karuizawa, ready to have another go at making proper malt whisky.

KARUIZAWA DISTILLERY: THE EARLY DAYS

Daikoku Budoshu started constructing their new distillery in Karuizawa in 1955. They got a new malt mill and lauter tank, installed eight epoxy-lined concrete washbacks, moved the pot still from Shiojiri to the new location and added several more. There are conflicting reports about the number of pot stills in use in the early years. According to Sekine, there were four (between 2.5 and 4kl); however, documentation published by Sanraku states that there were only three, with a fourth (3kl) installed in 1963 to increase production capacity.

The first distillation took place in February 1956, following test runs that were done the previous month. One of the things that Daikoku was struggling with was getting ahold of malted barley. At the time, foreign trade (especially trade connected with farm products) was strictly controlled by the government. Seeing as there were virtually no Japanese agricultural products that could compete on even terms with imports, the government's protectionist strategy was simple: most agricultural imports were banned. This was the case with barley, malted or not. The established whisky makers obviously had contracts with domestic suppliers, but Daikoku—being new to the malt whisky game—had to make do with what they could cobble together. In 1957, they really struggled, so much so that they had to mix malted and unmalted barley on occasion.

This handicap became an advantage in 1958 when restrictions on barley (and other) imports were eased somewhat. Whereas the other whisky makers had contracts to honor, Daikoku Budoshu could immediately take advantage of the opening and import malted barley from Scotland. They were, in fact, the first to import malted barley from abroad. This allowed them to increase their whisky production and become a more serious competitor in the marketplace. By 1961, about half of the malted barley used at Karuizawa distillery was imported.

Sekine and his colleagues carried out lots of R&D in the early years of Karuizawa distillery. They used American whiskey yeast as well as yeast sourced from Scotland, experimented with yeast pitching rates, various distillation temperatures and so on. They got their hands on books on brewing and distilling published abroad and increased their know-how on the fly. By November 1959, they managed to produce a "Scotch-type distillate."

THE MERGER AND THE END OF YAMANASHI DISTILLERY

By the end of the 1950s, whisky production had become increasingly important to Daikoku Budoshu. In 1960, whisky constituted 53 percent of their total production and 59 percent of sales. Their whisky range consisted of: Gloria Ocean, Old Ocean (both special grade), Black Ocean (1st grade) and various 2nd grade products, including White Ocean, Ocean Deluxe and Ocean Kakubin. Wine was no longer their main business and the Ocean brand was everywhere, so in 1961, the company decided to change its name to Ocean Whisky Co., Ltd., to reflect that state of affairs.

In 1962, Sanraku Shuzo and Ocean Whisky merged. This was a big story at the time. Both companies had spent considerable resources on advertising and promotion, so they had to cut costs elsewhere. Sharing the same distribution network was one way. Another was for Ocean Whisky to use the blending alcohol made by Sanraku Shuzo in its products. In the end, a merger seemed beneficial to both parties. On July 1, 1962, the new company was registered as Sanraku Ocean.

Obviously, some aspects of production needed to be restructured. Both companies had just set up a malt distillery. There was no need for the new company to have two malt distilleries, not at a time when malt whisky constituted a low percentage of most blends. The decision was made to compare distillate from both distilleries that had been in wood for one year. The Karuizawa distillate was deemed fine, the Yamanashi distillate "problematic." Sekine was dispatched to the Yamanashi distillery to see what the cause might have been.

As soon as he arrived, he knew what was wrong. The two pot stills at Yamanashi distillery were huge (14.5kl and 7.2kl) and made out of . . . stainless steel. That's why the distillate stank—apparently, literally! The people at Sanraku knew that certain parts of a copper still, especially the swan neck, had to be replaced every so often because copper wears out. Stainless steel doesn't, so being a rational and pragmatic company, they figured they were being clever. It didn't occur to them that there was a reason why nobody in Scotland or in France was distilling in stainless steel pots.

Following Sekine's visit, the staff at Yamanashi distillery experimented with adding copper chips to new-make for a while. They also tried to stir new-make with copper strings. Apparently, it helped a bit but it was still far from good. The people in management must have realized it was best to bet on Karuizawa distillery, so the decision was made to concentrate production of malt whisky there. In 1964, production capacity was increased at Karuizawa, so the stainless steel stills at Yamanashi could be put to rest. Unexpectedly, between 1967 and 1969, Yamanashi distillery was needed again so whisky was produced at both distilleries for a short period of time. Mercifully, that was the last of Yamanashi distillery. After 1969, it was converted into a warehouse.

KAWASAKI DISTILLERY

Towards the end of the 1960s, Sanraku Ocean set out to fix the one thing that prevented them from offering products that wouldn't pale in comparison with the average blended whisky coming out of Scotland: the lack of grain whisky. Whisky drinkers in Japan were starting to appreciate good—read: imported and therefore, because of the tax system, expensive—whisky, so comparisons were bound to be made.

Masataka Taketsuru had brought the first Coffey stills into the country. In 1967, Sanraku Ocean followed suit and sent one of its people to Scotland to investigate the possibilities of making grain whisky in-house. Things went well and in 1969, a Coffey still made by McMillan Coppersmiths was shipped from Scotland to Japan. The Kawasaki factory was the obvious place to install this unwieldy piece of equipment. Next door, at Ajinomoto, huge amounts of corn were being used to produce seasoning products, so it was a small matter to divert some of that corn to the grain whisky factory.

Grain whisky production at Kawasaki distillery started in June 1969. White maize imported from South Africa was the main ingredient. That made up 80 percent of the mashbill. To this, 20 percent malted barley was added late in the mashing stage. Initially, they were taken aback by what came out of the Coffey still, something that smelled (in Sekine's words) like fish oil (*"sakana no abura"*), but they made the necessary adjustments and managed to produce grain whisky that was close in quality to what they knew from Invergordon distillery in Scotland.

The standard procedure was to distill the mash to an abv of 94% and then bring it down to 59% by adding water before filling it into wood. The average maturation time was three to four years. In the beginning, the grain whisky was filled into ex-bourbon barrels and stored at the Kawasaki factory. They soon ran out of space and decided to use the old Yamanashi distillery site for storage. According to the last master distiller of Karuizawa distillery, Osami Uchibori, who spent a couple of months at Kawasaki distillery, everything was sent to Yamanashi and filled into the same sort of wood that was used at Karuizawa, namely, ex-sherry. Summers in Yamanashi can be very warm, so the thinking was the climate would speed up maturation.

Kawasaki distillery is long gone but it's unclear when exactly it stopped producing and when it was dismantled. Ichiro Akuto of Venture Whisky purchased the last remaining casks of Kawasaki. He was alerted to this opportunity by the staff at Karuizawa distillery in 2006. In the wake of the acquisition of Mercian by Kirin, the Yamanashi warehouse was going to be modified for the purpose of storing wine casks. There was genuine concern among the Karuizawa staff ("they were real whisky guys," as Ichiro put it)

Rarest of the rare: the oldest vintage of Kawasaki single grain bottled to date and bottle number 1

that the precious Kawasaki stock would have been redistilled or otherwise gotten rid of. Ichiro has used it for some of his premium blends and has also released a handful of single cask bottlings. The oldest vintage he has released is 1976, the youngest 1982.

It's highly likely that grain whisky was still being made at Kawasaki distillery in the mid-1980s. As mentioned elsewhere, 1983 was the peak of whisky consumption in Japan. After that, sales started dropping. In the book published to commemorate the 50th anniversary of Sanraku, no mention is made of Kawasaki distillery being closed or demolished and that was in 1986. Most likely, production was phased out during the latter half of the 1980s or in the early 1990s.

KARUIZAWA DISTILLERY: RISE AND FALL

Throughout the 1960s and 1970s, Karuizawa factory (as it was called then) was a workhorse for Sanraku Ocean's cheap blends. Supplying the malt whisky used in those blends was its raison d'être, plain and simple. Obviously, given the very low malt ratio in the recipes, the impact it had on the quality of the final product was very limited.

In 1977, Karuizawa Factory was renamed Ocean Karuizawa Distillery. This may seem like a trivial detail, but a few things that happened around this time indicate it was a reflection of a slightly changed view of the place—a revaluation, so to speak. In July 1976, Sanraku Ocean had released its first Karuizawa single malt whisky (¥15,000, 720ml). In fact, it was the very first malt whisky released as such in Japan. The company used the highest-quality malt maturing in the warehouses and had a special hand-blown crystal decanter designed for it. Because good (read: mature) malt stocks were very limited, the company could only produce 10,000 bottles of Karuizawa Single Malt per year, and they never actually promoted the brand, seeing as they didn't want to create more demand than they could

Uncanny resemblance: Suntory Kakubin and Sanraku-Ocean Bright 5 (released in 1971)

possibly satisfy. This partly explains why Karuizawa has been written out of the history of single malt whisky in Japan. (A much bigger company claimed to be the first, eight years later.)

There's an interesting anecdote connected with the first Karuizawa Single Malt. Japan's former emperor Akihito, crown prince at the time, was given a bottle of it while on holiday in Karuizawa with his wife in the summer of 1978. Apparently, he liked it so much that he had more bottles ordered later. Today, that would be a marketing department's dream, but tight stocks of suitably aged whisky in the Karuizawa warehouses meant Sanraku Ocean was in no position to make a big deal out of all this. Another product was added to the portfolio in 1977, this time a "premium blend" *avant la lettre*. Named Asama, after the volcano that towers over Karuizawa, it came in a bottle that looked like a piece of rock. It was limited to 30,000 bottles and sold around Tokyo only (¥10,000, 720ml).

Between 1977 and 1981, much of the infrastructure at Karuizawa distillery was upgraded. In order of replacement, the distillery got new washbacks, a new malt mill, a more efficient boiler and a new lauter tank. Over and beyond raising production volume, there was a clear commitment to quality. We are now reaping the rewards of that commitment as evidenced by the superb quality of casks from the early 1980s vintages, recently bottled by Number One Drinks. At the time, however, it was a case of pearls before swine. The love for whisky in general was fading away in Japan from the mid-1980s onwards, and the whisky that still managed to find some affection was the polar opposite of Karuizawa: light, soft, "smooth" and characterless—whisky trying to pretend it was vodka or shochu.

Ocean Sanraku anticipated this development with a product released in November 1984: MOO (as in "smooth"). Almost colorless, bottled at 35%abv and presented in a modern, cheap minimalist style, it was trying to appeal to the kids coming of age in the bubble years. It came in 450 and 900ml bottles and was dirt-cheap (¥500 and ¥1,000, respectively). Great for partying on a budget, it was whisky that was trying to hide the fact that it was whisky.

In 1985, Sanraku Ocean shortened its corporate name to Sanraku. Five years later, it became Mercian. Again, this reflected changing priorities. Whisky was becoming old hat and wine was the new cool kid on the block. In the spring of 1990, a survey was carried out to check what the corporate image of Sanraku was in the eyes of the Japanese people.

A shocking 99 percent of people surveyed considered Sanraku to be an old and traditional Japanese liquor producer. Just 15 percent knew that Sanraku also produced wine and that Mercian was part of Sanraku. Suntory, on the other hand, was regarded as the premier wine maker in Japan. This was painful news to the management at Sanraku. Hoping to be able to redress that situation, Tadao Suzuki announced in June 1990 the change in the company name to Mercian. In a shot across Suntory's bow—whose patronage of music, fine arts and literature was widely known—Suzuki established the Mercian Musée d'Art Karuizawa in the same year. The museum was on the distillery grounds and it quickly became a big attraction in the area. Most of the people visiting the site were actually there for the museum rather than the distillery.

Throughout the 1990s, Mercian tightened its whisky focus more and more on the single malt category. Finally, Karuizawa distillery could showcase its qualities. Its day in the spotlight had come as far as what it was capable of producing, but unfortunately the audience for it was largely gone. Production had been scaled back steadily since the mid-'80s. On December 31, 2000, they called it a day. The distillery was mothballed and the three people working there now spent their days tending to the grounds and hand-bottling casks for the distillery shop from time to time.

It wasn't all doom and gloom, however. In 2001, Karuizawa Pure Malt Whisky 12yo picked up a gold award at the International Wine and Spirits Competition in London. This, along with a Yoichi 10yo single cask winning *Whisky Magazine*'s "Best of the Best" the same year, heralded the beginning of an era in which Japanese whiskies would routinely capture the highest honors at prestigious whisky and spirits competitions worldwide.

At the end of 2006, Mercian became a consolidated subsidiary of Kirin. The same year, a company was set up that would play an instrumental role in bringing Karuizawa and other quality Japanese whiskies from smaller producers to the attention of whisky fans abroad. David Croll and Marcin Miller, based in Japan and England respectively, set up Number One Drinks and started bottling exceptional single casks for sale in Europe and, later on, other foreign markets as well. When

Facing page: Karuizawa Distillery in the spring of 2008. Clockwise from the top: empty casks, the faded heads of two of them revealing their origins ("The Macallan-Glenlivet Disty."); retired casks in front of Warehouse No.2; the main distillery building; the stillroom; inside Warehouse No.1; the path to the distillery

Karuizawa casks at Chichibu Distillery

they shipped their first Karuizawa bottlings westwards, very few people outside Japan knew about the distillery. A few years later, people would trample on each other just to get a shot at buying a bottle.

In the summer of 2010, Mercian became a wholly owned subsidiary of Kirin. People had been hopeful in 2006 that Kirin's involvement would be a good thing for Karuizawa, that the cobwebs would be blown away and the stills fired up again. By 2010, it had become clear that that wasn't going to happen. Kirin was interested in Mercian's wine business, not in their little mothballed distillery in Nagano. As far as whisky was concerned, Kirin was happy with what they had going at Fuji Gotemba distillery.

Number One Drinks and at least one other seriously interested party tried to buy the distillery from Kirin, but they wouldn't let it go. Kirin wasn't interested in reviving Karuizawa distillery, but they weren't keen on seeing it in production again in someone else's hands either. Number One Drinks figured that maybe Kirin could be persuaded to sell the entire remaining inventory. In August 2011, after long and arduous negotiations, Number One Drinks managed to purchase all remaining Karuizawa casks. Not that there was much left of Karuizawa distillery's legacy by then. All that remained were 364 casks.

The next step was stocktaking. A retired blender went through everything and separated the wheat from the chaff. Fortunately, there wasn't too much of the latter. The majority was of sufficiently high quality to be bottled as single casks; 77 casks (all from the 1999 and 2000 vintages) were earmarked for vatting and a couple of faulty casks were sent back.

Shortly after Number One Drinks had acquired the Karuizawa inventory, they were informed by Kirin that the distillery site would be sold and were asked to remove their casks. After being told it wasn't for sale, this came as a big surprise to Number One Drinks. Fortunately for them, Ichiro Akuto, who had just built a new warehouse on the Chichibu distillery annex site, had a temporary home for the casks. By the end of 2011, the tiresome process of regauging and moving all casks there had been completed and the endgame could begin.

The most high-profile release was unveiled at the Tokyo International Bar Show/Whisky Live in 2013. Cask #5627, a 250-liter hogshead, was filled in 1960 and bottled on New Year's Day 2013. It was not only the oldest Karuizawa cask within the inventory, but also—once in glass—at the time, the oldest Japanese single malt ever bottled (52 years). Unsurprisingly, it was also the most expensive Japanese whisky ever sold, at 2 million yen a bottle—twice the price of the previous record holder, Yamazaki 50yo. As Marcin Miller put it, "The angels of Karuizawa were relatively thirsty, so we only had 41 bottles." It set a further record at Bonhams in Hong Kong 2½ years later, when a bottle was sold for HK$918,750 (about US$118,500), the most ever paid for a single bottle of Japanese whisky at auction, at the time.

If wood could speak...

THE LAST OF KARUIZAWA DISTILLERY: A MEMOIR

The year 2016 marked the end of a chapter in Japanese whisky history. In February and March of that year, scrappers demolished all the buildings at Karuizawa distillery. By the time they were done—March 15, to be precise—there was nothing left to remind us of the 60-year history of the distillery: of the years of struggle and hard toil; the years of glory, decline and then neglect; the years the distillery's work was taken for granted or ignored, and then appreciated, but too late, by a growing circle of whisky fans abroad and eventually also at home. It's ironic that by the time the bulldozers had finished their job, Karuizawa was at the top of many whisky lists all over the world. Reviewers were reserving their highest praise and scores for Karuizawa whiskies, and bottles were changing hands for obscene amounts of money. Karuizawa distillery had become one of a handful of truly iconic whisky distilleries—and the first non-Scottish one in that pantheon—as the final nail was put in the coffin.

The year before, in late November, the distillery was stripped of all its equipment. It had been sold as one lot at a public auction where Taiko Nakamura of Gaia Flow had bought it for a little over 5 million yen. Most of it was not going to be of much use anymore, but some key pieces of equipment were in good enough condition to be able to get a new life at the distillery Nakamura was setting up in Shizuoka. A week before Karuizawa distillery was gutted, I had the chance to walk through the distillery one last time. I had been there many times, but this was the most emotional visit of all. I was, of course, aware that it was the last time I would see it, but what made it all the more heartrending was the fact that I was going to be in the company of a man whose life was intimately entwined with that of the distillery, from the glory days of the 1960s and '70s all the way through the decline and mothballing, who knew the place like the back of his hand, the last "Malt Master," Osami Uchibori.

Uchibori didn't plan on working in the whisky industry. In fact, he wasn't keen on alcohol in general. "Even though I started smoking when I was in fourth grade, I didn't drink liquor at all," he laughs. "I couldn't stand liquor. The smell alone was enough to make me sick. My old man drank, but I guess I took after my mother." His original plan was to work at a gasoline stand and, with that in mind, he had acquired a license to

The path to Karuizawa Distillery, soon no more (2015)

handle hazardous materials while still in high school. Upon graduating from high school, a senior who worked at Daikoku Budoshu advised him to apply for a position at his company. The salary was good, but it wasn't easy to get in. The odds of getting hired were one in eight. Fortunately, Uchibori found himself on the left side of that ratio.

Uchibori started in April 1960 and joined a team of about 50 people working in three shifts at the distillery. It was a busy place: 7 "boiler men" took care of the energy supply (coal in those days); 8 people were in charge of the mashing and fermentation; another 8 handled the distillation; 6 people worked at the cooperage; 8 people worked in the warehouses and 10 people were kept busy in the testing and administration department. Over the years, Uchibori found himself working in all of these areas, except the cooperage. He got a boiler license, handled the mashing, distillation, cask selection, and bottling and took care of liquor tax matters as well.

Walking around the distillery, a lot of the equipment and infrastructure brought back memories for Uchibori: things that used to be there, but were no longer; challenges that were thrown at the workers and overcome; funny stories and sad stories. As we enter the main production building, Uchibori points out one of the most valuable pieces of equipment at the distillery: the Porteus malt-mill. This was imported from England and installed in 1989. Better milling meant better mashing; according to Uchibori, the new mill had a noticeable impact on the quality of the distillate. As he admires it in silence, he shakes his head. Later, he explained that the mill itself was easily worth 20 million yen, four times the hammer price Gaia Flow paid for the complete distillery equipment at auction earlier that year. "What a bargain," Uchibori sighs.

Another piece of equipment that's still in good condition is the mash tun, a lauter tank with a capacity of 1.2kl (they only filled it with 1kl when the distillery was operative). The five Oregon pine washbacks, however, are no longer salvageable, having been neglected for a decade. They were made to order in Scotland, then shipped to Yokohama, trucked to the distillery and installed in 1992. Before that, epoxy-lined tanks were used for the fermentation; prior to that, steel tanks; and in the early days, eight open concrete troughs. The fermentation time was three to five days and the distillery used both brewers and distillers yeast, including Mercian's proprietary yeast strain. The habit was to use a "starter." A small amount of wort was transferred to a little tank and yeast was added to it. When this starter was active, it was added to the rest of the wort in the washback along with a bit of extra yeast.

Of the four pot stills, only the most recently installed one (the 1975 spirit still) is in good enough shape to be put to work again. The very first still was made in Scotland and used at Shiojiri distillery before being moved to Karuizawa. Miyake Seisakusho, the Japanese copper-and-steel specialist, then made a replica of that spirit still. In the early 1960s, two wash stills and a new spirit still were ordered from Scotland. The new spirit still replaced the very

The original pot still

first one, which later became a little monument outside. In the distillery's heyday, all four still stills were used around the clock. Towards the end, they were only using three of the four, and only for a few months a year. As far as Uchibori remembers, the stills were always indirect-heated with steam.

The stills were equipped with shell-and-tube condensers. Water quality was obviously not as important for the condensers as it was for the distillation. Quantity, on the other hand, was. This reminds Uchibori of an interesting episode that took place in 1977, when the current buildings of Miyota Kita Elementary School were constructed, just a tenth of a mile/200 meters down the road from Karuizawa distillery. "When they built the new school, they also built a swimming pool. Shortly after, we noticed that, on certain days, the temperature of the water in the condensers rose by as much as 5.4°F/3°C. We had no idea what was going on. Keeping the water temperature in the condensers steady was

Osami Uchibori reminiscing about his life at Karuizawa Distillery (November 2015)

crucial, of course. That requires a lot of water. So does changing the water in a swimming pool. After a while, we put two and two together. Apparently, when the school was built, a piping mistake had occurred, which led to our water supply being docked to theirs. When the water in the school pool was changed, there wasn't enough to keep supplying our condensers with a steady stream. As soon as we had figured this out, we went to the city office and requested that the school change the water in the pool in the evening. After that, we never had trouble with the condensers again."

Right from the start, most of the spirit produced at Karuizawa distillery was filled into ex-sherry wood. Initially, they purchased casks from Spain through Hayakawa Bussan. At some point in the 1960s, they decided to make their own "sherry casks" in-house and set up a cooperage on site. In addition to craftsmen hired from Tochigi and Ibaraki, they got half a dozen people who had previously worked for the wine section of Daikoku Budoshu in Shiojiri to come to Karuizawa for that purpose. They also used a few local Karuizawa craftsmen who had experience making wooden baths. At the cooperage, new casks were made, which were then seasoned with sherry from Mercian. The staff opened the casks, opened bottles of sherry, poured the sherry into the casks and left things for 6 to 12 months before emptying the casks and filling them with whisky. Occasionally, they would use refill casks, but according to Uchibori, "The good stuff went into first-fill casks."

As we enter one of the ivy-festooned stone warehouses that gave the distillery site much of its picturesque quality, we are greeted by a beguiling aroma of incredible weight and intensity. Our voices echo in the empty warehouse. The casks are all gone. Soon the heavy scents, accumulated over decades of dunnage-style maturation, would vanish as well.

Because of the way the wooden racks in the warehouses were set up, the coopers at Karuizawa distillery developed their own size of sherry cask. Slightly smaller than a butt (450 as opposed to 500 liters), this made it possible to fit two casks in the racks. The oldest warehouses on site held 400 casks, arranged four high, with the fourth level being reserved for slightly smaller-sized casks (barrels and hogsheads).

Karuizawa Distillery's last winter

The "newest" warehouse (no. 8) was built in the late 1990s. It was the only one that was not of the dunnage type and the only one that was fully automated. Because of this, it was no longer necessary to make the casks smaller in size. In the new warehouse, regular-sized butts could be accommodated without any problem. Racks could be moved mechanically, and there was room for over 2,000 casks. The plan was to convert other warehouses along the same lines, but history decided otherwise. After the distillery was mothballed, warehouse no. 8 was used as a book depot. Now, this state-of-the-art warehouse was earmarked for demolition, just like most of the other distillery buildings. "What a waste," Uchibori sighs.

An interesting aspect of warehousing at the distillery was the practice of vatting when the whisky had turned 8 to 10 years old. To focus the maturation and arrive at a certain consistency, a hundred-odd casks would be vatted together and then returned to the same casks for further maturation. Some of the liquid spent its entire life in one cask, but most of the whisky maturing at Karuizawa was subject to this intermediate vatting process.

In recent years, the early 1980s vintages (1981-84) have come to be seen as the "Golden Age" of Karuizawa distillery. Asked if he could think of any reasons for that (any changes in production) Uchibori-san points to the water filtering system, which was changed around that time. "We had been using diatomaceous earth filtration to purify our water until the beginning of the '80s. In 1981, we installed a new mash tun (a lauter tank) and, around that time, we switched to a system that just took the clean top layer of the water without filtering it to death. The old filtration system resulted in very polished water, but maybe, some of the elements that helped contribute flavor during the initial stages of the whisky-making process were lost because of that. That's the only explanation I can think of, really."

Asked about his personal "Golden Age" at Karuizawa, Uchibori's face lights up: "The last decade of production there, the '90s, without a doubt. Until then, I was just a *salaryman*, but when I became Malt Master, I could do what I wanted." One of his projects from that time was the Rouge Cask experiment. In 1995, he brought in 20 casks that had contained red wine from Mercian's winery in Katsunuma and refilled them with Karuizawa spirit. He carefully monitored the maturation process and gradually began to release them when they were 12 years old. From 2007 onwards, they could be picked up at the distillery shop for a few thousand yen. Now people would sell their mother to get hold of one those precious Rouge Cask Karuizawas.

Uchibori was keen to run more experiments—because unless you mature whisky for more than 10 years, you can't really tell what the effect is—but whisky making at the distillery was gradually being faded out towards the end of the '90s. In the end, it was a "three-man whisky factory," as shown on the labels, in production for just two or three months a year, a far cry from the days when 50 people were keeping the spirit flowing around the clock.

After the last official day of production (December 31, 2000) Uchibori and his two colleagues essentially became groundskeepers. They took care of the property and hand-bottled many of the single casks that have now become the stuff of legend (not to mention some of the most expensive whisky on the planet), but the fun was over. In the summer of 2006, the stills were running again for a short while. Someone wanting to set up his own distillery was keen to "practice" a bit and spent a month at the distillery, honing his skills with Uchibori. That man was Ichiro Akuto and his story is elsewhere in this book. Ichiro's internship at Karuizawa wasn't exactly textbook. The mash tun was rusty and the stills were in such a lamentable condition that vapor came out during distillation. True to the Karuizawa character, Ichiro used 'Golden Promise' barley.

As soon as Ichiro's new distillery was ready, he got Uchibori to help him out with the technical side of the operation. It was a bit of a trek from Karuizawa to Chichibu, however. Eventually, wanting to work a bit closer to home, Uchibori found something literally in his backyard: making beer at Yo-Ho Brewing. Not a bad deal for someone who doesn't drink whisky but is partial to a beer or two after work.

After putting the chain on the distillery parking lot for the last time, we head back to the Uchibori residence, a 15-minute drive from the distillery, and settle in the tatami room. Alongside a seemingly endless procession of culinary delights, courtesy of Mrs. Uchibori, bottles start appearing on the table: Karuizawa whiskies from the 1960s and '70s, as well as various commemorative releases in weird and wonderful decanters. Later in the evening, I ask about the character of the Karuizawa new-make. "Why don't you tell me," Uchibori says with a complicit smile. He disappears for a few minutes and comes back with a distillate sample dated 2006. This was the last spirit to ever run off the stills at Karuizawa, the spirit made by Ichiro Akuto under the tutelage of

Uchibori. When Ichiro set up his internship, it was part of the deal that he would purchase the spirit he made at Karuizawa distillery. He did but the interesting thing is that he filled it into a variety of casks types, including one *mizunara* cask. One day, a *mizunara* Karuizawa will see the light of the day, but it will be a while. As Ichiro told me, "The spirit was very . . . characteristic, not clean at all, so it will need a lot of time in wood." As I sip the 2006 Karuizawa new-make alongside the first new-make produced at Chichibu (from 2008), I understand what he means. I know that it will be worth the wait, though.

Less than four months after that unforgettable day, Karuizawa distillery was gone forever. Various people tried to save the distillery, even at the eleventh hour, but it wasn't to be. The city of Miyota wanted a brand new administration building on the site and they got one. In the process, the city lost its one and only claim to fame. The irony is probably lost on the powers that be.

Some of the equipment is now put to good use at Shizuoka distillery, so at least something lives on, albeit in a different place. The dream of making whisky in Karuizawa is not completely dead, though, and several companies are currently in the process of establishing new whisky distilleries in the Karuizawa area, but they won't be in exactly the same location and they won't have the same equipment. "The water is key," says Uchibori, "that and the climate." Will it ever be possible to recreate the unique character of the Karuizawa spirit? "It may be," Uchibori smiles, "as long as I'm around . . . but it will never really be the same."

HANYU DISTILLERY (TOA SHUZO/VENTURE WHISKY)

Toa Shuzo, the company behind Hanyu distillery, set up a liquor production plant in the village of Hanyu in November 1941, a month before the attack on Pearl Harbor. It was an extension of the Akuto family's sake business in Chichibu, which dates back to 1626. Initially, the Hanyu plant was used to produce shochu and sake. After the war, there was significant demand for whisky in Japan and Isoji Akuto (Ichiro's grandfather) decided to try and respond to that. He obtained a license to make whisky in April 1946 and started experimenting using a homemade still. Things didn't go very well and there were times when most of the production at the Hanyu plant was liquor destined for use as an ingredient in baked goods.

The old Hanyu wash still, now at Chichibu Distillery

Towards the end of the 1970s and beginning of the 1980s, whisky consumption in Japan skyrocketed. Like most smaller whisky "producers" in Japan, Toa Shuzo relied heavily on malt whisky imported in bulk from Scotland. The higher the quality (and price tag) of the product, the more Scotch whisky was used. The Toa Shuzo portfolio in the early '80s, from premium to bottom shelf, was as follows: Golden Horse 100 (containing 100 percent Scottish malt whisky), Golden Horse Excellent (40 percent Scotch malt whisky), Golden Horse Special (23 percent), Golden Horse Grand (16 percent) and Old Halley (11 percent). The bulk of this imported Scottish malt whisky was three years old and then aged for another year and a half in Japan. For Golden Horse 100, they purchased five-year-old malt whisky, then matured it for another two years in Japan. The blending alcohol/grain whisky was produced in-house (made from wheat and assorted grains, but not corn) and although the company felt two years' maturation in white oak was ideal, there was so much demand for whisky that most of the blending alcohol used for the products mentioned above was less than one year old. Today, we see an interesting reversal of this domestic grain/imported Scotch malt situation among craft whisky distillers in Japan. Now, the malt whisky is produced in-house while the grain whisky tends to be imported.

This little history lesson serves to underscore why, unlike Scotch whisky, old bottles of Japanese whisky are of little or no interest to collectors, other than as historical curiosities. When one buys an old Golden Horse bottling, and when the quality is relatively high, one is in fact buying mostly Scotch whisky, primarily Aberlour, in the case of Golden Horse. Examples are legion for many other Japanese whisky producers. The only difference is that, while Toa Shuzo was very open about the composition of their products, others weren't, so exactly what is in many old bottles of Japanese whisky is anyone's guess in most cases.

In the early 1980s, at the height of the whisky boom, Toa Shuzo decided to up their game and enter the field of malt whisky. On their trips to Scotland to buy whisky in bulk in the late 1970s/early '80s, Ichiro's father and grandfather had taken notes on malt whisky distillation. They also visited many distilleries in Japan and made sketches of the pot stills in use there. Based on those sketches, they commissioned a pair of copper pot stills from Miyake Industries. In 1983, the stills were installed and production of malt whisky "in the Scottish tradition" at Toa Shuzo could finally begin. Since the company already had a whisky license, they could start as soon as everything was hooked up.

The production specs were fairly typical: non-peated barley, lantern-shaped pot stills (4kl and 2kl), shell-and-tube condensers and mostly hogshead maturation. Since Toa Shuzo imported Scotch whisky in casks, they had a good supply of hogsheads. After the casks coming from Scotland had been disgorged, they could be refilled with Hanyu new-make. This means that most of the Hanyu production was actually matured in second-fill casks, which would be an unusual default wood program today. About 80 percent of production went into refill hogsheads. The remainder was filled into virgin American white oak puncheons made by Maruesu, a local independent cooperage.

In the beginning, everything went according to plan. Unfortunately, the tide quickly turned against Toa Shuzo. In the early 1980s, the yen was very weak, so importing Scotch became quite expensive. Setting up a distillery (i.e., becoming self-sufficient in terms of malt whisky supply) made a lot of economic sense in that climate. The September 1985 Plaza Accord reversed that situation dramatically, however. The yen's sharp appreciation after the Plaza Accord suddenly made it much more costly to produce malt whisky in-house, at least on a small scale, compared with importing it in bulk. Another setback was the decline in overall consumption of whisky in Japan starting in 1984.

The liquor tax change of 1989 was the proverbial final nail in the coffin. One of the results of the tax change was that Scotch whiskies (meaning bottled products, not bulk imports) suddenly became much cheaper. Competition was tougher and profits smaller. After the 1991 season, they switched the stills off at Hanyu distillery. Over at Hombo Shuzo's Mars Shinshu distillery, the same scenario was playing out at exactly the same time.

In 1996, someone appeared on the scene who would help breathe life into Hanyu distillery again, if only for a short while: Ichiro Akuto. After graduating from the Tokyo University of Agriculture, Ichiro started working for Suntory. His father, a friend of Keizo Saji's, recommended he apply for a job there. Ichiro was keen to work at Yamazaki distillery, but at the time, only people with a graduate degree were considered for a position in production there. The interviewer recommended a job in the sales and marketing division and Ichiro accepted. He became brand manager for imported liquors (Jack Daniel's, Early Times, Macallan, etc.) and was in charge of developing strategies for the sales team. This was easier said than done. Ichiro lacked experience in the field, so the strategies he suggested weren't always welcomed by the people in sales. He requested a transfer in order to get firsthand experience in the field and spent the rest of his time at Suntory working in sales. He enjoyed it, but after more than six years at the company, he was starting to get bored. More than anything, he wanted to work in the manufacturing division. It was around this time (1996) that his father asked him to come back to help out in the family business.

Toa Shuzo wasn't doing very well, so Ichiro's sales experience was most welcome. Toa Shuzo being a small family-owned company, Ichiro soon found himself working in every department. One of the key problems he identified was that the whiskies sold by Toa had "too much character." Even the sales people at Toa Shuzo complained that the character was too bold for the market. They were not the easy-drinking whiskies that most consumers wanted. Ichiro tried some Hanyu malt straight from the cask and felt it had a "unique and interesting character." Keen to get some independent feedback, he took samples to bars around Tokyo. Bartenders were impressed, so Ichiro felt the way to go was to release products where "character" was an asset, not a liability. Up until 2000, all

Ichiro Akuto in front of the old Hanyu wash still with one of the first Hanyu's released by his new company, Venture Whisky

malt whisky produced at Hanyu distillery was destined for blends. On Ichiro's advice, a single malt Golden Horse Chichibu 8 Year Old was launched that year. It was named Chichibu in reference to the water used at Hanyu distillery, which was brought in from Chichibu, the Akuto family's hometown. (This is a bit confusing to the unsuspecting collector, given the fact that there's now a new distillery in Chichibu.) Though it didn't sell a huge volume, it was clear there was a market for a more flavorful whisky.

After the 1999/2000 sake-making season had ended, the pot stills at Hanyu distillery were fired up again and malt whisky production resumed. Ichiro joined the team and started making whisky for the first time. Those months in the spring of 2000 would turn out to be the last time Hanyu distillery was active. The Golden Horse Chichibu single malt range was extended with a 10, 12 and 14 year old, but the company couldn't survive economically on the sales of just those niche products.

Facing page, clockwise from top left: Four Ichiro's Malt "cards": the Eight of Spades; the Four of Hearts; the Queen of Hearts; and the Eight of Clubs; and the final two Ichiro's Malt "cards," the Jokers

Before Ichiro had joined Toa Shuzo, his father had borrowed money to invest in a big, brand-new sake-brewing machine. Unfortunately, the sake market was shrinking, too. There were lots of competitors and price slashing was the order of the day. The company was in dire financial straits and it became clear, among other things, that it wouldn't be possible to resume whisky production again, following the 2000 season.

In 2004, the business was sold to a Kyoto-based shochu producer who took over the Toa Shuzo company name. The new owner was interested in the sake and shochu arm of the business, but couldn't care less about the whisky. They wanted to run Toa Shuzo as an efficient business. Whisky, with its long turnaround time, didn't fit that bill, and the new owner was soon looking to offload the whisky maturing in the warehouse, either selling it or disposing of it. Ichiro couldn't let that happen. As he said, "Some of the whisky was almost 20 years old—that's like children approaching their coming-of-age."

The new owner of Toa Shuzo had asked Ichiro to stay on, but for Ichiro that was out of the question; his passion was for whisky. He felt his new mission was to save the maturing Hanyu stock. He called several liquor companies in the Kanto area, but everyone responded in the same way: whisky didn't sell and they had to reduce their own whisky stocks so they couldn't even consider buying someone else's. Eventually, he got in touch with Tetsuzo Yamaguchi, CEO of Sasanokawa Shuzo in Koriyama, Fukushima prefecture. Sasanokawa happened to have an empty warehouse and they also had a whisky license. Ichiro found a way to buy most of the remaining Hanyu stock and had the casks (about 400, according to lore) moved to Sasanokawa. Some Hanyu whisky had to be left at Toa Shuzo because the company still had a few customers they had to keep supplying with whisky.

With investment help from a relative, Ichiro created a new company, Venture Whisky. Right from the start, the plan was to set up a new distillery. In the months

The "omnibus" Hanafuda Hanyu label

and years following Ichiro's courageous—some would have said reckless—act, he was spotted at bars around the country with increasing frequency, trying to interest bartenders in the saved Hanyu stock one cask, one case or even just one bottle at a time. Some of the most collectable Hanyu bottles come from these years, simply because the outturn of these releases was so low (24 or 60 bottles). It was during one of these visits that the idea for the Card Series was born (see page 319). In 2008, when Ichiro's new distillery was ready, the Hanyu stock was moved there. A few casks are still slumbering in the Sasanokawa warehouse, but in time, they too will be moved to Chichibu distillery to join the rest of the family.

Even though Hanyu distillery as such is gone, traces still remain. Initially, the Hanyu equipment was moved to a warehouse in Chichibu. Ichiro's father wanted to have a go at making shochu in the Hanyu stills, but he was getting on in age and eventually gave up on that plan. The spirit still was moved to Chichibu Kojiro, a sake brewery run by one of Ichiro's relatives, where it's used to make shochu. The wash still was purchased by Ichiro and turned into a monument at the entrance of Chichibu distillery: it's a beautiful metaphor, the past guarding the present and the future. There's not much Hanyu left in the warehouses at Chichibu distillery. One day in the not so distant future, the last drop of Hanyu will be bottled and then it will be gone forever. For a brief but intense moment, its past will come alive every time someone pours some Hanyu into a glass and listens to what the spirit has to say.

Trivia for Hanyu Fans

- There are only six Hanyu vintages: 1985, 1986, 1988, 1990, 1991 and 2000. Whisky wasn't produced nonstop at Hanyu. During the 1980s, whisky was made as and when the need arose. When stocks dropped, more was made. Simple as that. Between 1991 and 2000, no whisky was produced at Hanyu.

- Post-2004, the Hanyu stock was re-racked little by little in a plethora of different cask types—different in terms of type of oak, size and previous contents. Ichiro was a newcomer on the whisky scene, so he didn't have access to a large supply of casks. He bought half a dozen casks here, half a dozen there, and re-racked the Hanyu stock as he went along. The most exotic secondary maturation was #1702 (2000/2014), an ex-grappa cask.

- The youngest single-cask Hanyu bottled predates the Venture Whisky era. Bottled by Toa Shuzo in September 2002 as The Single Cask Chichibu, this was cask #6118, a virgin American white oak cask. It held distillate produced between October 1999 and May 2000, and was therefore just a little over two years old when bottled. The release was limited to 1,046 bottles (59%abv, 360ml).

- The youngest Hanyu bottled by Ichiro was cask #6076 (2000/2005), drawn from an American oak puncheon that used to contain grain whisky. There is also a private bottling of the same age, Gu Brath #9400 (2000/2005), bottled for the late Matthew D. Forrest, who bottled some extraordinary whiskies during his post-retirement transformation from banker to purveyor of fine whiskies.

- The oldest Hanyu hasn't been bottled yet. There is still some 1985 Hanyu maturing in the cask at the time of writing.

- Everyone knows about the Card Series but very few people know about the Hanafuda series (#9000, 2000/2007, 56.5%abv, 60 bottles). These were bottled for Bar Salvador in Takadanobaba. There were six different labels: five with a different *hanafuda* playing card motif and a sixth one that combines all five. A year before these were bottled, most of the liquid from cask #9000 was used for the Nine of Hearts but bottled at 46%. There is no complete set of the Hanafuda in existence anymore, but there are one or two bottles out there. They are rare as hen's teeth and a beautiful Japanese take on the Playing Card theme.

- The most collectable bottles of Hanyu date from the pre-Chichibu years, bottled before 2008. These were hand-bottled; because of that, they are an easy target for fakers. Fakes *are* circulating, so buyer, beware!

The first and last official Shirakawa single malt release

SHIRAKAWA DISTILLERY (TAKARA SHUZO)

Shirakawa Distillery was founded in the city of the same name in Fukushima prefecture, roughly 200km north of Tokyo, in 1939, but as so often with complex stories, the beginnings lie elsewhere and in times further past. As with the Karuizawa Distillery story, there are two lines intersecting—and interestingly, there is some overlap.

THE HISTORY

The first line starts in the Fushimi district of Kyoto, where in 1842, Unosuke Yomo started making sake. He wasn't the first. In fact, there were 28 other sake makers in the district when Unosuke started out—something about the water. In 1864, the Yomo family started making shochu and *mirin*, as well. The business grew and in 1925, Takara Shuzo Co., Ltd. was established, named after the brand the Yomo family had trademarked in 1897 to sell their *mirin*. In the course of the decade following its establishment, Takara Shuzo pursued further growth in the field of liquor production through mergers and acquisitions. In 1926, Takara Shuzo merged with Teikoku Shuzo. Three years later, the company acquired Taisho Seishu, and this is where whisky enters the narrative.

Taisho Seishu was established by Japanese entrepreneurs in Taiwan in 1915/16. In 1920, the company opened a plant in Oji, an old town in the north of Tokyo, and started making whisky. Exactly how whisky was produced there—at a time when Masataka Taketsuru was still learning the ropes in Scotland—is anybody's guess. The Oji Factory suffered major damage in the Great Kanto Earthquake (1923), but production was resumed eventually. In 1929, Takara Shuzo acquired Taisho Seishu, and in the process, also the Ideal Whisky trademark. There is no information about the equipment and/or processes used at the Oji Factory, but Takara Shuzo's company records indicate that there was "authentic malt whisky production" from the time they stepped into the picture.

Misfortune struck again in 1945, when the Oji Factory burned down in a bombing. A blurry photo of an old empty pocket bottle with a tin cup as bottle top and a newspaper advert in the *Asahi Shimbun* of February 8, 1930 featuring said bottle are the only traces of whisky production at Oji Distillery (as it was called on the label). This bottle is also the earliest known instance of the King brand, which would become Takara's flagship whisky brand. Interestingly, and not unusual in those early days of whisky marketing in Japan, the product was labeled as "Old Scotch Whisky."

Taisho Seishu was Takara Shuzo's second acquisition. In 1933, another liquor company came under the Takara umbrella, Shochikubai Shuzo, and the following year, two further acquisitions followed: Nihon Shuzo and . . . Daikoku Budoshu.

Here the line traced back in the Karuizawa chapter converges with the Takara line and, unsurprisingly, the plot thickens. In the early 1930s, business at Kaisan Shoten wasn't going well, but one of the company's suppliers, Takara Shuzo, came to the rescue. In 1934, Takara Shuzo acquired the company—now known as Daikoku Budoshu Co., Ltd.—as a subsidiary.

In 1938, Daikoku Budoshu established a factory in Shiojiri, in Nagano prefecture. The following year, a winery in Karuizawa, also in Nagano prefecture, was purchased. Both of these would feature in Japanese whisky history later and those stories are told in depth in the Karuizawa chapter of this book. However, 1939 also marks the year in which Shirakawa Factory was established. What types of liquor were produced at the Shirakawa Factory during those troubled times is unclear. Two years after the end of the Pacific War, the Antimonopoly Act (1947) was enacted and Takara Shuzo was forced to divest itself of Daikoku Budoshu as well as Shochikubai Shuzo. Keen to retain the Shirakawa Factory, Takara purchased this asset from Daikoku Budoshu. The factory was renovated and the production of shochu, wine, brandy, etc. began in earnest. According to company records, the production of malt whisky started in 1951.

As far as malt whisky production is concerned, the operational life of Shirakawa Distillery falls into three periods, followed by a long period of semi-retirement. The first period covers the years from 1951 to 1957. During that period, domestic barley was used and mashing was done in one go, with the water temperature between 55°C–65°C and then gradually increased to 80°C. The fermentation time was 4 days at 25°C and the distillation took place in two stainless steel pot stills heated with steam coils. Stainless steel pot stills are the standard for batch-distilled shochu, but whisky production and stainless steel are strange bedfellows. Based on the flavor profile of whisky made in stainless steel stills of the type used in shochu-making at other distilleries in Japan in the past, it's fair to assume the distillate would have been very "characterful," to use a euphemism. The middle cut averaged 65%abv. The spirit was then reduced to just under 60%abv and filled into 350-liter casks made domestically from Tohoku and Hokkaido mizunara.

The second period covers the years from 1958 to 1966 and the switch to copper pot stills would have resulted in a significant improvement in the quality of the spirit produced. During this period, the distillery kept working mainly with domestic malted barley, supplemented with the occasional load of imported malted barley. For the mashing they switched to two waters—the first at 62°C for 3 hours, the second at 65°C for 2 hours—and sometimes, most likely during the summer months, a short third-water phase—15 minutes at 80°C—to keep the wort free from bacterial contamination. The fermentation was increased to 5 days, and as mentioned, the distillation took place in twin copper pots. Spirit was collected at 73.1–57.1%abv, quite a wide middle cut, making for an average still strength of 66.7%. Domestic casks of the type mentioned above remained the go-to for maturation, but American white oak casks (presumably virgin-oak casks) and "imported casks" (it's unclear what exactly that meant) were also used from time to time.

The third period covers the last two years of the '60s, 1968–1969. During this time, the distillery used mainly imported malted barley.

For the mashing, they had settled on three phases: the first at 60°C for 3 hours, the second at 65°C for 2 hours and the third at 80°C for 15 minutes. The fermentation remained 5 days, but interestingly, they switched to distillers yeast (developed by Scotland's largest whisky company). It's unclear what type of yeast was used between 1951 and 1966, but a former employee who started working at Shirakawa Distillery in 1979 remembers that the distillery had only one whisky yeast (the distillers yeast) but lots of different wine yeasts. A cryptic "W-C" indication in company records for the yeast used in malt whisky production between 1951 and 1966 seems to suggest it may have been one of the company's wine yeasts. Most likely, we'll never know. What we do know is that, in 1968 and 1969, the middle cut was adjusted upward, with spirit collected at 74.6–60.8%abv, averaging 68.5%. There are no indications as to what cask types were used during this period. In the company records, instead, there is an interesting comment about the malt whisky produced during this short period: "The best quality among Shirakawa malts, we arrived at the level of Scotch-type malt."

Why, exactly, having reached a superior level of quality at the end of the '60s, malt whisky production was discontinued is a mystery. A Japanese whisky publication from 1983 relates that Takara Shuzo produced a lot of malt whisky from the mid-'50s onwards. One has to keep in mind, however, that the proportion of malt whisky in most whisky—blended whisky, by definition—sold in the '50s and '60s was very low. All things considered, Takura Shuzo may just have had more than enough Shirakawa malt in their warehouses by the end of the '60s.

Even though, on paper, malt whisky production was discontinued at Shirakawa Distillery after 1969, there are indications to the contrary. In the Takara Holdings Corporate History Museum, there is a photo showing racked casks with the heads stenciled with "Shirakawa Distillery" and the year "1981." One employee who worked at the distillery from April 1982 to March 1988—and who was in charge of shochu production and assorted technical duties—vaguely remembers that malt whisky was produced at Shirakawa Distillery in 1983 and 1985. He also remembers that in the early 80s, there was a feeling that the company might run out of malt stock if whisky consumption in Japan kept increasing and that some of the equipment was updated in 1984. As it happened, 1984 marked the beginning of a gradual decline in whisky consumption in Japan that would last 25 years. By the mid-'80s, however, Takara Shuzo had developed a close relationship with Tomatin Distillery (near

Inverness, Scotland) and therefore, there was no need to worry about access to quality malt whisky. Whisky production was shifted to Takara Shuzo's Takanabe Factory in 1985, and with that, the book was closed on malt whisky making at Shirakawa Factory. (In 1986, Takara Shuzo acquired an 80 percent stake in Tomatin Distillery. Later, this was boosted to 100 percent.)

By the end of the 20th century, many of the buildings at the Shirakawa Factory were decrepit and the equipment was old. Ideas and alternatives were discussed at Takara Shuzo, but none came to fruition. By the early 2000s, the Shirakawa Factory was on its last legs and merely used as a bottling facility. In 2003, it was closed and the buildings demolished. And with that a relatively small but significant part of Japanese whisky history was lost forever.

In the early afternoon of March 11, 2011, Japan was rocked by a 9.0-magnitude earthquake, the strongest ever recorded in Japan. The tsunami that followed devastated the coastal areas of the Tohoku region and claimed more than 15,000 lives. The natural disaster gave rise to a nuclear disaster at the Fukushima Dai-ichi nuclear plant, forcing the relocation of over 160,000 people. In June 2011, the Fukushima prefectural government through Shirakawa city asked Takara Shuzo if the Shirakawa Factory site could be used to build emergency housing to accommodate people displaced by the disaster. Takara Shuzo put 15,000m^2 of land at the disposal of the prefecture. Three years later, when it became clear that the evacuees would need much more time to rebuild their lives, the company decided to donate the land to Shirakawa city.

THE WHISKY

Even though Shirakawa Distillery was one of the pioneers of malt whisky making in Japan, it was never officially available as a single malt. That category didn't take off in Japan until the mid-'80s, and by that time, Takara Shuzo's focus lay elsewhere.

The expression that brought the consumer closest to the soul of Shirakawa Distillery was King Whisky Shirakawa Pure Malt 12yo (43%abv, 720ml), released in the 1980s. This contained 80 percent Shirakawa malt whisky from 1968–1969, the remaining 20 percent being made up of two 12-year-old Islay malts in equal measure. This was also the only expression from the Takara range not to have caramel added.

Sunset over Nanko Park in the city of Shirakawa

(Chill-filtration for 7–10 days at -10°C was standard procedure for all Takara Shuzo whisky products.)

Shortly after the Shirakawa Factory was closed, some single malt stock managed to reach the consumer, albeit in a highly unusual way. Vom Fass—a chain of gourmet food stores where oils, vinegars, spirits and liqueurs could be bought "straight from the cask" ("vom Fass" in German)—had half a dozen whiskies available for purchase in its heyday, i.e. roughly between 2004 and 2007. One of those was Shirakawa single malt. As a customer, you would purchase an empty glass bottle in the size of your choice (or go for a free plastic bottle), fill it with liquid from a small cask and then pay for the volume you had taken. It's hard to imagine such a scenario these days: being able to buy as much as you wanted of a Japanese single malt whisky that had never been available on the market before, at cask strength (55%abv) and aged for over 30 years, literally any day of the week. Most of these Vom Fass hand-fill bottles would have been emptied fairly soon after purchase, but Japanese bartenders tend to be good at hoarding, and it still happens, from time to time, that a small bottle with some info written on it with a white marker appears from behind the counter at a whisky bar.

Around the same time, full-sized (700ml) bottles were spotted left and right, with a beautiful label featuring a woodblock print image of a geisha. The info on the label specified: "Japanese Single Malt Whisky—King Whisky Shirakawa—Over 30 Years Old—The second half of the '60s—Cask Strength (55%abv)." Word on the street is that these bottles were homemade by an enthusiast and filled with liquid purchased from Vom Fass—probably someone who felt the liquid deserved a better presentation than a plastic bottle and some scribbles with a white marker. Whisky writer Jim Murray reviewed a 32-year-old Shirakawa Malt in his 2004 *Whisky Bible* (also 55%abv). Again, this must have been a DIY product, as there are no records at Takara Shuzo of an official single malt release.

It seemed unlikely we would ever have the chance to fully appreciate the Shirakawa malt, but seven decades after the start of malt whisky production at Shirakawa Distillery, the unlikely became a reality. At the end of August 2022, Tomatin Distillery Co., Ltd. announced the release of a Shirakawa 1958 (49%abv, 1,500 bottles). It officially went on sale on September 13, 2022. Until further notice, this is the earliest known single vintage Japanese whisky ever bottled.

Stephen Bremner, managing director of the Tomatin Distillery Co., Ltd., had become intrigued by parent company Takara Shuzo's history of malt whisky production in Japan. Very little was known about this aspect of the company's history but undeterred he kept asking questions and knocking on doors, hopeful that some liquid trace remained somewhere within the company. His persistence paid off and a parcel of 1958 stock was discovered in tanks at the company's Kurokabegura.

With regards to the liquid discovered, as with the history of the distillery itself, some pieces of the puzzle were missing. The liquid was first matured in wooden casks, but it was unclear what cask type(s) were involved and there were no records indicating for how long the whisky was aged in wood. Therefore, it came without an age statement. At some point, the whisky was transferred to the sort of large ceramic pots commonly used to age shochu. Then, and again this is common in shochu production, the liquid was moved to stainless steel tanks. When exactly is another mystery. Up until at least January 31, 2002, the whisky remained at its Shirakawa home. After that, either in the course of 2002 or in 2003 when the distillery was mothballed, the liquid was moved to Takara Shuzo's Takanabe Factory (renamed as Kurokabegura by the company in 2004) in Kyushu. There, the whisky remained in stainless steel tanks and was slowly forgotten about. As time passed, fewer and fewer people in the company were even aware it existed. It's best not to contemplate the—almost certainly unworthy—fate of the liquid in those tanks, had it not been for the appearance of a *deus ex machina* all the way from Scotland.

BRIAN BAR

花園一番街

ble
chige
¥1000
z

BRIAN
BAR
CHARGE
1000yen
DRINK
700yen~

Part 3

DRINKING JAPANESE WHISKY

A whisky thief in action at Mt Fuji Distillery

Ways of Drinking

In Japan, whisky is drunk in a variety of ways, depending on the setting, the time of day and individual preference.

STRAIGHT

This is not the most common way of drinking whisky in Japan, though it is the preferred way at specialist whisky bars. The casual drinker may gravitate towards this style later in the evening when out on the town, at a club or high-end bar.

ON THE ROCKS

In Japan, this will often take the form of whisky poured over one very large piece (rock) of ice in a classic whisky tumbler. The unsung hero here is the ice. In the Japanese bar world, the quality of the ice is of the utmost importance. Visit a handful of bars in Japan and you'll quickly notice that a seemingly inordinate amount of time is spent on "ice management."

A variant of this is the "whisky with an ice ball." Lots of Japanese bartenders spend years perfecting the art of hand-sculpting an ice ball. Cocktail designer Takayuki Suzuki explains his personal philosophy of the ice ball: "In the natural world, stones in a riverbed become spherical over long periods of time because of the flow of the water." An ice ball in a drink is not just there for effect. According to Suzuki, "It represents the stream of time."

HALF ROCK

This is a halfway between "on the rocks" and the two staples of Japanese whisky drinking, the highball and the *mizuwari*.

To make a "half rock" whisky, start with a whisky on the rocks, stir it to chill the whisky, then add an equal amount of mineral water or soda.

HIGHBALL

Basically, this is whisky with soda over ice. There's a bit more to it than that, but we'll delve into the complexities further below. At the moment, this is by far the most popular way of drinking whisky. It's not a new phenomenon, however.

From the mid-1950s, the highball reigned supreme at bars in Japan. On the back of the electrification boom (late 1950s/early 1960s), refrigerators—one of the "three holy durables" along with washing machines and black-and-white TVs—became ubiquitous in Japanese households and the highball started infiltrating the domestic sphere as well. In the early 1980s, the highball's popularity began to wane. It was considered an "old salaryman's drink" and younger people were more interested in beverages made with white spirits and/or fruity flavors. In 2008, Suntory launched their "Kaku-highball" campaign and a new generation of drinkers, for whom it didn't have any negative connotations (in fact, no connotations at all), discovered it as a refreshing alternative to beer. It sparked a veritable "highball boom" in Japan, which, after a decade and a half, shows no signs of waning. Maybe the highball is here to stay . . . for a while, at least.

The Kaku-highball recipe—now seen as the classic way of building a highball—is as follows: squeeze a wedge of lemon into a highball glass or beer mug, then throw the lemon rind in. Add lots of ice and 1 part whisky to 4 parts soda, pouring slowly; gently stir once. For their Chita Highball (which uses single grain whisky) Suntory recommends a ratio of 1:3.5 and no lemon. For a single malt highball, like the Hakushu Morikaoru Highball, Suntory suggests 1 part whisky to 3 parts soda, and a sprig of mint as garnish.

A radically different way of building a highball is the Samboa Highball, called after the bar chain in Kansai where it was the house drink. Rather than building the drink over ice, all the components are chilled before mixing, including putting the glass in the freezer. Pour 2 ounces/60ml of whisky into a highball glass; add a bottle (6 ounces/190ml) of Wilkinson

Tansan (soda); bend a slice of lemon peel around the tip of your forefinger and squeeze to express the oil. Serve without stirring. Since there is no ice involved, there's no dilution. This keeps the drink rich and flavorful.

In Tokyo, the best place to enjoy a Samboa-style highball is at Bar Rockfish in Ginza. More than 90 percent of the orders here are highballs of this type and the "master," Kazunari Maguchi, is very particular about his highballs. He swears by the old 43%abv version of the yellow Kakubin. Now Kakubin is only available at 40%abv. When Suntory discontinued the 43% version, Maguchi started scouring mom-and-pop stores all over the country to make sure he had the stocks to continue making his Rockfish Highball. In April 2013, Suntory paid tribute to Rockfish with a special limited edition of their Kakubin, featuring a retro label and bottled at 43%abv. The packaging featured Maguchi. That was a one-off special release, however, so unless you come across a

A Rockfish highball

dusty bottle of 43% in some forgotten backwater in Japan, you'll have to make do with the 40% one.

The highball is literally everywhere in Japan at the moment. You can even buy ready-to-drink canned ones at convenience stores around the country. They come in two sizes (12 and 17 ounces/350 and 500ml). The standard cans come at 7%abv, but there are also "premium" versions canned at 9%. There are seasonal flavored versions with lemon, *shikwasa* (a very sour citrus fruit from Okinawa) and so on as well. My impression, however, is that consumers prefer the regular, nonfruited ones.

MIZUWARI

Mizuwari literally means "divided by water" and that is what it is: whisky with water over ice. For those who need the recipe: Fill a Collins glass, or any glass at hand really, with ice; add between 1 and 1.5 ounces/30 and 45ml of whisky and stir to chill. Add mineral water (the whisky-to-water ratio should be in the area of 1:2–2.5); stir a couple of times and enjoy. Someone who was quite fond of his mizuwaris was Masataka Taketsuru. With food, he would drink sake, but afterwards he would switch to whisky. His preferred way of drinking it was 1 part whisky (usually Hi-Nikka) to 2 parts water, no ice.

The whisky *mizuwari* is actually an adaptation from shochu drinking culture. With shochu, the ratio of shochu to water is in the region of 3:2 or even 1:1. This has to do with the fact that shochu is bottled at a lower abv than whisky.

The advantage of the *mizuwari* is that you don't need soda. This may seem like stating the obvious, but it has implications. In restaurants, patrons can just help themselves once they've bought a bottle of whisky (or shochu) and been given a bucket of ice and water. It takes the strain off the bartender or whoever is in charge of making drinks and is also less costly than ordering individual highballs. For groups, it's a no-brainer. One bottle of whisky and everyone can partake. The *mizuwari* gained in popularity during the 1970s. Suntory's "Operation Chopsticks" may have had something to do with that (see page 61 for more on this). Nowadays, it's nowhere near as popular as the highball, however.

HOT WHISKY (OYUWARI)

This is the winter variation on the *mizuwari*. *Oyuwari* literally means "divided by hot water." Again, the name says it all. Take a hot toddy glass and warm it up with hot water; discard the water. Add whisky and

A hot whisky at Bar Keller in Kyoto

hot water in a ratio of 1:2–3, with the water at around 175°F/80°C. If so desired, a topping can be added. Among the more popular options are lemon, a cinnamon stick, cloves, a sprig of fresh basil or other herbs, a dollop of jam or a slice of dried apple.

Even though the *oyuwari* is also part of shochu drinking culture, it's actually a twist on the *atsukan* (hot sake). The earliest reference I could find to hot whisky in Japan was a Suntory advertisement for Torys from 1955. "*Hot ga umai*," it said. (Hot is delicious.) A more recent campaign promoting hot whisky dates from 1994, when Suntory started selling a new version of their bestseller Suntory Old. This was a bit more suggestive. A TV commercial showed the popular actress Yuko Tanaka (who was 39 at the time) in a romantic encounter with actor Nao Omori, who was 22. "Old is Hot" was the catchphrase.

The best whisky *oyuwari* I've had was served to me at Bar Keller in Kyoto—obviously in the winter (you wouldn't want to torture yourself with this in the hot, humid summer). Owner-bartender Minoru Nishida has developed his own way of preparing the perfect *oyuwari*. He starts by pouring a measure of whisky into a blender's flask, then adds water to the flask to bring the strength down to 13%abv (he's very precise about that). Next, he pours the contents of the flask into a small *kyusu* (teapot) and gently heats it. When it has reached the right temperature, he moves it to a special stand (which is revealed in front of the customer when part of the counter is removed) and serves it in a small glass of the kind used for drinking shochu and sake. The liquid in the teapot is kept hot by a small candle underneath it. Nishida developed this style (and even integrated it into the design of his counter) because he was dissatisfied with the traditional way of serving liquor *oyuwari* style, in a big glass. The problem with this is that the drink very quickly cools down and loses its appeal. For Nishida, the right temperature is the raison d'être for the *oyuwari* style and keeping it constant is crucial to the success of the whole experience. With his solution—simple as it is elegant: a small teapot, a small glass and a small candle—the initial sensation of sipping something *oyuwari* style is sustained for as long as you want.

MIST

This is a less common way of drinking whisky. Fill a rocks glass with crushed ice and add 1 to 1.5 ounces/30 to 45ml of whisky; squeeze a wedge of lemon over the glass and drop the wedge in the glass. A mist works best with blended whisky.

TWICE UP

This is quite simply whisky and mineral water in a 1:1 ratio at room temperature. A wine or tasting glass is ideal for this. "Twice up" is actually the way most professional blenders in Japan evaluate whisky. According to them, dropping the abv to about 20% prevents "alcohol burn" and allows the aroma of the whisky to come through better.

JAPANESE WHISKY COCKTAILS

A rather unfortunate side effect of the recent tendency to put Japanese whisky on a pedestal is that it's not considered as a candidate component of a cocktail as often as it should be. The following cocktails, specially created for this book, reveal a glimpse of the potential in this field. They all yield one drink.

5 ORIGINAL COCKTAILS BY TAKAYUKI SUZUKI

Takayuki Suzuki started working as a bartender when he was around 20 years old
(we are being deliberately vague here!).
He spent some time barhopping his way
from Vancouver to Miami, but had to
return to Japan because he couldn't get
a work visa. Suzuki spent a little over two
years working at a bar in Roppongi, and
then returned to the U.S. to study at the
International School of Bartending in New
York. He worked at various bars around
town but again couldn't get a work visa.
On returning to Japan, he was asked to
set up a bar at a small luxury hotel in the
Nasu Highlands. In April 2003, he became
manager of Bar Fifteen at the Shiba Park

Takayuki Suzuki carving an iceball

Hotel. In September of the same year, he set up a bar at the newly
opened Park Hotel in Shiodome. He still lives in Nasu where he comes
up with new creations at what must be the smallest, most remote bar
in Japan. The Black Tea Arbor is in the middle of a forest and seats
only one person. He works to spread Japanese bartending philosophy
through seminars all over the world. He is also the author of an exquisite
collection of autobiographical short stories entitled *The Perfect Martini*.

Bamboo Leaf Martini

This *mizuwari*-style cocktail tries to capture the transition from late winter to early spring. The liquid inside the leaf-cup suggests early spring, whereas the yuzu accent outside the cup acts as a memory of winter, when it is in season. Yuzu is a tart citrus fruit with a flavor reminiscent of grapefruit and a hint of mandarin orange.

1 bamboo leaf
White crème de menthe
1⅓ ounces/40ml Taketsuru Pure Malt Whisky
⅔ ounce/20ml soft water
1 teaspoon bamboo leaf syrup
1 small wedge of yuzu

Take a bamboo leaf and cut a small incision along the axis of the leaf; take one end of the leaf and pull it through the incision to make a "cup." Place the leaf-cup in a martini glass. Fill a mixing glass with ice and add white crème de menthe to rinse; discard the liqueur. Add the whisky, water and bamboo leaf syrup (simple syrup infused with a bamboo leaf). Stir to chill and drain into the leaf-cup in the martini glass. Squeeze a small piece of yuzu lightly outside the leaf-cup to add an accent to the liquid outside the leaf-cup.

Tatami Cocktail

This cocktail was inspired by the aromas and flavors of Yamazaki 12yo: cacao, tropical fruits and herbal citrus. The top layer, which splits in two after a while (since the whisky is lighter in gravity than the crème de cacao), is at room temperature, whereas the bottom tropical mix is ever so slightly chilled. In combination, the elements create the impression of a sun-soaked tatami room in fall.

1 ounce/30ml pineapple juice
⅔ ounce/20ml simple syrup
1 teaspoon apricot brandy
1 teaspoon fresh lemon juice
½ ounce/15ml Yamazaki 12yo
1 teaspoon dark crème de cacao
2 stalks (3 to 4 inches/7.5 to 10 cm long) lemongrass
Twist of lemon

Mix the pineapple juice, simple syrup, apricot brandy and lemon juice in a cobbler shaker; set aside. Mix the whisky and crème de cacao in a mixing glass; set aside. Take the lemongrass stalks and dip them in the bottle of Yamazaki whisky; set aside. Add ice to the cobbler shaker and shake lightly. Double-strain into a martini glass; carefully float the liquid in the mixing glass on top. Ignite the lemongrass with a lighter and shake to put out. Place the lemongrass stalks in the martini glass; garnish with a twist of lemon.

Rainy Season

This cocktail was inspired by the rainy season, which lasts from early June to mid-July. It's called *tsuyu* in Japanese (literally, "plum rain") because it coincides with the ripening of plums. Some of the malt that goes into Hibiki 12yo is finished in casks previously used to mature *umeshu*, the traditional Japanese plum liqueur. There's a little bit of *umeboshi* (pickled plum) in this cocktail, but the actual color of plums during the rainy season (light green) is provided by the cucumber.

1⅓ ounces/40ml Hibiki 12yo
1 teaspoon fresh lemon juice
4 slices cucumber
½ teaspoon *umeboshi*
⅓ ounce/10ml simple syrup
Sprig of fresh mint

Put the whisky, lemon juice and cucumber in a blender and blend into a purée. Add the *umeboshi* and blend some more; add the simple syrup and blend to incorporate. Add a small handful of ice and blend; repeat adding ice and blending until the mix has the consistency of a smoothie. Spoon into a margarita glass and garnish with a leaf or two of the mint.

Green Breeze

This cocktail was inspired by Hakushu, known as the "forest distillery." It uses Japanese mint (*hakka*), which contains more menthol than peppermint and has a clear, refreshing scent. There's no stirring involved in this cocktail. This is deliberate. For the first few sips, the scent of the mint is carried by the soda; then, the sweetness of the tonic comes through; then the tonic with the whisky; and, finally, the taste of the muddled mint. In short: a green breeze.

Fresh mint leaves
White crème de menthe
1 ounce/30ml Hakushu 12yo
Tonic water
Soda

Using a bar spoon, gently muddle the mint in crème de menthe in a conical highball glass; discard the liqueur. Carve an ice ball; the diameter should be such that the ice ball sits in the glass without touching the bottom. Add the whisky, then just enough tonic water so that it comes just a bit above the bottom of the ice ball. Top up with soda. Spank a few mint leaves and add as garnish.

Japanese Red Pine Highball

The *kyogi* is a key element of this highball. *Kyogi* are thinly shaved wooden sheets—mostly made of *akamatsu* (red pine)—that are traditionally used in Japan for wrapping food like raw fish, meat and rice balls (you can buy it online). In this cocktail, it conjures up the scent of *mizunara*. It's also suggestive of apricots, which is a prominent note of the Yamazaki. Tiny bubbles from the soda will cling to the surface of the *kyogi*, making it look almost like a vintage champagne.

Fresh mint leaves, preferably Japanese
White crème de menthe
1 sheet *kyogi*
1½ ounces/45ml Yamazaki Distiller's Reserve (NAS)
Soda
1 bamboo leaf (optional)

Using a bar spoon, gently muddle the fresh mint in crème de menthe in a Riesling glass; discard most of the liqueur. Roll up a sheet of *kyogi* and insert it in the glass so that it lines the inside of the glass; pull one end up so it sticks out of the glass. Place two large ice cubes in the glass. Add the whisky and top up with soda. Garnish with a bamboo leaf if you like.

5 ORIGINAL COCKTAILS BY HIROYASU KAYAMA

Hiroyasu Kayama started tending bar when he was 20. Following short stints at various bars, he became head bartender at Bar Amber in Nishi-Azabu, Tokyo. After six years, he decided to strike out on his own. He opened a bar in the Nishi-Shinjuku area of Tokyo in July 2013 and named it BenFiddich (a reversed translation of his last name in Gaelic). Kayama is a keen botanist, so it was wonderfully appropriate that he won the first prize at "The Botanist Foraged Cocktail Contest" in Japan in July 2015. He has picked up many more awards since and regularly guest-shifts around the world. His bar was the second-highest ranked Japanese bar (at number 32) in the 2021 World's 50 Best Bars list.

Hiroyasu Kayama building a Grain Market

Grain Market

Concord grapes are a good substitute if Kyoho grapes are not available. The Madeira used in the original recipe was a 1993 D'Oliveiras Bual.

6 to 7 Kyoho grapes
1½ ounces/45ml Nikka Coffey Grain Whisky
⅔ ounce/20ml medium-sweet Madeira

In a mixing glass, crush the grapes with a muddler. Add the whisky and Madeira. Shake with ice in a Boston shaker. Double-strain into a cocktail glass.

Maple Marriage

The whisky in this Japanese twist on the whisky sour is a vatted malt consisting of Hanyu (pre-2000) and Chichibu (post-2008). Initially, the batches leaned more towards the Hanyu (i.e., older malt); recently, there's proportionally more Chichibu (younger malt) in them. A little tweak to the recipe may be welcome, depending on the batch. The name of the cocktail refers to the fact that Chichibu is also renowned for its maple syrup.

1⅔ ounces/50ml Ichiro's Malt Double Distilleries (Leaf Label)
⅓ ounce/10ml maple syrup
⅓ ounce/10ml yuzu juice
1 egg white
8 dashes ginger bitters
Yuzu peel (optional)

Mix the whisky, maple syrup, yuzu juice and egg white in a large metal tumbler using a hand blender. Add ice and shake until frothy. Strain into a coupe glass. Carefully add the bitters to the foam's surface in a circular pattern; use the tip of a toothpick to connect the droplets. Garnish with yuzu peel, if you like.

Forest Flavor

This really captures the atmosphere of Hakushu, known as "the forest distillery." Hakushu 12yo also works a treat.

5 fresh sage leaves
1½ ounces/45ml Hakushu Distiller's Reserve (NAS)
⅓ ounce/10ml honey
⅓ ounce/10ml fresh lime juice
Soda

Thoroughly muddle 4 of the sage leaves in a mortar with a pestle (preferably a Japanese mortar, *suribachi*, with a wooden pestle, *surikogi*). Add the whisky and muddle some more; add the honey and lime juice and muddle some more. Transfer to a French cocktail shaker and shake with ice to chill. Fine-strain over ice into a highball glass. Top up with soda and stir gently; garnish with the remaining sage leaf.

Japonism

The *shiro-an* (sweet white bean paste) really ties this cocktail together. It is light in taste and is a basic ingredient in many Japanese sweets (*wagashi*). Matcha powder is finely ground green tea and readily available online and in stores.

1 egg, separated
30g shiro-an
2 teaspoons matcha powder
1½ ounces/45ml Fujisanroku 50° Non-Chill Filtered
⅔ ounce/20ml sake (clean and dry type)

In a bowl, whisk the egg white until foamy. In another bowl, beat the yolk, *shiro-an* and matcha powder until fully mixed together. Add the egg white foam and whisk a bit more to incorporate. Add the whisky and sake and whisk to incorporate. Transfer to a French cocktail shaker and shake with ice. Fine-strain into a *guinomi* (Japanese earthenware sake cup).

Aromatic Chichibu

Chichibu The Peated is a big, bold and intensely smoky whisky, released in small batches at varying strengths. This recipe was developed for the cask-strength 2015 version (62.5%abv). Adjust proportions based on the strength of the release at hand. The vermouth used was La Quintinye Vermouth Royal Rouge. The somewhat peculiar glass configuration is not for show. It is motivated by the desire to keep this cocktail chilled throughout but without the dilution that would result from serving it directly over ice.

1⅓ ounces/40ml Chichibu The Peated Cask Strength

⅔ ounce/20ml Benedictine

⅓ ounce/10ml sweet vermouth

⅓ ounce/10ml fresh black currant (cassis) purée

1 teaspoon Fernet Branca

Stir all the ingredients with ice to chill; strain into a Burgundy wine glass. Fill a stemless martini glass with crushed ice and place the bowl of the wine glass on the bed of ice.

An Insider's Guide to Japanese Whisky Bars

When whisky fans visit Japan, they usually have three things on their mind: visiting a couple of distilleries (that's easy); buying rare Japanese whiskies to take home (that's far from easy, in fact, well-nigh impossible); and going to bars to have some unforgettable drams, Japanese or other. The latter is the easiest of all and most rewarding. According to whisky writer *extraordinaire* Dave Broom, "The best whisky bars in the world are to be found in Japan." I'm glad he said it, so I don't have to. Being based in Japan, it would sound a bit biased coming from me. The truth is there are great bars everywhere in the country, even in the middle of nowhere. In particularly busy places like Ginza, you can go barhopping without leaving the building: you just take the elevator and move on to the next bar. As Broom says, "There's such a superabundance of them—packed into high-rises, lurking in basements, secreted in former janitor's closets—that the whisky hound's first visit to the country is both a chance to wander in the Elysian fields of whisky and be consumed by angst, believing that by having one more in this bar you are missing out on an even more extraordinary selection nearby." This bar guide is meant to relieve the angst a bit.

Although I can personally vouch for all the bars on the list that follows, it's not a list of "the best whisky bars in Japan," whatever that means. To be clear, all of these bars would be included in such a list if

Nikka's iconic King of Blenders logo at the entrance to Bar Augusta, Osaka

you had to draw one up, but there would be a great many others as well that didn't make it into these pages. The reason why places like The Bow Bar (in Sapporo), Bar Calvador (Kyoto), Bar Stag (Kita-Kyushu) and hundreds of other great watering holes are not listed here is because you wouldn't go there to drink Japanese whisky. Their focus lies elsewhere. The bars listed here have been spotlighted to help you try interesting Japanese whiskies that you would have a very hard time finding outside Japan. That was the main selection criterion.

Another important point: This is not a comprehensive list. I have done some dirty work for you and have visited way more bars than the number listed here, but I haven't visited every single whisky bar in Japan. If I had, I would be bankrupt or dead by now—probably both. There are literally thousands of whisky bars all over the country. Even after a lifetime of visiting two or three bars a night, one would still only have seen the tip of the iceberg. Don't assume that, just because a bar isn't listed here, it isn't worth going to. In fact, when it comes to bars in Japan, never assume! I have come across many little bars off the beaten track that no one had recommended to me but that turned out to be fabulous. Actually, the likelihood of coming across rare whiskies from yesteryear is higher at bars that are under the radar than at bars that everyone knows about, visits and then recommends to friends or on social media.

That last comment would seem to be an argument *against* including a bar list in this book. However, everybody needs pointers when they are new to a place and that is what this list is meant to be: to start you off on your journey. Once you're there, you'll be able to find your way to other good places. In general, bar folks in Japan are happy to recommend other places in the area based on your individual predilections. Very often, they'll even call the next bar to check if it's open and to let the staff there know you're coming so they can prepare. In many cities with a lively drinks scene, bars have joined forces and printed local bar maps to help you discover the variety the city has to offer. Kumamoto, Kagoshima, Sendai and many other cities have such handy maps.

It's often said that few countries are more resistant to change than Japan. There may be more than a grain of truth to this, but it certainly doesn't apply to the *mizu-shobai* (literally, the "water trade," a euphemism for the nighttime entertainment business). Bars come and go all the time. Sometimes, they move to different premises; other times, they disappear without a trace. I don't have a crystal ball, so please don't shoot the piano player if one or more of the bars I've recommended is no longer in business when you visit.

There are a few other caveats. The vast majority of bars in Japan are tiny (seating between 8 and 20 people) and in most cases, the person behind the stick is the owner of the place. When the owner has other business to attend to—urgent private matters or booze-related trips—he/she may have to close the bar for a day or two at very short (or without) notice or open later than usual. Grumbling doesn't really help. Chances are there's a great bar around the corner so go and drown your sorrows there.

The bars below were included based on their selection of Japanese whiskies. Other aspects of the experience—atmosphere, prices and the presence of pleasant and knowledgeable people on the other side of the counter—were taken into account, too, but the liquid on the shelves was the deciding factor. Two things need to be said about that. First, whiskies that are a revelation for one person may be old hat for another. If you find the latter to be the case at most of the bars listed below—something that is hard to imagine, but one never knows—you've probably been around the block a few times and don't need this bar map. Secondly, some bars are better at managing their stock than others. Japanese whisky is not the easily replenishable resource it once was, and while most owner-bartenders are clever enough to hold back bottles for a rainy day, it does happen that bars have a great selection of Japanese drams one day and then nothing the next. I trust that, should you find yourself in a situation like that at one of the bars listed below, there will be ample choice of quality amber nectar from other regions of the world to keep you in good spirits.

This brings us to something that may be hard to stomach for visitors from abroad: attitudes to smoking in Japan. Many people are shocked to see that smoking is still allowed in restaurants and bars in Japan. To put it crudely, 99 percent of bars—and this includes specialist whisky bars—in Japan allow smoking. Nonsmoking bars are the exception rather than the rule. Sometimes, accommodations for nonsmokers are *pro forma* only, as was the case at an eight-seat bar in Osaka I visited recently where the four seats on the left of the counter were smoking and the four seats on the right nonsmoking. You can imagine how effective that arrangement is when there are a couple of smokers in the bar. I've been in situations where I was drinking sublime, ultra-rare whiskies engulfed by secondhand smoke. The best way to deal with this is to see it as something akin to Tantric Buddhism, where meditation is practiced in unpleasant rather than pleasant circumstances or in difficult circumstances. The alternative is missing out on tons of stellar whiskies. In the list below, the few bars that are nonsmoking are indicated as such.

Another potential obstacle is the language barrier. The ability to communicate in English is not one of the national fortes in Japan. Like most people in Japan, bartenders tend to have limited English-language competence. Some will try to bridge the gap; others may greet you and immediately say they are hopeless at English (they'll be saying this in Japanese, of course). My experience is that, given some sensitivity from both parties, the liquid and the enjoyment thereof will help in building a bridge. In fact, sometimes the absence of a mutual language can be a blessing in disguise. As the American composer Morton Feldman once said, "Communication is when people *don't* understand each other, because then there is a consciousness level that is being brought out of you where an effort is made."

Finally, a few do's and don'ts.

1 Bars add a "service charge." This is usually between ¥500 and ¥1,000 per person, depending on the bar. At some places, you get little sandwiches and/or snacks for that; at others, just water and nuts. The service charge is standard practice, so you're not being had.

2 Standard pours in Japan are 1 ounce/30ml. If you're interested in trying a wide variety of whiskies at any given place, ask for half shots. In most cases, you will pay exactly half of what a full shot costs. Bars are very happy to oblige. In fact, with some very rare whiskies, the bar may ask you to be satisfied with a half shot. This is to make sure others after you also have a chance of trying it.

3 At most bars, it's futile to try and buy bottles, whether full, half-empty or empty. The bottles that people would be tempted to try and buy are invariably rare and worth lots of money. When there's liquid in the bottle, the bar needs it, because that's what draws people to the place. When it's empty, the bar still won't sell it. Prices for rare Japanese whiskies on the secondary market are positively mental these days, and bartenders are aware that an empty bottle given or sold to a customer could one day end up on an auction site, "refilled" and "resealed."

4 Some bars don't take credit cards, so it's best to check what the situation is before you sit down and order to avoid unpleasant surprises later on.

Bar folks in Japan are a creative bunch, as can be seen from the interesting names they come up with for their places. Be prepared for a weird and wonderful mix of uppercase, lowercase and punctuation marks in strange combinations. Just in case you're wondering: no, my editor hadn't taken the day off when this part of the book came in. Except for bars that incorporate Japanese characters in their names (which have been transcribed for your convenience), the names are printed following their preference.

HOKKAIDO

OTARU

Bar Bota
Hanzono, 1-11-3, Otaru-shi
0134-22-2858
19:30–24:00 Tue–Sat

Bar Bota has an incredible selection of long-gone, limited-edition Nikka releases, which makes this a mandatory stop on your pilgrimage to nearby Yoichi Distillery. If you like the great outdoors—camping, fishing and all that—you'll get on with the owner like a house on fire.

Bar Hatta
Hanazono 1-8-18, Otaru-shi
0134-25-6031
18:30–01:00 Mon–Sat

Yasuhiro Hatta opened his bar in 1983, when people in Japan were drinking more whisky than ever before. Hatta is a "Taketsuru Senior Ambassador" and the bar is nicknamed "No. 29" (there are 28 warehouses at nearby Yoichi Distillery), so you can imagine what the focus of this place is.

Nikka Bar Rita

Denukikoji Street, Ironai 1-1-17, Otaru-shi
0134-33-5001
15:00–22:00 Mon, Wed–Fri; 14:00–22:00 Sat–Sun

This chic, retro bar is named after Masataka Taketsuru's wife and almost everything liquid inside is from the Nikka/Asahi stables. It's in a very touristy part of Otaru, so you're bound to be in the neighborhood. My advice would be to drop in here for an aperitif and reserve more time after dinner for the two other bars in Otaru recommended above.

SAPPORO

Malt Bar Kirkwall

5.3 Bldg. 4F, Minami-Gojo Nishi-sanchome, Chuo-ku, Sapporo
011-511-6116
18:00–01:00 (until 2:00 day before national holiday), irregular closing day 3 times a month

As owner-bartender Tsutomu Iwamoto puts it, the concept behind his bar is "offering delicious whiskies at reasonable prices." I can attest that, on both counts, this place excels. Kirkwall is open every day of the week, so there's no excuse not to check it out.

the bar nano.gould.

J-BOX Bldg. 4F, Minami-Sanjo Nishi-yonchome, Chuo-ku, Sapporo
011-252-7556
18:00–24:00 Mon, Wed–Sun

Great whisky, delicious cocktails, a beautifully designed space *and* they love Glenn Gould here! Does it get any better than this? Not in my book.

NISEKO

Bar Gyu+ (aka The Fridge Door Bar)

167-21 Aza Yamada Kutchan
0136-23-1432 (no reservations)
19:00–24:00 Mon–Sun, Dec–March

If I had to choose one bar in Japan to live in, this would be it. I have to keep the superlatives in check, but this bar ticks all the right boxes: the setting is absolutely stunning, the drinks list is phenomenal and the people who run it (Hisashi and Ioanna Watanabe) are the best. It's only

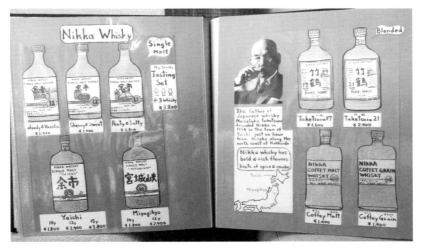

Two pages from the menu at Bar Gyu+ featuring drawings by owner Hisashi Watanabe

open during the winter, when skiers and snowboarders from all over the world come to play in Niseko, but the good news is that it is open every single day of the week during that period, including Christmas and New Year!

HONSHU

ISHIKAWA

Harry's Kanazawa

Honmachi 1-3-27, Kanazawa, Ishikawa
076-225-8830
18:00–24:00 Tue–Sat

Harry's Kanazawa opened during the pandemic, which is not the easiest thing to do, but a successful crowdfunding campaign made this project possible. The people behind it have close connections with Saburomaru Distillery and the head bartender, Kazuhiko Tajima, is one of the most engaging and knowledgeable bartenders in Japan, which is saying quite a bit. Behind the stunning Bubinga counter, more than 1,000 whiskies are available by the glass. A good bar was the only thing missing in Kanazawa and now there's a stellar one.

Pub Mahorobi

Chuo 1-13-1, Matsumoto-shi, Nagano
0263-36-3799
19:30–23:00 Tue–Sat (closed on national holidays)

This is not the sort of bar you just stumble into by accident. Even though it's supposedly in the geographical heart of Japan, it's in quite a remote location, about a three-hour drive from Tokyo. It's well worth a detour, though, especially when traveling to or from Mars Shinshu or Hakushu distillery. The bar has been open since 1978, which is quite a feat in a country where bars come and go all the time. Owner-bartender Teimei Horiuchi is a real Scotch aficionado (and historian) but he also has a very nice selection of Japanese whiskies.

SAITAMA

Bar Te Airigh

Dai-1 Ishida Bldg. 1F, Miyakawa-cho 8-4, Chichibu-shi
0494-24-8833
17:00–23:00 Mon–Tue, Thu–Sun

This bar is in Chichibu, so three guesses what distillery dominates the shelves at Te Airigh. Right . . . but there's way more to keep you glued to your chair here. Owner-bartender Takeshi Yokota tries to keep up with new releases of Japanese whisky as well as Japan-only releases of Scotch whiskey as best as anyone can. An added bonus is that you can order food from the restaurant upstairs and have it with your drams, or in between, whichever tickles your fancy. If you're really lucky, you may find yourself sitting next to one of the people from Chichibu distillery. It's their neighborhood bar, so they are known to pop in for a beer or something stronger from time to time.

Highlander Inn Chichibu

Higashimachi 16-1, Chichibu
0494-26-7901
Tue–Sun (weekdays from 15:00, weekend from 12:00, until 23:00)

The original Highlander Inn is in Craigellachie, Scotland, but this one (as well as the two branches in Tokyo, in Nakano-Sakaue and Ningyocho) is part of the same family. For those keen on bragging rights, there is a "Highlander Inn Challenge," which involves having a dram at a

Highlander Inn in Japan and in Scotland on the same day (doable with the time difference involved, but not easy). The Chichibu branch opened in September 2019 and is located in a beautiful, remodeled traditional house. Following the British pub model, The Highlander Inn Chichibu offers food, a variety of beers and a huge selection of whiskies, of course. It's popular also with the Chichibu Distillery staff, so it's not uncommon to run into people who actually make the amber nectar (of which there is plenty available by the glass).

Bar Craic
Miyakawacho 4-3, Chichibu
0494-22-5713
Tue, Wed, Fri 17:00–23:00 Sat–Sun 15:00–23:00

This bar is located near Chichibu station and it has one of the largest (if not the largest) selections of Chichibu whiskies available by the glass in Japan—which means, in the world. That's all you need to know, really.

MALT Bar Silkhat
Kinmeicho 246-16-2F, Soka-shi
048-932-6830
18:00–03:00 Mon–Sun

Owner-bartender Daisuke Hogyoku is a "Taketsuru Brand Ambassador," so if you happen to be in the area and are looking for some Nikka whiskies, this is a safe bet. He's also a massive Hombo Shuzo fan and has probably the largest selection of Mars Shinshu/Tsunuki whiskies in Japan. Silkhat is a very down-to-earth place, so don't expect any frills—just good whisky at decent prices.

TOKYO

Albion's Bar
Jujo-Nakahara 2-11-21, Kita-ku, Tokyo
03-3906-6700
18:00–24:00 Mon–Sun (irregular holidays)

If you find yourself in the northern reaches of the Tokyo metropolis, make a little detour to this bar. It caters to many types of drinkers: locals who pop in for a beer or something stronger on the way back from the supermarket or bakery, white-collar workers for whom this is an obligatory transit point on the way back home, regulars who are almost part of the furniture, but also people who know a good whisky when they see one. Word is the owner has a complete Ichiro's Card collection (all bottles with serial number 1), or maybe that should be "had", because he is known to crack open a few bottles from time to time.

Aloha Whisky Bar
Izumi Building 3F-B, 3-29-11 Nishi-Ikebukuro, Tokyo
03-6912-7887
18:00–23:30 Wed–Mon

Aloha Whisky Bar officially opened in September 2019 and in the short time since—extremely short when taking into account the successive states of emergency in Tokyo because of the COVID-19 pandemic—it has become one of the most respected whisky bars in Japan. Owner David Tsujimoto, who hails from Hawai'i, won Bartender of the Year and the bar itself won Bar of the Year in the Rest of the World category at the World Whiskies Awards 2020. The selection of Japanese whiskies is unparalleled. A large portion of the bar's clientele consists of whisky enthusiasts visiting from abroad, and because many of these loyal customers often come bearing gifts, there is a wide selection of bottlings for foreign markets (that you won't find at any other bar in Japan) available by the glass.

The Chichibu wall at Aloha Whisky Bar

Apollo Bar

Meiko Bldg. B1, Ginza 8-2-15, Chuo-ku, Tokyo
03-6280-6282
17:00–02:00 Mon–Fri, 17:00–24:00 Sat

Owner-bartender Hidenori Komatsu used to work for Suntory before he set up this bar. There is no other bar in Japan, and that means in the world, where you can see so many legendary historic Suntory whiskies gathered. Some of these specimens are incredibly rare, so not everything is available for tasting, but there's plenty that is. If you're partial to the music of Tom Waits, you have another reason to go to this bar: that's literally all you'll hear playing in the background.

Bar Espace Rassurants

Akasaka 2-13-8-207, Minato, Tokyo
03-6459-1556
17:00–23:30 Mon–Sat

This bar is in the busy Akasaka district. It's small but, if you want to try the latest Japan-only bottlings (both Japanese whiskies and bottlings of Scotch for the Japanese market), this is the place to visit. An added bonus is that prices are very reasonable. Owner-bartender Go Hashimoto is also a huge fan of The Arran Malt, so there is a wide selection of official Arran bottlings available by the glass, too.

Bar GOSSE Meguro

Meguro 2-10-15, Maison Takahashi 102, Meguro, Tokyo
03-3779-9779
Irregular

Bar Gosse is owned and run by the Yui brothers (Satoshi and Atsushi). They're bilingual (English/Japanese) and very laidback so there's no threshold whatsoever. The brothers both have busy full-time day jobs outside the drinks business, so it's best to check on social media whether they're open or not before you head out there. In addition to a well-curated selection of Japanese whiskies, there are also many limited-edition bottlings for the UK market. (The Whisky Exchange is well represented.)

Bar Groovy

Uchi-Kanda 3-17-6, Chiyoda-ku, Tokyo
03-3256-5556
17:00–03:00 Mon–Fri, 19:00–03:00 Sat

The selection here is quite basic but there's one exception. Owner-bartender Shigeo Fujishima is crazy about whiskies from the Venture Whisky stable here, so if you're looking for some Chichibu or Hanyu to sample, this is your place. He has a fabulous Hanyu bottled under the Kanda Bartender's Choice moniker here. That alone is worth a visit to Bar Groovy.

Bar High Five

Efflore Ginza5 Bldg. B1, Ginza 5-4-15, Chuo-ku, Tokyo
03-3571-5815
17:00–01:00 Mon–Sat

Bar High Five is one of the most respected bars in Ginza and owner-bartender Hidetsugu Ueno is a legend in the bar world. There's no menu, but Ueno and his staff know what you want better than you know it yourself. The focus is on classic cocktails but there's a very interesting selection of Japanese whiskies—recent and not so recent—on the shelves as well. If you plan on visiting a few bars in Ginza, it's best not to start here. You wouldn't make it to the second bar on your list.

Bar Kage

Sakae Bldg. B1, Ginza 6-3-6, Chuo-ku, Tokyo
03-6252-5044
18:00–03:00 Mon–Sat

Warm and intimate, this beautiful Ginza bar is the perfect place to unwind after a hard day's work. You wouldn't come here with your colleagues, though. You'd go on your own or with someone you feel really comfortable with. It's the kind of bar that's more comfortable than your living room or your man cave. Owner-bartender Takeshi Kageyama has a bit of a soft spot for Ichiro's Malts, so there's quite a bit of that on the shelves. Style and substance—it's not that easy to find a bar that excels in both departments. This one does.

Bar Nadurra

Park Heights Ikebukuro 203-2, Higashi-Ikebukuro 1-17-11, Toshima-ku, Tokyo
03-6914-3645
17:30–02:00 Mon–Fri, 15:00–01:00 Sat & holidays

This bar is open early—especially on Saturdays and holidays, which is great if you need some afternoon "tea"—and is nonsmoking. That's really all you need to know. As far as the rest is concerned, there is nothing to worry about: great selection, reasonable prices, a relaxing vibe and the nimble Noboru Matsudaira to tie everything together.

C-Shell

1F Wind Arakicho, 9 Arakicho, Shinjuku, Tokyo
03-6380-6226
Mon–Sun 18:00–24:00

C-Shell is located in the back alleys of Araki-cho, once a bustling geisha district, near Yotsuya. Owner-bartender Yu Makiura opened C-Shell in March 2009, after stints at many bars (including Wolfgang Puck Bar & Grill in Roppongi Hills and Joel Robuchon in Ebisu). The C refers to the many good things starting with that letter: cocktails, cigars, creativity, conversation, etc. There's no menu: conversation replaces that. According to Makiura, who is fluent in English and blessed with a great sense of humor, the atmosphere sets his bar apart from many other bars in Japan: "We're trying to create our own style—between classic and casual—which both start with C and that's what's inside our 'shell.'" There's a wide selection of Japanese whiskies as well as a display case with loads of Godzilla figures, for those who share Makiura's interest in Japan's most famous monster.

Campbelltoun Loch

Matsui Bldg. B1, Yurakucho 1-6-8, Chiyoda-ku, Tokyo
03-3501-5305
18:00–04:00 Mon–Fri, 18:00–23:30 Sat, Sun & holidays

This is the hardest bar to get into in Japan and I mean that literally. It's so small and cramped that, if you are fortunate to be sitting on one of the eight stools at the counter, you'll be rubbing elbows with the people sitting on either side of you. Again, this is not a figure of speech. It's worth trying to get in, though. Owner-bartender Nobuyuki Nakamura has a fabulous selection of whiskies on the shelves, which includes some that he has personally selected (ask for The Whisky

Hoop releases). Scotch vastly outnumbers Japanese whisky here but that's not a reason not to go. There's still plenty of the latter to keep you happy. Be warned though: Bottles don't last long here. So when someone raves about a certain whisky they tried there, don't assume it'll still be there a few weeks later. Then again, there'll be something else that you can rave about then.

Grand Cave (Isetan Shinjuku)
Isetan Shinjuku B1, Shinjuku 3-14-1, Shinjuku-ku, Tokyo
03-3225-2569
14:00–20:00 Mon–Sun

This is not a bar, it's a tasting counter in the basement of the posh department store Isetan in Shinjuku. So why is it included here? 1) You can try whiskies for a nominal fee and, if you like what you are drinking, pick up a bottle there and then. 2) They often have special whiskies exclusively bottled for Isetan—Scotch but also Japanese from time to time. Obviously, you will need to have luck on your side to drop by just when they have such special bottlings, but you never know. 3) The tasting bar is open from 2 p.m., which means you can stimulate the senses long before most bars open for business. 4) The staff is great. There you go—four good reasons to drop by.

J's Bar
Aoi Bldg. 2F, Nishi-Ikebukuro 1-34-5, Toshima-ku, Tokyo
03-3984-8773
01:00–24:00

J's Bar is a real feel-good bar. The selection is great—more often than not bottles are opened there the very day they are released—the prices are among the lowest you'll find in Tokyo, the atmosphere is casual and owner-bartender Hajime Hasumura is a very laid-back (but hugely knowledgeable) guy. The bar is a two-minute walk from the North exit of Ikebukuro station and surrounded by joints that cater to a wide variety of nightlife interests.

Ken's Bar Kyobashi
3-11-12-B1 Hatchobori, Chuo-ku, Tokyo
03-6869-7887
18:00–24:00

There's a Ken's Bar in Shinjuku's famous Golden Gai, but owner-bar-tender Ken Matsuyama's stock and ambitions outgrew that place so

Ken Matsuyama at his bar in Kyobashi

after 11 years in Golden Gai, he opened a second, much more spacious bar in Kyobashi on July 1, 2016. There's a small stage for music performances at the Kyobashi bar, so some nights there are top-notch performances by local musicians. Ken is a hardcore bourbon enthusiast, but in recent years, he has also become fanatical about Japanese whisky. He arranges bottlings of bourbon and Japanese whisky for his bars at a frequency nobody else on the Japanese bar scene can match.

M's Bar
Yaraicho 118, Shinjuku-ku, Tokyo
03-3269-0743
18:00–05:00 Mon–Fri, 19:00–05:00 Sat, 19:00–24:00 Sun & holidays

A great neighborhood bar in the elegant neighborhood of Kagurazaka. The selection here is superb, and the prices very reasonable. No frills and no nonsense, the whiskies do the talking here. There's not much more to say, other than that it has become my main reason for heading to Kagurazaka these days. The bar celebrated its 25th anniversary in March 2022. There's a reason for its longevity, as you'll find out when you go there.

Rockfish

Ginza 7-3-13-7F, Chuo-ku, Tokyo
03-5537-6900
15:00–20:30 Mon–Fri, 14:00–18:00 Sat, Sun & holidays

Rockfish is a one-trick pony, but what a trick. This place is all about the highball, made Samboa style (no ice, glass chilled, Kakubin chilled with soda and a twist of lemon). Ninety percent of what they serve is exactly that. There's a long menu of appetizers to go along with your highball(s). In fact, owner-bartender Kazunari Maguchi wrote a book on how to fix great appetizers to accompany your tipple of choice. You're in good hands here. The bar is popular with salarymen, keen to "refresh" themselves a bit before they head home, but it's also the perfect first stop on a barhopping tour of Ginza.

Shot Bar Zoetrope

Gala Bldg #4 3F, Nishi-Shinjuku 7-10-14, Shinjuku-ku, Tokyo
03-3363-0162
17:00–23:45 Mon–Sat

Zoetrope is all about Japanese whisky. There's also a smattering of Japanese rum, grappa and other assorted oddities. This place is an institution and nobody knows the field better than owner-bartender Atsushi Horigami. He's a walking encyclopedia of Japanese whisky. The ambience is one of a kind, too: old silent movies are projected on a screen and randomly coupled with more modern soundtrack music. Last time I was there, it was a Busby Berkeley choreography with a bit of Morricone spaghetti western music. Fabulous! The bar is in all the travel guides—deservedly so—but this means that, on an average night, you're more likely to be surrounded by foreigners than by Japanese enthusiasts of good liquor. Zoetrope doesn't take credit cards, so get some cash before taking the elevator up to the third floor.

The Mash Tun

Mikasa Bldg. B 2F, Kami-Osaki 2-14-3, Shinagawa-ku, Tokyo
03-3449-3649
19:00–02:00 Mon–Sat, 19:00–24:00 Sun & holidays

The Mash Tun has a very loyal fan base, which includes many whisky enthusiasts abroad who can't conceive of a visit to Tokyo without stopping by for an extensive dramming session. Owner-bartender Toru Suzuki has a lot to do with that. He knows whisky inside out and is one of those rare hosts who is 1) truly enthusiastic about what's on his shelves, and 2) has lots of really meaningful things to say about the liquid he pours, if you're interested in talking about what you're about to have/having, that is. If you're not, he'll leave you alone, so it's a win-win, whichever camp you fall in.

Wodka Tonic

Tamura Bldg. B1, Nishi-Azabu 2-25-11, Minato-ku, Tokyo
03-3400-5474
18:00~ Mon–Sun

As you may have suspected, this bar does not really specialize in vodka tonics. In fact, in all the years I've frequented this place I've never heard anyone order a vodka tonic. Why would you when you're surrounded by an amazing lineup of stellar whiskies, old and new? One word of caution: 99 percent of the whiskies they pour here are no longer available in the marketplace, so if that sort of situation tends to cause you heartache and pain, you should stay way. If you are happy to have drams you'll never forget but may never see or drink again in your lifetime, then you've come to the right place.

Wodka Tonic on a Saturday night

Bar Perch

Hotel Hut Walden, Moeginomura, Kiyosato 3545,
Takane-cho, Hokuto-shi
0551-48-2131
17:00–01:00 Mon–Sun

This bar is part of a mountain resort in Yamanashi called Moegi-no-mura. It's a bit of a trek—from Tokyo, that is—so the best thing to do is visit Hakushu Distillery, then drive to Moegi-no-mura, spend your evening at the bar and then the night at the hotel there. I have had the privilege of visiting the shed where the whisky stock is kept and it was like walking through decades of Japanese whisky history. There are a few bottles there that, when opened, I would move heaven and earth for to be able to try.

NAGOYA

Bar Barns

Amano Bldg. B1, Sakae 2-3-32, Naka-ku, Nagoya-shi
052-203-1114
17:00–23:30 Tue–Fri, 15:00–23:00 Sat, 15:00–22:30 Sun & holidays;
closed Mon and 2nd Wed

This is hands down the best bar in Nagoya. It excels in all departments: a warm décor, good vibe, perfectly executed cocktails, a fabulous assortment of whiskies (some bottled specially for the bar) and tasty finger food in case you build up an appetite between all those liquid marvels vying for your attention. Owner-bartender Toru Hirai is obsessed with *mizunara* (Japanese oak). When you're there, make sure you ask about the *mizunara* whisky "glasses" he crafts out of single pieces of wood in his free time. (And, no, they are not for sale . . . not yet, anyway.)

Rubin's Vase

Sakae 3-2-31-4F, Naka-ku, Nagoya
052-241-8633
Tue–Sat 17:00–24:00

Owner-bartender Fumihiro Ito opened Rubin's Vase on October 5, 2017. The selection is second to none and features lots of exclusive bottlings for the Japanese market (some of them selected by Ito himself) as well as many of the latest Japanese whisky releases.

Bar K6

Val's Bldg. 2F, Higashi-iru 481, Kiyamachi, Nijo, Nakagyo-ku, Kyoto
075-255-5009
18:00–02:00 Mon–Sun

Minoru Nishida, the man behind K6, is a legend in the bar world in
Japan. He has an extraordinary palate, which is great for us since he
has a habit of tracking down great casks of whisky (and grappa, too)
and then bottling them for his bar and/or liquor shop downstairs. K6 is
an elegant place, so the odds of getting in are better if you don't show
up with hiking boots or in tennis shorts.

Bar Keller

Val's Bldg. 1F, Higashi-iru 481, Kiyamachi, Nijo, Nakagyo-ku, Kyoto
075-253-0245
18:00–02:00 Mon, Wed–Sun

This is the sister bar of K6. It's located in the same building but on the
first floor. However, it's more exclusive than K6, so don't expect to be
able to get in just because you want to (and believe me, you want to!).
In the winter, they make a fabulous *oyuwari* whisky here, that's whisky
mixed with hot water but the way it's prepared here makes the average tea ceremony look basic. There are also some "casks in the wall"
at Bar Keller, with exclusive whiskies in them. But I should stop here, so
you don't feel too grumpy if you can't get in.

Bar Keller with its firmament of amber nectar

Bar SILENT THIRD

Kyara Bldg. 2F West, Goko-machi Rokkaku-sagaru Iseya-machi 354-1,
Nakagyo-ku, Kyoto-shi
075-746-6346
14:00–24:00 Mon–Sun

This spacious bar near Kawaramachi station in Kyoto is a real blessing. It's open from 2 p.m., so that means that, rather than a cup of green tea or a coffee at Starbucks, you can have something more stimulating when you need a break from playing the tourist. I have noticed that, since this bar opened, my breaks have become more frequent when I'm in that part of Kyoto. What can I say? The cocktails are superb and the whisky selection is fabulous.

Samboa

Gionmachi Minamigawa 570-186, Higashiyama-ku, Kyoto
075-541-7509
15:00–23:00 Tue–Fri, 15:00–22:00 Sat & Sun

One of the things I love about Samboa is the generosity. A full shot here is 2 ounces/60ml and a half is 1 ounce/30ml. I can't imagine many people asking for a double! This place is famous for its highballs and rightfully so. Start with that and then move on to other liquid thrills. There are 11 Samboa bars in Kansai (Kyoto and Osaka) and three in Tokyo, so chances are you will stumble upon one on your travels. I couldn't list all the addresses and since Tokyo has more than its fair share of bars listed already, I put this in the Kyoto section.

OSAKA

Bar Augusta Tarlogie

Arakawa Bldg. 1F, Tsurunocho 2-3, Kita-ku, Osaka-shi
06-6376-3455
17:00–24:00 Mon-Sun

Conveniently located in the Umeda district of Osaka, this bar opens at 5 p.m., which is early by Japanese standards, making this the perfect starting place for a bar crawl through the city. The bar is quite small but well stocked. Scotch is the order of the day, and owner-bartender Kiyomitsu Shinano knows the field inside out, but there is also an interesting selection of rare Japanese whiskies available at any given moment.

Bar, K

Koyo Bldg. B1, Sonezakishinchi 1-3-3, Kita-ku, Osaka-shi
06-6343-1167
18:00–24:00 Mon–Sat

Bar, K is located in the heart of Osaka, about a 10-minute walk from Umeda station. To get there, you will have to duck hostesses, scouts and assorted drunks left, right and center, but once you find the place, descend the stairs and open the door, you will enter an oasis of tranquility and intimacy. Here, the focus is on the drinks and the attention to detail is second to none. Don't leave without having a cocktail or two, even if you are a malt *otaku* (maniac, geek, nerd, take your pick!).

BAR whiskycat1494

Showa-cho 1-10-1-2F, Abeno-ku, Osaka-shi
06-6623-1494
18:00–02:00 Tue–Wed, Fri–Sun

This is a small and low-key place but there are some real gems here. The prices are unbeatable but I'm not going to shout that from the rooftops, since this bar only seats eight people and I still want to be able to get in next time I'm in town. There are many bars named "Whiskycat" in Japan, so owner-bartender Mitsuo Yoshimura added "1494"—the earliest historical reference to distilling in Scotland— to make sure you get to the right one.

BAR whiskycat1494 is open for business

The Court

Shibakawa Bldg. 1F, Fushimi-machi 3-3-3, Chuo-ku, Osaka-shi
06-6231-3200
15:00–02:00 Mon, 12:00–02:00 Tue–Sun

The Court has the feel of a Scottish pub, but, mercifully, this place is devoid of random tartans and endless streams of bagpipe music. The people who run The Court are obsessed with Nikka whiskies, so you'll find plenty of those here. There's also a little museum in the basement with lots of Nikka memorabilia. That's by appointment only, unfortunately. They're not very bureaucratic here, so just be nice to the folks behind the stick and chances are they'll reciprocate and give you an "appointment."

KOBE

The Nineteenth Bar
Stella Luce Kitanozaka 2F East, Nakayamate Street, 1-22-18, Chuo-ku,
Kobe City
078-242-0019
17:00–01:00 Mon–Sat

Owner-bartender Kazuya Miyamori opened this bar in 2019 and it has quickly become the best place in Kobe to kick back and enjoy some Japanese whisky. There is a particularly wide selection of Chichibu whiskies. The master also runs an interesting YouTube channel, which includes reports of his visits to whisky (as well as rum and gin) distilleries all over Japan. It's in Japanese but his enthusiasm will get the message across, even if Japanese is all Greek to you. His channel is "Bar studio TV by ミヤモリ."

SHIKOKU

TAKAMATSU

Bar Shamrock
Kiuchi Bldg. 2F, Minami-shinmachi 10-1, Takamatsu-shi
087-835-0995
19:00–02:00 Mon–Sat

Shikoku is not exactly the best place for the wandering whisky lover in Japan. Even in Takamatsu, it's hard to find a bar that has a decent whisky selection. Fortunately, there's Shamrock. The whisky selection is massive, but there is an enormous range of interesting beers here, too, especially Belgian brews. Unless you're traveling with teetotalers, everyone will be pretty happy here.

MARUGAME

Silence Bar
Minato-machi 307-32, Marugame-shi
087-724-3646
19:00–03:00 Mon–Sun

This place is so dark they give you a torch so you can find your glass on the counter and read what's on the bottle label. Thankfully, however, the silence isn't as heavy as the darkness, otherwise it would be a rather spooky experience. There is no menu and since you can't see what's on the shelves, you will have to make a little wish list in your head before you go in. The great thing is that the master will retreat to the bottomless black hole that is the backroom and come back with suggestions that are way better than anything you could have imagined. There are lots of interesting bottles from yesteryear at this bar, so if you like liquid time travel, you'll love this place.

KYUSHU

FUKUOKA

Bar Higuchi
Tamon Bldg. '83 1F, Nakasu 3-4-6, Hakata-ku, Fukuoka-shi
092-271-6070
19:00–01:00 Mon–Sat

This bar is an absolute delight. The attention to detail and level of service is unparalleled. I've never seen a bar that is run as smoothly and with so much grace and elegance as this one. Owner-bartender Kazuyuki Higuchi is a key figure on the Kyushu drinks scene. He's also the mastermind behind Whisky Talk Fukuoka, which is, hands down, the best whisky festival in Japan. If it seems tempting to combine the two—a visit to Bar Higuchi and Whisky Talk Fukuoka—I can assure you, you'll need a great deal of luck to be able to get into the bar the weekend of the festival. However, any other time of the year, there's no excuse not to drop by.

Bar Kitchen
Grand Park Tenjin 1F, Maizuru 1-8-26, Chuo-ku, Fukuoka-shi
092-791-5189
16:00–01:00 Mon–Sun

In October 2015, this bar was the site of an epic tasting of Ichiro's complete Card Series, co-organized by yours truly. I don't think there is any other bar in the world where this could have been done, and definitely not at reasonable prices, so that should give you an idea of what a treasure trove Bar Kitchen is. Since that tasting, the Card Series is no longer complete. In fact, our group killed quite a few bottles and several more have been finished off since then, but there's still more than plenty to keep you happy. Incidentally, this bar doesn't have a kitchen, so get some grub before you head on over.

Whisky Bar Leichhardt
Watanabe-dori 2-2-1-5F, Chuo-ku, Fukuoka-shi
092-215-1414
19:00–24:00 Tue–Sun

With more than 1,000 whiskies on the shelves, including a good many rare Japanese ones, and a bartender with phenomenal cocktail-building skills, you know you've come to the right place as soon as you walk through the door. The master, Yu Sumiyoshi, is fluent in English. In fact, his bar is named after the suburb of Sydney where he lived as a student. Yu is a "Taketsuru Senior Ambassador" and if you try his original cocktail "The 8th Journey," which uses Taketsuru NAS as a base, you'll understand why. Don't even think about leaving Fukuoka without spending some quality time here.

KUMAMOTO

Bar:Colon
Utsunomiya Bldg. B1, Shimotori 1-9-4, Chuo-ku, Kumamoto-shi
096-355-2468
20:00–03:00 Mon–Sat

I know, it's a bit of an unfortunate name. But consider this: Before the bar moved to its present location, it used to be near a place called Cabbages & Condoms. More than a few people must have wondered what part of town they were in. The new space is a bit more compact but the selection is just as good, although stocks are dwindling a bit. Owner-bartender Takeshi Tsuruta used to have a complete set of the Suntory Vintage series, but now he's down to a handful of bottles. There are plenty of other treats on the shelves, though, including some fabulous bottlings for the Kumamoto Bar Society, not to be confused with the Kumamoto Bar Association (which is a group of lawyers).

Bar Ricordi
Dai-ichi Ginnan Bldg. B1, Hanabata-cho 13-26, Chuo-ku, Kumamoto-shi
096-327-2115
19:00–03:00 Mon–Sun

A very stylish bar with impeccable service and a well-curated selection of whiskies. There is more in the walk-in closet at the end of the counter, so it may pay to make subtle enquiries. Subtle is the keyword here. Good luck!

Honda Bar
Ginnan Kaikan 2F, Hanabata-cho 12-8, Chuo-ku, Kumamoto-shi
096-354-0363
20:00–04:00 Mon–Sat

This is not the sort of bar where bottles stare at you from all angles, but what it lacks in quantity, it makes up for in quality. Owner-bartender Kosuke Honda's selection won't disappoint. The ambience is nice, too—very cozy and intimate—so just the right place for a little night-cap . . . or two or three.

Bar Masquerade
Yudachi Bldg. B1, Shin-shigai 3-2, Chuo-ku, Kumamoto-shi
096-356-8166
19:00–03:00 Mon–Sat

If the phantom of the opera had been into booze, this would have been his favorite bar: dark, in the basement and with a glass counter full of bright red roses underneath. Make no mistake, though, this bar is not just about mood, although there's plenty of that. The whisky selection is top notch.

KAGOSHIMA

B.B.13 Bar
Yutaka Sangyo Bldg. 2F, Izumi-cho 16-13, Kagoshima-shi
099-223-4298
18:00–03:00 Mon–Sun

This is a great place to visit if you're traveling with someone who is not into whisky, or even when you're with a teetotaler, as it's a proper restaurant. Kagoshima is the home base of Hombo Shuzo, so there's quite a bit of Mars whisky on the shelves. Substitute the "13" in the name for what it would be in a deck of cards and you know which blues legend they worship here.

Ernest

Yoshinaga Bldg. B1, Yamanokuchicho 11-21, Kagoshima City
080-5608-3499
18:00–02:00 Mon–Sun

Ernest (a reference to Hemingway and his daiquiri, of course) is probably the most fun whisky bar in Japan, which has a lot to do with owner-bartender Mayumi Hashiguchi's bubbly personality and quirky sense of humor. Kagoshima whiskies feature prominently at her bar, but there is a wide range of whiskies from other parts of Japan/the world and other spirits, too. Maybe not the best place for wallflowers and navel-gazers but if you like a good dash of humor with your whisky, this is the place to go.

OKINAWA

Bar poco rit

Matsuyama 2-10-1-B1, Naha, Okinawa
098-943-2893
18:00–03:00 Tue–Sun

Owner-bartender Shin Miyazato opened his bar in 2021, in the midst of the COVID-19 pandemic. Miyazato had dreamed of opening his own bar since he was 15, and spent a decade working at bars in Kyushu (including a five-year stint at Bar Higuchi) after graduating from high school, so he wasn't going to let a pandemic stop him. Miyazato returned to his home prefecture of Okinawa and, in less than a year's time, his bar has become the best place to drink whisky there. The name of the bar—short for *poco ritardando* (the Italian term used in music to tell the performer(s) to "slow down a little")—captures the ethos of the place where he grew up: in Okinawan dialect *yonna yonna* (slowly, don't rush).

A rare Kawasaki bottling at Bar poco rit with some *awamori* paraphernalia

ICHIRO'S CHOICE

1981

- ▪ Bottled
  CHICHIBU

- ▲ Warehouse
  YAMANASHI

- Distillery
  KAWASAKI

SINGLE GRAIN WHISKY
KAWASAKI

CASK TYPE : REFILL SHERRY BUTTS
Distillery KAWASAKI
Distilled 1981 / Bottled 2009
Warehouse

Cask Strength
Non chill-filtered Non coloured
Bottling # **656** / 710

700 ml

Iconic Japanese Whisky Series

The most common way of dealing with the bewildering multiplicity of things out in the world is grouping them—connecting the dots, as it were. Obviously, it helps if things are offered to us in groups or clusters. In the world of whisky, this takes the form of series. Individual releases are contextualized by the series and become part of a narrative that draws us in. In what follows, we put the spotlight on eight iconic series of Japanese whiskies.

THE CASK OF YAMAZAKI/HAKUSHU (SUNTORY)

In July 2002, Suntory offered three single cask Yamazaki bottlings through its online shop: 1979 Mizunara, 1984 Sherry Cask and 1991 Bourbon Cask. These were bottled at cask strength and with minimal filtration. The prices were unbelievable—just ¥18,000 plus tax for the 1979 Mizunara. A survey carried out after the launch showed that people were very keen on these bottlings and that they wanted Suntory to make more single casks available. Suntory obliged—those were the days!—and put a new trio together. This second edition sold out in 30 minutes. Whisky fans were hooked, that much was clear.

In June 2003, three The Cask of Hakushu releases went on sale, together with a new The Cask of Yamazaki. This time round, the Hakushu bottles were gone in 10 minutes. In this day and age, special editions sell out in seconds, but this was two decades ago when Japanese whisky was not nearly as popular as it is now.

In November 2004, Suntory started its Owner's Cask program which allowed individuals or companies to buy and bottle private single casks, so from that point onwards, there was an alternative option for those with a keen interest in single cask whiskies. "The Cask of . . . " series was resumed in 2005 and a few more casks followed in 2007. The series was wrapped up in 2008. Fittingly, Suntory finished with a 1979 Mizunara. The circle was closed.

Suntory "The Cask of" Series (2002–2008) (official bottlings)

The Cask of Yamazaki	*	Year of Release	*	The Cask of Hakushu
1979 Japanese oak cask	2	2002		
1984 Sherry cask	2	2002		
1991 Bourbon cask	2	2002		
1993 Bourbon cask	2	2002		
1991 Sherry cask		2002		
1980 White oak cask		2002		**The Cask of Hakushu**
1980 Sherry cask		2003		1988 Bourbon cask
1990 Hogshead		2003		1982 Sherry cask
1993 Hogshead		2003		1984 White oak cask
1990 Hogshead		2005		1989 Sherry cask
1993 Hogshead		2005		1994 Bourbon cask
1993 Heavily-peated malt	2	2007		
1990 Sherry Butt	4	2007		
1993 Heavily-peated malt	4	2008	5	1993 Heavily-peated
1990 Sherry butt	3	2008	3	1993 Bota corta
1979 Japanese mizunara oak**		2008	5	1998 Hogshead

* number of different single casks, if more than one

** travel retail release

VINTAGE MALT SERIES (SUNTORY)

The Vintage Malt Series is atypical in that it was sold all at once. There was a reason for this. The idea behind the series was summed up in the sales tagline: "a vintage malt for the anniversary year in your life." Sixteen successive vintages—from 1979 to 1994—were made available so people could choose a year that held special significance for them: coming-of-age, graduating from college, marriage, the birth of a child and so on.

What was interesting was that each of the vintages was given a specific character. Each vintage release was defined in terms of distillery (Yamazaki or Hakushu), cask type, whether the washbacks used for fermentation were made out of wood or stainless steel, the type of pot stills used for distillation and the warehouse where the whisky was laid down. This obviously invited comparison, meaning you would have wanted to have more than one vintage on hand.

The series went on sale on October 19, 2004. A hundred complete sets were available for purchase at the quite frankly ridiculous price of ¥443,000 plus tax. Now you'd have to be very lucky to be able to buy the 1979 alone at auction for that price. A second edition went on sale a year later. To accommodate those who had a 10-year anniversary to celebrate in 2005, a 1995 vintage was added. This time around, no complete sets were made available.

Suntory Vintage Malt Series (2004–2005)
(official bottlings, 56%)

Vintage	Distillery	Cask Type	Washbacks	Still Type	Warehouse	Outturn rel. 2004 (btls)	rel. 2005 (btls)
1979	Yamazaki	mizunara butt	stainless	straight head	Yamazaki	300	150
1980	Yamazaki	Spanish oak sherry butt	stainless	straight head	Ohmi	300	150
1981	Hakushu	Spanish oak sherry butt	wood	lantern head	Ohmi	300	150
1982	Hakushu	white oak puncheon	wood	lantern head	Ohmi	300	150
1983	Yamazaki	white oak sherry butt	stainless	straight head	Ohmi	300	150
1984	Yamazaki	Spanish oak sherry butt	stainless	straight head	Ohmi	600	300
1985	Hakushu	white oak hogshead	wood	lantern head	Yatsugatake	600	500
1986	Yamazaki	Spanish oak sherry butt*	stainless	straight head	Yamazaki	300	500
1987	Hakushu	Spanish oak sherry butt	wood	lantern head	Ohmi	300	300
1988	Hakushu	white oak hogshead	wood	lantern head	Hakushu	300	300
1989	Yamazaki	white oak hogshead	wood	straight head	Ohmi	2,000	500
1990	Hakushu	white oak barrel	wood	lantern head	Hakushu	2,000	500
1991	Yamazaki	white oak barrel	wood	bulge	Ohmi	2,000	500
1992	Yamazaki	white oak hogshead	wood	bulge	Ohmi	2,000	500
1993	Hakushu	white oak hogshead	wood	lantern head	Yatsugatake	2,000	500
1994	Yamazaki	white oak barrel	wood	bulge	Ohmi	2,000	500
1995	Yamazaki	Spanish oak sherry butt	wood	straight head	Ohmi	x	1,000

(*transferred to white oak hogshead in 1988)

YOICHI/MIYAGIKYO 20YO (NIKKA)

In December 2004, Nikka released a limited edition Yoichi from the 1984 vintage. Over the next six years, they repeated this idea of releasing a single-vintage 20 year old at the end of the year. The releases were priced fairly reasonably (¥20,000 a bottle, which is peanuts now, but at the time it was the upper end of the spectrum) and very well received by whisky fans in Japan.

In 2007, the 1986 vintage was crowned "Best Japanese Single Malt" whisky at the World Whiskies Awards. By the time they got the award, all 500 bottles were gone, so Nikka released a special WWA edition of the 1986 in May 2007. The year after, the same problem presented itself. This time around, the 1987 vintage was named "Best Single Malt

in the World" at the WWA 2008. Even though Nikka had upped the outturn to 2,000, they found themselves in the same boat as the year before. They responded by releasing a non-chill filtered edition of the 1987 in May 2008.

In January 2009, the first Miyagikyo following the same concept was released. Sadly, the series came to a close at the end of 2010. It was the same old refrain: stocks of mature whisky were getting tighter and priorities had to be reevaluated. The series pre-dates the Japanese whisky boom so most of the bottles were bought for the purpose of drinking. Because of that, they are not an uncommon sight on bar shelves in Japan even in this day and age.

Nikka 20yo Single Malt Series (2004–2010)
(official bottlings)

	Released	Outturn (btls)	Abv (%)
Yoichi 1984	12.2004	500	55
Yoichi 1985	12.2005	500	55
Yoichi 1986	12.2006	500	55
Yoichi 1986 WWA	5.2007	430	55
Yoichi 1987	11.2007	2,000	55
Yoichi 1987 NC	5.2008	1,350	55
Yoichi 1988	11.2008	3,500	55
Yoichi 1989	11.2009	3,500	55
Yoichi 1990 NC	11.2010	3,500	50
Miyagikyo 1988	1.2009	1,500	50
Miyagikyo 1989	12.2009	1,000	50
Miyagikyo 1990 NC	11.2010	1,000	48

(NC = non-chill filtered)

ICHIRO'S CARD SERIES

The year was 2005; the place, Bar Panacee in Ebisu, Tokyo. Takeshi Abe—a whisky fan with a background in graphic design—was introduced to Ichiro Akuto by a mutual friend. Ichiro had just single-handedly saved the legacy of his grandfather's failing whisky business (Hanyu Distillery) by buying up several hundred casks of whisky that would otherwise have been reprocessed into shochu. The whisky was safe but he couldn't just sit on it. The next challenge was to bottle and sell it, little by little. Struck by how difficult it was to pick whiskies at a bar, Akuto and Abe started brainstorming.

The question was: How do people choose a whisky to drink at a bar? The first conclusion they came to was that most people who don't know very much about whisky make their pick based on appearance, namely, the label. The bottle had to visually jump out of the backbar. It also had to come with a bit of a story so the bartender could talk about it with the customer. In other words, a bottle had to be a conversation starter of sorts. The third conclusion they came to was that, presented as a series, the appeal would be bigger: People would instinctively connect them as part of the same "family" and it would appeal to the collector gene as well. The theme they came up with was as simple as it was ingenious: a deck of cards. Visually, anyone can relate to that. People could just ask for an "Ace of Spades" or a "Two of Hearts," and if they liked it enough to want to drink it again later or buy a bottle, that would be all they needed to remember it.

The rest, as they say, is history. Akuto picked the casks and Abe designed the labels. With the exception of the last two—the Jokers—this was done in groups of four. Although the playing card theme ran through the whole series, each quartet had a different visual style and a different subtheme or secondary element (e.g., flowers, constellations, etc.). The first "card" was the King of Diamonds, released in 2005; the last release the two Jokers (2014; Monochrome and Color). In those 10 years, many things changed on the Japanese whisky scene. If the first dozen releases lingered on the shelves of liquor stores around the country for years, trying to get ahold of the last couple of Cards was akin to looking for a four-leaf clover. If Cards released in the early years of the new century were bought primarily for drinking, those released after 2010 were being treated increasingly like collector's items (with all that this entails: fetishized, unopened, resold). By the time the series came to an end, bottles were going for 20 to 30 times their original price on the auction circuit.

In 2015, two complete collections were sold for the price of an average house in Japan. Having the opportunity to try any of these whiskies was clearly becoming more and more unlikely for the aficionado. Unhappy about this state of affairs, I decided to organize a complete tasting of the Card Series. With the assistance of Scott van Leenen and Tomoyuki Oka of Bar Kitchen in Fukuoka, I set up "Ichiro's House of Cards." Thirty people flew in from all over the world to take part in this epic tasting. Spread over two days (October 11–12, 2015) and eight sessions, we tasted and scored the entire series. It was the first time this had been done. Unfortunately, it is highly likely it was also the last time. Skyrocketing prices and the increasing fetishization of the series—not to the mention the appearance of fakes on the secondary market—make a repeat of "House of Cards" anywhere in the world a very unlikely prospect.

Organizing the series into flights that made sense—i.e., that were neither too monolithic nor too eclectic—proved to be a challenge.

For the benefit of others interested in organizing a partial tasting of the Card Series, the following table lists the flights as I organized them. The names of the flights are tongue-in-cheek references to aspects of the maturation process (the size, type of wood and/or previous contents of the casks used for secondary maturation). In each flight, the card in bold is the one that got the highest average score.

Session 1: The Spanish Inquisition
    D-A, C-10, **H-K,** S-A, S-9, D-7, D-8

Session 2: France vs. America Part 1
    D-K, D-J, H-5, **C-9,** Joker-C, S-7, D-9

Session 3: The Portuguese on the Way to the New World
    S-Q, H-3, H-10, C-4, **H-2,** S-2, H-J

Session 4: Big Sizes
    C-A, **S-4,** H-6, C-8, D-10, S-10

Session 5: Japanese & American Pigs
    S-2, S-J, **Joker-M,** C-Q, C-7, S-3, C-5

Session 6: Big Butts: Spanish vs. American Oak
    C-J, D-5, D-4, **H-A,** H-9, S-8, H-8

Session 7: 262,800 Seconds (Give or Take)
    H-Q, H-7, C-3, **D-3,** S-K, S-6, C-6

Session 8: France vs. America Part 2
    D-6, **C-K,** D-Q, H-4, S-5, D-2

The top three at "Ichiro's House of Cards," in descending order, were the Monochrome Joker, the Queen of Clubs and the Jack of Spades. Needless to say, everyone had their own personal favorites. Curious to see whether the collective top three matched Ichiro's own personal favorites, we texted him from the event in Fukuoka. His reply was: "It is difficult to choose a favorite because they are all my children. In fact, I like everything. If I was really pushed to pick some that I thought were interesting or special, I would say the Two of Clubs and the Ace of Clubs, as they were matured in *mizunara* casks. The Color Joker is unforgettable, too. For this, I blended casks from 1985 to 2000 and the blend worked surprisingly well. It has deep and complex flavors and the character changes every single second." Abe's personal favorites from the series, in terms of label design, are the first four.

Ichiro's Card Series (2005–2014)
(Hanyu distillery, bottled by Venture Whisky)

	Vintage	Bottled	Abv (%)	Cask #	Age (years)	Finished (months	2nd Cask type
Hearts							
A	1985	2007	56.0	9004	22	22	American oak sherry butt
2	1986	2009	56.3	482	23	2	Madeira hogshead
3	2000	2010	61.2	465	10	15	Port pipe
4	2000	2011	59.2	529	11	25	Cognac cask
5	2000	2008	60.0	9100	8	36	Cognac cask
6	1991	2012	57.9	405	21	40	American oak puncheon
7	1990	2007	54.0	9002	17	6	American oak sherry butt
8	1991	2008	56.8	9303	17	42	Spanish oak oloroso sherry butt
9	2000	2006	46.0	9000	6	15	American oak sherry butt
10	2000	2011	61.0	463	11	18	Madeira hogshead
J	1991	2010	56.1	378	19	11	Red oak heads hogshead
Q	1990	2005 2006	54.0	482	15 16	6 17	Cognac cask
K	1986	2009	55.4	9033	23	13	Spanish oak PX sherry butt
Diamonds							
A	1986	2008	56.4	9023	22	1	Spanish oak cream sherry butt
2	1991	2008	58.1	9412	17	24	Bourbon barrel
3	1988	2007	56.0	9417	19	6	Bourbon barrel
4	2000	2011	56.9	9030	11	28	Spanish oak PX sherry butt
5	2000	2012	57.7	1305	12	18	Spanish oak sherry butt
6	2000	2007	60.5	9410	7	11	Bourbon barrel
7	1991	2010	54.8	9031	19	25	Spanish oak PX sherry butt
8	1991	2009	57.1	9302	18	55	Spanish oak oloroso sherry butt
9	1985	2009	58.2	9421	24	31	Bourbon barrel
10	1990	2011	54.9	527	21	25	American oak puncheon
J	1988	2008	56.0	9103	20	36	Cognac cask
Q	1985	2007	58.5	9109	22	29	Cognac cask
K	1988	2005 2006	56.0	9003	17 18	6 16	American oak sherry butt

	Vintage	Bottled	Abv (%)	Cask #	Age (years)	Finished (months)	2nd Cask type
Clubs							
A	2000	2012	59.4	9523	12	59	Mizunara puncheon
2	2000	2007	57.0	9500	7	18	Mizunara hogshead
3	2000	2009	61.1	7020	9	6	New American oak puncheon
4	1991	2009	58.1	9802	18	5	American oak rum cask
5	1991	2009	57.4	371	18	3	Mizunara hogshead
6	2000	2009	57.9	9020	9	14	Spanish oak cream sherry butt
7	2000	2008	59.0	7004	8	13	Refill American oak hogshead
8	1988	2011	57.5	7100	23	67	American oak puncheon
9	1991	2011	57.3	401	20	30	Bourbon barrel
10	1990	2008	52.4	9032	18	2	Spanish oak PX sherry butt
J	1991	2005 2006	56.0	9001	14 15	6 17	American oak sherry butt
Q	1988	2008	56.0	7003	20	31	New American oak hogshead
K	1988	2010	58.0	9108	22	67	Cognac cask
Spades							
A	1985	2005 2006	55.0 55.7	9308	20 21	4 15	Spanish oak sherry butt
2	1991	2011	55.8	477	20	18	Port hogshead
3	2000	2007	57.0	7000	7	23	New American oak hogshead
4	2000	2010	58.6	60	10	23	Mizunara puncheon
5	2000	2008	60.5	9601	8	22	American oak refill sherry butt
6	2000	2011	58.6	1303	11	8	Spanish oak oloroso sherry butt
7	1990	2012	53.8	525	22	35	Cognac cask
8	2000	2008	58.0	9301	8	34	Spanish oak sherry butt
9	1990	2010	52.4	9022	20	25	Spanish oak cream sherry butt
10	1988	2006	46.0	9204	18	14	American oak puncheon
J	1990	2007	54.2	7002	17	27	New American oak hogshead
Q	1990	2009	53.1	466	19	4	Port pipe
K	1986	2007	57.0	9418	21	6	Bourbon barrel
Jokers							
Monochrome							
	1985	2014	54.9	1024	29	28	Mizunara hogshead
Color							
	vatting	2014	57.7	n.a.	14-29	various	Vatting of 14 casks

THE NOH SERIES

The Noh Series is the brainchild of David Croll and Marcin Miller of Number One Drinks. The labels feature masks and costumes used in Noh, a form of traditional Japanese theater originating in the four-teenth century. Almost all of the releases in the series are Karuizawa single casks.

The first Noh bottlings were 200ml bottles produced for the Japanese market, that is to say, specifically for sale at performances of the Noh troupe Kamiasobi. David Croll explains: "The relationship with the Kamiasobi troupe came about purely by accident when we were asked if we were interested in sponsoring a performance of their whisky play "Bakuryu." It was just before Whisky Live 2008 and they very kindly agreed to come along to Big Sight [the venue] and perform an act from their play. We had requests for labels other than the Karuizawa Distillery labels and the Number One Drinks label, so the Noh costumes and masks seemed a very obvious and appropriate place to go. Several of the troupe were enthusiastic and knowledgeable whisky drinkers and they were delighted to become involved in this venture, from which a royalty is paid from each bottling to support their activities."

Interestingly, the very first Noh bottlings were not Japanese whisky, but Scotch. The troupe's first mini-bottle—labeled as Kamiasobi's Original Single Malt Whisky—was a 12-year-old Royal Brackla from 1993 (46%abv). They subsequently selected three single casks (partial bot-tlings, obviously), one from Caol Ila Distillery (a 12-year-old from 1995, 46%abv), and two from Karuizawa distillery: a 13-year-old (1997/2010, cask #3312, 60.2%abv) and a 19-year-old (1991/2010, cask #3206, 60.8%abv). All of the other releases in the series were full-sized and bottled for retailers abroad.

Noh Series (2008–)

(Karuizawa & Hanyu distillery, bottled by Number One Drinks)

All Karuizawa distillery, single cask and 700ml, except where otherwise indicated.

	Vintage	Bottled	Abv (%)	Outturn (btls)	Cask #	Cask Type	
30yo	1977	2008	62.8	528	7026	Sherry butt	
13yo	1995	2008	63.0	246	5007	Wine cask	
12yo	1995	2008	63.0	186	5004	Wine cask	
32yo	1976	2009	63.0	486	6719	Sherry butt	
14yo	1995	2009	59.4	222	5039	Wine cask	
32yo	1977	2010	60.7	190	4592	Sherry butt	
15yo	1994	2010	62.7	480	270	Sherry butt	
Multi-Vintage	1981 1982 1983 1984	2011	59.1	1,500	6405 4973 8184 6437	Sherry butts and bourbon casks	
32yo	1980	2012	50.4	102	7614	Sherry butt	
31yo	1981	2012	58.6	186	4676	Sherry cask	
29yo	1982	2012	58.8	411	8529	Bourbon cask	
28yo	1983	2012	57.2	571	7576	Sherry butt	
41yo	1971	2013	63.7	82	1842	Bourbon cask	
32yo	1980	2013	59.2	335	3565	Sherry butt	
31yo	1981	2013	58.9	207	348	Sherry butt	
31yo	1981	2013	66.3	94	4333	Sherry butt	
31yo	1981	2013	62.5	196	8775	Sherry butt	750ml
31yo	1981	2013	56.0	595	155	Sherry butt	
29yo	1983	2013	59.4	205	5322	Sherry hogshead	
29yo	1983	2013	54.3	130	8552	Bourbon cask	
23yo	1989	2013	63.9	302	7893	Sherry butt	
13yo	1999	2013	57.7	500	869	Sherry butt	750ml
30yo	1984	2014	61.4	279	3032	Sherry cask	
30yo	1984	2015	58.2	522	2030	Sherry cask	
15yo	1983	2015	62.2	495	2326	Sherry cask	
21yo	1994	2016	63.6	380	6149	Sherry cask	
35yo	1981	2017	56.5	486	6183	Sherry cask	
35yo	1981	2017	60.6	226	4059	Sherry cask	

Mini Bottles

	Vintage	Bottled	Abv (%)	Outturn (btls)	Cask #	Cask Type	
19yo	1991	2010	60.8	n/a	3206	Sherry butt	200ml
13yo	1997	2010	60.2	n/a	3312	Sherry butt	200ml

Hanyu Distillery

	Vintage	Bottled	Abv (%)	Outturn (btls)	Cask #	Cask Type	
21yo	1988	2009	55.6	625	9306	Spanish oak sherry butt	
10yo	2000	2010	61.0	463	6066	Puncheon	

The founders of Number One Drinks established The Kyoto Distillery, the first ever Japanese distillery to specialize in gin, in 2014 and the Noh Series was further developed there. "We decided to resurrect the Noh Series," Croll relates, "to draw attention to the cask-aged gins we were producing and also to underline the links between what we were doing with gin and what had gone before at Number One Drinks: the same founding team; the KI NOH BI bottle (which was based upon the classic Karuizawa Distillery design, with minor tweaks); and the use of ex-Karuizawa casks for aging." The first edition of KI NOH BI was for Isetan Department Store (August 2017). At the time of writing, they were on edition 26.

THE GAME

The Game is a series of bottlings of Hanyu/Chichibu single casks selected by Japanese liquor retailer Shinanoya. In January 2009, Tsuyoshi Kitakaji, then spirits buyer at Shinanoya, visited Ichiro Akuto to arrange a private bottling. The year before, Shinanoya had launched their flagship series of store-exclusive Scotch bottlings, The Chess. Right from the start, Kitakaji wanted the Hanyu to be the first in a new series. The common ground shared by Ichiro's Card Series and Shinanoya's Chess series became the focus of the new series: The Game.

For the label design, Shinanoya secured the services of the designer of the Card Series, Takeshi Abe. The label of the first release simply combined the playing card and the chess theme. From the second release onward, they wanted to visually emphasize the fact that these were Japanese whiskies selected by and bottled for a Japanese liquor shop. This motivated the integration of *ukiyoe* (Japanese woodblock prints) in the label design of the subsequent releases. The games featured were dice (no. 2), sumo (no. 3), shooting (no. 4) and a space puzzle (no. 5).

To tie the series together, Abe took his inspiration from another Japanese game: *shiritori*. This is a word game in which players take the last *kana* (syllable) of the previous word and make it the first *kana* of the new word. Visually this was translated by integrating the previously released bottle as an element of the label of the new release.

The first five releases in the series were all from the final vintage of Hanyu, 2000. The sixth one was from 1988. Interestingly, this was bottled in 2014, but not released until 2017. From the seventh release onwards, the series migrated to Chichibu single casks.

The Game (2009–)
(Hanyu (#1–6) & Chichibu (#7–) distillery, single cask bottlings, selected by and bottled for Shinanoya)

	Vintage	Bottled	Abv (%)	Outturn (btls)	Cask #	Cask Type
1st	2000	2009	61.2	476	6081	Grain whisky puncheon
2nd	2000	2011	59.4	312	917	Finished in a hogshead fitted with mizunara heads
3rd	2000	2012	57.5	309	360	Finished in a hogshead fitted with red oak heads
4th	2000	2012	59.0	235	9805	Finished in rum wood
5th	2000	2013	59.5	302	1302	Finished in mizunara wood
6th	1988	2014*	51.9	192	471	Hogshead, *released in 2017
7th	2011	2017	61.3	260	1370	Madeira hogshead
8th	2008	2019	61.4	n.a.	215	Bourbon barrel

JAPANESE ENDANGERED ANIMALS SERIES

Whisky Talk Fukuoka is an annual whisky festival, held in June in Fukuoka, Kyushu. At each one, there are a few special festival bottlings. The one constant is the Japanese Endangered Animals series. The first one, featuring the Japanese wolf, was released at the first edition of Whisky Talk Fukuoka in 2011. Since then, every year one has been added to the series. All of the bottlings come from the Venture Whisky stable (Hanyu & Chichibu Distilleries). The labels have all been designed by—who else?—Takeshi Abe.

Three Chichibu bottlings from the Endangered Animals series

Japanese Endangered Animals Series (2011–)
(bottled for Whisky Talk Fukuoka)

	Distillery	Vintage	Bottled	Endangered Animal on Label	Abv (%)	Outturn (btls)	Cask Type
1st	Hanyu	2000	2011	Japanese Wolf	58.7	181	1st cask: hogshead; 2nd cask: quarter cask
2nd	Hanyu	2000	2012	Japanese Crested Ibis	60.1	446	American oak puncheon
3rd	Chichibu	2009	2013	Japanese River Otter	60.8	221	1st cask: 1st fill barrel; 2nd cask: 3rd fill barrel
4th	Chichibu	2009	2014	Tsushima Leopard Cat	60.2	225	1st cask: 1st fill barrel; 2nd cask: 3rd fill barrel
5th	Chichibu	2010	2015	Blakiston's Fish Owl	60.8	593	1st cask: 1st fill barrel; 2nd cask: 3rd fill puncheon
6th	Chichibu	2010	2016	Japanese Giant Salamander	59.4	306	1st cask: 1st fill barrel; 2nd cask: Oloroso Spanish oak hogshead
7th	Chichibu	2011	2017	Asiatic Black Bear	59.5	242	1st: first-fill bourbon barrel, 2nd: beer barrel
8th	Chichibu	2010	2018	Eastern Barbastelle (Chichibu Bat)	62.3	292	Ex-Hanyu hogshead
9th	Chichibu	2012	2019	Green Turtle	62.2	183	Bourbon barrel
10th	Chichibu	2013	2020	Ezo Chipmunk	62.9	212	Bourbon barrel
11th	Chichibu	2015	2021	Japanese Grouse	63.0	216	First-fill bourbon barrel
12th	Chichibu	2016	2022	Sea Otter	62.0	259	Wine cask

THE GHOST SERIES

It may seem a little immodest to include a series in this section that I'm personally responsible for. I make no apologies for this, though, but I also won't take too much credit for it. First of all, I didn't make these whiskies. (I wish I had, though, because they are stunning.) Also, a series is made iconic by whisky fans and collectors, not by the person behind it; otherwise, they would all be iconic series. It's called The Ghost Series because the labels feature artwork taken from the last great *ukiyoe* artist Yoshitoshi's final series of woodblock prints, "New Forms of 36 Ghosts" (1889–1892).

There are a few aspects that make this series rather special. First of all, it shows the quirky side of Japanese whisky history. In one way or another, all of these releases are somewhat unusual or one of a kind. The first release was a Karuizawa but not the sort of Karuizawa people had gotten used to: bold, robust, oily and richly fruited. Cask #3681 showed a different side of the distillery character: light, elegant and subtle. The second release was another Karuizawa, but one matured in a cask that used to contain Japanese red wine. Only 20 such casks were ever filled in the history of the distillery, all in 1995, and #5022 was the last one to be bottled and also the oldest. The third release was a Hanyu, and the only instance until further notice of a Japanese whisky finished in an ex-grappa cask. The fourth was a single grain whisky from the long-gone Kawasaki distillery, and the only surviving cask from the 1980 vintage to have come to light so far. The fifth was inspired by the photographic technique of time stacking, layering multiple images of the same subject taken at different time points over one another to create a quasi-impressionist effect. It was a vatting of malt distilled over a period of four decades at Karuizawa distillery, from 1960 right up until the last vintage (2000), which was then returned to wood for marrying before being bottled. The sixth was a cask-strength bottling of a solera whisky made by Ichiro Akuto. It is the only instance of a cask-strength solera bottling coming out of Japan that I am aware of. The seventh release was a blend of Karuizawa malt and Kawasaki grain from the late 1970s that was discovered in a forgotten warehouse up in the cold north of Japan, which—having slumbered in glass for over three decades—was refilled into a freshly disgorged ex-Karuizawa cask for a period of seven months to reinvigorate the whisky. It's a true "time slip" whisky. The eighth one is a cask-strength version of Ichiro's Double Distilleries, a vatting of older Hanyu malt and younger Chichibu malt. Yoshitoshi's series has 36 ghosts, so it's far from over.

Another aspect that makes this series special is that, unintentionally, the outturn for most of these releases was very low. The most limited one was the second release. What was left in the cask at the time of bottling yielded a mere 22 bottles. Obviously, the highly limited nature of the individual releases increased the appeal of the series in collectors' circles. Unfortunately but inevitably, it also drove prices on the secondary market to astronomic heights. In early 2016, a single bottle of Ghost 2 was sold at auction for over US$25,000. To keep things exciting and to be true to the theme, elusiveness is built into the series. Ghost 6 was only made available to selected bars in Japan. Bottles were hand delivered by yours truly, opened there and then, and a dram was ordered straight away. This made the series a completist's worst nightmare.

On the occasion of the Japanese publication of this book, three bottles were released (#9–11), selected together with Hideo Yamaoka, the co-translator of the book. Since then, we have selected a handful of other releases in the series.

At the time of writing, the Ghost Series has reached the halfway point. Inevitably, the series reflects the changing landscape of the Japanese whisky scene in that the recent releases tend to be younger. The project is, by nature, unhurried and open to serendipity, so there is no telling where the second half of the journey will take us.

A selection of bottlings from the Ghost Series

The Ghost Series (2013–)
(selected by Stefan Van Eycken, some in association with Hideo Yamaoka)

		Type of Whisky	Abv (%)	Outturn (btls)	Cask #	Cask(s)
1st	Karuizawa 16yo	single cask malt 1996/2013	59.5	140	3681	Sherry cask
2nd	Karuizawa 18yo	single cask malt 1995/2013	61.9	22	5022	Red wine cask

3rd	Hanyu 14yo	single cask malt 2000/2014	59.9	120	1702	Grappa finish
4th	Kawasaki 33yo	single cask grain 1980/2014	59.6	60	6165	Sherry butt
5th	Karuizawa "4 Decades"	single malt (btld. 2014)	61.8	24	4556	Marrying cask: sherry butt
6th	Ichiro's Malt WWR	vatted malt (btld. 2015)	59.5	28		Wine Wood Reserve Cask Strength
7th	Karuizawa + Kawasaki	blended (btld. 2015)	43.0	282	6432	Marrying cask: sherry butt
8th	Hanyu + Chichibu	vatted malt (btld. 2016)	60.1	26		Double Distilleries Cask Strength
9th	Hanyu + Chichibu (+Peated)	vatted malt (btld. 2018)	61.3	129		Double Distilleries Cask Strength
10th	Eigashima 3yo	single cask malt 2015/2018	61.5	500	101520	Sake Cask Finish
11th	Komagatake 3yo	single cask malt 2015/2018	60.0	200	5141	First-Fill Bourbon Barrel (Tsunuki Aging)
12th	Chichibu 10yo	single cask malt 2009/2019	61.9	157	554	First-fill Bourbon Barrel
13th	"Kaisen"	cask-aged Kyoto dry gin	48.0	24	(no cask nr)	Marrying casks: ex-Karuizawa, mizunara puncheon & ex-Kilchoman bourbon barrel
14th	Eigashima 4yo	single cask malt 2015/2020	61.0	394	61791	Cabernet Franc Finish
15th	Eigashima 4yo	single cask malt 2016/2021	61.5	849	61966	Tawny Port Cask Finish
16th	Kanosuke 3yo	single cask malt 2018/2022	58.0	271	20081	Second-Fill Chardonnay Finish
17th	Tsunuki 4yo	single cask malt 2017/2022	61.1	192	T431	First-Fill Bourbon Barrel
18th	Eigashima 3yo	single malt 2018/2022	62.0	631	101857/8	First-Fill Bourbon Barrel (Heavily Peated)

Into The Glass:
33 Shades of Liquid Gold

Compiling a list of must-try Japanese whiskies is a bit like putting together a list of Italian soundtracks to listen to before you die. Where do you start and where do you draw the line, especially with something as subjective as whisky and music? Taste is involved, so any "best of" list is bound to be hopelessly subjective, subjective because one person's thrill is another person's "whatever"; subjective also because who has tried every whisky out there? There are always more marvels waiting to be discovered.

And yet, many of us do want to know what the brightest stars in the firmament are. To make the selection that follows slightly more objective, I have used the trick of collating many subjectivities. I went about this by asking people with a wide-ranging experience of Japanese whisky—bartenders, retailers, independent whisky reviewers, early fans of Japanese whisky, etc.—for their personal top 10. I then put these top 10s side by side and looked for bottles that featured on many of the lists. That still doesn't mean this is an authoritative list—whatever that is—but it is more than just one guy's opinion.

In compiling a meta top 10, which turned out to be a list of 33 whiskies, I wanted to make sure it covered the whole spectrum of Japanese whisky. Most producers are represented; whiskies of all styles—blended, blended malt, single malt, single grain and in the latter two categories also single casks—are included; some whiskies are very old, some are very young, others somewhere in between; some are peat/sherry monsters, others are subtle and quiet.

All but two of the whiskies listed were released in this century. That's not a pragmatic choice. Japanese whisky is better now than it has ever been. I say this based on many years of research in bars in every nook and cranny of the country, trying to find an old Japanese whisky that would invalidate that blanket statement. I have yet to find it. The fact that most of the whiskies listed below were released recently doesn't mean it will be easy to find them. However, to those who are inclined to think this is an impossible bucket list, I say: hope springs eternal. Sure, it's not easy to find them, and some of them cost a pretty penny, but it is not undoable to experience them in the wild.

The list is organized by producer—in the same order as the distilleries profiled in the middle section of this book—and where there are multiple entries for one producer, the bottles are listed depending on the type of whisky (blends first, then blended malts, then single malt/ grain and, finally, single cask releases) and within each type from older to newer releases. For some listings, alternatives of the same quality and similar style are suggested.

Reading whisky reviews can be a bit like listening to someone else's holiday stories. The good thing about the printed word, however, is that you can quickly read between the lines to ascertain whether a whisky is likely to appeal to you or not and even skip the bits you are not so interested in.

KEY

(N) **nose**

(P) **palate**

(F) **finish**

Suntory Whisky President's Choice
(blended whisky, 43%abv, rel. 1980s)

As it says on the label: "This whisky was specially selected and blended by the president of Suntory Limited from choice malt and grain whiskies." The president at the time was Keizo Saji.

N The harmony is so exquisite it's almost impossible to isolate key notes; subtly suggestive of dried persimmon, meadows after rain, honeydew melon, communion wafers, old magazines; hints of mustard and fresh dill.

P This is like a Rothko panel, but behind a semi-transparent veil: apricot liqueur, *ichigo daifuku* (strawberry and red bean mochi) and sage—don't get this wrong: the flavors are not full-on but precariously hovering over your palate, if that makes sense.

F Gently lingering, initially with a touch of fudge; in the afterglow, green plums emerge.

You would expect the President's Whisky to be a bold and brash dram. This couldn't be further from that: gentle, understated, supremely elegant and beautifully poetic. It's also a master class in blending. It's not just that the whole is greater than the sum of its parts; you can't even imagine what the parts were here. At Suntory, the president of the company is also the master blender. Try this and you'll understand that's more than just a title on a business card.

Hibiki 30yo
(blended whisky, 43%abv)

Originally released in November 1997, this comes in a bottle with 30 facets, unlike the other Hibiki expressions, which have 24 (symbolizing the 24 small seasons and the 24 hours in a day). The 30 year old also comes with a hefty price tag, if you can find it. The original price was 80,000 yen—the good old days!

N Blind, nobody—except those who've had this before—would guess this was a blended whisky; most people would take it for a superb old single cask bottled at cask strength. The initial impressions are *rancio charentais* (a term used in the cognac trade to describe the complex aromas and flavors from long ageing in oak casks, evocative of old leather, overripe banana, mushrooms, soy sauce, walnut oil, dried fruits, etc.), furniture polish, orange marmalade, walnuts, dried figs, raspberries and freshly grated nutmeg. After a while, it opens up more, revealing gingerbread, mincemeat, balsamic glaze, green apple peel, horseradish and a hint of thyme; give it another quarter of an hour and you get a prominent strawberry milkshake note.

P Beautifully dynamic: It makes a journey across the palate from sweet (fruit candy) to dry (that's the wood speaking). In the middle of the journey, bitter and sour elements—fresh citrus, citrus peel, grape skins and burnt caramel—intertwine in perfect harmony; the palate becomes progressively spicier (white pepper and aniseed).

F Long and woody on candied orange peel, roasted chestnuts, prune jam, dark chocolate and a touch of mint; the finish morphs into white grapes as it fades out, a surprising yet subtle afterglow.

Some people prefer Hibiki 21 to the 30. With whisky this old, there's bound to be some batch variation, so don't write the 30 year old off too quickly. I'm sure there is a batch with your name on it somewhere. I know I've had more than a few with mine.

[Yamazaki] Age Unknown
(over 25yo, single malt whisky, 43%abv, rel. 1989)

In 1989, Keizo Saji was awarded the First Class Order of the Sacred Treasure, Japan's highest honor. To mark the occasion, Saji created this whisky, which was given to guests at a party held in his honor. It dates from the time when Suntory used the nomenclature "pure malt" to refer to what were technically single malts.

N A phenomenal *mizunara*-and-sherry duet; first, the *mizunara* leads with incense, sandalwood and coconut butter, then the sherry takes over with lychee, passion fruit, canned apricots, overripe kiwifruit and dates. There are also some very subtle floral notes in the background and a teeny tiny bit of dried thyme and fennel. Given time in the glass, a gorgeous strawberry sorbet note emerges.

P Very complex: watermelon on the attack, then *crêpes suzette* and limoncello, followed by diced candied mixed fruit, sweet red bean paste, dried dates, pine nuts and a drop of crème de menthe.

F Very long and slightly drying with candied grapefruit peel and grilled lotus root transforming into a sustained *biwa* (loquat) afterglow.

The standard Yamazaki 25yo was launched as a permanent addition to the Yamazaki range in the same year as this whisky. The core range 25yo used to be 100% matured in ex-sherry Spanish oak, but from the mid-2010s onwards it became noticeably more tannic and aggressive. In the summer of 2021, Suntory chief blender Shinji Fukuyo announced that the company was abandoning the monolithic design of the 25yo in favor of a broader palette of wood types (American, Spanish and Japanese oak). The bottle featured on the following page was said to have been the inspiration for the reformulated recipe, but this Age Unknown could have provided some pointers, too.

Yamazaki 1984
(48%abv, 2,500btls, rel. 2009)

Released to commemorate the 25th anniversary of the Yamazaki brand, this is a vatting of malt distilled in 1984 and matured primarily in *mizunara* as well as European and American oak. Suntory got a truckload of awards for this expression, including some of the highest accolades in the business (Supreme Champion Spirit at the 2010 ISC and World's Best Single Malt Whisky at the 2011 WWA).

N Sandalwood, beeswax, sour plum jam and orange marmalade, pork rillettes (with loads of brandy), balsamic-stewed strawberries, pear drop candy and green apple peel, cinnamon, incense and subtle hints of *sansho* (known as Japanese pepper but really the seedpods of the prickly ash—very hot and citrusy at the same time) and nail polish remover. Water brings out fresh stone fruits and a young Karuizawa-like metallic quality.

P *Kabosu* and yuzu fruit (both citrus fruits used in Japanese cooking) in fortissimo with orange oil, ruby grapefruit-infused olive oil, licorice and herbal elements in smaller doses, and a distinct passion fruit top note. Water dials up the sour level, resulting in a great mix of fresh citrus fruits and citrus zest joined, after a while, by caramelized onion and fresh peaches.

F Long and slightly drying, on yuzu marmalade, plum jelly, old Cognac and black pepper. With water: sour candy, matcha powder, fruit yogurt and over-ripe melon.

Huge and extrovert but with more than enough substance to keep you glued to your glass for an hour or more.

Yamazaki 50yo

(single malt whisky, 57%abv, 150btls, rel. 2011)

This is a very expensive whisky—a million yen plus tax for a bottle originally and much more on the auction circuit now—so you will pardon me, dear reader, for the absence of detailed tasting notes. There's simply no room for that when you have this in your hand, and that's not an excuse, even though it sounds like one.

N + **P** + **F** A transcendental experience

If I was forced to pick one Japanese whisky to take to a desert island, this would be it. I had the chance to buy a bottle of Yamazaki 50 a couple of years ago, at the original price. I didn't because I figured there were better ways to spend a million yen. I was wrong. Fortunately, there are some bars in Japan—not many, but there are a few—where you can drink this by the glass. And no, I'm not telling you where. Liquid gold of this caliber demands to be stumbled upon by accident, the thrill of the discovery adding to the ecstasy of the moment.

Yamazaki 1986/2007
Owner's Cask Mizunara
(mizunara butt #6B0018, 49.0%abv, 424btls)

A single cask *mizunara* release from The House of Suntory. I remember the days when you could pick one up from a big electronics retailer with branches all over Japan any day of the week. Now finding one available at a bar by the glass is like winning the lottery.

Toasted coconut flakes, coconut macaroons, pineapple cake, brown pine tree needles and mild Middle Eastern spices; after a while, mashed strawberries, sage, wet grass, wood shavings and something between ground coffee and incense ash. With water, it becomes slightly sweeter and fruitier (mango pudding).

P Gentle citrus notes (dried orange slices), subtle bitter notes (bitter melon morphing into thick green tea), vanilla, a gentle green sappiness, subtle peppery notes and hints of white chocolate mousse and newspapers (don't pretend you don't know what newspapers taste like!)—gentle and subtle are the key words here; it really is a beautifully controlled assemblage of flavors.

F Initially a gentle crescendo of matcha, gooseberries, rhubarb jam and a bit of agave syrup; in the wake of its *adieu*, we get some subtle wood smoke notes.

Supremely elegant and intensely beguiling, this is my personal favorite from the handful of 1986 Yamazaki *mizunara* single casks released over the years. That said, I would never pass up the chance to savor any of the others listed below, because at this level, "preference" is like saying you like Bach's Cello Suite No.6 better than the other five.

✦ Yamazaki 1986/2006 Owner's Cask Mizunara *(mizunara butt #6G5029, 60.0%abv, for La Maison du Whisky 50th Anniversary)*

✦ Yamazaki 1986/2007 Owner's Cask Mizunara *(mizunara butt #6G5020, 57.0%abv, for Bar Barns 5th Anniversary)*

✦ Yamazaki 1986/2009 Owner's Cask Mizunara *(mizunara butt #6B0021, 51.0%abv)*

Yamazaki 1989/2011 Owner's Cask Futakata III

(hogshead #9W70427, 59%abv, 113btls)

This was bottled by Osamu Futakata, who ran the legendary Malt Bar South Park in Tokyo until his untimely death in April 2018. The bar itself closed a year and a half later. Before he even thought about opening a bar, Futakata bought a few Owner's Casks from Suntory. This, his third selection, is a small miracle.

 Dynamic in the extreme; like a chameleon, it keeps changing: It starts off savory with lemon-rosemary grilled chicken, porcini stock, fennel and freshly roasted almonds, then turns subtly fruity: Kyoho grapes, green apples, overripe persimmons and a hint of passion fruit. After that, there's herbal tea and a bit of potpourri but the savory elements stay (now reminiscent of beef tongue jerky and *foie gras*); give it time and you get roasted peaches and orange liqueur custard, then a cup of caramel tea . . . and after a really long time, beautiful overripe peaches. An extraordinary journey.

P Takes no prisoners, a massive collision of bitter, sour and spicy intensities. Quite resistant to analysis because the impact is so strong and sustained. There's *yuzu kosho* (a fermented Japanese condiment made from yuzu juice and zest, chili peppers, and salt), assorted candied citrus peel, caramelized *crème brulée* crust, a hint of *sansho* and plenty more.

F Follows you all the way to the parking lot: citrusy and slightly herbal again, sustained by ginger and spice. It's here that the wood speaks but in just the right register, so it doesn't ruin things for the caraway seeds and the cardamom, the aniseed and the tamarind. After a few minutes, you'd swear you were munching on some licorice allsorts.

For my money's worth, this is the best Suntory Owner's Cask. I obviously haven't tried them all, or I'd be dead. Speaking of dough, this cask cost 2 million yen in 2011. Back then, that seemed like a lot of money. Now, people would trample each other to get their hands on a cask like this, even if it cost a multiple of what Futakata paid for it.

Yamazaki 1993/2012

(first-fill sherry butt #3T70070, 57.5%abv, 444btls, for La Maison du Whisky)

The people at Suntory are very particular about their sherry casks (well, they're very particular about many things). They regularly send wood specialists to forests in the north of Spain to look for the right trees; then they have the wood prepared and coopered to their specifications by local craftsmen with extraordinary oversight. After that, they have the casks sent to top bodegas in Jerez, where they are seasoned with sherry for at least three years. The best of those are sent back to Japan to be filled at Suntory's warehouses. If you think sherried Yamazakis are a bit expensive, now you know why.

N First, dark chocolate mousse, *mole* sauce, spiced *speculaas* cookies and macadamia nuts; then the fruit enters: apricot jam, Moro blood oranges, sultanas, dried prunes, brandy-soaked cherries and strawberries macerated with balsamic vinegar. A little later, other elements start to emerge: spices (nutmeg, cloves), freshly polished leather, Frangelico liqueur, a hint of *foie gras* and a distinct floral note.

P The perfect triad of sour, sweet and bitter: sweet as in candied orange peel, Turkish delights, *crema catalana* and tiramisu; sour featuring lime and *yama-mikan* (a peculiarly sour Japanese variety of mandarin orange); and the bitterness of Seville oranges, dark chocolate and tannins from the oak.

F Long and lingering on Napoleon III truffles, *orangettes* (candied orange peels dipped in chocolate), Korean *kimchi* chocolate, chestnut cream cake and a touch of garam masala.

The label features an elephant. If you've had this, you know why.

Yamazaki 2003/2014 119.14 Raspberry Imperial Stout
(11yo, 1st fill bota corta, 53.9%abv, 538btls, Scotch Malt Whisky Society release)

In March 2015, the Scotch Malt Whisky Society released 11 Japanese single cask bottlings. The Japan chapter of the Society dubbed them the "11 Samurai." I remember being at the launch party in Tokyo and this Yamazaki seemed to be the darling of the crowd there, which meant something, given the caliber of the other 10 samurai.

N All things dark: dark fruits, dark chocolate, strong black coffee, dark forest notes, dark rum, dark wine cellars. On top of all those dark elements, there's some pipe tobacco, brown sugar syrup, *tarte tatin* and balsamic-blackberry *crème brulée*.

P We're in deep sherry territory here: stewed berries, prune jam, cherry sauce, dates, dark chocolate, freshly grated nutmeg, clove, espresso jelly, candied ginger and a bit of menthol, all superbly balanced; rich and dense but nothing beyond the pale.

F Not very long, but that's not a problem since it coaxes you into having another sip, and another, and another. You get chocolate-dipped orange peel, marzipan, figs, a bit of lime zest and a touch of aniseed; slightly drying towards the end, but again, that just encourages you to have a bit more.

It's not the most complex whisky in this list, but it does what it does very well.

It's intense without being extreme, dense without being one-dimensional and bold without being offensive. There are no big surprises but it's intriguing and engaging from start to finish. My bottle didn't last long, I can tell you.

The Cask of Hakushu 1993 Spanish Oak Bota Corta

(#3C40789, bottled 2008, 60.0%abv, 571btls)

Many bartenders in Japan have a soft spot for this bottling from Suntory's "The Cask of . . ." series. Take a sip and you'll know why: it's a great whisky that happens to be heavily sherried, rather than a great heavily sherried whisky, which, as we all know, is not the same thing.

Massive sherry—stewed plums, raisins, blackberries, coffee liqueur and spices galore (clove, aniseed, cardamom)—but in harmonized plenitude; in the background, some *katori senko* (incense coils used to keep mosquitoes away, very common in Japan in summer); after a while, hints of sweet soy sauce and *crème de violette*.

Wonderfully decadent with prune jam, sour cherries, dark chocolate and a touch of menthol, but there's more going on than that; there's also a subtle vegetal dimension (grilled burdock and king trumpet mushrooms) as well as suggestions of beef stock, *umeboshi*, eel sauce (*unagi tare*) and a little bit of *sansho*.

Medium long on tiramisu, prunes, a fig log, essential citrus oils and chocolate with mint.

Don't go looking for distillery character here. This is cask-driven whisky. It's not hard to "do heavy sherry," but it is very hard to do it well, meaning, do it so that 1) the whisky is not crippled or obliterated by the wood, 2) it's not merely an exercise in style and 3) the enjoyment of the experience is not dependent on a subconscious quasi-macho privileging of "the extreme." This Hakushu single cask does it really well and that's why it's in this little list.

Chita 2011/2014 G13.1
A complete revelation

(single grain whisky, virgin oak puncheon, 58.3%abv, 622btls, Scotch Malt Whisky Society release)

This is the first and, at the time of writing, the only single cask grain whisky from Chita distillery.

N Very much cask-driven. Like entering a candy store, then the plot thickens with banana bread, *crème anglaise*, something between *advocaat* (a Dutch liqueur made from eggs, sugar and brandy) and *amazake* (a sweet, non- or low-alcohol Japanese drink made from fermented rice), rum-raisin cream sandwich cookies, a hint of young rye whiskey, new furniture and dried flowers.

P Spices and sweet elements beautifully entwined, with cinnamon, cloves, nutmeg and a tiny bit of fennel keeping this from becoming a one-sided sweet-tooth affair (toasted marshmallows, banana fudge, eggnog, chocolate-coconut macaroons, grilled rum-soaked pineapple and white chocolate mousse).

F Long and intense on coconut tapioca with some dried orange slices (lightly dipped in milk chocolate), lemon-ginger gummy bears, rum baba and licorice allsorts on the side.

If everything they make at Chita develops into something this extraordinary in just four years, we are in trouble.

The Nikka 40

(blended whisky, 43% abv, 700btls, rel. 2014)

This contains some of the oldest stock available at Nikka's distilleries, including Yoichi malt distilled in 1945 and Miyagikyo malt laid down in 1969, and it is very malt-heavy (containing only about a third grain whisky).

N A hermetic mystery—to name but a few of the elements in play: an antique shop (wood polish and old leather), an autumn forest after rain, Turkish delights and *marzipankartoffeln*, mint-and-balsamic-marinated strawberries, caramelized apples and hints of very old calvados, pine nut cookies with rosemary, *chinsuko* cookies (Okinawan shortbread), potpourri (featuring lavender but very subtly), grilled rum-infused figs, apricot-thyme jam, cinnamon French toast, black sesame paste. Then, after a while, *crema catalana*, dried apple-mango, subtle floral notes, Yubari King melon Hi-Chew (soft candy) and faint whiffs of tea (Darjeeling, rooibos).

P Extremely silky mouthfeel: bergamot tea, candied yuzu peel, *kabosu crème brûlée,* blood orange jam, gentle woody notes, again, communion wafers, chocolate truffles. After a while, tiny hints of maraschino cherries, roasted almonds, *kinako* (roasted soy flour)-dusted tofu, pink peppercorns and lots more.

F Develops a lovely bitterness, with grapefruit albedo and apple-kale juice—like a green ray. White chocolate rusk and menthol segue into an afterglow too beautiful for words.

An undisputed masterpiece of blending (and of Mother Nature!).

Taketsuru 35yo

(blended whisky, 43%abv, 10,800btls,
rel. yearly from 2000–2011, except 2010)

There is a little bit of confusion about this whisky, but the confusion is understandable. All "Taketsuru" releases are vatted malts (i.e., blends of Yoichi and Miyagikyo malt whisky), except for this one. This also contains some Coffey grain distilled at Nishinomiya distillery, making it a blended whisky. Exactly why Nikka decided to break the mold with this, the oldest Taketsuru, is anybody's guess, but who cares? It's an absolutely stunning whisky and that's what matters.

N Rich mango pudding drizzled with old cognac, passion fruit jam, *crème d'anjou, nama* (soft) caramel and overripe cantaloupe; after a while, hot chocolate spiked with orange liqueur and a cinnamon stick; in the background, mild pipe tobacco and licorice allsorts—a fabulous nose unlike any other Japanese whisky.

P The first thing you notice is how intensely creamy this whisky is; then you get soft tropical fruit notes, raspberry coulis, old cognac, saffron and salted caramel tea. There's also a lovely touch of pink pepper and a tiny bit of yuzu zest involved.

F Not very long but the immediate retro-olfaction is amazing—grapefruit and mango give the whisky an Irish touch for a second or two, then you get a leaf of fresh mint before it fades on peach-pineapple (an Okinawan fruit).

After a while, there's a subtle hint of very weak green tea, the sort you would get after the fourth or fifth infusion.

Up until 2006, this was sold for ¥50,000 plus tax; from 2007, the price was raised slightly, to ¥70,000 plus tax. The good old days . . . If you see this at a bar—and it is still out there in the wild!—don't hesitate to order it.

Yoichi 1990/2001
(10yo, #223639, 62%abv)

This is the single cask that sent shock-waves through the whisky community abroad and made people take notice of what was going on in Japan. It was named "Best of the Best" at *Whisky Magazine*'s first contest in 2001, the first time a non-Scottish whisky was named best in the world. That's happened a few times since, but this is the one that started it all.

N Beautifully balanced with damp, foresty notes, sweet baked goods (apricot Danish, butterscotch, spice cake), apple-prune compote, gentle peat and soft leather; after a while, hints of smoked herring, grilled rice balls and a subtle metallic note. Water makes the smoke a bit more prominent.

P Smooth and velvety, it doesn't feel like 62%abv at all. Starts off with a gentle, fruity sweetness that's sustained all the way through; then other flavor partials are brought out: lemon zest and a splash of lime, followed by candied grapefruit peel and some walnut skin, and, finally, a touch of spice (*shichimi togarashi*—also known as Japanese seven spice—and white pepper) and a tiny bit of smoke. Water brings out underripe peaches.

F Not that long but a perfect echo of the palate.

A master blender's wet dream, except here the cask was the master blender. This probably happens once in a blue moon in the warehouses, but kudos to the people at Nikka for spotting this cask and bottling it at just the right moment.

Yoichi 1988/2013

(virgin oak butt #100215, 62%abv, for La Maison du Whisky)

Brace yourself for a little exercise in extremes: this is a heavily peated Yoichi that has spent a quarter of a century in virgin oak.

N Pencil shavings, new plank, almond milk jelly and furniture polish—that's the virgin oak speaking—as well as barnyard smells (reminiscent of some Port Charlotte single casks), heavily smoked nuts (beech nuts, peanuts, almonds) and a bit of fruit (apple butter). The combination of new oak, heavy peat and that typically "dirty" Yoichi character works a treat.

P Sour cherries, smoked duck, marzipan, rhubarb jam, milk chocolate, smoked nuts again and the last of a summer campfire. Time has integrated the peat beautifully—it's not as front and center as you would expect from a heavily peated malt.

F Long and lingering, with the peat smoke more pronounced and a slight hint of orange peel. It works well with water, too, delivering a bit more fruit.

On paper, this looks like a whisky on steroids; in reality, it's a little miracle of nature—"extremes that were made to meet," Aldous Huxley would say.

✦ Yoichi 1988/2013 *(virgin oak butt #100212, 62%abv)*

✦ Yoichi 1991/2014 *(virgin oak puncheon #129459, 62%abv, for LMdW)*

Worst Whisky in the World?

On paper, it ticks all the right boxes: a single malt from 1983 from an obscure Japanese distillery, bottled at cask strength (64%abv). In reality, Usuikyou 1983, distilled at Monde Shuzo in Yamanashi, often finds itself in the company of the likes of Loch Dhu and Lost Spirits' Leviathan in lists and discussions of the worst whisky ever made anywhere on earth. If it had been available more widely, and therefore tried by more people, there's no doubt it would be the undisputed "King of Nasty."

The good folks at the Los Angeles Whiskey Society tasted Usuikyou in 2010 and came up with the most hilarious tasting notes you will ever read. Unfortunately, they are spot on. Here's a selection from their comments, quoted with permission.

> *"The nose gives you metal, some sherry and old garbage left out in the sun; drifting farts in a kitchen where someone made cinnamon toast while using oily power tools to cut chemically treated lumber; wet cardboard, vinyl that hasn't degassed fully, neoprene, incredibly chemical."*

> *"The flavor is distinctly that of burnt rubber, like when a semi slams on the breaks; cinnamon toast again with pollution smoke; tastes like something you'd keep under your kitchen sink mixed with whatever Erin Brockovich was fighting against."*

> *"The finish is bitter and metallic and lasts seemingly forever; splinters, menthol and nightmares; this is what I imagine licking the ash off of burnt wood or eating dirt and chalk would taste like."*

It's unclear how this horrifying, cringeworthy stuff was made. Monde Shuzo is basically a winery that dabbles in other types of liquor. Located in the town of Isawa in Yamanashi prefecture, they've been selling "whisky" since the late 1960s.

Monde Shuzo used to buy malt whisky from Toyo Jozo in Shizuoka prefecture. Toyo Jozo was a fairly sizeable distilling enterprise, equipped with several continuous stills and a pair of pot stills. However, it seems like their malt whisky was nothing to write home about. For their special and 1st-grade blends, they used homemade malt whisky mixed with malt whisky imported from Scotland; for their 2nd grade products, the malt whisky they used was all made in-house. That speaks volumes. Toyo Jozo was merged with Asahi Chemical in 1992 (now Asahi Kasei) and, mercifully, gave up on making whisky.

There's another possibility. Monde Shuzo apparently also made "malt whisky" inhouse, and the label of Usuikyou does say "distilled at Monde Shuzo in Yamanashi." Nobody at Monde has ever clearly explained how exactly whisky was made there and, given the quality of what they sell, quite frankly, it's in their own best interests to keep the past as misty as possible. The only still on the premises is a 2,000-liter stainless steel still used to make grappa and brandy. Judging from the taste, it's highly likely that the malt may have been distilled in that contraption. It definitely tastes like it's never been near copper.

We'll never know and the mystery is part of its perverse appeal. You can still find Usuikyou or one of its brethren (including, shudder to think, a 1.8-liter bottle!) at bars around Japan. It's often drunk as a dare or served as a practical joke. If you see it, muster up all the courage you can and go for it. You don't really know the lower depths of whisky until this vile liquid has passed your lips.

Miyagikyo 1988
(50%abv, 1,500btls, rel. 2009)

A vatting of lightly peated and non-peated malt matured in recharred, remade and ex-sherry casks, this was the first Miyagikyo release in Nikka's iconic 20-year-old vintage single malt series.

Gentle smoke and vegetal notes (steamed beetroot and potato peel), then green, fruity notes: honeydew melon (with smoked ham), green apples and freshly squeezed Niagara grapes, complemented by Monaka wafers and a spoonful of rice pudding.

 An orchard during harvest time: green apples drizzled with lemon and pear sorbet with some fresh blackberries, Danish pastries and brandy butter on the side. Much less peaty on the palate than the nose suggested.

 Roasted apple pie and a few drops of lime juice with gentle smoke coming through in the retro-olfaction, almost like a little campfire the day after.

A whisky that speaks low, but has some really lovely things to say.

Miyagikyo 1996/2014

(remade hogshead #66535, 62%abv, for La Maison du Whisky)

This is a lightly peated Miyagikyo single cask selected by the sharp noses at La Maison du Whisky and released as part of their 2014 quartet.

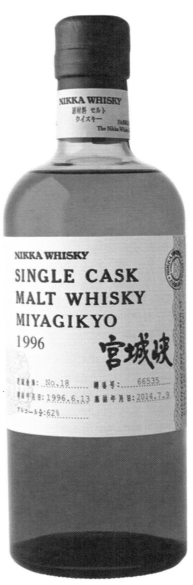

N An explosion of fruit (apricot jam, pear drops, green apples, grape skin) but with lots of intriguing secondary notes floating by, too: pumpkin pie (with a good dose of nutmeg), smoked dried pineapple, maraschino cherries, honey doughnuts and a little bit of bacon in the background. The peat is very subtle; on the nose it adds something reminiscent of the smell of barbecue clinging to your clothes the day after or a campfire doused with water.

P The same fruits spotlighted by the nose but surrounded by sour (*kabosu, shikwasa* jam) and bitter (grapefruit peel, walnut skin) elements. It evokes *crêpes suzette* but it's also markedly spicy (chili peppers, *sansho*) and everything comes wrapped in a lovely blanket of faint peat.

F Long and intense, it leaves an afterglow of woody aromas and it's here that the light peat comes through most cleanly and clearly.

A quirky take on the classic Miyagikyo profile and the last official single cask bottling from the distillery for the time being.

✦ Miyagikyo 1999/2013 *(recharred hogshead #67223, 61%abv, for LMdW)*

Miyagikyo 1996/2014 124.4 Full of Secret Pleasures

(17yo, 1st fill PX sherry butt, 60.0%abv, 479btls, Scotch Malt Whisky Society release)

Miyagikyo and sherry wood is a combination that works a treat. Unfortunately, there aren't many single cask bottlings out there. This one was selected by the good folks at the Scotch Malt Whisky Society. They thought it was "full of secret pleasures." Well, we concur!

This Miyagikyo is of the same caliber as Karuizawa, but whereas Karuizawa has its feet firmly planted on the ground—in the earth, I would say—this Miyagikyo is floating 10 inches off the ground, if that makes sense.

N The initial impressions are golden raisins, raspberry coulis, hazelnuts, antique furniture and wood smoke; after a while, you get wine-soaked figs, truffle oil, cold coffee, a bit of walnut liqueur and a subtle hint of beef stock. There are lots of tiny tertiary elements that add complexity and a subtle burnt rubber note—nothing extreme and certainly not off-putting.

P Very seductive: red fruits galore, Bonfire toffee, Christmas pudding, rum-soaked raisins, chili-and-nutmeg dark chocolate bark, peanut sauce, cinnamon, and some fennel candy.

F Long and mouth-coating on stewed berries, *mole* sauce and barbecued meat; a piercing citrus top note emerges, which quickly travels up the back of the mouth and into the nasal cavity, almost as if you'd had a teaspoon of wasabi. The afterglow is beautifully nutty, especially after a sip of water, and is accompanied by faint hints of secondhand smoke and guitar cables (rubber).

Fuji Gotemba Single Grain Whisky 25yo Small Batch

(46%abv, rel. 2015)

At the moment, Fuji Gotemba is the undisputed master of grain whisky in Japan. In fact, this little beauty was crowned "World's Best Grain Whisky" at the World Whiskies Awards in 2016, and deservedly so. Unfortunately, it was pretty much sold out by then. Those who knew it was a winner before the *Whisky Magazine* folks in London said so are probably smiling now.

N Our inner kid goes bananas . . . also, literally: there's banana bread, cream puffs, maple-pecan pancakes, butterscotch and loads of all that, but it's not too much (but then the inner kid would say that, wouldn't they?). There's more: digestive biscuits, eggnog, freshly grated nutmeg as well as subtle notes of dried apricots, dried flowers, balsamic glaze and both new plank *and* antique furniture.

P Rich and sweet—custard, roasted coconut flakes, rice pudding with honey, *crème anglaise,* baklava, you get the gist, but the oak brings a bit of spice to the party, which is most welcome.

F Long and mouth-coating on pumpkin pie but with the spices gaining in presence as the sweetness fades, making it almost rye-like (rye whiskey, that is).

This small-batch single grain was launched together with a small batch single malt. The latter was 17 years old and a very fine whisky, indeed, but everyone I know preferred the single grain. Single grain whisky used to be the ugly duckling of the industry, not just in Japan, but in Scotland as well. Well, the times they are a-changing.

The Malt of Kagoshima 1984
(25yo, matured in sherry casks, 46%abv, 3,018btls, rel. 2009)

You can count the number of bottlings of Kagoshima single malt on the fingers of one hand and all of them are long gone. This is the pick of the bunch.

Beautifully "dirty," like the best coming out of Glen Scotia distillery over in Scotland—the equivalent of eating a fruit salad in a car repair shop: fresh apples and pears, ripe prunes, canned apricots and peach yogurt, but also hints of pumpkin pie and mashed turnips against a background of dirty overalls, toolboxes, oil spills, old rags and rope, cardboard and gravel. Suggestions of saffron, cardamom, ashtrays, sake lees and bread dough rising. Beguiling and utterly original aromatic combinations and, strange as it may sound, nothing clashes.

P Initially slightly grassy and vegetal, but then the spices come in (cumin, coriander seeds, porcini powder, curried fruit) together with burnt cinnamon toast, Brazil nuts, a bit of Christmas pudding and salted caramel sauce. It falls apart when you add water, so don't.

F Medium-long, salty and rather dry, with citrus zest and canned black coffee quickly fading into something between almond and macadamia butter. It keeps surprising even after you swallow, because in the retro-olfaction you get some gentle but sustained dried chili pepper heat.

In 2015, the staff at Hombo discovered a dozen cases of this whisky in one of their warehouses. For some reason, they had been completely forgotten about. Seeing as the bottles couldn't be dropped into the market without causing confusion, the decision was made to rebottle them (from 720ml into 500ml bottles) and make them available to bartenders in Kyushu. Those 111 bottles represent the very last of Kagoshima distillery, unless . . .

✦ Maltage Satsuma 12yo *(40%abv, rel. 1996)*

✦ Maltage Satsuma 15yo *(43%abv, rel. 1998)*

Mars Maltage 3+25
(blended malt whisky, 46%abv)

This beauty was named "Best Blended Malt Whisky in the World" at the World Whiskies Awards 2013, a dark horse if ever there was one. I still remember, it was the first year I had the pleasure of being part of the Japanese panel for the World Whiskies Awards, and nobody had any idea what this fabulous whisky was. Some of us even suspected it was a decoy—a 1970s BenRiach slipped in to test our whisky-tasting acumen.

Malt" at the WWA2013, you couldn't pick up a bottle if your life depended on it. People are so easily led, except in this case, they were led to a truly fabulous whisky.

N The nose of a glorious old Speysider: apricots galore, grilled pineapple, a bit of dried persimmon, custard, fudge, barley sugar, subtle spices (masala chai and chutney) and old library notes (leather-bound books and old wood); after a while, lemon zest, beeswax, Brazil nuts with a bit of engine oil in the background.

P Gorgeous and generous, endlessly giving: rhubarb jam, dried mango, apple and pear peel, lemon tart, lime zest, beech nuts and a touch of allspice; it is also reminiscent of old Local Barley Springbank releases.

F A stunning finish: dried apricots and marzipan—a little 1960s Bowmore-like— with some white pepper, candied ginger and lingonberries in the background; as it fades, it morphs into rich milk chocolate with a whiff of wood smoke.

This was on the shelves of liquor stores in Japan for ages and nobody bought it. The day after it won "Best Blended

Mars Komagatake 1987/2014 Salon de Shimaji

(27yo, ex-Scotch whisky American white oak cask #479, 59%abv, 249btls, for Pen & Shinanoya)

Katsuhiko Shimaji was the chief editor of *Weekly Playboy* in Japan in the 1980s. In September 2012, he opened a "salon" on the eighth floor of the posh department store Isetan (Men's Store) in Shinjuku, Tokyo. In April 2020, he moved his salon to a new location in the trendy Azabu area. This bottling was selected by Shimaji for his salon and released in association with Japanese liquor retailer Shinanoya.

N Pulls out all the stops: fruity notes, big vegetal and herbal notes, spicy notes and, surrounding all of that, old tatami and damp warehouse aromas; you get blueberries, golden raisins, sour plums, beetroot, cold ratatouille, sage, thyme, cumin, coriander powder, a hint of balsamic glaze and lots more. After a while, a complex sweetness develops. The most amazing thing about the nose is the way all these different aromatic partials—to continue the pipe organ analogy—blend together.

P Peppery throughout—white and a bit of cayenne—accompanied by cough syrup, Dutch Dubbel Zoute (double-salted) licorice drops, caramelized onions, eggplant chutney, gingerbread cookies and rhubarb jam.

F Extremely long and incredibly spicy with hints of cranberry sauce, cough syrup again and some "old bottle effect"; it's quite salty but what makes it really special is the sustained triad of white pepper, dried chili and candied citrus peel. The finish is so relentlessly spicy, it almost brings tears to your eyes; again, it's more like a pipe organ than a piano sound, or rather like a "freeze pedal" on an electric guitar: it prolongs the resonance with unfading intensity. A truly mesmerizing experience.

When Mr. Shimaji visited Mars Shinshu to select a cask from the few remaining pre-1991 specimens, the distillery manager included this cask sample but secretly hoped his esteemed visitor wouldn't go for it since he had a soft spot for it himself. His hopes were quickly dashed. For us drinkers, this may have been a good thing. It was bottled at exactly the right time and offered at a reasonable price (¥24,000 plus tax). If this had been in the cask for a couple more years, it could have been over the hill and would have been priced much, much higher. Much appreciated, Mr. Shimaji.

Chichibu 2011/2015

(ex-beer barrel #3303, 59.7%abv, 267btls,
for La Maison du Whisky)

When local craft brewers seeking to barrel-age some of their suds in ex-whisky casks came knocking on Ichiro Akuto's door, rather than giving or selling them, he decided to lend them out. After the brewers are done with them, Ichiro gets his casks sent back and reuses them to (partially) age his Chichibu whiskies. It's a clever move on his part, as these type of Chichibus tend to be spellbinding.

N Tons of manuka honey and baklava, as well as assorted pastries (apricot Danish and marzipan tart), *yuanxiao* (a kind of sweet dumpling), grapefruit jelly, *hitotsubu no muscat* (sugar-coated muscat grapes), yuzu peel, bergamot tea and a tiny hint of duck *a l'orange*. A sweet tooth's dream . . .

P There's still plenty of sweetness, but there's a light savory dimension that is most welcome: steamed endive, pear-ginger chutney, cider-glazed turnips and apples with a bit of sage. The mouthfeel is incredibly creamy, suggestive of *crème d'anjou*, white chocolate mousse and oatmeal. Citrus (candied grape-fruit peel, Seville oranges, *sudachi*—a Japanese citrus fruit) takes over the palate after a few seconds and leads the dance all the way through the very long finish, with a touch of rosewater in the afterglow.

Extreme and unusual but irresistible, especially if you like artisanal honey. Doesn't take water well, so enjoy as is.

✦ Chichibu 2011/2015 *(ex-beer barrel #3292, 57.6%abv, 261btls, for Chichibu Whisky Matsuri 2015)*

Karuizawa 1964/2012

(48yo, 400l ex-sherry cask #3603, 57.7%abv, 143btls, Number One Drinks for Wealth Solutions Poland)

This is one of my all-time favorite Japanese whiskies, but I'll let the liquid do the talking.

Starts off with a prelude of *annin dofu* (almond tofu) and maraschino cherries, which soon gives way to a triple fugue of forest, tree fruit and waxed wood notes. The initial interplay is between the forest notes, suggestive of a forest in spring after rain, incredibly fresh, with hints of pine trees, boulder fern, sandalwood and a faint eucalyptus note. Soon after, seemingly out of nowhere, fruit notes start to appear: overripe apricots, Yubari King melon, *nashi* (Japanese pears), and some dates in the background. There are also subtle hints of blood orange and ruby grapefruit. On the back of these fruit notes, something reminiscent of a recently polished chapel starts to develop, with some freshly baled hay, heather honey and a hint of freshly crushed pink peppercorns thrown in the mix. Water tends to push notes of green apples and underripe peach to the fore; it also brings some wet grass drying in the sun to the party.

The nose sets up certain expectations, but the palate gracefully sidesteps these expectations, only to reveal a whole new dimension; such is the complexity of this whisky. Neat, the initial impressions are acerola (West Indian cherry), blackberries, gooseberries and orange liqueur. There's also a distinct *kashiwa mochi* (rice cake wrapped in oak leaf) note. The sour—pleasantly so—flavors soon give way to an equally pleasant and seductive bitterness: bitter melon (*goya*), walnut skin, kale-and-green-apple juice, and an ever so slight licorice note. Water brings out a prominent *sudachi* note.

Medium-long with hints of kiwi jam, also lingonberry jam, sweet-and-sour sauce, bitter melon again, and an incredibly delicate sweetness at the center of it all.

I am fortunate to have tried all the early 1960s Karuizawa single cask bottlings—including some from the pre-Number One Drinks days—and for me, this is the pick of the bunch. It is one of those rare whiskies that creates a world of its own and holds it together so beautifully it's almost like an image of nature at its best.

Karuizawa Noh 1980/2012
(32yo, sherry butt #7614, 50.4%abv, 102btls, for Taiwan)

There aren't very many Karuizawas from the 1980 vintage—less than a dozen, to be precise—and maybe that is part of the reason why there is a tendency among fans of the distillery to think of its "Golden Age" as being the period from 1981 (not 1980) to 1984. We're certainly spoiled for choice as far as stellar single cask bottlings from those years are concerned. And yet, for me, this superb Noh bottling eclipses anything I've tried from the "Golden Period" and that's saying something.

N Like a diva's dressing room: lovely perfumy notes, flowers, fresh fruit, loads of nuts, raspberry mousse, strawberries with balsamic vinegar, After Eights, old manuscripts, with everything exquisitely balanced. This is the sort of rare whisky in which every aroma has an air of being glad to be together.

P The main tonalities are sweet and sour: lemon curd, grapefruit jelly, green apples drizzled with lemon, tart cherries and chocolate, acerola juice, cranberry granola with rhubarb jam. If you are a fan of this sort of yin-yang interplay of sweet and sour, you will love this whisky.

F Reveals a lovely herbal dimension—mint, thyme and eucalyptus—against a seemingly endless afterglow of *sudachi* (a signature note of old Karuizawas, here in full HD) and candied lemon peel.

This is a real *tour de force* of a whisky: incredibly fresh, vibrant and intense but so beautifully balanced.

Karuizawa 45yo Water of Life 1967/2012

(sherry butt #2725, 59.6%abv, 310btls, for Taiwan)

Writing tasting notes for old Karuizawas is an exercise in setting limits. You have to know when to stop, because you *could* go on forever—but nobody wants that. Incidentally, the color on this is absolutely magnificent: dark mahogany with a slight shade of candy apple red. Karuizawa engages all the senses. Texturally, it's quite something as well: so thick you can almost cut it with a knife.

N Aged balsamic vinegar, figs, old leather-bound books and chapels, but also plum jam, prune chutney, stewed berries and a gorgeous mimolette cheese note; if you really give it time, you may even find something akin to bacon-wrapped parmesan-stuffed dates—incredibly voluptuous.

P Very dense and concentrated: prune juice, hazelnuts, mince pies, chocolate-dipped orange peel, pine resin, licorice and a lovely tangy *suda-chi* note, which is a sort of signature note of very old Karuizawas.

F The finish? Well, there is no finish. It just goes on and on and on. It's mouth-coating to the extent that it will just stay with you for hours after, which, in a case like this, is exactly what you want.

You can spend hours with a dram of this and feel like the luckiest person on earth—and that's not empty hyperbole. If ever you have a chance to try this and find yourself disagreeing with me, drop me a line.

Karuizawa 1995/2013

(18yo, Japanese red wine cask #5022, 61.9%abv, 22btls, Ghost Series no.2)

In 1995, master distiller Osami Uchibori got 20 ex-red wine casks delivered to Karuizawa distillery and filled them with new-make. Most of these were bottled for the distillery shop between 2007 and 2011. I have always had a soft spot for these Rouge Casks so I was thrilled to be able to bottle the last and oldest one. As it turned out, it was also the last of the 1995 vintage.

N Raspberries, blackberries, blood orange jam, dried apricots, dried leaves, antique furniture, then, after a while, candied lime peel, dark chocolate-covered acai with blueberry, red miso, old leather-bound books, and cigar boxes but also lychee liqueur and hints of manuka honey, mint, eucalyptus and fennel. Just gorgeous—a whisky with many tiny aromatic surprises in its folds.

P Loads of berries again, very thick and concentrated, like jam, with propolis throat candy, licorice allsorts, spice cake *(peperkoek)* and rooibos tea added to the mix; then, an explosion of fresh citrus mid-palate: *sudachi* most prominently, also a bit of lemon and grapefruit and some strawberry sauce in the background. On the back of all that, spices (cloves, aniseed, nutmeg) and then a lovely, subtly bitter transition (kale-apple juice, endive) to the finish.

F Strawberry macarons and Turkish delight, a sweetness so delicate yet intense it breaks your heart to feel it

fade, but in the afterglow, you get these little reminders of what the nose and palate have spoken to you about.

This is the whisky equivalent of *One Thousand and One Nights*. Unfortunately, there were only 22 bottles left in this, the last Rouge Cask when it was bottled, so finding it is not going to be easy. However, there are a few sister casks out there. If you see a Karuizawa from the 1995 vintage and the cask number starts with 50, you've found one.

Karuizawa 1984/2015 Artifices

(ex-sherry cask #8838, 61.6%abv, 151btls, for La Maison du Whisky)

This is an extraordinary specimen from the "Golden Age" of Karuizawa distillery, 1981 to 1984. I've always wondered what it was about these four years in the early 1980s that produced such phenomenal whiskies. The distillery is gone and the few people who used to work there at the time don't remember, so probably we'll never know.

N Knocks you off your socks; a beautiful blueberry-raspberry sauce top note and underneath hundreds of aromatic thrills: Dutch *stroopwafels*, strong café mocha, coffee-flavored caramel candy, burnt hay, cigar boxes, beef tendon stew *(gyusuji nikomi)*; it also conjures up something between an old rum and an old Armagnac. With water, it becomes more damp, earthy and autumnal; it reminds me of the smell of the empty Karuizawa dunnage-style warehouses.

P *Shikwasa* and endive on the attack (an unusual combo!), then, hazelnut liqueur, licorice and *kuromitsu* (Japanese black sugar syrup). It's much more defined with a bit of water added: stewed prunes, red currants, grilled burdock, coffee beans (the actual beans), gravy, eggplant chutney and much, much more. Menthol and chili pepper act as a bridge to the finish.

F Long and intense on *café Guillermo* (hot espresso poured over a slice or two of lime), acacia gum, candied *amanatsu* peel and the aftertaste of crème de menthe; after a long time, it even develops some OBE (old bottle effect).

This is the whisky equivalent of Henry Rollins: super-intense, uncompromising and relentlessly stimulating. What a wild ride. This is whisky that demands time and undivided attention. There's no room for any other thoughts when you are sipping this.

✦ Karuizawa 1983/2015 Nepal Appeal *(ex-sherry cask #3557, 59.1%abv, 50btls, for The Whisky Exchange)*

Kawasaki 1980/2014

(33yo single grain whisky, sherry butt #6165, 59.6%abv, 60btls, Ghost Series no.4)

This is the only known Kawasaki specimen from the 1980 vintage. It's one that I found—or rather, it found me—and bottled for my Ghost Series, but it wouldn't be right to discriminate against it for that reason. The liquid is what it is—out of this world—and that's why it's spotlighted here.

The initial impressions are a Middle Eastern spice shop, old rum, polished wood and a multitude of sweet delicacies: butter tablet (a Scottish sweet similar to but not exactly the same as fudge), coconut butter, *crema catalana* and *chinsuko* cookies. But there's a lovely savory side to the whisky as well: apple balsamic-glazed spare ribs, *rafte* (Okinawan simmered pork belly) and some *foie gras* with apricot preserves. Dig deeper and you will find loads of other tiny aromas: overripe Yubari King melon, baked vanilla custard with nutmeg, *tupig* (Filipino sticky rice logs with coconut cream and molasses, wrapped in banana leaves), Dutch spice cake and hints of rosemary, eucalyptus, spearmint and maraschino cherries.

P Nothing prepares you for the intense citrus attack on the palate: grapefruit, yuzu peel, kumquat and Seville orange are out in full force! As the citrus settles down, other fruit notes emerge: ripe mango and balsamic roasted stone fruits (peaches, plums and cherries). You do get a bit of the sweetness hinted at by the nose (coconut scones and vanilla custard) but not as much as you would think. You definitely get more of the savory notes and lots of spice (cloves, cinnamon and nutmeg). A subtle bitter transition (grapefruit albedo) leads into the finish.

F Long with echoes of the citrus along with brown sugar on toast, lychees, fig sorbet and hints of ginger and After Eights.

Incredibly complex and lush, this is the grain equivalent of the best early 1980s Karuizawas.

✦ Kawasaki 1976/2009 Ichiro's Choice *(33yo, refill sherry butts, 65.6%abv, 95+432btls)*

Hanyu Queen of Clubs 1988/2008

(1st cask: hogshead, 2nd cask: new American oak hogshead #7003, 56.0%abv, 330btls, Ichiro's Card Series)

This is a really beautiful whisky and conceptually intriguing as well. Putting new-make in virgin oak, and then transferring it to a refill cask is nothing to write home about: You beef up the whisky and speed up the maturation process in the initial stage and then slow it down, so the wood doesn't overpower the spirit in the long run. This is an upside-down world: over 17 years in refill wood, and then an intense reinvigoration period of two and a half years in virgin American oak.

There's no underlying "scheme" in the Card Series but Ichiro has said that he had a habit of reserving "high cards" (the Ace and face cards) for casks of exceptional quality. I've tasted the whole series and all I can say is: I believe him.

N Incredibly heavy on blueberry jam, roast venison with cranberry sauce, *foie gras* with apricots, ground coriander, blood sausages with black cherry sauce and apricot frangipane tart; after a while, you get baklava, cola cubes and thyme. Water brings out more seasoning, but it also delivers a selection of Danish pastries and *Far Breton* (custard cake with prunes).

P Very fiery, with lots of white pepper on the attack and a little bit of grapefruit albedo; after that, it's like an impromptu feast in a damp forest: wild game meat, berries, nuts, dried fruits, curried bread, dried herbs, tons of spices—a bit of *crema catalana* and some acacia gum, too. Water dials up the citrus (Seville orange and ruby grapefruit).

F Long and intense on citrus zest, rhubarb jam and cotton candy; the retro-olfaction suggests exotic wood, aromatic incense and essential oils.

Hanyu 1985/2009

(#1732, 57.1%abv, 61btls, for La Maison du Whisky)

This is a bottling from "way back in the day" when Japanese whisky was considered an acquired taste. Now, every man and his dog would want a bottle like this.

N Seductive and enigmatic. The initial impressions are cantaloupe, mango chutney, *shibukawa-ni* (Japanese-style boiled chestnuts soaked in liquor), *guimauve* (French marshmallows) and cumin, followed by hints of ginger preserves, pine resin, assorted herbs (including Japanese mint), mixed spices, wood shavings and lemon-honey tea. Give it half an hour in the glass and you get whiffs of postage stamp gum, whiteboard markers and marzipan—an eclectic mix but the balance is exquisite.

P Salty and insanely spicy: *shichimi togarashi* and cayenne morph into *yuzu kosho*; then, the citrus becomes more dominant (kumquats), helped along by some freshly grated ginger. As the whisky travels across the palate, slightly bitter notes develop (bitter melon, radish sprouts) together with a bit of potato peel. Water brings out more herbs and a touch of rosewater. The palate is the proverbial iron fist in the nose's velvet glove.

F Endless—spicy and peppery with a citrus kick (like sucking on a slice of lemon), initially with a bit of bitterness (grape pips) and a hint of bamboo shoots and oregano. As it calms down, it becomes more mineral and slightly drying.

With single cask Hanyu, it's good to have a bit of water handy to try and find the sweet spot for yourself. Be careful with this particular bottling, though. In spite of its intensity, it's quite fragile, so if you add a few drops too much it loses much of its beguiling charm.

Hanyu King of Clubs 1988/2010

(1st cask: hogshead, 2nd cask: Cognac cask #9108, 58.0%abv, 417btls, Ichiro's Card Series)

This is a bottle from the famous Card Series. I've tried them all and it's a thankless task to pick the best of the best from the entire set. This is one of my personal favorites. The liquid spent three-quarters of its life in a refill hogshead, and a quarter in an ex-Cognac cask, so no quick "cosmetic" finish but a proper secondary maturation here. It seems to have worked wonders.

N Lush and intense with tamarind jam, spiced persimmon chutney, mashed turnip, duck *à l'orange,* balsamic-glazed peaches, candied *amanatsu* peel, caramelized onions and mixed citrus; suggestive of a Middle Eastern spice shop next to a diva's powder room (perfumy notes). After a while, you get *crêpes suzette*, maraschino cherries and a touch of manuka honey; a joy for the imagination.

P Very salty (like licking your lips after a day on the beach) and very savory—couscous, falafel, turkey breast with a dab of *raiyu* (Chinese hot chili oil), some celery seed powder; lots of concentrated fruit notes, too: blood orange-rosemary marmalade, brandy-soaked raisins, dates and plenty more. Water dials up the fruit.

F Long and spicy—think chili pepper, fenugreek, turmeric—with hints of chocolate-covered raisins, Vietnamese coffee, rich beef stock, cardamom and papaya. What makes the finish really alluring is the *kabosu* note (a Japanese citrus fruit) running through it like a gentle drone. Water tames the spices.

Hanyu is whisky for foodies, chock-full of flavors from all corners of the world. Sometimes this is at the expense of coherence and balance, but with the best casks, the eclectic elements are sewn together into an elaborate liquid quilt. This is one of those casks.

Hanyu The Game III 2000/2012

(12yo, red oak heads hogshead finish #360, 57.5%abv, 309btls, for Shinanoya)

Red oak is uncommon in the whisky industry. Unlike its ubiquitous white oak cousin, red oak has no tylose in its pores, making it highly penetrable to liquids and therefore not suitable for tight cooperage. Keen to see what sort of impact red oak would have on the whisky maturation process, Ichiro found a way around the leaking problem by fitting regular hogsheads with heads made out of red oak. Judging by the handful of casks released so far, it's more than worth the risk.

N Muscular, complex and hyper-fragrant: a whole spice rack (nutmeg, cinnamon, cumin and much more), mimolette cheese, baby back ribs with bourbon-cranberry barbecue sauce, apple-gorgonzola pizza drizzled with honey, chai tea, digestive biscuits, *Far Breton*, clotted cream, coconut flakes and distinct notes of stewed white peaches and kiwi jam, all against a background of beautifully pronounced wood notes (Japanese temples, new lacquerware, antique furniture) and a hint of smoke.

P Very creamy in terms of mouthfeel, with the same interplay of fruity/spicy and sweet/savory notes. There's a whole pantry of flavors waiting to be discovered here: red fruits, chutneys, jams (blood orange, most prominently), exotic sweets, chocolate, various kinds of tea, syrups (maple, *kuromitsu*), baked goods (herb scones, carrot cake) . . . the list goes on and on.

F Extremely long and peppery with candied orange peel, dates, raisins and curried pineapple slowly fading into milk caramel candy and rosemary chocolate chip shortbread.

Shortly after releasing The Game III, Shinanoya collaborated with Tokachino Fromages to produce a cheese washed in this particular whisky. If you're wondering what that was like, get ahold of a camembert and start washing. If you need a substitute whisky, any of the below will do nicely.

✦ Hanyu 1991/2010 Jack of Hearts *(red oak hogshead finish #378, 56.1%abv)*

✦ Hanyu 1991/2010 *(red oak hogshead finish #377, 56.0%abv, The Nectar of the Daily Drams)*

✦ Hanyu 2000/2015 *(red oak hogshead finish #358, 56.5%, for Isetan)*

Local Chichibu barley

References

Abe, Atsuko, 1999. *Japan and the European Union. Domestic Politics and Transnational Relations*, London & New Brunswick, NJ: The Athlone Press, 86-117.

Asai, Shogo, 2003. "The Introduction of European Liquor Production to Japan," in: Umesao, Tadao et al. (ed.), *Senri Ethnological Studies*, 64, 49–61.

Asano, Hajime, 2014. *Nikka Whisky Seihin List 2014nenhan* [Ver.2014/11/2], Kashiwa: privately published.

Buxrud, Ulf, 2008. *Japanese Whisky: Facts, Figures & Taste*, Malmö: DataAnalys Scandinavia AB.

Checkland, Olive, 1998. *Japanese Whisky, Scotch Blend*, Edinburgh: Scottish Cultural Press.

Fukuyo, Shinji & Yoshio Myojo, "Japanese Whisky," in: Russell, Inge & Graham Stewart (ed.), 2014. *Whisky: Technology, Production and Marketing*, 2nd edition, Amsterdam: Elsevier Ltd, 17–26.

Hozumi, Tadahiko, 1983. *Tsuukai! Ji-Whisky Sengen*, Tokyo: Byakuya Shobo.

National Tax Agency, 2016. [National Tax Agency Reports], www.nta.go.jp/kohyo/tokei/kokuzeicho/tokei.htm.

Nonjatta, www.nonjatta.com.

Sanraku Co. Ltd. 1986. *Sanraku 50nen Shi*, Tokyo: Sanraku Co. Ltd.

Sekine, Akira, 2004. *Aru Yoshuzukuri no Hitokoma*, Osaka & Tokyo: Taru Shuppan Co. Ltd.

Sugimori, Hisahide, 1986. *Bishuichidai: Shinjiro Torii Den*, Shinchosha Publishing.

Suntory Liquors Ltd., 1999. *Hibini Aratani—Suntory 100nen Shi*, Tokyo: Suntory Ltd.

Suntory Holdings Ltd., 2014. *Tales of the Founders—The Origins of Suntory II*, Tokyo: Suntory Public Relations Department.

Suntory Liquors Ltd., 2014. *The Founder of Japanese Whisky—Shinjiro Torii*, Tokyo: Suntory Spirits Division, Whisky Department.

The Nikka Whisky Distilling Co. Ltd., 2015. *Nikka Whisky 80nen Shi*, Tokyo: The Nikka Whisky Distilling Co. Ltd.

Van Eycken, Stefan, 2013. "Future Dream Drams," in: *Whisky Magazine,* 116: 20–25.

Van Eycken, Stefan, 2016. "The Japanese Boom" in: *Whisky Magazine,* 135: 48–50.

World Trade Organization, 1987. "Japan—Customs Duties, Taxes and Labelling Practices on Imported Wines and Alcoholic Beverages" [Report of the Panel adopted on 10 November 1987], www.wto.org.

Glossary

abv

Stands for "alcohol by volume" and indicates how much alcohol (ethanol) is contained in a given volume of an alcoholic beverage when measured at 68°F/20°C. It is expressed as a percentage of the total volume.

angels' share

The poetic industry term for the portion of whisky that evaporates from the cask in the course of the maturation process, expressed as the percentage of the total volume in the cask lost per year. In general, the warmer the climate, the higher the angels' share is. In Scotland, the average angels' share is around 2 percent. At Amrut in Goa, India, the angels' share can average as much as 12 to 15 percent.

beer column

The first column in a multi-column still.

chill-filtering

A process whereby whisky is chilled and filtered before bottling to remove compounds that can form hazes and deposits when stored or drunk at low temperature (which can happen when the abv of a bottled product is below 46%). The number of producers who believe this negatively affects flavor and mouthfeel—and who bottle some or all of their products non-chill-filtered—is growing, but big brands maintain it is a cosmetic necessity.

Coffey still

A continuous still of the type invented by Aeneas Coffey and patented in 1830. It consists of two linked columns. The first column—called the "analyzer"—has steam rising and wash descending through several levels. Alcohol vapors rising to the top of the analyzer then travel down to the base of the second column—called the "rectifier"—where they rise up, chamber by chamber, until they are drawn off at the desired strength. Originally Coffey stills were used by rectifiers and gin distillers in the U.K. During the mid-1840s, Scottish distillers started using Coffey stills to make grain whisky. Masataka Taketsuru brought the first Coffey still to Japan in 1963.

column/continuous still

An apparatus used to produce light or almost neutral spirit. It is much faster (being a continuous process as opposed to the "batch" process of distillation in pot stills) and much more economical than pot still distillation. Most grain whisky is produced in a column/continuous still.

condenser

A cooling device attached to a still to condense the vaporized spirit back into liquid form. The traditional method is a worm tub (a coiled copper tube of decreasing diameter immersed in a tub filled with continuously running cold water). Most distilleries nowadays use the modern "shell and tube" condenser (a tall, copper drum—the "shell"—with dozens of narrow bore copper pipes—the "tubes"—through which cold water runs). The latter is considered to be more efficient and provides much more copper contact—resulting in a "cleaner" spirit—but some distilleries still use the old-fashioned worm tubs because "light and clean" is not what they are after.

dunnage warehouse

A term used in Scotland for traditional whisky warehouses—usually low-rise with thick, brick or stone walls, an earth or cinder floor and a slate roof. Casks are stacked three or four high on wooden runners. Running costs are much higher compared with racked or palletized warehouses, not only because of the space constraints but also because moving casks in and out of a dunnage warehouse is a more laborious process.

expression

An individual product from a distillery or a specific release within a brand portfolio that is clearly defined in terms of one (or more) salient aspect(s) of production, e.g., age, maturation regime and/or peating level.

filling strength

The strength at which the spirit is filled into the cask (known in the United States as "entry proof"). In Scotland, filling strength is typically 63.5%abv.

kiln

An area for drying malted barley. Most kilns have a distinctive pagoda chimney. This has become such an iconic distillery image in Scotland that—even though very few distilleries do their own malting nowadays—the pagoda is often kept/integrated as an architectural element.

lyne arm
The pipe that connects the head of a pot still with the condenser. Also known as "lye arm/pipe," the orientation, angle and diameter have an influence on the character of the resulting spirit, more reflux and copper contact resulting in a lighter spirit and vice versa.

mash
As a verb, this refers to the process of steeping grist (ground-down malted barley) with hot water to extract the sugars. As a noun, it refers to the mix of grist and hot water.

mash tun
A large vessel in which the mashing takes place.

outturn
The number of bottles a particular release is limited to.

ppm
Stands for "parts per million." In the context of whisky, this usually refers to the level of peating in malted barley, expressed as phenol parts per million. Lightly peated malt is generally below 15ppm, medium-peated around 20ppm, heavily peated more than 30ppm and super heavily peated above 50ppm.

reflux
The alcohol vapors and heavier aromatic compounds that condense and fall back into the still during distillation before they reach the condenser. The shape of the still, the height and width of the neck and the orientation of the lyne-arm are all factors affecting the degree of reflux. The more reflux, the lighter the spirit.

rummager
A device consisting of rotating chains of interwoven copper rings used in direct-fired wash stills to keep solids moving at the bottom of the still and prevent scorching (which would result in undesirable notes in the spirit).

sake (*nihonshu*)
A Japanese filtered or pressed fermented alcoholic beverage made with rice, koji (sake mold) and water. In the industry, this is referred to as "seishu" (literally, clear alcohol). The average abv of bottled sake is 15–16%. By law, it must be under 22%abv.

shochu

A Japanese distilled beverage made from a very wide range of base ingredients. Some of the more orthodox varieties are rice *shochu*, barley *shochu*, sweet potato *shochu*, buckwheat *shochu* and brown sugar *shochu*. In terms of production method, there are two types: *korui shochu* (class A) which is distilled in a continuous still to a very high abv and then diluted for sale to an abv of less than 36%, and *otsurui/honkaku shochu* (class B, "authentic shochu"), which is distilled once—usually in a stainless still—to an abv of no more than 45%.

umeshu

A traditional Japanese liqueur made by steeping whole, unripe *ume* fruit in alcohol and sugar. It's available wherever alcohol is sold, but also commonly made at home. Between 10% and 15%abv, it's usually served on the rocks, mixed with soda or as a "'sour" (in the Japanese sense of the word, i.e., mixed with *shochu* and soda).

wash

Strictly speaking, wort becomes wash as soon as it's been cooled down and yeast is added to start fermentation, but most people in the industry think of wash as the liquid at the end of the fermentation process (which is known in the United States as "'distiller's beer").

washback

The vessel in which the fermentation takes place. In Japan, as in the United States, the equivalent "'fermenter" is more prevalent.

wort

Essentially barley juice, this is the liquid that is drawn off from the mash tun after the mashing process has been completed. It contains the sugars from the barley that will be converted into alcohol during the fermentation process.

whisky loch

A term coined in the mid-1980s to refer to the enormous surplus in whisky stock maturing in warehouses in Scotland created by overproduction of malt and grain whisky during the late 1970s and early 1980s while consumption of whisky, both at home and abroad, was declining and drinkers' preferences were shifting to other categories (most notably, white spirits).

Cask Chart

	Liters	U.S. Gallons	
Port Pipe	550–600	145–158	Used in the port industry, these casks are huge, tall, and difficult to handle, store and get hold of; in the whisky world, they're mostly used for secondary maturation purposes
Butt	500	132	Butts tend to be synonymous with ex-sherry, but Nikka, for example, makes butts that have never been near sherry (e.g., virgin oak butts)
Puncheon	500	132	Holds about the same volume as a butt, but shorter and fatter than a butt; can vary quite a bit in size
Bota Corta	480	126	Slightly shorter and squatter than a butt; Spanish oak ex-sherry casks of this type are used by Suntory; the shortened butts that were commonly used at Karuizawa distillery can also be seen as falling into this category
Cognac Cask	350	92	Cognac casks come in a wide variety of sizes; this is the most commonly used size

	Liters	U.S. Gallons	
Hogshead	250	65	Made using staves from ex-bourbon barrels; breaking down five barrels and reassembling the staves will give you four hogsheads (which will need to be fitted with new heads)
Barrique	225	59	The default cask type used in the wine industry
Barrel	195	53	The default cask type used in the bourbon industry (American Standard Barrel); the most commonly used cask type in the whisky industry in Japan, as elsewhere
Chibidaru	130	34	A type of quarter cask made and used at Chichibu distillery; basically, a shortened hogshead

All cask sizes are approximate. These are hand-crafted vessels and the actual size can vary from cooperage to cooperage.

Index

Maps

ACTIVE DISTILLERIES (established before 2017)

1   Akkeshi
2   Yoichi
3   Miyagikyo
4   Asaka
5   Saburomaru
6   Nukada
7   Chichibu
8   Hakushu
9   Mars Shinshu
10 Mt Fuji
    (Fuji-Gotemba)
11 Shizuoka
12 Nagahama
13 Chita
14 Yamazaki
15 Eigashima
16 Okayama
17 Mars Tsunuki

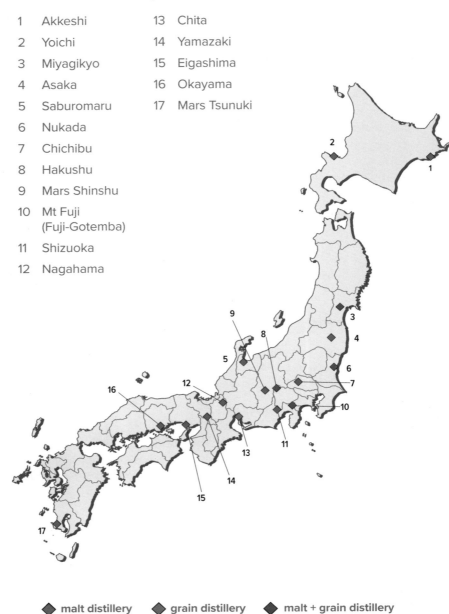

◆ malt distillery   ◆ grain distillery   ◆ malt + grain distillery

ACTIVE DISTILLERIES (established 2017–)

18	Kamui Whisky	31	Tamba
19	Niseko	32	Rokkosan
20	Yuza	33	Kaikyo
21	Niigata Kameda	34	Sakurao
22	Nozawa Onsen	35	Setouchi
23	Yasato	36	Shindo
24	Hanyu	37	Kuju
25	Hikari	38	Yamaga
26	Chichibu II	39	Osuzuyama
27	Fuji Hokuroku	40	Osumi
28	Ikawa	41	Kanosuke
29	Kurayoshi	42	Hioki ◆
30	Kyoto Miyako	43	Ontake

◆ LOST DISTILLERIES

1 Shirakawa Distillery

2 Karuizawa Distillery

3 Hanyu Distillery

4 Shiojiri Distillery

5 Yamanashi Distillery (Hombo)

6 Yamanashi Distillery (Sanraku)

7 Kawasaki Distillery

8 Kagoshima Distillery (Hombo)

○ OTHER LOCATIONS

A Tochigi Factory (Nikka)

B Miyake Industries (Copper & Steelworks)

C Kashiwa Factory (Nikka)

D Yatsugatake Aging Cellar (Suntory, demolished)

E Ohmi Aging Cellar (Suntory)

F Nishinomiya Factory (Nikka)

G Ariake Barrel (Independent Cooperage)

H H Yakushima Aging Cellar (Hombo)

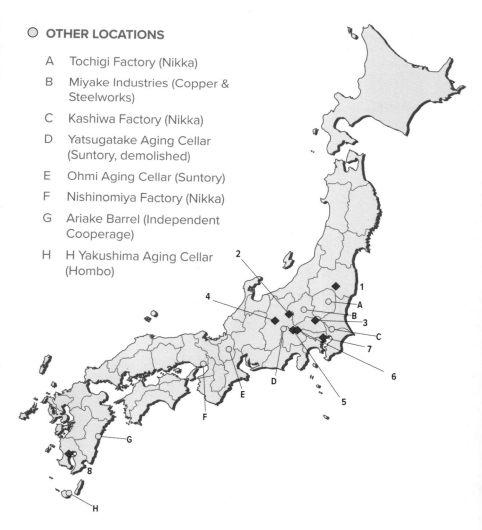

Photo Credits

About the Author

Stefan Van Eycken grew up in Belgium and Scotland and moved to Japan in 2000. He was the chief editor of Nonjatta, the foremost online resource on Japanese whisky, until its discontinuation in 2016. He is regional editor (Japan) for *Whisky Magazine UK* and regularly contributes to a variety of whisky-related publications in English, French and Japanese. He is responsible for the annual updates to the Japanese section of the *Malt Whisky Yearbook* and has been on the Japanese panel of the World Whiskies Awards since 2012. He is also the man behind the Ghost Series, an ongoing series of bottlings of rare Japanese whiskies, and the biannual charity event Spirits for Small Change. He regularly hosts tastings in Japan and abroad and is co-founder of a (somewhat secret) transpacific bourbon club. The first edition of *Whisky Rising* has been translated into Chinese and Japanese. Aside from his work in the field of whisky, he is also a full-time music teacher and occasionally manages to find time to compose music for the concert hall. He lives in Tokyo with his wife and two sons.

About the Foreword Writer

Jim Meehan worked at some of New York City's most popular restaurants and bars, including Gramercy Tavern and the Pegu Club, before opening the James Beard Award–winning bar PDT in 2007. The former editor of *Food & Wine* magazine's annual cocktail book and the *Mr. Boston Bartender's Guide*, Meehan is the author of The *PDT Cocktail Book* and *Meehan's Bartender Manual*. He and his family reside in Portland, Oregon, where he operates his consulting firm Mixography Inc.

ABOUT CIDER MILL PRESS BOOK PUBLISHERS

Good ideas ripen with time. From seed to harvest, Cider Mill Press brings fine reading, information, and entertainment together between the covers of its creatively crafted books. Our Cider Mill bears fruit twice a year, publishing a new crop of titles each spring and fall.

"Where Good Books Are Ready for Press"

501 Nelson Place
Nashville, Tennessee 37214

cidermillpress.com